CONSTRUCTING THE AMERICAN PAST

A SOURCE BOOK OF A PEOPLE'S HISTORY

Sixth Edition

VOLUME 2

Elliott J. Gorn
Brown University

Randy Roberts
Purdue University

Terry D. Bilhartz
Sam Houston State University

PEARSON
Longman

New York San Francisco Boston
London Toronto Sydney Tokyo Singapore Madrid
Mexico City Munich Paris Cape Town Hong Kong Montreal

Executive Editor: Michael Boezi
Executive Marketing Manager: Sue Westmoreland
Production Manager: Denise Phillip
Editorial Assistant: Vanessa Gennarelli
Project Coordination, Text Design, and Electronic Page Makeup: Electronic Publishing Services, Inc., NYC
Cover Design Manager: Wendy Ann Fredericks
Cover Designer: Susan Koski Zucker
Cover Art: © 1978 George Ballis/Take Stock
Photo Researcher: Photosearch, Inc.
Senior Manufacturing Buyer: Alfred C. Dorsey
Printer and Binder: R. R. Donnelley & Sons / Crawfordsville
Cover Printer: R. R. Donnelley & Sons / Crawfordsville

Cataloging-in-Publication data on file with the Library of Congress.
Library of Congress Cataloging-in-Publication Data

Constructing the American past : a source book of a people's history / [edited by] Elliott J. Gorn, Randy Roberts, Terry D. Bilhartz. -- 6th ed.
p. cm.
Includes bibliographical references and index.
ISBN 0-321-48474-6 (v. 1) -- ISBN 0-321-48203-4 (v. 2)
1. United States--History--Sources. I. Gorn, Elliott J., 1951-
II. Roberts, Randy, 1951- III. Bilhartz, Terry D.
E173.C69 2007
973--dc22 2007015064

Please visit us at www.ablongman.com

ISBN 13: 978-0-321-48203-7
ISBN 10: 0-321-48203-4

2 3 4 5 6 7 8 9 10—DOC—10 09 08 07

For our children

Jade Rachel Yee-Gorn

Alison MacKenzie Roberts

Kelly Rankin Roberts

Teri Noel Bilhartz

Rocky Bilhartz and Lindsey Lee Bilhartz

CONTENTS

PREFACE

Every historian knows the feeling. You're working in an archive, sleepy and bored, when something jumps out at you. Maybe a letter written by someone who has been dead a hundred years boldly states an idea that was just a glimmer in your mind; or a diary that turns up unexpectedly takes you into the inner life of someone who seemed so unknowable before; or an eyewitness account of clashing armies makes you see and hear and smell the battlefield. Doing history can be as exciting as any act of discovery and exploration.

We developed this anthology to communicate some of that excitement to students. All three of us take pride in our work as teachers and writers of history. Sometimes, however, those two sides of the historian's job seem terribly distant from each other. Bridging that gap is our task here. We have tried to put some of our best teaching between these covers. We hope students will learn the challenges, the rigors, and the joys of hands-on history. Our goal is to present students with exciting documents on a series of topics that will help them learn to think critically.

Each chapter centers on a particular problem in American history. The introductions, documents, and study questions direct students to participate in the past. What was it like, for example, to be at a religious revival at the beginning of the nineteenth century? Who attended them and why? Our chapter on camp meetings offers eyewitness accounts. To give another example, what really happened at Wounded Knee, South Dakota, in 1890? Students read descriptions of the clash between the Sioux and the U.S. cavalry from a variety of vantage points: the voices of the Sioux, the letters of military officers, and the statements of government officials.

The sixth edition of *Constructing the American Past,* volume 2, contains several new features. The chapter on the Progressive era has been restructured to focus on two hotly-debated topics–the meatpacking industry and birth control–to allow students to understand the nature of reform movements. We include a whole new chapter on World War II, which includes Franklin Roosevelt's famous "Four Freedoms" speech, as well as documents about the war's impact on Japanese Americans, African Americans, and Mexican Americans. We also include new documents on World War I, the Cold War, and on the environmental movement.

As we compiled these volumes, we also compiled debts. We want to thank the library staffs at Purdue, Miami, Stanford, and Sam Houston State Universities; at the Museum of the City of New York; the Western College Archives; the archives of the Southern Regional Council, Atlanta; the Library of Congress; the New York Public Library; the Newberry Library; the American Antiquarian Society; the Huntington Library; and the Wisconsin Center for Film and Theater Research.

Many colleagues and graduate students have made suggestions and corrected us when we went astray. We especially acknowledge the assistance of Arthur Casciato, Allan Winkler, Jack Kirby, Mary Frederickson, James Hamill, Lynn Dumenil, Joshua Brown, Margo Horn, Timothy Gilfoyle, Paul Hutton, Howard Shorr, Gary Bell, Greg Cantrell, James Olson, Roseanne Barker, Ken Hendrickson, Caroline Crimm, Ty Cashion, Joseph Rowe, and Robert Shadle.

Terry Bilhartz still remembers with appreciation the following teachers and colleagues in a 1987 National Endowment for the Humanities Summer Institute on Classic Texts in Early American History who gave inspiration for the first edition of this work: Richard D. Brown, Karen O. Kupperman, Harry S. Stout, John P. Demos, Robert A. Gross, Stephen Nissenbaum, R. Kent Newmyer, Phillip Boucher, Alan V. Briceland, Jerald Combs, Donald R. Hickey, Richard L. Hillard, Graham Hodges, John Ifovic, Thomas W. Jodziewicz, Lawrence Kazura, Patricia O'Malley, Jacqueline Peterson, Bruce Stuart, William Swagerty, Alan S. Thompson, Louis P. Towles, Kerry A. Trask, James A. Trask, and Daniel E. Williams.

Several outside readers have strengthened our work. We acknowledge with gratitude the comments we received from Carson Cunningham, DePaul University; Todd Estes, University Oakland; Dana Goodrich, Northwest Vista College; Jennifer Green, Central Michigan University; Bradley J. Gundlach, Trinity College; Marianne Holdzkom, Southern Polytechnic State; Maggie Lowe, Bridgewater State College; Laura Robinson, Foothill College; Asa L. Rubenstein, Pace University.

Many of the events and documents in this collection were first used in our own classrooms. We thank all of our students over the years who have helped teach us about teaching. We dedicate this work to our children, our representatives in the next generation, who will construct their own pasts in order to understand themselves and their future. To this illustrious list, which includes Jade Rachel Yee-Gorn, Alison MacKenzie Roberts, Kelly Rankin Roberts, Teri Noel Bilhartz, Rocky Bilhartz, and Lindsey Lee Bilhartz.

Elliot J. Gorn
Randy Roberts
Terry D. Bilhartz

INTRODUCTION

Constructing the Past

History is *constructed;* human beings make their lives. The generation that decided to end slavery in America, for example, chose that path, just as generations before had opted to continue enslaving African Americans. The discipline of history assumes that the unfolding of the past is not ordained by God or nature, but by humankind.

But there is another meaning to the phrase "*constructing* the American past." There is no single correct narrative for any given historical episode. Historians have interpreted the Civil War for over a hundred years, and they continue to argue over what were the causes of the war, why the North won and the South lost, whether or not the war might have been averted, and countless other questions. It is not true that one interpretation of history is as valid as another; some historians argue with better logic, larger context, more evidence than others. But no written history is perfect because the past is so complex, because documentation is always incomplete and contradictory, and because historians are never totally free of socially shaped assumptions and their own personal biases.

Constructing the American Past, volume II, challenges you to become an historian. Each chapter provides background information and documentary evidence for a particular historical episode. Your goal is to reconstruct what happened, to put events in context, and to explore their meanings. Was being an immigrant at the turn of the century a positive or negative experience? What was at stake in the Scopes "Monkey" trial in the 1920s? What was it like to live through the Great Depression? There are no easy answers, but the sources allow you to construct an historical story and offer your own ideas.

Each chapter begins with a brief essay that sets the historical context for the episode. Following the essay is a selection of primary documents, with each document or group of documents preceded by an introductory headnote. Three sets of study questions follow the documents. The "Defining Terms" section invites readers to review the chapter's key figures, events, and ideas; "Probing the Sources" questions raise specific points about the sources; "Interpreting the Sources" questions seek more speculative responses about the meaning and importance of the chapter's subject. "Additional Reading" provides suggestions for further reading. Above all, we invite you to read the documents and become your own historian.

1

Reconstruction and the Rise of the Ku Klux Klan

Historical Context

In a letter to the House of Representatives dated April 19, 1872, President Ulysses S. Grant described a "grand system of criminal associations pervading most of the Southern States." Investigations by the attorney general, by the Joint Committee of Congress upon Southern Outrages, and by local officials all revealed that a terroristic organization known as the Ku Klux Klan, or KKK, exercised enormous influence in the South and worked in defiance of federal Reconstruction. Grant alleged that members swore oaths of obedience and secrecy that they considered more binding than their allegiance to the United States. "They are organized and armed," the president declared. "They effect their objects by personal violence, often extending to murder. They terrify witnesses, they control juries in the State courts, and sometimes in the courts of the United States." Klansmen spied on, murdered, and intimidated their enemies and thereby destroyed the rule of law. Their goals, according to Grant, were

> by force and terror, to prevent all political action not in accord with the views of the members, to deprive colored citizens of the right to bear arms, and of the right of a free ballot, and to suppress the schools in which colored children were taught, and to reduce the colored people to a condition closely allied to that of slavery.

The Ku Klux Klan, in other words, threatened to seize by terror what the South had lost on the battlefield. Voting, bearing arms, education, free thought—all were integral to democracy, and all were menaced by the Klan.

The KKK originated in informal organizations that Confederate men joined immediately after the Civil War. The agenda of these organizations became increasingly political as Andrew Johnson's Reconstruction policies were replaced by the more stringent ones of the so-called radical Republicans in Congress. The South was now occupied by federal troops, its cities burned, farms barren, elected officials disgraced, and population decimated. Those who had been slaves, black men and women stigmatized as ineradicably inferior, were now to be treated as equal citizens of a democracy. There was even talk of confiscating southern agricultural land and redistributing it so that blacks and poor whites could become independent farmers, a plan, as it turned out, too radical for most radical Republicans, whose devotion to private property—even that of former rebels—brooked no exceptions.

For African Americans, the era of Reconstruction was a time of relative freedom. Many took the opportunity to leave the land they had been bound to and sought opportunity in southern cities and in the North. Certainly some whites feared the possible loss of their labor force. Equally threatening, the former slaves were more free to worship, work, learn, and acquire power and money than ever before. Many whites alleged that blacks were incapable of handling freedom, that black politicians were corrupt; black workers, slothful; and black masses, ignorant. But the unspoken and perhaps deeper fear was that African Americans were indeed capable of good citizenship and would compete with their former masters. In other words, the comforting idea that any white, no matter how degraded, was "better than a nigger" no longer held. If radical Reconstruction failed to secure real economic opportunity for the former slaves, it did insist that African Americans be treated as equal citizens under the law, an idea antithetical to the old southern economic and social structure, indeed to white southern identity.

But it was not just the new position of blacks that threatened white southerners. Republican rule included policies for changing the region to conform more with the tone of northern society. The "carpetbaggers" and "scalawags" generally were not corrupt individuals but people who genuinely believed that the South's salvation would come through railroads, new industries, and public schools—in short, institutions associated with economic progress in the free-labor North. Radical Reconstruction not only proposed to change racial mores but aimed to make a premodern social and economic system modern. Such drastic changes, imposed, as it appeared to many white southerners, by upstart blacks and alien Yankees, were terrifying.

The Ku Klux Klan was a response to the social, cultural, and economic changes that many white southerners found so disturbing. It might best be seen as the extreme wing of the "redeemers," those whites who sought political redemption from Reconstruction. African Americans and southern Unionists, with the aid of the federal government and the Republican party, were able to govern several states for a few years after the Civil War, but eventually the political experience, popularity, and just plain brutality of the redeemers won the day. The Klan specialized in the latter.

Klansmen typically dressed in white robes and hoods, and they tried to convince their black victims that they were the ghosts of the Confederate dead. Blacks were intimidated, not so much by the transparent ghostly ruse, but by the violence the Klansmen dealt out. By the 1860s, their pattern was clear: several Klansmen would surround a victim's house at night, shoot into the windows, set fire to the structure, poison livestock, or simply drag the inhabitants out and shoot, whip, or hang them. Usually the victims were individuals who had stood up for their rights, blacks who voted, ran for office, or refused to take whites' insults. Occasionally there was open warfare between Klansmen and black militias. White citizens, too, who dared support blacks or who expressed Unionist sympathies were terrorized by the night riders.

It is impossible to know how many southern men ever joined the Klan—it was, after all, a secret organization—but through the late 1860s and into the early 1870s, the Klan was very successful in intimidating both blacks and whites. When the federal government outlawed the organization and began prosecuting its members, the Klan lost some of its effectiveness, but by then violence, along with social ostracism and economic coercion, had become part of the arsenal of redeemer politics. Redemption came to state and local government but succeeded only because the federal government lost its resolve to make sure that all citizens were treated, as promised in the Constitution, with equality. Slowly, African-Americans' rights to vote, to speak out freely, and to participate equally in social life were stripped away.

Perhaps even more important than the political disenfranchisement of African-Americans that followed Reconstruction was their reduction to economic peonage. Slavery died at Appomattox, but new forms of economic and political servitude soon took its place, and they lasted for a century. In the years following the Civil War, most blacks became tenant farmers with no land of their own, and most of these sharecropped, work that offered little more freedom or material comfort than slavery. As a sharecropper, a former slave might farm a white man's land; buy tools, supplies, and food from him; and rent a shack for the family from him. Owner and renter would split the proceeds of the harvest, but the black farmer's debt for the goods that the white man had furnished would almost certainly exceed any profit. Indebted to the white planter, former slaves would be unable to leave; year after year they would have to stay on the land, trying to pay off a debt that grew ever larger.

THE DOCUMENTS

The following documents reveal the Ku Klux Klan from various points of view. The initiation oath of the Knights of the White Camelia (a part of the Klan) reveals the style, tone, and purposes of this organization. Despite the Klan's high rhetoric of defending southern honor, the passages from the narratives of former slaves and from congressional hearings give testimony to how the Klan used violence to accomplish its goals. Note here the reasons for which the victims felt they were being attacked. Congressman Stevenson's speech summarizes the federal findings on the scope of Klan activities and reveals the conflict over values and ideology between southern redeemers and northern Reconstructionists. Finally, *Experience of a Northern Man Among the Ku-Klux* gives a good sense of how northerners viewed the South and how some of them even visualized colonizing it and remaking its society to conform to northern norms. As you read these selections, ask yourself how and why the problem of race relations spilled over into issues related to ideology, economics, and labor.

Introduction to Document 1

The initiation oath of the Knights of the White Camelia reveals the attraction of such organizations. The Knights originated during the early days of the Klan in the late 1860s. Note the claims to religious faith and patriotism and the chivalric mandate: to protect the weak and defenseless against the outrages of "lawless" blacks. Aside from the reassertion of crude white supremacy, the KKK must have been very popular for its sense of mystery, pageantry, and special rituals; individuals were made to feel that they belonged to something splendid and grand. To whom would such appeals be most compelling?

DOCUMENT 1 *Initiation Oath of the Knights of the White Camelia*

I do solemnly swear, in the presence of these witnesses, never to reveal, without authority, the existence of this Order, its objects, its acts, and signs of recognition; never to reveal or publish, in any manner whatsoever, what I shall see or hear in this Council; never to divulge the names of the members of the Order, or their acts done in connection therewith; I swear to maintain and defend the social and political superiority of the White Race on this Continent; always and in all places to observe a marked distinction between the White and African races; to vote for none but white men for any office of honor, profit or trust; to devote my intelligence, energy and influence to instil these principles in the minds and hearts of others; and to protect and defend persons of the White Race, in their lives, rights and property, against the encroachments and aggressions of an inferior race.

I swear, moreover, to unite myself in heart, soul and body with those who compose this Order; to aid, protect and defend them in all places; to obey the orders of those, who, by our statutes, will have the right of giving those orders. . . .

The oath having been taken by the candidate, the C[ommander] shall now say:

Brother, by virtue of the authority to me delegated, I now pronounce you a Knight of the [White Camelia]. . . .

Brothers: You have been initiated into one of the most important Orders, which have ever been established on this continent: an Order, which, if its principles are faithfully observed and its objects diligently carried out, is destined to regenerate our unfortunate country and to relieve the White Race from the humiliating condition to which it has lately been reduced in this Republic. It is necessary, therefore, that before taking part in the labors of this Association, you should understand fully its principles and objects and the duties which devolve upon you as one of its members.

As you may have already gathered from the questions which were propounded to you, and which you have answered so satisfactorily, and from the clauses of the Oath which you have taken, our main and fundamental object is the *maintenance of the supremacy of the white race* in this Republic. History and physiology teach us that we belong to a race which nature has endowed with an evident superiority over all other races, and that the Maker, in thus elevating us above the common standard of human creation, has intended to give us over inferior races, a dominion from which no human laws can permanently derogate. The experience of ages demonstrate that, from the origin of the world, this dominion has always remained in the hands of the Caucasian Race; whilst all the other races have constantly occupied a subordinate and secondary position; a fact which triumphantly confirms this great law of nature. Powerful nations have succeeded each other in the face of the world, and have marked their passage by glorious and memorable deeds; and among those who have thus left on this globe indelible traces of their splendor and greatness, we find none but descended from the Caucasian stock. We see, on the contrary, that most of the countries inhabited by the other races have remained in a state of complete barbarity; whilst the small number of those who have advanced beyond this savage existence, have, for centuries, stagnated in a semi-barbarous condition, of which there can be no progress or improvement. And it is a remarkable fact that as a race of men is more remote from the Caucasian and approaches nearer to the black African, the more fatally that stamp of inferiority is affixed to its sons, and irrevocably dooms them to eternal imperfectibility and degradation.

Convinced that we are of these elements of natural ethics, we know, besides, that the government of our Republic was established by white men, for white men alone, and that it never was in the contemplation of its founders that it should fall into the hands of an inferior and degraded race. We hold, therefore, that any attempt to wrest from the white race the management of its affairs in order to transfer it to control of the black population, is an invasion of the sacred prerogatives vouchsafed to us by the Constitution, and a violation of the laws established by God himself; that such encroachments are subversive of the established institutions of our Republic, and that no individual of the white race can submit to them without humiliation and shame.

It, then, becomes our solemn duty, as white men, to resist strenuously and persistently those attempts against our natural and constitutional rights, and to do everything in our power in order to maintain, in this Republic, the supremacy of the Caucasian race, and restrain the black or African race to that condition of social and political inferiority for which God has destined it. This is the object for which our Order was instituted; and, in carrying it out, we intend to infringe no laws, to violate no rights, and to resort to no forcible means, except for purposes of legitimate and necessary defense.

As an essential condition of success, this Order proscribes absolutely all social equality between the races. If we were to admit persons of African race on the same level with ourselves, a state of personal relations would follow which would unavoidably lead to political equality; for it would be a virtual recognition of *status*, after which we could not consistently deny them an equal share in the administration of our public affairs. The man who is good enough to be our familiar companion, is good enough also to participate in our political government; and if we were to grant the one, there could be no good reason for us not to concede the other of these two privileges.

There is another reason, Brothers, for which we condemn this social equality. Its toleration would soon be a fruitful source of intermarriages between individuals of the two races; and the result of this *misceganation [sic]* would be gradual amalgamation and the production of a degenerate and bastard offspring, which would soon populate these States with a degraded and ignoble population, incapable of moral and intellectual development and unfitted to support a great and powerful country. We must maintain the purity of the white blood, if we would preserve for it that natural superiority with which God has ennobled it.

To avoid these evils, therefore, we take the obligation *to observe a marked distinction between the two races*, not only in the relations of public affairs, but also in the more intimate dealings and intercourse of private life which, by the frequency of their occurrence, are more apt to have an influence on the attainment of the purposes of the Order.

Now that I have laid before you the objects of this Association, let me charge you specially in relation to one of your most important studies as one of its members. Our statutes make us bound to respect sedulously the rights of the colored inhabitants of this Republic, and in every instance, to give to them whatever lawfully belongs to them. It is an act of simple justice not to deny them any of the privileges to which they are legitimately entitled; and we cannot better show the inherent superiority of our race than by dealing with them in that spirit of firmness, liberality and impartiality which characterizes all superior organizations. Besides, it would be ungenerous for us to undertake to restrict them to the narrowest limits as to the exercise of certain rights, without conceding to them, at the same time, the fullest measure of those which we recognize as theirs; and a fair construction of a white man's duty towards them would be, not only to respect and observe their acknowledged rights, but also to see that these are respected and observed by others.

Introduction to Documents 2 and 3

Despite the Klan's lofty rhetoric, the following testimonies by its victims reveal the terrorism for which the organization was renowned. Ask yourself who became Klan victims and why. The three statements in Document 2 were made by former slaves looking back on their experiences from a distance of several decades; the statements are taken from oral histories collected during the 1930s by the Federal

Writers Project. The two statements in Document 3 come from testimony before a congressional committee investigating Klan activities in the early 1870s.

DOCUMENT 2 TESTIMONY OF VICTIMS OF THE KU KLUX KLAN

Pierce Harper

After de colored people was considered free an' turned loose de Klu Klux broke out. Some of de colored people commenced to farming like I tol' you an' all de ol' stock dey could pick up after de Yankees left dey took an' took care of. If you got so you made good money an' had a good farm de Klu Klux'd come an' murder you. De gov'ment built de colored people school houses an' de Klu Klux went to work an' burn 'em down. Dey'd go to de jails an' take de colored men out an' knock dere brains out an' break dere necks an' throw 'em in de river.

Dere was a man dat dey taken, his name was Jim Freeman. Dey taken him an' destroyed his stuff an' him 'cause he was making some money. Hung him on a tree in his front yard, right in front of his cabin. Dere was some young men who went to de schools de gov'ment opened for de colored folks. Some white widder woman said someone had stole something she own', so dey put these young fellers in jail 'cause dey suspicioned 'em. De Klu Kluxes went to de jail an' took 'em out an' kill 'em. Dat happen de second year after de War.

After de Klu Kluxes got so strong de colored men got together an' made a complaint before de law. De Gov'nor told de law to give 'em de ol' guns in de commissary what de Southern soldiers had use, so dey issued de colored men old muskets an' told 'em to protect theirselves.

De colored men got together an' organized the 'Malicy [Militia]. Dey had leaders like regular soldiers, men dat led 'em right on. Dey didn't meet 'cept when dey heard de Klu Kluxes was coming to get some of de colored folks. Den de one who knowed dat tol' de leader an' he went 'round an' told de others when an' where dey's meet. Den dey was ready for 'em. Dey'd hide in de cabins an' when de Klu Kluxes come dere dey was. Den's when dey found out who a lot of de Klu Kluxes was, 'cause a lot of 'em was killed. Dey wore dem long sheets an' you couldn't tell who dey was. Dey even covered dere horses up so you couldn't tell who dey belong to. Men you thought was your friend was Klu Kluxes. You deal wit' 'em in de stores in de day time an' at night dey come out to your house an' kill you.

Sue Craft

My teacher's name Dunlap—a white teacher teachin de cullud. De Ku Klux whupped him fo' teachin' us. I saw de Ku Klux ridin' a heap dem days. Dey had hoods pulled ovah dere faces. One time dey come to our house twict. Fus' time dey come quiet. It was right 'fore de 'lection o' Grant jus' after slavery. It was fus' time cullud people 'lowed t' vote. Dey ast my father was he goin' to vote for Grant. He tell 'em he don' know he goin' vote. After 'lection dey come back, whoopin' an' hollerin. Dey shoot out de winder lights. It was 'cause my father voted for Grant. Dey broke de do' open. My father was a settin' on de bed. I 'member he had a shot gun in his han'. Well, dey broke de do' down, an' then father he shoot, an' dey scattered all ovah de fence.

Morgan Ray

. . . I heard a lot about the Klu Klux, but it warn't till long afterwards dat I evan see 'em. It was one night after de work of de day was done and I was takin' a walk near where I worked. Suddenly I hear the hoof beats of horses and I natcherly wuz curious and waited

Ku Klux Klan "mode of torture." (Library of Congress)

beside de road to see what was comin'. I saw a company of men hooded and wearin' what looked like sheets. Dey had a young cullud man as dere prisoner. I wuz too skairt to say anything or ask any questions. I just went on my sweet way. Later I found out dey acclaimed de prisoner had assaulted a white woman. Dey strung him up when he wouldn't confess, and shot him full of holes and threw his body in de pond.

DOCUMENT 3 *Congressional Inquiry into Klan Activities*

Atlanta, Georgia, October 25, 1871.

Joseph Addison (White) Sworn and Examined

BY THE CHAIRMAN:

Question: What is your age, where were you born, where do you live, and what is your present occupation?

Answer: I am about twenty-four years old; I was born in Muscogee County, and now live in Haralson County; I have been living there ever since I was a little bit of a boy; I am a farmer.

Question: During the war which side were you on?

Answer: I never fought a day in the rebel army; I was not in it at all.

Question: Which side were your feelings on?

Answer: My feelings were on the side of what you call the radical party now.

Question: What did they call it then?

Answer: I was what you call a Union man then.

Question: Were your opinions well known?

Answer: Yes, sir; I reckon I am well known.

Question: Have you seen any people, or do you know of any, in your county, called Ku-Klux?

Answer: Yes, sir.

Question: Tell us what you know about them.

Answer: Do you want me to state just about all how they did?

Question: Yes.

Answer: I will tell you how they did me. . . . My wife looked out and said, "Lord have mercy! Joe, it is the Ku-Klux." I jumped out of the door and ran. One of them was right in the back yard, and he jabbed the end of his six-shooter almost against my head, and said, "Halt! God damn you." I said, "I will give up." I asked them what they were doing that for; they said that I had been stealing. I said, "You men here know I have not." They said, "We gave you time once to get away, and, God damn you, you have not gone; now, God damn you, you shall not go, for we allow to kill you." I said, "If you do not abuse me or whip me, I will go the next morning." They said they would not abuse me or whip me, but they would kill me. I said, "Let me go and see my wife and children." They said, "No, God damn you." I turned away from the man; he jammed his pistol in my face, and said, "God damn you, go on, or I will kill you." They took me about eighty or ninety yards from there into a little thicket. The man on my right was a high, tall man; the one on my left was a low, chunky fellow. The man on my right stepped back, and said to the little fellow on my left, "Old man, we have got him here now; do as you please with him." There were some little hickories near him; he looked at them, but did not take them. They were all standing right around me with their guns pointing at me. Just as he turned around, I wheeled and run; but before I had run ten yards I heard a half a dozen caps bursted at me. Just as I made a turn to go behind some buildings and little bushes, I heard two guns fired. I must have gone seventy or eighty yards, and then I heard what I thought was a pistol fired. I heard a bullet hit a tree. I run on eight or ten steps further, and then I heard a bullet hit a tree just before me. Every one of them took after me, and run me for a hundred and fifty yards. I ran down a little bluff and ran across a branch. When I got across there, I could not run any further, for my shoes were all muddy. I cut the strings of my old shoes, and left them there. I stopped to listen, but I never saw anything more of them. I then went around and climbed up on the fence, and sat there and watched until dark. I then went to the house and got some dry clothes, and then went back where I had fixed a place in the woods to sleep in, and went to bed. That was the last I heard of them that night. They came back Sunday night before court commenced on Monday, in Haralson County. My wife would not stay there by herself, but went to her sister-in-law's, Milton Powell's wife. They came in on them on Sunday night, or about two hours and a half before day Monday morning. They abused her and cursed her powerfully, and tried to make her tell where I was. They said that if she did not tell them they would shoot her God-damned brains out. I was laying out close by there, and I stood there and heard them. They shot five or six shots in the yard; some of them said they shot into the house. They scared my wife and sister-in-law so bad that they took the children and went into the woods and staid there all night. That was the last time they were there. . . .

Question: Have they ever molested you since then?

Answer: No, sir; they have never been on me any more since then.

Question: Do you still stay there?

Answer: No, sir; I have done moved now. I moved off, and left my hogs and my crop and everything there, what little I made. I did not make much crop this year, for I was afraid to work, and now I am afraid to go back there to save anything.

Atlanta, Georgia, October 26, 1871.

Thomas M. Allen (Colored) Sworn and Examined

BY THE CHAIRMAN:

Question: What is your age, where were you born, and where do you now live?

Answer: I am now thirty-eight years old. I was born in Charleston, South Carolina, and I am living here at present; that is, my family is here; I am pastor of the Baptist church at Marietta, Jasper County.

Question: How long have you been living in this State?

Answer: I came to this State the year that James K. Polk died, about 1849.

Question: How do you connect your coming here with his death?

Answer: I landed in Savannah at the time they were firing cannon there, and asked what was the matter.

Question: Were you a slave?

Answer: Partly so. My father was a white man and he set us free at his death. They stole us from Charleston and run me and my brother and mother into this State. He left us ten thousand dollars each to educate us, and give us trades, and for that money they stole us away.

Question: Were you kept in slavery until the time of emancipation?

Answer: Yes, sir; I was held as a slave; I hired my time.

Question: You never were able to assert your freedom before emancipation?

Answer: No, sir, I could not do it. . . .

Question: Have you been connected with political affairs in this State since the war?

Answer: Yes, sir. When the constitutional convention was called, I took an active part, and did all I could, of course. Afterwards I ran for the legislature and was elected.

Question: In what year?

Answer: I was elected in 1868; the colored members were expelled that year.

Question: From what county were you elected?

Answer: From Jasper County.

Question: Were you reinstated in your seat in the legislature?

Answer: Yes, sir.

Question: Have you witnessed any violence towards any of your race, yourself or any others?

Answer: Yes, sir. After we were expelled from the legislature, I went home to Jasper County; I was carrying on a farm there. On the 16th of October, a party of men came to my house; I cannot say how many, for I did not see them. . . . About 2 o'clock my wife woke me up, and said that there were persons all around the house; that they had been there for half an hour, and were calling for me. I heard them call again, and I asked them what they wanted, and who they were. . . .

They asked me to come out. At this time my brother-in-law waked up and said, "Who are they, Thomas?" I said, "I do not know." . . .

He put on his shoes and vest and hat; this was all he was found with after he was killed. He opened the door and hollered, "Where are you?"

He hollered twice, and then two guns were fired. He seemed to fall, and I and my wife hollered, and his wife hollered. I jumped up, and ran back to the fire-place, where I started to get a light, and then started to go over the partition to him. I threw a clock down, and then I thought of the closet there, and went through it to him, and my wife closed the door. I hollered for Joe, a third man on the place, to come up and bring his gun, for Emanuel was killed. He did not come for some time, and then I was so excited that I could not recognize his voice. After a time I let him in. We made up a light, and then I saw my brother-in-law laying on his back as he fell. I examined him; there were four or five number one buck-shot in his breast. . . .

Question: What do you know about this organization of men they call Ku-Klux?

Answer: I have never seen one in my life; I have seen a great many people who have seen them. I have a Ku-Klux letter here that I got on the day of the election for the constitution.

Question: Will you read it?

Answer: Yes, sir; this is it.

To Thomas Allen:

Tom, you are in great danger; you are going heedless with the radicals, against the interest of the conservative white population, and I tell you if you do not change your course before the election for the ratification of the infernal constitution, your days are numbered, and they will be but few. Just vote or use your influence for the radicals or for the constitution, and you go up certain. My advice to you, Tom, is to stay at home if you value your life, and not vote at all, and advise all of your race to do the same thing. You are marked and closely watched by K.K.K. (or in plain words Ku-Klux.)

Take heed; a word to the wise is sufficient.

By order of Grand Cyclops.

Question: Where did you get this?

Answer: It was dropped in the shop the morning of the election, when I was running for the legislature. I showed it to a great many men in town; I showed it to Colonel Preston, a friend of mine. He asked where I got it, and I told him. He said, "Tear it up." I said, "No, it may be of service to my children if not to me." He said, "You need not talk so slack about it; there may be heaps of Ku-Klux in the State, and they might get hold of your talk. . . ."

Question: What is the feeling of your people in regard to their personal safety?

Answer: They do not consider that they have any safety at all, only in the cities; that is the truth. In a great many places the colored people call the white people master and mistress, just as they ever did; if they do not do it they are whipped. They have no safety at all except in a large place like this. If I could have stayed at home I would not have been here. I left all my crops and never got anything for them. My wife had no education, and when I came away everything went wrong. There are thousands in my condition.

Question: Is that the reason so many of your people come to the large cities?

Answer: Yes, sir, that is the reason. Mr. Abram Turner, a member of the legislature, from Putnam County, the county adjoining mine, was shot down in the street in open day. He was a colored man. They have elected another in his place, a democrat.

Question: When was he elected?

Answer: Last fall.

Question: He has been killed since?

Answer: Yes, sir, shot down in broad open day. . . .

Question: Was he a republican?
Answer: Yes sir, I knew him very well; he was a good man, a harmless man; I married him to his wife.
Question: Do the people of your race feel that they have the protection of the laws?
Answer: By no means.
Question: What is their hope and expectation for the future?
Answer: They expect to get protection from the Federal Government at Washington; that is all. You ask any one of my people out there, even the most ignorant of them, and they will tell you so. . . . I believe that many of the jurymen, and lawyers too, are members of the Ku-Klux; I believe it positively; I would say so on my deathbed.
Question: How much have you been over the State?
Answer: I have traveled all over the State.
Question: Have you communicated pretty freely with the people of your own race?
Answer: Yes, sir.
Question: Have you received information from them about the Ku-Klux?
Answer: Yes, sir, occasionally.
Question: In how large a portion of the State do you find reports of Ku-Klux operations?
Answer: I find it in the counties of what is known among us as the Black Belt. Wherever the negroes are in the majority, there the Ku-Klux range more than in any other places. Up in Cobb County they are very peaceable. The democrats are always elected there to the general assembly. The whites have about seven hundred majority. The colored people get along splendidly there. In those counties where the whites are largely in the majority, the colored people get along very well; but go into the counties where the negroes are in the majority, and there is always trouble; for instance, in Monroe County, or Warren County, or anywhere in the Black Belt, there is always trouble between the whites and the colored people.
Question: Are the colored people riotous in disposition? Are they inclined to make trouble?
Answer: I suppose the colored people are as peaceable as any people in the world. The colored people of Madison, when the white people went to the jail and murdered a man there, could have burned up the town and killed all the white people there.

Introduction to Document 4

Congressman Job E. Stevenson from Ohio delivered the following address in the House of Representatives on May 30, 1872. He argued that the Klan was not merely a brutal organization devoted to terror, but part of a political conspiracy to overthrow Reconstruction and reenslave African Americans. As you read the excerpts from this speech, note Stevenson's characterization of the newly conquered South. Why did he believe that the North must stop the Klan? What were his political motivations for opposing the Klan?

DOCUMENT 4 *Speech to the House of Representatives*

Hon. Job E. Stevenson of Ohio

Mr. Speaker: The gravest question before Congress is the Kuklux Conspiracy, its origin and extent, character and actions, plans and purposes, condition and prospects.

Origin

It originated in hostility to the Government, in enmity against the Union. It is the successor of the southern confederacy, rebellion in disguise, war at midnight. It rose like an exhalation from the unsodden grave of the "lost cause." . . .

A Political Conspiracy

Such being the origin . . . of this great conspiracy, we may well inquire against whom its terrors are aimed. It strikes exclusively at the Unionists of the South, principally at the freedmen. No man can deny that it is political. The oath swears the member to oppose Radicalism, to oppose the Radical party, to oppose the political equality of the races.

General Forrest said: "It is a protective political military organization. Its objects originally were protection against Loyal Leagues and the Grand Army of the Republic; but after it became general, it was found that political matters and interests could best be promoted within it, and it was then made a political organization, giving its support, of course, to the Democratic party." . . .

It appears that in the States of Georgia, Louisiana, Tennessee, and South Carolina from the spring election in 1868 to the election for President in 1868, the Republican vote was reduced eighty-five thousand by intimidation and violence. . . .

Commanders

The forces of the conspiracy are controlled by such men as Generals Gordon, Hampton, and Forrest, and under them by inferior officers, running down from grade to grade, to captains of companies, or chiefs of klans or cyclops of dens. The organization begins at the den and extends to the precinct, the county, the congressional district, the State, the South. It is compact, connected, consistent, moving as a perfect body from the head to the humblest member, as an army in the field, with sterner discipline than that of an army. . . .

Authority

These commands bind the members by an oath enforced by fear; administered with strange ceremonies, emphasized by penalty of death. At midnight the member is led blindfold to the den, and there, on his knees, hears the ritual and takes the oath. And as the bandage drops from his eyes he sees circles of men in frightful disguises armed with revolvers leveled on his head, and the Grand Cyclops says: "And this you do under penalty of a traitor's doom, which is death! death! death!" In some dens there are symbols of horror. In one in North Carolina, two skulls, one of a white man, a Union soldier, whose grave was rifled and his skull taken for the den; and the other the skull of a freedman, who had been murdered; and a vial of blood of the colored victim; the member is sworn "by these skulls and this blood."

Thus members are sworn to obey their superior officers on penalty of death, and under that oath they are compelled to take the field at the command and to do any deed he may order, even to murder. Scores of members have confessed and testified that they have committed outrages and murders at the command of their officers.

Outrages

The outrages vary from threats and intimidations to scourging, wounding, maiming, and killing by shooting, drowning, hanging, and burning. If we could know the whole truth it would appear that since the war this conspiracy has outraged more than thirty thousand men, women, and children—peaceful, innocent, defenseless citizens of the Republic. . . .

Excuses

Among the excuses made by those who control and defend this organization is that they feared the negroes; yet all Southern men of intelligence testify that the negroes of the South have behaved better than any other people ever did under similar circumstances. . . . They pretend that the Government of the United States has oppressed them, yet that Government, to which they had forfeited property, liberty, and life, spared their lives, allowed them their liberty, and returned them their property. No confiscated estates are withheld from their owners; although some abandoned property was taken, the only rebel estate remaining in the hands of the Government is Arlington [Robert E. Lee's estate], and gentlemen in both Houses of Congress propose to remove the remains of our soldiers and give that cemetery back to its rebel owners. No life has been taken for treason. Jefferson Davis is as free as the air, a citizen of the Republic. Few political privileges are denied, few leaders are unamnestied. The only issue that can be made on amnesty is whether the remnant should be forthwith relieved. The difference between parties on this question is whether the Republican party has been derelict in not restoring to political power even Jefferson Davis. . . .

Financial Results of Reconstruction

What has been the financial result of reconstruction? The Government and the peoples of the North forgave to the people of the South and caused them to repudiate debts amounting to more than twenty-five hundred million dollars. We relieved them by constitutional amendments, and by the generosity of our people, of debts nearly double the property their own crimes had left. If the Government and the people of the North had merely withheld their hands from the South, and left the conquered rebels to their own financial devices, the South would have sunk in bankruptcy and ruin as a man thrown into the sea with a millstone at his neck. The Government and people of the North rescued them, fed them, advanced money and property, restored peace and order, and gave them the opportunity to revive their fortunes.

The white people of the South continually upbraid the colored people, saying, "The negro will not work." Yet wherever you go you see scores of white men lounging on the piazzas of the hotels, shifting their chairs to keep out of the sun, moving only to get "refreshments," while freedmen are laboring in the fields earning money to enable the whites to lounge. The laborers of the South have produced in cotton and other agricultural products since the war nearly $4,000,000,000, more than double the value of property in 1865. And the people have saved so much of these gains, that they had in 1870 $2,700,000,000 against $1,600,000,000 at the end of the war, having increased their property since the war over $1,000,000,000. And they had in 1870, $6,000,000 more than their State assessments in 1860, excluding slaves. That is the financial result of reconstruction. . . .

Financial Effects of Kuklux

They have not yet ceased reckless destruction of their own property. The Kuklux conspiracy is fatal to values. It disturbs business, disorganizes labor, paralyzes industry and commerce. The documents show the fall of property in those States where the conspiracy has been acting by the millions. . . . The Kuklux conspiracy has cost the South more than all the carpet-baggers of all the States (including the Louisiana leader of the new movement), have been able to misappropriate.

Depopulation

The conspiracy is driving away the people. Here is a copy of the *Freedmen's Repository*, giving an account of the emigration from this country to Liberia, showing that last fall a ship took out of the country from Virginia one passenger; from Florida, five; from North Carolina, five; from Georgia, sixty-six; and from Clay Hill, York county, South Carolina, one hundred and sixty-six. And at the head of this South Carolina party was Rev. Elias Hill, a description of whom is given here, a Baptist preacher, a cripple, whom the Kuklux scourged because he preached the gospel, taught school, and belonged to the Republican party. He was driven with a colony of one hundred and sixty-six souls out of South Carolina, out of the United States of America, even to Liberia.

Here were two hundred and thirty-eight industrious people driven at once from the United States to Africa.

Before the war these colored people—men, women, and children—were valued by their owners at $500 each. Now they are driven out of the country by outrage, scourging, and murder; and we are told that the United States Government must not interfere to protect them. Imagine Elias Hill in the wilds of Africa, telling the bushmen how the great American Republic protects its citizens.

Present Condition of the Conspiracy

But, Mr. Speaker, what is the present condition of this organization? . . .

Those who imagine that because the conspirators are now still, they will remain so, do not understand them. In South Carolina the members of this organization raided in 1868, outraged and murdered Union people, and changed votes by scores of thousands. From that time until 1870 they were quiet, and then they raided again until more than three thousand outrages were committed in less than six months. The conspiracy is so organized that it may remain quiescent for a year or for two years, ready to be called into the field by the blast of the bugle, or by the click of the telegraph. Within one week this "military political" organization could throw into action a quarter of a million men, armed with the revolver, the bowie-knife, . . . with bayonets captured from State militia, and revolving rifles furnished from New York city.

Its Power

Shall we trust them? Are we blind—blind to the red rivers of blood they have shed; deaf to the cries of their thousands of victims? Are we mad to forget our own interests and safety? These conspirators have power, if they dare—and they are men who have dared death at the cannon's mouth—to sweep the whole South at the next presidential election; and if the result depends on the South, they can seat their candidate in the presidential chair. . . . *Whoever shall be the Democratic candidate will be the candidate of the Kuklux conspiracy*. If the *Democrats elect the next President it will be by Kuklux votes and violence; and the man thus elected will be the Kuklux President*.

INTRODUCTION TO DOCUMENT 5

Benjamin Bryant's *Experience of a Northern Man Among the Ku-Klux* argues that, while the South had been defeated, the region's way of life remained stubbornly unchanged. Bryant began with the problem of education, stating that the southern planter aristocracy kept both African Americans and poor whites in ignorance. The Klan had arisen to maintain this situation. Keeping the masses poor and ignorant, according to Bryant, was the Klan's main goal. Document 5 contains excerpts from Bryant's book.

DOCUMENT 5 **From Experience of a Northern Man Among the Ku-Klux**

Benjamin Bryant

In order to better inform my readers of my intention for writing a book, I will say before entering into the main body of the work, that I have just returned from a long visit in the South, and have witnessed things which have occurred in the States late in Rebellion, and have kept a record of all, for the interest of the Northern people, and also, to give in detail the present situation of the people who are living there. . . .

As education is the great aim of every true American citizen, I will first inform you of its progress. The South has not had the advantages to aid in the development of education like the people of the North; but it has always been discouraged by the aristocracy of the South; and in so doing they have deprived the poor white people of education and other intelligences, as well as the black man. . . .

A great many freedmen are working on shares with their former masters, and are generally doing well, but are working for one-half, one-third, or one-fourth of their former pay, and are working under their master's hand, calling their former masters, "master," and denouncing the Proclamation of Emancipation. They hate that "old Northern woman" who is teaching the "nigger school," and resist all aid to free schools, and say, "I can live without education; I don't want it and will not have it."

"You are a good negro, and you may live on my land all your life-time."

That black man will work there for some time, and make one or two bales of cotton and give it to his master, as he calls him, to sell; and he will sell it and bring Tom, the good and smart negro, what he has a mind to.

Well, some day Tom will walk by the school-house and have a word or two with the teacher. Tom will tell him about his cotton. The teacher will say, "How much cotton did you have?"

"So much."

"How much money did you get?"

Tom says, "I got fifty dollars."

The school teacher will say, "Is that all? You should have more than that."

"How much more?"

"You should have twenty-five dollars more."

Tom says, "I am going to see him." . . .

[Tom's former master asked who told him he deserved more money.]

"The school teacher told me so."

"Who, that damn'd Yankee?"

"Yes sir."

"He told you that you could get more pay if you should go North, did he?"

"Yes sir. He told John, that black boy that lives with Mr. Brown, that he was free and should go to school. Yes, master, he told all the colored people to send their children and let them learn something." . . .

"Where is he from?"

"Massachusetts."

"We will fix him," says Tom's master. "Hitch up my horse; I am going away."

He will then go to the fork of the roads and tell everybody about what the damn'd Yankee school teacher told his niggers. If he stays here long he will have every nigger in the place think that he is as good as a white man. Well, we must run him away. Send him word to leave by Monday. If not, we will fix him.

Monday has come—Tuesday has come. The nigger-school teacher has not gone yet. We must get together. (This is not talked in the presence of Tom, but Tom is in the next room and hears it all.)

"Tom, you go and tell Mr. Brown and Mr. Bond to come here, and on your way back go round by the Pugh Place and tell Mr. Pollock to come, too, and bring every one that he can."

They will all meet and talk the matter over, and agree to meet on Wednesday night at 10 o'clock, all dressed in uniform, ready to commence their secret midnight demonstration. They went to his house and took him out, and tied a large rope round his neck, and he was seen down on his knees praying. But the party who saw him was a colored man (in the woods), and he says that he could go to the spot where he was hung with his feet up, tied to the branch of an oak tree, and a log of wood round his neck, and his tongue from five to seven inches out of his mouth. This punishment will be applied to that class of Northern people who will go South and settle, and have not received full information how to act. You know it is an old saying, and a good one too, when you are in Rome, act as a Roman, and when you are in the South, you must act as a Southern man. What are these actions? First, I will say, you must act with the majority, let their actions be good or bad. You must denounce all free schools for white or black children. You must not come South and pay more for labor than the established price, which is all the way from five to ten dollars per month, but an extra good hand, who has always been farming, may in some cases get from fifteen to sixteen dollars per month. Never give a black man, or a poor white man who cannot read, any advice to post themselves upon matters pertaining to their own welfare. Never speak a good word for New England, because her States demand human rights before the law, for all men. Never say anything about Bunker Hill, because that is in Massachusetts. Never express your political opinion, let it be Republican or Democratic, for we know that both parties wanted to maintain the Union. And, above all, you must hate niggers. There has been many a good enterprising Northern man driven from the newly established homestead because he did not know the existing circumstances. This organization, known as the "Invisible Empire," or Ku-Klux, does exist in the Southern States. There is a number of Northern people in both of the political parties that have manifested a strong unbelief in regard to the Ku-Klux Klans, but I will say a word on a verified fact, and truth, which is today being witnessed by every peace-loving and upright citizen.

Introduction to Document 6

In *The Grand Army of the Republic Versus the Ku Klux Klan,* W. H. Gannon proposed that 100,000 former soldiers be allowed to colonize the South. These men would be given land and money, and, presumably, their example would show southerners the value of Northern industriousness and the free-labor system. Such a plan would also help alleviate the unemployment caused by swings of the business cycle. The following excerpts are taken from the chapter "How to Extirpate Ku-Kluxism from the South" in Gannon's book.

DOCUMENT 6 *"How to Extirpate Ku-Kluxism from the South"*

W. H. Gannon

. . . In view of the fact, that the present phase of the difficulty between the North and the South has already continued for eight long and dreary years, whereas half that time sufficed in which to annihilate the whole of rebel armies, the conclusion is inevitable that the Northern People are making some very serious mistake in conducting their case in its present form; and consequently, that they must make some radical change in their Southern policy, before they can hope to gain their cause at the South. . . :

(1.) That the fatal mistake of the Northern People in their Southern policy since the dispersion of the rebel armies, has been their reliance upon United States Marshals and United States soldiers, almost exclusively, to represent them at the South; (2.) that their true course to pursue towards the South is to colonize it with at least One Hundred Thousand (100,000) intelligent, respectable, and industrious Northern Working Men; (3.) that, inasmuch as the Federal Government found no very great difficulty, any time during the late war, in inducing a million of Northern men to exchange the security, peace, and enjoyment of their homes for the dangers and privations of prolonged active warfare in the face of a determined and powerful enemy at the South and to remain there year after year, until the overthrow of their antagonists left them free to return to their homes,—there are 100,000 of those same men who would gladly return South now with the implements of peace in their hands, to make their homes there, provided they had the means to enable them to do so; (4.) that One Thousand (1000) Dollars per man would be all sufficient to establish them comfortably there; (5.) that the required funds would readily enough be forthcoming, were the proper parties to ask the public for them; and (6.) that the proper parties to collect the required funds, and to select the proposed colonists, and superintend the suggested undertaking, generally, are the GRAND ARMY OF THE REPUBLIC, and the various WORKING MEN'S SOCIETIES throughout the North. . . .

All purely patriotic considerations aside, the success of this plan would, in a mere speculative and economic point of view, prove highly beneficial to the industrial and business interests of the North. Its operations, if extended to anything like National proportions, would necessarily open a vast field for utilizing the immense mass of well disposed and intelligent, but adventurous young energy now wandering aimless about the North; they would provide acceptable and remunerative employment, at the South, for multitudes of Northern working people who find it impossible to secure the means of a decent support for themselves and their families in their present abodes. For, while individual Northern enterprise in that direction is not just now advisable, yet throughout the whole civilized world, there is not another so favorable an opening for co-operative Northern enterprise, if it be united, systematic, and of a legitimate character, as the South, in its present condition, offers to it. Every associated enterprise, such as this plan suggests, if judiciously located and properly managed for developing the natural resources of the South, instead of (as some have done) plunging into mad attempts at competition with great Northern industries, would handsomely compensate the laborer for his work, besides, after the first year, paying cent-per-cent, per annum on every dollar of capital invested in it. Once settled at the South, the colonist, amidst congenial social surroundings that this plan would secure to him, could not, with a tithe of the industry, fail to secure an ample competency for themselves and their dependents, without that incessant toil which, for even a scanty and precarious support, the North exacts from every person who depends solely upon manual labor, for their livelihood within its great centers of population. Thus they would materially benefit themselves in all the relations of life, and, at the same time, leave a freer field to, and open a new market for, the industry of those of their fraternity who are established at the North. It would, also, give a new and lasting impetus to legitimate business of all kinds throughout the whole country. Therefore, leaving Southern interests and political considerations out of the question altogether, this plan deserves the serious attention of the Working men and the Business men of the North.

QUESTIONS

Defining Terms

Identify in the context of the chapter each of the following:

racism	Reconstruction
redeemers	carpetbaggers and scalawags
sharecroppers	Knights of the White Camelia
Job Stevenson	Benjamin Bryant
miscegenation	Liberia

Probing the Sources

1. Who were the victims of Klan violence? Why were whites sometimes attacked by the Klan in addition to African Americans?
2. Under what political circumstances did the Klan arise?
3. What were its stated goals? What were its goals as you can infer them by its members' actions?
4. How did northerners characterize southerners? How did southerners characterize northerners?

Intrepreting the Sources

1. Who opposed the Klan and why? Was the Ku Klux Klan a political organization? A terrorist organization?
2. Did the Klan's racist ideology fulfill goals beyond the simple expression of irrational hatred?
3. Did opponents of the Klan want to stop racism, or did they have an additional agenda?
4. Was the Klan successful? Why or why not?

ADDITIONAL READING

On the Ku Klux Klan, see Allen Trelease, *White Terror: The Ku Klux Klan Conspiracy and Southern Reconstruction* (1971), and David Mark Chalmers, *Hooded Americanism: The History of the Ku Klux Klan* (1981). For various interpretations of Reconstruction, see John Hope Franklin, *Reconstruction After the Civil War* (1961); Kenneth M. Stampp, *The Era of Reconstruction, 1865–1877* (1965); and Eric Foner, *Reconstruction: America's Unfinished Revolution, 1863–1877* (1988). On African Americans during Emancipation, see W. E. B. DuBois, *Black Reconstruction* (1935); Leon F. Litwack, *Been in the Storm So Long: The Aftermath of Slavery* (1979); and Litwack, *Trouble in Mind* (1999). For the era's legacy, see Jay R. Mandle, *Not Slave, Not Free: The African American Economic Experience Since the Civil War* (1992). On the reborn Klan of the 1920s, see Leonard Moore, *Citizen Klansmen* (1992) and Nancy MacLain, *Behind the Mask of Chivalry: The Making of the Second Ku Klux Klan* (1994). For a popular history of the old Klan and the new, try Wyn Craig Wade, *The Fiery Cross* (1987).

2

The Great Strike of 1877

Historical Context

The year 1876 was one of celebration. The centennial of the Declaration of Independence was heralded with speeches, fireworks, and prayers. In Philadelphia, a great exhibition made palpable the nation's progress in technology and the arts. Self-congratulation seemed in order, for the Union had been preserved, the railroad now linked both coasts, and new inventions like the telephone and the Corliss engine promised a bright and prosperous future.

Yet these were not altogether happy times. Reconstruction in the South seemed more and more torturous as the Ku Klux Klan continued its rampage of violence and whites found ways to limit blacks' newly won freedom. In the summer of 1876, word came from out west that General George Armstrong Custer and over two hundred cavalrymen had been wiped out at the battle of the Little Bighorn, and during the following year, Chief Joseph and his Nez Percés tribe gave the army all it could handle. Moreover, corruption tainted business and government at the highest levels, as a series of scandals rocked the Grant administration, Wall Street, and especially the nation's largest business, the railroads.

Worst of all, a severe economic depression continued into its fourth year. Millions were unemployed, and many who had jobs experienced severe wage cuts. In New York City, roughly one-quarter of the labor force was out of work, and police brutally dispersed angry crowds of the unemployed. Some workers questioned the logic of celebrating a hundred years of freedom when families went hungry in the streets, and a handful of laborers even began calling for a second American Revolution. In the best of times, the concentration of wealth in the hands of relatively few entrepreneurs raised questions in many workers' minds. These were not the best of times.

Labor organizing and militancy had a long history in America. Before the Civil War, as the old artisan system broke down, as the division of labor grew more specialized, and as manufacturing wealth began to concentrate—in other words, as the dividing line between employers and employees grew ever sharper—labor unions formed in several crafts and industries. Their record was spotty; sometimes they succeeded in gaining worker control over wages, hours, and hiring practices; sometimes they failed. Some workers and labor leaders criticized the system of production and distribution itself, asking why a relative handful of individuals should own so much wealth while most families barely scratched out a living.

But nothing on the scale of the Great Strike of 1877 had ever happened before. In the middle of that year, most of the nation's vast new transcontinental railroad system—the very symbol of American progress, wealth, and modernity—was shut down by angry employees. Tracks, engines, and switching yards were destroyed, related businesses were forced to close, and workers in other industries organized themselves for strikes. Rather suddenly, America looked less like a special land of opportunity for all and more like the London of Charles Dickens, where poverty ground down the working class, or like Paris, where the masses organized themselves for bloody revolution.

The strike began on July 16, in the town of Martinsburg, West Virginia. The Baltimore & Ohio Railroad on that day announced a 10 percent wage cut for all employees, the second such cut in eight months and part of the policy for all railroads across the country. Workers grumbled that companies continued to pay generous dividends to stockholders during the depression, but that those who labored were forced to take starvation wages. Men gathered and talked through the day. When the crew of one train abandoned their posts, other men refused to replace them, and soon everyone threw down their tools. Workers then rode all of the engines into the roundhouse and announced to B&O officials that no trains would move through Martinsburg until their pay was restored.

Local sheriffs and militia were powerless to get the engines running, for the strikers grew too numerous. As they left Wheeling, state troops sent by the governor of West Virginia were met by angry workers, and when they got to Martinsburg, they found themselves overwhelmed by an orderly but determined crowd. Equally important, the soldiers themselves came mostly from laboring families and were sympathetic to the strikers. Finally, at the urging of the governor of West Virginia and the president of the B&O line, President Hayes dispatched three hundred federal troops, who guarded strikebreakers sent from Baltimore. But by now thousands had gathered, including miners and canal workers, all angered by the conditions of labor in their industries. The federal soldiers managed to get trains moving out of Martinsburg, but soon strikers were ambushing these, side-railing and detaining them. Worse, the strike was spreading. Workers, one Baltimore leader declared,

> know what it is to bring up a family on ninety cents a day, to live on beans and cornmeal week in and week out, to run in debt at the stores until you cannot get trusted any longer, to see the wife breaking down under privation and distress, and the children growing up sharp and fierce like wolves day after day because they don't get enough to eat.

The incidents begun in Martinsburg were repeated across the country. The strike was not well organized; during the depression, the small gains made by unions in previous years had been nearly wiped out, and the workers' organizations that did exist tended to be very conservative. The faith of many workers in equal opportunity meant that unions generally were not terribly strong, and as the need for labor solidarity in the face of ever larger companies grew apparent, owners used lockouts, blacklists, scabs, espionage, firings, and prosecutions to keep unions out of their shops. The lack of organization and preparation for a major strike gave the upheaval considerable spontaneity, as workers in various communities responded to local situations and did their best to control events. But sometimes things got out of hand.

The strike reached its climax in Pittsburgh. The Pennsylvania Railroad was America's largest private enterprise, controlling 6,000 miles of track and creating over 20,000 jobs. Three days after the Martinsburg incident began, Pennsylvania Railroad managers ordered that all trains running east from Pittsburgh be "doubleheaders," meaning that two engines pull twice the usual number of cars. Doubleheaders meant harder work, increased danger of accidents, and more layoffs. Once again, brakemen, conductors, flagmen, and others walked off the job, and they were joined by angry workers from other industries. Once again, the state militia was called in, but as an officer explained, "The sympathy of the people, the sympathy of the troops, my own sympathy, was with the strikers proper. We all felt that those men were not receiving enough wages." Soon the soldiers laid down their weapons and fraternized with the strikers. But then 600 fresh troops from Philadelphia were called in; since they were not from the local area, they had less sympathy for the workers. A crowd of 6,000, including women and children there to support their husbands and fathers, began jeering and throwing rocks; the militia opened fire and, in five minutes, killed 20 people. When the soldiers retreated to the roundhouse, strikers armed themselves and attacked them, burned the roundhouse, tore up tracks, and destroyed over 2,000 cars and 100 engines.

And so the upheaval rolled across the country; in St. Louis, Chicago, Cincinnati, Buffalo, and countless other towns, workers from various industries refused to accept low wages, authoritarian owners, or armed coercion. For a few days, workers stopped the wheels of business and rejected the sovereignty of management. The general strike that had begun with the railroads gripped all parts of industry.

But the strike ended as quickly as it began. Lacking organization, the workers failed to make their demands clear, and the ability of laborers to counter management quickly eroded. The federal government mobilized thousands of troops, and cities reorganized their police forces. Soldiers rolled into a town, drove off strikers, secured management's property, allowed strikebreakers to restart businesses, then moved on to the next town. Occasionally workers won concessions from management; more often, not. In all, over a hundred laborers were killed.

The strikes threw disturbing new features of American life into bold relief. At the time of the uprising, about fifty corporations controlled eighty thousand miles of line, and employed hundreds of thousands of workers. As companies competed and sometimes drove each other out of business, the railroads were concentrated in fewer and fewer hands. A handful of men enjoyed private fortunes and paid themselves dividends even during depressions, but most of their employees would be wage laborers for life and would never rise to become independent entrepreneurs, that status so exalted by journalists and orators. And the railroads, it was clear, had merely led the way, for America now was no longer the land of small shopkeepers and apprentices, but of capitalists and workers.

The notion that America had escaped the curse of class conflict—Europe's curse of a rich upper class and an oppressed working class—seemed no longer plausible, if it had ever been true. The events of 1877 made it abundantly clear that a deep chasm divided and would continue to divide the rich and the poor in America. The Great Strike also gave a glimpse of how government would respond to this state of affairs. In the past, civic officials had often taken the part of the workers, for they represented local control rather than the distant power of faceless corporations. But in 1877, as in future conflicts (and there would be many intense labor struggles in

Strike of 1877: People standing amongst debris. (Carnegie Library of Pittsburgh)

the coming decades), state and federal power were the creatures of the rich and powerful. When the government intervened, it was to protect private property against the claims of workers.

THE DOCUMENTS

Introduction to Documents 1 and 2

The documents in this section are as much about how individuals responded to the strike as about the strike itself. Document 1 appeared in a leading journal of the day, the *North American Review,* in September 1877. It is a letter written by an anonymous striker justifying the actions of those who had taken part in the uprising. Document 2 is an article that the *North American Review* solicited from Colonel Thomas Scott, the president of the Pennsylvania Railroad. Note how both identified their own interests with those of the nation. Compare the striker's assumption that all value is created by labor with the railroad president's belief that the best interests of his company and of the nation were one. How did each writer define patriotism? How did they differ on what constitutes fairness? What common ground did they share?

DOCUMENT 1 *"Fair Wages"*

by a Striker

The newspapers have fallen into line to defend the railway companies, who thus have brought all the great guns of public opinion to bear on one side of the fight, so the strikers have got the worst of it before the community. We have been so handled that if a workingman stands out to speak his mind, the public have theirs so full of pictures of him and his doings in the illustrated papers, that he is listened to as if he was a convicted rough pleading in mitigation of penalty, instead of an honest and sincere man asking for a fair show. I would not have any one mistake what my principles are and have been. I don't envy any man his wealth, whether it is ill-gotten or not. I am a workingman, therefore an honest one, and would refuse a dollar I did not earn, for I am neither a beggar to accept charity nor a thief to take what belongs to another, however he came by it. If it be his according to law, I, for one, am ready to protect him in his legal rights, and in return I want to be protected in what I believe to be mine.

Forty years ago my father came over to this country from Sweden. He had a small business and a large family. In Europe business does not grow as fast as children come, and poverty over there is an inheritance. He heard that North America was peopled and governed by workingmen, and the care of the States was mainly engaged in the welfare and prosperity of labor. That moved him, and so I came to be born here. He, and millions like him, made this country their home, and their homes have mainly made this country what it is. Until lately the States kept their faith and promise to the people, and we, the people, showed ours when trouble came; an assessment of blood was made on our shares of liberty, and we paid it. That is our record. We did not fight for this party or that party, but for the country and against all that were against the United States. . . .

So it was before the war, but since then, it seems to me, the power has got fixed so long in one set of hands that things are settling down into a condition like what my father left behind him in Europe forty years ago, and what stands there still. I mean the slavery of labor. The landed aristocracy over there made the feudal system, just as the moneyed men of this continent are now making a ruling class. As the aristocracy used to make war on each other, so in our time the millionnaires live on each other's ruin. As the feudal lords hired mercenary soldiers to garrison their strongholds and to prey on the common people, so the railway lords and stock-exchange barons hire a mercenary press to defend their power, the object of both being the same: the spoils of labor. It looks very like as though this country was settling down into the form and system we fled from in Europe.

The rights and value of labor were acknowledged here forty years ago because the country wanted hands. Now we have made it rich, it turns our own earnings against us, and its prosperity becomes our disaster. We are told to look at Europe and perceive that this condition of affairs is the inevitable result of growth, of population, of wealth; but we look over there, and find that discontent, rebellion, and war are also the inevitable results, and it was to avoid such results these States declared themselves free, that Americans should have a government that was not a conspiracy.

That government has been regarded by the laboring classes of Europe and by our people as the stronghold of the workingman, and in this our present difficulty we are referred to its Constitution which should afford us a remedy for our grievances, the ballot-box is the panacea for all and every complaint. It is not so; and those who point to the remedy know it to be a sham,—they know they can buy idlers and vagabonds enough to swell the ranks of wealth and run up a majority whenever a show of hands is required. They recruit the very men that wrecked Pittsburgh, and would pillage New York if they dared to face us, the workingmen, that fill the ranks of the militia.

We are sick of this game, we are soul-weary of looking around for some sympathy or spirit of justice, and, finding none, we turn to each other and form brotherhoods and unions, depots of the army of labor, officered by the skilled mechanic.

This organized force is now in process of formation, and prepared to meet the great questions of the age: Has labor any rights? If so, what are they? Our claim is simple. We demand *fair wages*.

We say that the man able and willing to work, and for whom there is work to do, is entitled to wages sufficient to provide him with enough food, shelter, and clothing to sustain and preserve his health and strength. We contend that the employer has no right to speculate on starvation when he reduces wages below a living figure, saying, if we refuse that remuneration, there are plenty of starving men out of work that will gladly accept half a loaf instead of no bread.

We contend that to regard the laboring class in this manner is to consider them as the captain of a slave-ship regards his cargo, who throws overboard those unable to stand their sufferings. Let those who knew the South before the war go now amongst the mining districts of Pennsylvania, and compare the home of the white laborer with the quarters of the slave; let them compare the fruits of freedom with the produce of slavery!

But we know the question is a difficult one to settle,—we do not want to force it on with threats. The late strike was not intended to break out as it did; things broke loose and took a direction we regretted. We find ourselves answerable for results we had no share in or control over. Nevertheless we accept the event as a symptom of the disorder that is consuming our body and pray the country to look to it,—it is not a passing complaint. Let me put this matter in a plain way, as we understand it, and use round numbers instead of fractions, as we have to deal with hundreds of millions,-dividing the subject into sections.

1. In the United States the amount of capital invested in railway property last year was $4,470,000,000, made up of $2,250,000,000 capital stock and $2,220,000,000 bonded debt. The gross earnings were $500,000,000, or about eight and a half per cent on the capital. The running expenses (of which the bulk was for labor) were $310,000,000, leaving $185,000,000 as [profit] interest to the capitalist, or barely four per cent on his investment.

Labor is admitted into this enterprise as a preferential creditor, to be paid out of gross earnings before the most preferred mortgagee or bond holder receives a dollar. For as capital could not build the roads nor equip them without labor, so the enterprise, when complete, cannot be run without labor.

Capital, therefore, takes a back seat when it comes to the push, and acknowledges not only that labor has the largest interest in the concern, but takes the first fruits.

I take the railroad as a sample out of all enterprises, and if we could get at figures, there is no doubt it is a fair sample of the crowd. If, then, labor is the more important and essential factor in the result, when it comes to the question which of the two shall suffer in moments of general distress, the capitalist in his pocket or the laborer in his belly, we think the answer has been already settled by the rights assumed by one and acknowledged by the other.

2. It is manifestly unjust that the workingman should be subject to under wages in bad times, if he has not the equivalent of over wages in good times. If railroad companies in concert with the laboring class had established a tariff of labor, and paid a bonus on wages at every distribution of dividends, that bonus being in proportion to the profits of the road, so that each man becomes a shareholder in his very small way, then he would have submitted to bear his share of distress when all were called on to share trouble, but to share it equally and alike.

3. When folks say that labor and capital must find, by the laws of demand and supply, their natural relations to each other in all commercial enterprises, and neither one has any rights it can enforce on the other, they take for granted that the labor "market" is, like the produce market, liable to natural fluctuations. If that were so, we should not complain. But it is not. The labor market has got to be like the stock and share market; a few large capitalists control it and make what prices they please. This sort of game may ruin the gamblers in stocks, and injure those who invest, but the trouble is confined mostly to those who deserve to lose or those who can afford it.

But not so when the same practice operates in the labor market. The capitalist must not gamble with the bread of the workingman, or if he does, let him regard where that speculation led France one hundred years ago, when the financiers made a corner in flour, and the people broke the ring with the axe of the guillotine.

4. When the railway companies obtained privileges and rights over private property, and became by force of law the great landowners of the state, holding its movable property as well, and controlling every avenue and department of business, public and private, they became powerful monopolies. The state endowed them with powers to frame laws of their own and deprived citizens of their property, means, facilities of transport, to vest it all in these corporations. Thus endowed, they cannot pretend they are no more than ordinary commercial enterprises. They are responsible to the state for the result of their operations, if they disturb fatally the order of our concerns. They are not independent. The state has claims upon them it has not on private concerns. They may not accept liabilities and then decline responsibility. It behooves the state to decide what the people are entitled to in return for all they have conceded to these companies, and to enforce such claims.

5. The English Parliament legislated on the question of the number of hours a workingman should labor. It limits them to so many. It legislates for his health and supply of light and water. In all these matters the capitalist has an interest. (He does as much for his horse.) But when it comes to the question of a proper amount of food and clothing, of warmth and shelter, the government declines to interfere. It leaves the question of fair wages to be adjusted between employer and employed.

And so I leave it, fearing I have put the matter in rough language, but not intentionally rude, having a deep and loyal faith in the humanity and justice that abide in the hearts of all this community, and wishing that God had given me the power to touch them.

A "*Striker*"

DOCUMENT 2 ***"The Recent Strikes"***

by the President of the Pennsylvania Railroad

Philadelphia, August 13, 1877

Allen Thorndike Rice, Esq.,
Editor of the *North American Review*

My *Dear Sir,*

On the 16th of July it became known that the firemen and freight brakemen of the Baltimore and Ohio Railroad were on a strike at Martinsburg, West Virginia, and that no freight trains were allowed to pass that point in either direction. This proved to be the beginning of a movement which spread with great rapidity from New York to Kansas, and from Michigan to Texas, which placed an embargo on the entire freight traffic of more than twenty thousand miles of railway, put passenger travel and the movement of the United States mails at the mercy of a mob, subjected great commercial centres like Chicago and St. Louis to the violent disturbance of all their business relations, and made the great manufacturing city of Pittsburgh for twenty-four hours such a scene of riot, arson, and bloodshed as can never be erased from the memory of its people. . . .

I do not wish, and happily it is not necessary, to fill your pages with the mere recital of the distressing cases of violence and outrage which marked the course of these riots unexampled in American history. Suffice it to say that the conduct of the rioters is entirely inconsistent with the idea that this movement could have been directed by serious, right-minded men bent on improving the condition of the laboring classes. How wages could be improved by destroying property, the existence of which alone made the payment of any wages at all possible, it is difficult to understand. Nothing but the insanity of passion, played upon by designing and mischievous leaders, can explain the destruction of vast quantities of railroad equipment absolutely necessary to the transaction of its business, by men whose complaint was that the business done by the full equipment in possession of the railways did not pay them sufficient compensation for their labor. . . .

It must not for a moment, however, be understood that the greatest portion, or, indeed, any considerable portion, of the outrages upon life and property which have disgraced our recent history were actually committed by railway employés. It is not true that the majority, or even any large portion, of these men have been disloyal to the trust reposed in them. Probably ninety per cent of the men on all the important lines of the country where strikes occurred were faithful to their duties, and either remained at work, or stood ready to resume it as soon as they were relieved from the actual intimidation to which they were subjected by the rioters and their leaders. It was the dissatisfied element—which exists in that branch of industry as in all others—which perpetrated or allowed the perpetration of most of the overt acts of violence, such as stopping trains, forcing men therefrom, uncoupling cars, disconnecting engines, and other lawless doings of the kind, and which made itself amenable also to the charge of directly attacking the interests of the government and society at large as well as of the railway companies.

As General Hurlbut of Illinois so forcibly expresses it, in a paper recently published, "they permitted themselves to be the nucleus around which the idle, vicious, and criminal element could gather. Reinforced by these dark and disreputable allies, they destroyed property, stopped commerce, deranged the mails, burned great public buildings, broke up tracks, and thus paralyzed the natural circulation of the Commonwealth." It is in the menace to the general interests of society involved in these disturbances that the real gravity of the situation with which this country is now called to deal exists. "The railroad system is today a supreme necessity to maintain life, furnish ready markets, and to bring about the enormous interchange of products which makes the country one. Stop it, and in ten days many parts of the country would near the starvation-point, and within a month there would be no hamlet in the vast territory drained by these channels but would feel to the core of its business the effects of the stoppage of this regular and unusual circulation."

The enormous mechanical changes and progress of the past century have brought about a complete revolution, so gradual that perhaps it has not been generally apprehended, in the very condition of things in the United States. The water lines, which, at the date of the framing of the Constitution, were our important channels of internal commerce, have been almost superseded by the new iron highways. Upon these is borne a traffic so essentially national, so closely interwoven with the interests not only of our own but other countries, that it demands the most efficient and speedy protection against all unlawful interference. . . .

It is well known that the government uses the railway lines of the country, both as postal and military highways, in such form as its interests may require. The Constitution of the United States imposes upon the government the duty of thoroughly protecting inter-State commerce. When it is considered that the stock and bond holders of the various railway companies, whenever the interests of the government required it, paid taxes upon their coupons, their dividends, and their gross receipts, that they promptly met every call made by the Federal authorities, and that the entire equipment of the various lines was often placed at the disposal of the government for the prompt movement of the national forces and their supplies, to the exclusion often of other and more profitable traffic, it would seem but a matter of equity that the government should insure such protection to these railways as would preserve their usefulness and keep them always in condition to render similar services when they may be required. But over and beyond such considerations as these, the absolute dependence of the whole community upon this great system of railways for almost its very existence as a civilized body would seem to impose upon the Federal government in the last resort the supreme duty of preventing any lawless and violent interference with the regular and certain operation of every railway in the United States.

This insurrection, which extended through fourteen States, and in many cases successfully defied the local authorities, presents a state of facts almost as serious as that which prevailed at the outbreak of the Civil War. Unless our own experience is to differ entirely from other countries,—and it is not easy to see why it should, with the increasing population of our large cities and business centres, and the inevitable assemblage at such points of the vicious and evil-disposed,—the late troubles may be but the prelude to other manifestations of mob violence, with this added peril, that now, for the first time in American history, has an organized mob learned its power to terrorize the law-abiding citizens of great communities. With our recent experience before us, it is believed that no thoughtful man can argue in favor of delay by the proper authorities in dealing with lawless and riotous assemblages. Delay simply leads to destruction of property, and may lead in the end to the destruction of life. . . .

With the approach of winter, and the loss of outdoor employment which severe weather even in the most prosperous times entails, the country will have to deal not only with the deserving among the unemployed, who can be reached and helped through local organizations, but with vast numbers of idle, dangerous, and in many cases desperate men, who have been allowed unfortunately to catch a glimpse of their possible power for mischief. Such men, unless confronted by a thorough organization in the cities, States, and other communities, backed by the power of the Federal government and an unmistakable public opinion, will need but little urging to renew the scenes which have already brought such disgrace upon the American name. . . .

The magnitude of the evil to be met and dealt with can hardly be overstated. The remedy to be provided should be equally prompt and effective. It must be discussed and adopted in the interest of the whole country, and not of any particular class; for the interests of all classes of our citizens are the same in the maintenance of domestic peace and civil order. . . .

My own railway experience, extending over a period of thirty years, leads me to believe that the managers of American railways in general may fearlessly appeal to their past relations with the faithful among their employés, to prove that they at least have always endeavored to treat the interests of employers and employed as identical, and have never failed to take into prompt and respectful consideration every grievance which has been fairly and properly presented to them. I am sure that it has been the purpose of the company with which I am connected to at all times pay its employés the best compensation that the business of the country would warrant; and I have no doubt that this will be the policy of the company for all future time, as it is founded on sound business principles no less than upon the instincts of humanity.

Very truly yours,
Thomas A. Scott

Introduction to Documents 3 and 4

The next two documents come from Allan Pinkerton and Samuel Gompers. Pinkerton became famous as a private detective. During the Civil War, his company provided the federal government with (often incorrect) intelligence reports of Confederate troop strength and movements. After the war, Pinkerton's agency sold its services to private businesses, providing industrial espionage, guards, strike-breakers, and agents provocateurs. Pinkerton assumed that the Great Strike of 1877 was part of a much larger conspiratorial plot, imported to the United States from Europe and designed to destroy the country. The excerpt reprinted here is from a book entitled *Strikers, Communists, Tramps and Detectives* (1878).

Samuel Gompers, on the other hand, worked as a cigar maker in New York City during the strike. He eventually rose from worker, then local union leader, to president of the American Federation of Labor, a coalition of craft unions founded in 1886. In his later life, Gompers always insisted that organized labor must stay out of politics, must eschew socialism, and must not question owners' rights to hold property and manage it; unions existed to improve wages and working conditions, not to make workers co-owners or managers. Gompers's passage was written fifty years after the Great Strike and published in his memoirs.

DOCUMENT 3 *From Strikers, Communists, Tramps and Detectives*

Allan Pinkerton

It was everywhere; it was nowhere. A condition of sedition which can be located, fixed, or given boundaries, may, by any ordinary community or government, be subdued. This uprising, in its far-reaching extent, was so alarmingly sudden that it seemed like the hideous growth of a night. It was as if the surrounding seas had swept in upon the land from every quarter, or some sudden central volcano had upraised its hideous head and belched forth burning rivers that coursed out upon the country in every direction. No general action for safety could be taken. Look where we might, some fresh danger was presented. No one had prophesied it; no one could prevent it; no one was found brave enough or wise enough to stop its pestilential spread. Its birth was spontaneous; its progress like a hurricane; its demise a complete farce.

But, looking over the destruction wrought, the consideration of the now clearly established fact, that our country has arrived at such an age and condition that it contains the dormant elements which require only a certain measure of turbulent handling to at any moment again bring to the surface even a stronger and more concentrated power of violence and outlawry, becomes not only a most wise policy, but an urgent necessity. . . .

The great strike has left everybody poorer. Who has been bettered? Who can point to a single instance where a body of workingmen has been benefited by their participation?

Who shall pay for the enforced idleness of millions; the ruin to vast business interests; the misery brought upon innocent working men and women; and for the hundreds of lives sacrificed upon this altar of human ignorance, blindness, and frenzy?

Looking at the matter from any point of consideration, no good thing can be seen in it, unless it may be judged a good thing to know that we have among us a pernicious communistic spirit which is demoralizing workingmen, continually creating a deeper and more intense antagonism between labor and capital, and so embittering naturally restless elements against the better elements of society, that it must be crushed out completely, or we shall be compelled to submit to greater excesses and more overwhelming disasters in the near future.

The "strike" is essentially an institution of continental Europe, and, like all other good and bad emanations from that part of the world, gradually but surely found its way into England, Scotland, and Ireland, and from thence was transplanted to this country. Riot, which has always existed, has become the constant companion of the strike everywhere. Through my Scotch and English experiences I have become well acquainted with the characteristics of strikes in those countries. One marked difference in them there is in the fact that women, in almost every instance after the strike is inaugurated, seem the most savage in preventing the breaking of the strike by the employment of "nobs," as the "scabs" are called there, and in both inciting and participating in riots. . . .

A good deal has been written and said regarding the causes of our great strike of '77. To my mind they seem clear and distinct. For years, and without any particular attention on the part of the press or the public, animated by the vicious dictation of the International Society, all manner of labor unions and leagues have been forming. No manufacturing town, nor any city, has escaped this baleful influence. Though many of these organizations have professed opposition to communistic principles, their pernicious influence has unconsciously become powerful among them. Other organizations have openly avowed them. They have become an element in politics. The intelligent workingmen, not being altogether ready for the acceptance of these extreme doctrines, have given them no political support, and their violent propagators have been obliged to fall back upon agitation of subjects which would antagonize labor and capital. For years we have been recovering from the extravagances of the war period. Labor has gradually, but surely, been becoming cheaper, and its demand less. Workingmen have not economized in the proportion that economy became necessary. Want and penury followed. Workingmen consequently have become discontented and embittered. They have been taught steadily, as their needs increased, that they were being enslaved and robbed, and that all that was necessary for bettering their condition was a general uprising against capital. So that when, under the leadership of designing men, that great class of railroad employees—than whom no body of workingmen in America were ever better compensated—began their strike, nearly every other class caught the infection, and by these dangerous communistic leaders were made to believe that the proper time for action had come.

DOCUMENT 4 ***". . . A Declaration of Protest in the Name of American Manhood . . ."***

Samuel Gompers

During the summer of 1876 the unemployment situation grew steadily worse. A feeling of desperation was growing as week after week slipped by and still the unemployed had no dependable means of earning a livelihood. The city authorities selected that time to suspend improvements on public works. The workingmen protested against this course as a harmful, cruel policy. Our next effort was in the form of demonstrations. First, we called a mass meeting in Tompkins Square early in August. Crowds met quietly on the appointed day. We had police protection instead of police aggression. . . .

Mass meetings for organization and as unemployment demonstrations continued. We tried to organize discontent for constructive purposes. Mayor Ely paid no more attention to our needs than other Mayors had done, but wageearners did heed our gospel of organization and solidarity. I am recounting in some detail a picture of cumulative misery in order to bring out why revolt brought a whisper of hope. The crash that broke the months of strain came in the revolt of the railroad workers in July, 1877. That was in the pioneer period of railroading. The Union Pacific had been completed but a short time before, uniting the eastern and western coasts in a new effort to conquer distance. The railway unions were but fledglings. In fierce competitive fights, railroad managements cut passenger and freight rates far below the maintenance level. They were preparing to shift the resulting losses upon their employes by wage cuts. In 1873, wages of railroad workers had been reduced ten per cent; a similar wage reduction was announced for June 1, 1877. Railroad officials had organized and united upon a uniform policy. They did not even consider consultation with their employes. They handed down an order that meant another ten-per-cent reduction in the standards of living of their employes. Although both employment and pay on the railroads were irregular, unemployment was general in all other lines of work, and railroad workers were obliged either to accept conditions, bad as they were, or join the already large ranks of tramps. In addition to cutting wages, the railroads announced employes were to be required to use company hotels which still further reduced real wages.

Made desperate by this accumulation of miseries, without organizations strong enough to conduct a successful strike, the railway workers rebelled. Their rebellion was a declaration of protest in the name of American manhood against conditions that nullified the rights of American citizens. The railroad strike of 1877 was the tocsin that sounded a ringing message of hope to us all.

The railroad rebellion was spontaneous. In those days before the establishment of collective bargaining as an orderly system for presenting grievances to employers as the preliminary to securing an adjustment based on mutuality, the only way the workers could secure the attention of employers was through some demonstration of protest in the form of a strike. The strike grew steadily until it surpassed in numbers and importance all previous industrial movements. Strikers and sympathetic workmen crowded into the streets. The New York papers said at the time that so far as the arguments were concerned, the workers had the best of the situation, but that they could not win because of the weakness of the unions. The authorities grew apprehensive and asked for military protection. Then the fight was on. Long pent-up resentment found vent in destruction. The primitive weapons, fire and violence, were labor's response to arbitrary force. . . .

When the co-operative factory was abandoned with the close of the strike, I could have continued to work there, but, of course, I had neither the desire nor the willingness to act as superintendent or foreman for the factory although requested by them to do so, so I applied to Hirsch for my old job. That had been filled and there was really no opportunity for work with him. The Cigar Manufacturers' Association had declared that under no circumstances would any leaders of the strike be employed for at least six months. As a consequence, for nearly four months I was out of employment. I had parted with everything of any value in the house, and my wife and I were every day expecting a newcomer in addition to the five children we already had.

My family helped in every way possible. Part of the time they were hungry and without the necessaries of life. Never once did my wife falter. Blacklisted, I desperately sought employment, going home at night where my brave wife prepared soup out of water, salt, pepper, and flour. One night when there was no food in the house and our little girl was very ill I returned home to find a fellow-worker, Jack Polak, had called and offered my wife $30 a week for three months if she would persuade me to give up the union and return to work. I turned to my wife and said, "Well, what did you tell him?" My wife, indignant at the question answered: "What do you suppose I said to him with one child dying and another coming? Of course I took the money." Stunned by the blow I fell in a chair. My wife, all tenderness and sympathy, seeing I didn't understand exclaimed: "Good God, Sam, how could you ask such a question? Don't you know I resented the insult?"

Occasionally, my wife suggested the commissary—but I refused that help, for I wanted to fight my own way. My mother worried over our need. She used to tell brother Al and the younger children to go over and find out whether we had food. Sophia always kept covered pots on the stove—but sometimes they contained only water. The children would accidently brush aside the covers to fulfill their mission of kindness. Many times my mother sent us food from her none too bountiful supply.

Once I was ready to commit murder. All the children were ill, probably because of winter cold and under-nourishment; they were subject to illness and fever. I walked around looking for work and could not find it, and as I left my wife in the morning again to look for work there were indications that the newcomer was about due, but by previous experience I thought that that condition would last a couple of days. But when I came home, my sister-in-law, who was living with us and sharing whatever little we had, told me that the child was born. There had been nobody to help the mother or the child. I stood by, dazed, and then rushed to the man who had acted as our physician. He was the physician paid by the Hand-in-Hand Society. But he was not in and like a madman I rushed back, but the situation was the same as it was before.

It dawned on me that there was a physician on the next block and I went to him and told him of the condition and that I wanted him to come down and attend to my wife. He asked me if I had money. When I told him I did not, he replied that he was not our regular physician. I said I knew that but my wife was in such a serious condition and the child there and I wanted him to come to attend her right away. He said, "Well, I do not feel like it and I won't do it."

I walked up to him, looked him square in the eye and said, "Yes you will, you will come and see my wife now." He said, "Well, I will not." I put my hand on his coat collar and said, "You will come now with me or you will never make another move." He said he wanted me to pay him and I said: "I have got no money. I have been out of work, but I will promise to pay you everything I can gather tonight, but you will come with me without another minute's hesitation or I will not be responsible for what I will do to you. Come along." He put on his hat and coat and he went with me. While he was attending the mother and child, I went around among the members of my family and gathered up two dollars and gave it to him. He prescribed some medicine and I did not have the money to get the prescription filled and finally prevailed upon the druggist with whom I was acquainted through living in the neighborhood to trust me for it and we pulled her through. The baby was my Al. He was our strike baby, born in the forenoon of February 28, 1878.

Introduction to Documents 5 and 6

Like Samuel Gompers, Mary Harris "Mother" Jones was a labor organizer, and, in the following excerpt from her autobiography, she remembers the strike from a distance of fifty years. Unlike Gompers, Jones was not a political moderate but a socialist known for her militant oratory. She was over forty years old when the strike broke out, and it was her first direct involvement in a labor action. She would be at the eye of the storm as an organizer for another fifty years. Like Gompers, she accused company agents of fomenting the violence and destruction. Note also her point that local businessmen as well as laborers resented big national corporations like the Pennsylvania Railroad.

Document 6 comes from a *New York Times* report on the sermons of Reverend Henry Ward Beecher during the strike. Beecher's congregation, Plymouth Church in Brooklyn, was very wealthy, and Beecher was one of the most famous clergymen in America. Beecher's harsh judgment of the strikers grew out of his attachment to the social Darwinist assumption that the law of living is survival of the fittest, which just happened to flatter his very successful congregants.

DOCUMENT 5 *The Great Uprising*

Mary Harris "Mother" Jones

One of the first strikes that I remember occurred in the Seventies. The Baltimore and Ohio Railroad employees went on strike and they sent for me to come help them. I went. The mayor of Pittsburgh swore in as deputy sheriffs a lawless, reckless bunch of fellows who had drifted into that city during the panic of 1873. They pillaged and burned and rioted and looted. Their acts were charged up to the striking workingmen. The governor sent the militia.

The Railroads had succeeded in getting a law passed that in case of a strike, the train-crew should bring in the locomotive to the roundhouse before striking. This law the strikers faithfully obeyed. Scores of locomotive were housed in Pittsburgh.

One night a riot occurred. Hundreds of box cars standing on the tracks were soaked with oil and set on fire and sent down the tracks to the roundhouse. The roundhouse caught fire. Over one hundred locomotives, belonging to the Pennsylvania Railroad Company, were destroyed. It was a wild night. The flames lighted the sky and turned to fiery flames the steel bayonettes of the soldiers.

The strikers were charged with the crimes of arson and rioting, although it was common knowledge that it was not they who instigated the fire; that it was started by hoodlums backed by the business men of Pittsburgh who for a long time had felt that the Railroad Company discriminated against their city in the matter of rates.

I knew the strikers personally. I knew that it was they who had tried to enforce orderly law. I knew they disciplined their members when they did violence. I knew, as everybody knew, who really perpetrated the crime of burning the railroad's property. Then and there I learned in the early part of my career that labor must bear the cross for others' sins, must be the vicarious sufferer for the wrongs that others do.

These early years saw the beginning of America's industrial life. Hand and hand with the growth of factories and the expansion of railroads, with the accumulation of capital and the rise of banks, came anti-labor legislation. Came strikes. Came violence. Came the belief in the hearts and minds of the workers that legislatures but carry out the will of the industrialists.

DOCUMENT 6 *"There Is No Rich Class and No Working Class Under the Law"*

Henry Ward Beecher

The Pulpit on the Situation

REV. HENRY WARD BEECHER CONDEMNS THE STRIKE AND DECLARES THAT A FAMILY CAN LIVE ON A DOLLAR A DAY

What right had the working men, the members of those great organizations, to say to any one, 'You shall not work for wages which we refuse.' They had a perfect right to say to the employers, 'We shall not work for you,' but they had no right to tyrannize over their fellow-men. They had put themselves in an attitude of tyrannical opposition to all law and order and they could not be defended. The necessities of the great railroad companies demanded that there should be a reduction of wages. There must be continual shrinkage until things come back to the gold standard, and wages, as well as greenbacks, provisions, and property, must share in it. It was true that $1 a day was not enough to support a man and five children, if a man would insist on smoking and drinking beer. Was not a dollar a day enough to buy bread! Water costs nothing. [Laughter.] Man cannot live by bread, it is true; but the man who cannot live on bread and water is not fit to live. [Laughter.] When a man is educated away from the power of self-denial, he is falsely educated. A family may live on good bread and water in the morning, water and bread at midday, and good water and bread at night. [Continued laughter.] Such may be called the bread of affliction, but it was fit that man should eat of the bread of affliction. Thousands would be glad of a dollar a day, and it added to the sin of the men on strike for them to turn round and say to those men, 'You can do so, but you shall not.' There might be special cases of hardship, but the great laws of political economy could not be set at defiance.

Communism Denounced

HENRY WARD BEECHER'S OPINIONS ON THE LABOR QUESTION

We look upon the importation of the communistic and like European notions as abominations. Their notions and theories that the Government should be paternal and take care of the welfare of its subjects and provide them with labor, is un-American. It is the form in which oppression has had its most disastrous scope in the world. The American doctrine is that it is the duty of the Government merely to protect the people while they are taking care of themselves—nothing more than that. "Hands off," we say to the Government; "see to it that we are protected in our rights and our individuality. No more than that." The theories of Europe in regard to the community of property we reject because they are against natural law and will never be practicable. God has intended the great to be great, and the little to be little. No equalization process can ever take place until men are made equal as productive forces. It is a wild vision, not a practicable theory. The European theories of combinations between workmen and trades-unions and communes destroy the individuality of the person, and there is no possible way of preserving the liberty of the people except by the maintenance of individual liberty, intact from Government and intact from individual meddling. Persons have the right to work when or where they please, as long as they please, and for what they please, and any attempt to infringe on this right, and to put good workmen on a level with poor workmen—any such attempt to regiment labor is preposterous. . . .

Our theory is that the Government protects men in their rights, and not Government, but God, gave them those rights. The Government gave me no right of liberty, but God did. The Government protects me in that right. All that the Government has the right to say is, you shall use your rights so as not to injure another's; to secure to every man the liberty that God gave him. Clear the arena! Let each man go into it for what he is! Let him reap what he can sow! Let the Government see that there is fair play between man and man and citizen and citizen! When I hear men say that the Government shall take charge of the railroads, of the telegraphs, and of other forms of industry, and that the proceeds shall be distributed equally among the working men, I say that if all citizens were angels this would be folly. But as men are, only a theorist insane by nature and thrown by meditation into delirium tremens could have invented such a theory. No human being on earth has any rights resulting from the fact that he belongs to a class. In the eye of the law we have rights, but simply of men. The law rubs out all the European distinctions of class and says all men are born equal. We hear of the rich class being arrayed against the working class. There is no rich class and no working class before the law. The way in which these terms are coming now to be used is undemocratic, unphilosophical, and false in fact. It is an American doctrine that every man is to have the full ownership of himself, and the right to develop himself if he can do it.

QUESTIONS

Defining Terms

Identify in the context of the chapter each of the following:

centennial	Martinsburg
Thomas Scott	labor unions
"fair wages"	Allan Pinkerton
Samuel Gompers	*Strikers, Communists, Tramps and Detectives*
Mother Jones	"a family can live on a dollar a day"

Probing the Sources

1. Who were the strikers? What were their goals?
2. What, according to the writers of the documents in this chapter, were the causes of the Great Strike?
3. How did the law and government react to the crisis? Were they consistent? Evenhanded?
4. What did Gompers mean by "American manhood"? Why did he use that phrase?

Interpreting the Sources

1. If they could argue with Gompers, Jones, and the anonymous striker, what do you think Scott, Pinkerton, and Beecher would say? How would Gompers, Jones, and the striker respond?
2. Take the position of either workers or management, and argue over the merits of the strike.
3. Which tactics do you think are justified and which unjustified in civil disputes like labor conflicts?
4. Do you think that the strikers were successful or unsuccessful?
5. What patriotic appeals did each side make? How did they differ?

ADDITIONAL READING

On the 1877 strike, see Philip Foner, *The Great Labor Uprising of 1877* (1977); David O. Stowell, *Street Railroads and the Great Strike of 1877* (1999); and Robert V. Bruce, *1877: Year of Violence* (1959). For discussions of particular aspects of labor in this era, see Melvyn Dubofsky, *Industrialism and the American Worker, 1865–1920* (1985); Herbert Gutman, *Work, Culture and Society in Industrializing America* (1976); Gutman, *Power and Culture: Essays on the American Working Class* (1987); and David Montgomery, *The Fall of the House of Labor: The Workplace, the State, and American Labor Activism, 1865–1925* (1987). An international perspective is provided by Eric Hobsbawm. *The Age of Capital, 1848–1875* (1975); and *The Age of Empire* (1987). On the poor, see Jacqueline Jones, *The Dispossessed: America's Underclass from the Civil War to the Present* (1992). For politics in the era of rapid economic growth, try Richard Franklin Bensel, *The Political Economy of American Industrialization* (2000). For a discussion workers in American fiction, see Laura Hapke, *Labors Text,* (2001).

3

When Cultures Collide

Wounded Knee

Historical Context

"The 'Great American Desert,' " Charles Nordhoff wrote in 1873, "has disappeared at the snort of the iron horse. . . . The very desert becomes fruitful, and in the midst of the sagebrush and alkali country, you will see corn, wheat, potatoes, and fruits of different kinds growing luxuriantly." For Nordhoff, as for his fellow Americans, settling the West was a poetic ideal, a hymn of progress:

> One can not help but speculate upon what kind of men we Americans shall be when all these now desolate plains are filled; when cities shall be found where now only the lonely depot or the infrequent cabin stands; when the iron and coal of these regions shall have become, as they soon must, the foundation of great manufacturing populations; and when, perhaps, the whole continent will be covered by our Stars and Stripes.

Americans' prose soared as they contemplated their prosperous and powerful republic stretching from sea to shining sea.

In the most concrete sense, the expansion of white settlers westward was part of the same set of processes transforming the rest of society. Imagine, for example, a Nebraska farmer purchasing a Currier and Ives lithograph for his home in 1875, perhaps a scene of pioneers making their way across the continent. He buys the lithograph from a store in Omaha, where the pictures just came off the train from New York. He sells his wheat in the same city, and some of it may find its way onto the tables of railroad workers, who at that moment are worried about rumors of an impending wage cut. Or perhaps our farmer looks at the lithograph and chooses not to buy it, because the low price he will get for his wheat means another lean year in these troubled economic times. He wonders for a moment how he will ever pay off the bank for the new threshing machine that allowed him to grow more wheat. Farmers mechanize, he muses, and grow bigger crops, and, as a result, prices go down. The point, of course, is that industrialization, urbanization, and commercial exchange were all part of a related set of processes. The railroad was one of the ties that bound western farmers to eastern laborers. And underlying the entire transformation—manufacturing, shipping, growing, processing, and financing—was the market economy.

As the quotation from Nordhoff reveals—and as Currier and Ives lithographs of westward expansion made palpable—prosperity, progress, productivity, and individual betterment were highly charged ideals. The marketplace was not just a system of exchange; it generated its own ideology. But shining visions of progress usually did not include those whose land was taken; rather, the myth of progress justified the taking.

When white colonists first came to British North America, there were already millions of native people living in this "uninhabited" land, this "desert," as some colonists called it. European diseases, to which the indigenous peoples had no immunity, quickly wiped out many of them. As whites colonized the new lands, then, they faced greatly weakened tribes that, when not outnumbered, were outgunned. Some groups, after resisting the whites, were simply destroyed, such as the Pequots of New England. The large southeastern tribes—the Creeks, Cherokees, Choctaws, and Chickasaws—were finally conquered during the presidency of Andrew Jackson and forced to relocate west to lands that would be theirs "forever."

By the late nineteenth century, the Sioux of the northern plains were one of the largest and most powerful tribal cultures remaining. During the colonial era, they had occupied lands between Lake Superior and the headwaters of the Mississippi River, but the Ojibwas, armed by the French, drove them west to the plains. The Sioux adapted well to the new environment, cultivating their skills as horsemen and hunters and following the enormous herds of buffalo that roamed the western prairies. Until the Civil War, they ranged from Minnesota to the Rockies and from the Yellowstone River to the Platte, and, with millions of buffalo and thousands of horses, they were masters of these lands.

In 1868, with settlement of the plains by whites accelerating, the federal government sought direct control over the native inhabitants. The Sioux agreed to a treaty granting them the western half of the present state of South Dakota and portions of Nebraska and Wyoming, "for their absolute and undisturbed use and occupation," along with rights to hunt for buffalo beyond reservation boundaries. The treaty seemed to provide not only an endless supply of food, but also peace. "From this day forth," the treaty stated, "all wars between the parties of this agreement shall cease forever." In a few years, however, marksmen and trappers had hunted the buffalo to near extinction, while masses of white settlers had poured in on the new railroads. When gold—"the yellow metal that they worship and that makes them crazy," as one Sioux called it—was discovered on the tribal reservation in the Black Hills, a massive new influx of whites into the region commenced.

Bands of Sioux resisted the occupation of their lands, but as sporadic violence broke out on both sides, the government sent in the army to round up the "hostiles." George Armstrong Custer led the Seventh Cavalry into the Sioux country as part of a larger expedition under the command of General Alfred Terry. In the spring of 1876, Custer divided his forces into three groups to assault the enemy near the Little Bighorn. The entire regiment—over 250 men—was killed by a force of at least 2,500 Indians. The government promptly sent in more troops, who arrested several chiefs and chased the main leader of the uprising, Sitting Bull, and his people into Canada.

Government officials from the military and from the Bureau of Indian Affairs (under the Department of the Interior) now drew up a new treaty, and an accommodating chief, Red Cloud, signed for the tribe. The Sioux lost one-third of their reservation, including the sacred Black Hills. A people who had been hunter-gatherers, with no experience, habits, or capital for agriculture, were left on poor land, without the buffalo herds that had provided food, shelter, clothes, and goods for barter. After another decade of land speculators greedy for profits, railroads coveting rights of way, and squatters clamoring for land, the federal government in 1889 seized half of the remaining Sioux territory and, in the process, divided the one large reservation into five separate units.

In exchange for all of these concessions, the government promised to supply food (which often never came), clothing (which always arrived after the arctic cold), schools for Indian children (where tribal ways were demeaned), and reservation administrators (who were often incompetent political hacks). The old way of life was undermined: agents of the federal government forbade warrior societies and honors, usurped the powers of the chiefs, and banned tribal religious customs, holidays, and ceremonies. The Sioux and other tribes were forced to trade the freedom of the plains for broken promises and confinement to the reservation.

In the midst of this crisis, a new religion swept through the tribes of the western United States, a religion containing both Christian and Native American elements, as seen in the two names given to the movement: the Messiah Craze, as whites called it, and the Ghost Dance. By 1890, word had spread to the plains of a Paiute chief in Nevada named Wavoka who claimed to be "the Christ," returned to earth as an Indian. Throughout the western territories, Native Americans of various tribes listened to Wavoka's message and followed his advice. He promised to renew the earth to what it had been before the coming of the whites. In the spring of 1891, when the grass grew knee-high, the earth would be covered with fresh soil, running water, trees, and buffalo. And all of the old Indians who had died would return as young men and women. Those who did the Ghost Dance would be lifted into the sky, and the new soil would roll over the old and bury the whites; the dancers would then descend to earth and dwell there with their ancestors.

Native Americans across the West donned ghost shirts, painted with symbols that allegedly made them impervious to white men's bullets, and they danced the Ghost Dance. For the Sioux—starved and humiliated, their numbers depleted—the promise of living in peace and plenty was irresistible. Widows would be reunited with their husbands, hunting bands would once again be able to provide food, and an *Indian* messiah would take revenge on the white oppressors. With promises like these, the reservations resounded with the songs and steps of the sacred dance.

Reports of the "Messiah Craze" greatly alarmed whites. There is no doubt that the new religion gave Native Americans the confidence to assert themselves in ways that reservation agents found alarming and citizens saw as threatening. Certainly the idea of a Native American messiah offered tribal members a sense of pride and a new militancy. Many whites, on the other hand, jumped to the conclusion that the Ghost Dance merely proved how wild and barbaric the Native Americans were or that the new religion was a cover for a treacherous attack. Soon army troops were again streaming west, and Native American bands, feeling threatened, began leaving the reservations. The scene was set for tragedy.

THE DOCUMENTS

Introduction to Document 1

Anthropologists call phenomena like the Ghost Dance *revitalization movements.* In times of social stress, people often go back to important elements of their culture

and reshape them in powerful ways. The rejuvenated customs or beliefs become a focus of group solidarity and cultural revival.

Z. A. Parker, a teacher on the Pine Ridge reservation in South Dakota, described the Ghost Dance she witnessed at White Clay Creek, June 20, 1890.

DOCUMENT 1 *"The Ghost Dance Observed"*

Z. A. Parker

We drove to this spot about 10.30 oclock on a delightful October day. We came upon tents scattered here and there in low, sheltered places long before reaching the dance ground. Presently we saw over three hundred tents placed in a circle, with a large pine tree in the center, which was covered with strips of cloth of various colors, eagle feathers, stuffed birds, claws, and horns—all offerings to the Great Spirit. The ceremonies had just begun. In the center, around the tree, were gathered their medicine-men; also those who had been so fortunate as to have had visions and in them had seen and talked with friends who had died. A company of fifteen had started a chant and were marching abreast, others coming in behind as they marched. After marching around the circle of tents they turned to the center, where many had gathered and were seated on the ground.

I think they wore the ghost shirt or ghost dress for the first time that day. I noticed that these were all new and were worn by about seventy men and forty women. The wife of a man called Return-from-scout had seen in a vision that her friends all wore a similar robe, and on reviving from her trance she called the women together and they made a great number of the sacred garments. They were of white cotton cloth. The women's dress was cut like their ordinary dress, a loose robe with wide, flowing sleeves, painted blue in the neck, in the shape of a three-cornered handkerchief, with moon, stars, birds, etc., interspersed with real feathers, painted on the waist and sleeves. While dancing they wound their shawls about their waists, letting them fall to within 3 inches of the ground, the fringe at the bottom. In the hair, near the crown, a feather was tied. I noticed an absence of any manner of head ornaments, and, as I knew their vanity and fondness for them, wondered why it was. Upon making inquiries I found they discarded everything they could which was made by white men.

The ghost shirt for the men was made of the same material—shirts and leggings painted in red. Some of the leggings were painted in stripes running up and down, others running around. The shirt was painted blue around the neck, and the whole garment was fantastically sprinkled with figures of birds, bows and arrows, sun, moon, and stars, and everything they saw in nature. Down the outside of the sleeve were rows of feathers tied by the quill ends and left to fly in the breeze, and also a row around the neck and up and down the outside of the leggings. I noticed that a number had stuffed birds, squirrel beads, etc., tied in their long hair. The faces of all were painted red with a black half-moon on the forehead or on one cheek.

As the crowd gathered about the tree the high priest, or master of ceremonies, began his address, giving them directions as to the chant and other matters. After he had spoken for about fifteen minutes they arose and formed in a circle. As nearly as I could count, there were between three and four hundred persons. One stood directly behind another, each with his hands on his neighbor's shoulders. After walking about a few times, chanting, "Father, I come," they stopped marching, but remained in the circle, and set up the most fearful, heart-piercing wails I ever heard—crying, moaning, groaning, and shrieking out their grief, and naming over their departed friends and relatives, at the same time taking up handfuls of dust at their feet, washing their hands in it, and throwing it over their heads. Finally, they raised their eyes to heaven, their hands clasped high above their heads, and stood straight and perfectly still, invoking the power of the Great Spirit to allow them to see and talk with their people who had died. This ceremony lasted about fifteen minutes, when they all sat down where they were and listened to another address, which I did not understand, but which I afterwards learned were words of encouragement and assurance of the coming messiah.

When they rose again, they enlarged the circle by facing toward the center, taking hold of hands, and moving around in the manner of school children in their play of "needle's eye." And now the most intense excitement began. They would go as fast as they could, their heads moving from side to side, their bodies swaying, their arms, with hands gripped tightly in their neighbors', swinging back and forth with all their might. If one, more weak and frail, came near falling, he would be jerked up and into position until tired nature gave way. The ground had been worked and worn by many feet, until the fine, flour-like dust lay light and loose to the depth of two or three inches. The wind, which had increased, would sometimes take it up, enveloping the dancers and hiding them from view. In the ring were men, women, and children; the strong and the robust, the weak consumptive, and those near to death's door. They believed those who were sick would be cured by joining in the dance and losing consciousness. From the beginning they chanted, to a monotonous tune, the words—

Father, I come;
Mother, I come;
Brother, I come;
Father, give us back our arrows.

All of which they would repeat over and over again until first one and then another would break from the ring and stagger away and fall down. One woman fell a few feet from me. She came toward us, her hair flying over her face, which was purple, looking as if the blood would burst through; her hands and arms moving wildly; every breath a pant and a groan; and she fell on her back, and went down like a log. I stepped up to her as she lay there motionless, but with every muscle twitching and quivering. She seemed to be perfectly unconscious. Some of the men and a few of the women would run, stepping high and pawing the air in a frightful manner. Some told me afterwards that they had a sensation as if the ground were rising toward them and would strike them in the face. Others would drop where they stood. One woman fell directly into the ring, and her husband stepped out and stood over her to prevent them from trampling upon her. No one ever disturbed those who fell or took any notice of them except to keep the crowd away.

They kept up dancing until fully 100 persons were lying unconscious. Then they stopped and seated themselves in a circle, and as each one recovered from his trance he was brought to the center of the ring to relate his experience. Each told his story to the medicine-man and he shouted it to the crowd. Not one in ten claimed that he saw anything. I asked one Indian—a tall, strong fellow, straight as an arrow—what his experience was. He said he saw an eagle coming toward him. It flew round and round, drawing nearer and nearer until he put out his hand to take it, when it was gone. I asked him what he thought of it. "Big lie," he replied. I found by talking to them that not one in twenty believed it. After resting for a time they would go through the same performance, perhaps three times a day. They practiced fasting, and every morning those who joined in the dance were obliged to immerse themselves in the creek.

Introduction to Document 2

The Ghost Dance spread, and by autumn, government officials in the West had made their fears known in Washington. The following letters were sent by agents on the reservations to their superiors in the Office of Indian Affairs. The letters give a sense of the anxiety that the Ghost Dance was engendering among whites. It was on the basis of such information that military forces were dispatched to prevent a Sioux outbreak.

DOCUMENT 2 *Letters from Reservations by United States Agents*

Commissioner of Indian Affairs, Washington, D.C.

United States Indian Service, Office of Indian Agent
Pine Ridge Agency, S. Dak., October 12, 1890

Sir:

In assuming charge of this agency I did so under embarrassing circumstances. I feel that my administration will be badly handicapped owing to the sad mess into which affairs have gotten here. These ghost dances have assumed such proportions that they become very serious. . . . The mistake was made by not nipping it in the bud four months ago when it was in its infancy. They have been permitted to continue in these foolish and harmful practices until they are entirely beyond the control of the police. As yet I have taken no definite action in the matter, my object being to thoroughly acquaint myself with the situation, so that I could act intelligently and wisely when I did make a move. . . .

I intend to act very cautiously until I am convinced that it can not be suppressed without the military, and then I trust I will have the hearty cooperation of the Department.

It is useless for me to undertake to describe the foolish manner in which they conduct themselves during these dances. I can only say it injures them physically, mentally, and morally, and undoes all the Department has done for them in the past. What makes the situation so serious is that every Indian on the reservation is armed with a Winchester rifle, and when they are requested to stop these dances they strip themselves and are ready to fight. Why any Indian on the reservation is permitted to have a gun I am not informed. They certainly have no use for them except to endanger the lives of those who try to suppress them in some wrongdoing. If it were not for this fact alone, we would not have any trouble in controlling them with the police. . . .

Very respectfully,
D. F. Royer
United States Indian Agent

Hon. T. F. Morgan
Commissioner of Indian Affairs, Washington, D.C.

United States Indian Service
Rosebud Agency, S. Dak., November 2, 1890

Sir:

I deem it my duty to call the attention of the Department to the extremely disaffected and troublesome state of a portion of the Indians on this and other Sioux agencies.

The coming new order of things as preached to this people during the past seven months is the return to earth of their forefathers, the buffalo, elk, and all other game, the complete restoration of their ancient habits, customs, and power, and the annihilation of

Oglala Sioux Ghost Dance, drawing by Frederic Remington. (The Ghost Dance by the Ogallala Sioux at Pine Ridge Agency, Dakota, *by Frederic S. Remington, supplement to the Harper's Weekly, Dec. 6, 1890. Amon Carter Museum Library, Fort Worth, Texas.)*

the white man. This movement, which some three weeks ago it was supposed had been completely abandoned, while not so openly indulged in, is continually gaining new adherents, and they are daily becoming more threatening and defiant of the authorities.

This latter phase of the case may in a measure be attributed to the scant supply of rations, to which my attention has been almost daily called by the Indians, and especially to the reduction in the quantity of beef as compared to the issue of former years. They kill cows and oxen issued to them for breeding and working purposes, make no secret of doing so, and openly defy arrest. They say that the cattle were issued to them by the Great Father and it is their right to do as they please with them. This evil is increasing daily and if not checked there will be but very few of this class of stock left on the reservation by spring. During the past week it is reported to me that two Indians in the Red Leaf Camp on Black White Creek had killed their cows for a feast at the ghost dance. I sent a policeman to bring them in; they refused to come.

The following day I sent two officers and eight policemen, and they returned without the men, reporting that after they arrived at the camp they were surrounded by seventy-five or more Indians, well armed and with plenty of ammunition, and they unanimously agreed that an attempt to arrest the offenders would have resulted in death to the entire posse. On Friday I sent the chief of police, with an interpreter, to explain matters and endeavor to bring the men in. They positively refused to come, and the chief of police reports that the matter is beyond the control of the police. This is one case which could be repeated indefinitely by attempting the arrest of parties guilty of the same offense.

The religious excitement aggravated by almost starvation is bearing fruits in this state of insubordination; Indians say they had better die fighting than to die a slow death of starvation, and as the new religion promises their return to earth, at the coming of the millennium, they have no great fear of death. To one not accustomed to the Indians, it is a hard matter to believe the confident assurance with which they look forward to the fulfillment of their Prophet's promise.

The time first set for the inauguration of the new era was next spring, but I am reliably informed that it has since and only lately been advanced to the new moon after the next one, or about December 11.

The indications are unmistakable; these Indians have within the past three weeks traded horses and everything else they could trade for arms and ammunition, and all the cash they became possessed of was spent in the same way.

One of the traders here reports that Indians within the last few days have come to his store and offered to sell receipts for wood delivered at the agency, and for which no funds are on hand to pay them for one-third the value *in cash*. When asked what urgent necessity there was for such a sacrifice of receipts for less than their face value, they answered that they wanted *the cash* to buy ammunition.

These are some of the signs of the times and strongly indicate the working of the Indian mind.

To me, there appears to be but one remedy (and all here agree with me) unless the old order of things (the Indians controlling the agency) is to be reestablished, and that is a sufficient force of troops to prevent the outbreak which is imminent, and which any one of a dozen unforeseen causes may precipitate.

Very respectfully, your obedient servant,
E. B. Reynolds
Special United States Indian Agent

The Commissioner of Indian Affairs
Washington, D.C.

United States Indian Service
Western Shoshone Agency, Nev., November 8, 1890

Sir:

The Indians of this reservation and vicinity have just concluded their second medicine dance, the previous one taking place in August last. They are looking for the coming of the Indian Christ, the resurrection of the dead Indians, and consequent supremacy of the Indian race. Fully one thousand people took part in the dance. While the best of order prevailed, the excitement was very great as morning approached, when the dancers were worn out mentally and physically. The medicine-men would shout that they could see the faces of departed friends and relatives moving about the circle. No pen can paint the picture of wild excitement that ensued; all shouted in a chorus, "Christ has come!" and then danced and sung until they fell in a confused and exhausted mass on the ground. The more intelligent ones freely admit that it is all foolishness, but dare not disobey the order of the medicine-men to attend. I apprehend no trouble beyond the loss of time and the general demoralizing effect of these large gatherings of people.

Several of the leading men have gone to Walker Lake to confer with a man that calls himself Christ; others have gone to Fort Hall to meet Indians from Montana and Dakota, to get the news from that section; in fact, the astonishing part of the business "is the fact that" all the Indians in the country seem to possess practically the same ideas and expect about the same result. So universal is this that I can not think but some designing white man or men are at the bottom of the whole matter, and yet there seems to be nothing beyond the merest suspicion to base that opinion on. . . .

Very respectfully,
William I. Plumb
United States Indian Agent

The Commissioner of Indian Affairs
Washington, D.C.

United States Indian Service, Office of Indian Agent
Pine Ridge Agency, S. Dak., November 12, 1890

Sir:

The condition of affairs at this agency when I took charge, whether intentional or not, were to render my administration a failure. Orders of constitutional authority are daily violated and defied, and I am powerless to enforce them. The condition of affairs is going from bad to worse. Yesterday in attempting to arrest an Indian for violation of regulations the offender drew a butcher knife on the police and in less than two minutes he was reënforced by two hundred ghost dancers all armed and ready to fight, consequently the arrest was not made. To-day I received a communication from the offender stating that the policeman who attempted to enforce my orders must be discharged or I could expect trouble, and I was given four weeks to do it.

The police force are overpowered and disheartened; we have no protection; are at the mercy of these crazy dancers.

The situation is serious. I urgently request that I be permitted to proceed to Washington at once and confer with you personally, as a correct idea of the situation can not be conveyed otherwise. The Indians have received their beef and rations, and are going home, and there is no immediate danger until next big issue (four weeks from today). I can leave now without the service being injured, and I do hope you will grant my request, or let the blame rest where it belongs. I have no other object in view save the best interest of the service.

Royer, Agent

Commissioner of Indian Affairs
Washington, D.C.

Pine Ridge Agency, S. Dak., November 15, 1890

Indians are dancing in the snow and are wild and crazy. I have fully informed you that employés and Government property at this agency have no protection and are at the mercy of these dancers. Why delay by further investigation? We need protection and we need it now. The leaders should be arrested and confined in some military post until the matter is quieted, and this should be done at once.

Royer, Agent

Introduction to Document 3

William T. Selwyn was a full-blooded Sioux who worked for the U.S. government on the Yankton reservation as a policeman. When he learned that a man named Kuwapi from the Rosebud reservation was at Yankton teaching the Ghost Dance, Selwyn arrested him. He then interviewed his prisoner and reported his findings to Colonel E. W. Foster on November 22, 1890.

DOCUMENT 3 ***". . . No White People in the Other World . . ."***

Selwyn's Interview with Kuwapi

Q. Do you believe in the new messiah?—A. I somewhat believe it.

Q. What made you believe it?—A. Because I ate some of the buffalo meat that he (the new messiah) sent to the Rosebud Indians through Short Bull.

Q. Did Short Bull say that he saw the living herd of roaming buffaloes while he was with the son of the Great Spirit?—A. Short Bull told the Indians at Rosebud that the buffalo and other wild game will be restored to the Indians at the same time when the general resurrection in favor of the Indians takes place.

Q. You said a "general resurrection in favor of the Indians takes place"; when or how soon will this be?—A. The father sends word to us that he will have all these caused to be so in the spring, when the grass is knee high.

Q. You said "father;" who is this father?—A. It is the new messiah. He has ordered his children (Indians) to call him "father."

Q. You said the father is not going to send the buffalo until the resurrection takes place. Would he be able to send a few buffaloes over this way for a sort of a sample, so as to have his children (Indians) to have a taste of the meat?—A. The father wishes to do things all at once, even in destroying the white race. . . .

Q. What other object could you come to by which you are led to believe that there is such a new messiah on earth at present?—A. The ghost dancers are fainted whenever the dance goes on.

Q. Do you believe that they are really fainted?—A. Yes.

Q. What makes you believe that the dancers have really fainted?—A. Because when they wake or come back to their senses they sometimes bring back some news from the unknown world, and some little trinkets, such as buffalo tail, buffalo meat, etc.

Q. What did the fainted ones see when they get fainted?—A. They visited the happy hunting ground, the camps, multitudes of people, and a great many strange people.

Q. What did the ghost or the strange people tell the fainted one or ones?—A. When the fainted one goes to the camp, he is welcomed by the relatives of the visitor (the fainted one), and he is also invited to several feasts.

Q. Were the people at Rosebud agency anxiously waiting or expecting to see all of their dead relatives who have died several years ago?—A. Yes.

Q. We will have a great many older folks when all the dead people come back, would we not?—A. The visitors all say that there is not a single old man nor woman in the other world—all changed to young.

Q. Are we going to die when the dead ones come back?—A. No; we will be just the same as we are today.

Q. Did the visitor say that there is any white men in the other world?—A. No; no white people.

Q. If there is no white people in the other world, where did they get their provisions and clothing?—A. In the other world, the messenger tells us that they have depended altogether for their food on the flesh of buffalo and other wild game; also, they were all clad in skins of wild animals.

Q. Did the Rosebud agency Indians believe the new messiah, or the son of the Great Spirit?—A. Yes.

Q. How do they show that they . . . believe in the new messiah?—A. They show themselves by praying to the father by looking up to heaven, and call him "father," just the same as you would in a church.

Q. Have you ever been in a church?—A. No.

Q. Do you faithfully believe in the new messiah?—A. I did not in the first place, but as I became more acquainted with the doctrines of the new messiah . . . I really believe in him.

Q. How many people at Rosebud, in your opinion, believe this new messiah?—A. Nearly every one.

Q. Did not the Rosebud people prepare to attack the white people this summer? While I was at Pine Ridge agency this summer the Oglalla Sioux Indians say they will resist against the government if the latter should try to put a stop to the messiah question. Did your folks at Rosebud say the same thing?—A. Yes. . . .

Q. You do not mean to say that the Rosebud Indians will try and cause an outbreak?—A. That seems to be the case. . . .

Introduction to Documents 4 and 5

The following petitions were submitted by citizens' committees to the federal government. The first, addressed to the president of the United States from Mandan, North Dakota, makes clear the contest over resources between white settlers and native peoples. How did the issues of safety, economics, race, and culture blur together? The second petition, from Chadron, Nebraska, insists that all Sioux be disarmed and that their horses be taken away. Under what justification did the citizens of these towns expect government intervention in their behalf?

Document 4 *". . . Indians Armed to the Teeth . . ."*

Mandan, N. Dak., November 18, 1890

Dear Sir:

. . . The settlers who live in the country surrounding Mandan desire to urge strongly that the Indian Department from henceforth deny to Indians the right to carry arms or ammunition off their reservations. Game off the reservations belongs to the white men anyway. . . .

While this is being written there are camped within the city limits of Mandan over one hundred Indians, armed to the teeth, and our wives and our children are asking why these red men are allowed to molest and overawe and annoy us. Our people have stood the ravages of prairie fires, drought, and blizzards for a number of years and are still hopeful; but if, added to their other troubles, they are to be subjected to the depredations of Indians who are supposed to be under the control and subject to the Government they will have to leave the country.

The most conservative men in this community will be powerless to suppress the determination of the majority of the settlers to kill off every Indian that presents his face in this county in the future unless the Government does something to protect us. There are scores of men in this immediate neighborhood who were sufferers by the Minnesota massacres in 1862, and they don't propose to be annoyed and harassed any longer. Their property has been destroyed and their children and wives frightened by these worthless nomads, who are permitted by a lax Government to prowl over the country with arms that would not be allowed on the person of a white man. They will stand it no longer, and we ask that something be done to tighten the rules and regulations governing the actions of the Indians who are under the Indian agents of this locality.

R. M. Tuttle, Chairman
Jesse Ayers
P. B. Wickham
Joseph Miller

DOCUMENT 5 ***". . . Defrauding Us of Vested Rights . . ."***

Chadron, Nebr., November 26, 1890

Dear Sir:

I am instructed by a meeting of the citizens of this town and county, held last evening, to forward you a copy of resolutions unanimously adopted at that meeting, which copy I herewith respectfully submit in print.

Very obediently,
A. A. McFadon

Secretary of the Interior
Washington, D.C.

"*Resolved,* That we respectfully demand of the Government that such steps be taken at this opportune time as shall effectually dispose of the Indian outbreak subject on the Sioux Reservation, and restore to the citizens the confidence the Government may demand of him.

"*Resolved,* That the allowing of thousands of savages to be armed to the teeth in the center of a sparsely settled agrarian State is a condition improvident and unreasonable.

"*Resolved,* That the leaders and instigators of criminality in savages should receive at the hands of the Government the punishment the law provides for traitors, anarchists, and assassins.

"*Resolved,* That in our judgment the exigencies of the occasion demand nothing short of the complete disarming of the Indian and making it a crime for any person to furnish him with arms or implements of war, and we respectfully suggest that the shortest route to the satisfactory settlement of the question would be to deprive the savages of their horses, substituting therefor oxen trained to the plow.

"*F. S. Little,*
"*W. Rucker,*
"*E. S. Ricker,*
"*A. C. Putnam,*
"*A. Bartow,*
"*Committee on Resolutions*"

Introduction to Documents 6 through 8

The violence exploded as the year 1890 ended. Military forces that were sent to round up hostile Sioux engaged a band under Chief Big Foot camped at Wounded Knee Creek. Document 6 is an account taken from the Annual Report of the Commissioner of Indian Affairs for 1891. Document 7 is a set of three letters written by military leaders in the field; it is taken from the same congressional report as Document 2. Document 8 is a series of eyewitness reports from Indians who were interviewed by the Office of Indian Affairs. How do the accounts in Documents 6 through 8 differ? Which do you find most believable, and why? Were there white and Indian views?

DOCUMENT 6 ***Annual Report of the Commissioner of Indian Affairs, 1891***

The "Messiah Craze"

Early in November reports received from the agents at Pine Ridge, Rosebud, and Cheyenne River showed that the Indians of those agencies, especially Pine Ridge, were arming themselves and taking a defiant attitude towards the Government and its representatives, committing depredations, and likely to go to other excesses, and November 13 this office recommended that the matter be submitted to the War Department, with request that such prompt action be taken to avert an outbreak as the emergency might be found by them to demand. . . .

DEATH OF SITTING BULL

At daybreak, December 15, 39 Indian police and 4 volunteers went to Sitting Bull's cabin and arrested him. He agreed to accompany them to the agency, but while dressing caused considerable delay, and during this time his followers began to congregate to the number of 150, so that when he was brought out of the house they had the police entirely surrounded. Sitting Bull then refused to go and called on his friends, the ghost dancers, to rescue him. At this juncture one of them shot Lieutenant Bullhead. The lieutenant then shot Sitting Bull, who also received another shot and was killed outright. Another shot struck Sergeant Shavehead and then the firing became general. In about two hours the police had secured possession of Sitting Bull's house and driven their assailants into the woods. Shortly after, when the United States troops, under command of Capt. Fechet reached the spot the police drew up in line and saluted. Their bravery and discipline received highest praise from Capt. Fechet. The ghost dancers fled from their hiding places to the Cheyenne River Reservation, leaving their families and dead behind them. Their women who had taken part in the fight had been disarmed by the police and placed under guard and were turned over to the troops when they arrived. The losses were six policemen killed (including Bullhead and Shavehead who soon died at the agency hospital) and one wounded. The attacking party lost eight killed and three wounded. . . .

INDIANS CONCENTRATE IN THE BAD LANDS

Groups of Indians from the different reservations had commenced concentrating in the "bad lands," upon or in the vicinity of the Pine Ridge Reservation. Killing of cattle and destruction of other property by these Indians almost entirely within the limits of Pine Ridge and Rosebud reservations occurred, but no signal fires were built, no warlike demonstrations were made, no violence was done to any white settler, nor was there cohesion or organization among the Indians themselves. Many of them were friendly Indians who had never participated in the ghost dance but had fled thither from fear of soldiers, in consequence of the Sitting Bull affair, or through the over persuasion of friends. The military gradually began to close in around them, and they offered no resistance, and a speedy and quiet capitulation of all was confidently expected.

FIGHT AT WOUNDED KNEE CREEK

Among them was Big Foot's band belonging to the Cheyenne River Agency, numbering with others who had joined him, about 120 men and 230 women and children. They had escaped to the bad lands, after arrest by the military at Cheyenne River, but soon started from the bad lands for the Pine Ridge Agency, and with a flag of truce advanced into the open country and proposed a parley with the troops whom they met. This being refused they surrendered unconditionally, remained in camp at Wounded Knee Creek over night, expecting to proceed next morning under escort of the troops to Pine Ridge, whither most of the quondam bad-land Indians were moving. The next day, December 29, when ordered to turn in their arms, they surrendered very few. By a search in the teepees 60 guns were obtained. When the military—a detachment of the Seventh Cavalry (Custer's old command), with other troops—began to take the arms from their persons a shot was fired and carnage ensued. According to reports of military officers, the Indians attacked the troops as soon as the disarmament commenced. The Indians claim that the first shot was fired by a half crazy, irresponsible Indian. At any rate, a short, sharp, indiscriminate fight immediately followed, and, during the fighting and the subsequent flight and pursuit of the Indians, the troops lost 25 killed and 35 wounded, and of the Indians, 84 men and boys, 44 women, and 18 children were killed and at least 33 were wounded, many of them fatally. Most of the men, including Big Foot, were killed around his tent where he lay sick. The bodies of women and children were scattered along a distance of two miles from the scene of the encounter.

Frightened and exasperated, again the Indians made for the bad lands. Indians en route thence to the agency turned back and others rushed away from Pine Ridge.

DOCUMENT 7 *Three Letters by Military Leaders*

Camp Pine Ridge Agency
December 31, 1890

Acting Assistant Adjutant General
Headquarters Department of the Platte
In the field

Sir:

I have the honor to report the following in connection with the movements of my command on the night of December 28th and during the following day. Pursuant to verbal orders from the Commanding General of the Department, I moved my command from this point to the crossing of the Wounded Knee by the main trail to the Rosebud Agency, leaving here at 4:40 P.M., and arriving there at about 8:30 P.M. Major Whitside's battalion of the 7th Cavalry and detachment Light Battery E, 1st Artillery, had that day captured Big Foot's band of Indians, and when I arrived had them in his camp. My command, consisting of Regimental Headquarters and the second battalion, detachment of Light Battery E, 1st Artillery, went into camp for the night. At about 7:30 the next morning, after considerable trouble, the bucks of Big Foot's band, numbering 106 were collected away from their camp, and after explaining to them that having surrendered they would be treated as prisoners of war, but that as such they must surrender their arms. Squads of twenty were cut off, and told to bring them to a designated place. The result of this was very unsatisfactory, but few arms being brought. Keeping the bucks collected, details of soldiers were made under officers to search the Indian camp. While this was in progress, one Indian separated a little from the rest, and in ghost dance costumes, began an address, to which I paid no attention, as the interpreter said he was telling the Indians to be quiet and submit. After a short while, however, the interpreter told me that he was talking of wiping out the whites. I then made him cease his address. Just after this, the search through their camp having proved almost fruitless, I gave orders to search the persons of the bucks, again telling them that they must do as white men always do when surrendering, that is, give up their arms.

At the first move to carry out the order last referred to, the bucks made a break, which at once resulted in terrific fire and a hot fight, lasting about twenty minutes, followed by skirmish firing of about one hour. From the first instant the squaws parted for the hills and it is my belief that comparatively few of them were injured. Some bucks succeeded in getting away and three troops were sent in pursuit. They overtook and captured five bucks (all badly wounded), nineteen squaws and children, and killed one buck. Very soon after the force was attacked by about 125 bucks, supposed to be from the agency. . . . As accurate estimate as could be made of the dead Indians, bucks in and near the camp, was 83, which added to the 7 before mentioned, makes 90 as the number of bucks killed. . . .

Chief Big Foot lying dead in the snow at Wounded Knee. (National Anthropological Archives, Smithsonian Institute (55,018))

Our loss was one officer (Captain Wallace), six non-commissioned officers and eighteen privates killed, and two officers (Lieuts. Garlington and Gresham, the latter slightly, 7th Cavalry, and Lieut. Hawthorn, 2d Artillery), eleven non-commissioned officers and twenty-two privates wounded. . . .

In closing this report, I desire to express my admiration of the gallant conduct of my command in an engagement with a band of Indians in desperate condition, and crazed by religious fanaticism. . . .

Very respectfully,
Your obedient servant,
James W. Forsyth
Colonel 7th Cavalry Commanding

Headquarters Division of the Missouri
In the field, Pine Ridge, S.D.
January 21, 1891

To the Assistant Adjutant General
Headquarters Division of the Missouri
Pine Ridge, S.D.

Sir:

I have the honor to report that in obedience to verbal orders of the Division Commander, I proceeded this morning at 7 A.M., under escort of a detachment of the 1st Infantry, mounted, to White Horse Creek, about eleven miles distant, where I found the bodies of one woman, adult, two girls, eight and seven years old, and a boy of about ten years of age.

They were found in the valley of White Horse Creek, in the brush, under a high bluff, where they had evidently been discovered and shot. Each person had been shot once, the character of which was necessarily fatal in each case. The bodies had not been plundered or molested. The shooting was done at so close a range that the person or clothing of each was powder-burned.

The location of the bodies was about three miles westward of the scene of the Wounded Knee battle. All of the bodies were properly buried by the troops of my escort.

From my knowledge of the facts, I am certain that these people were killed on the day of the Wounded Knee fight, and no doubt by the troop of the 7th Cavalry, under command of Captain Godfrey. Tracks of horses shod with the Goodenough shoes were plainly visible and running along the road passing close by where the bodies were found. . . .

Very respectfully,
Your obedient servant,
Frank D. Baldwin
Captain 5th Infantry, A.A.I.G.

Headquarters Division of the Missouri
Chicago, Illinois, January 31, 1891

Respectfully forwarded to the Adjutant General of the Army . . .

Certain features of the affair at Wounded Knee Creek were so unusual and extraordinary, and such injurious reports were current immediately thereafter, so to imperatively demand an investigation in order to ascertain and record as accurately as possible all the facts, so that an intelligent opinion might guide in the bestowal of commendation or censure. The testimony elicited shows the following facts: First, that Colonel Forsyth had received repeated warnings as to the desperate and deceitful character of Big Foot's band of Indians, and repeated orders as to the exercise of constant vigilance to guard against surprise or disaster under all circumstances.

Secondly, that these warnings and orders were unheeded and disregarded by Colonel Forsyth, who seemed to consider an outbreak of the Indians as being beyond the pale of possibility, in the presence of the large force of troops at hand. The disasters that have occurred to our troops in the past from the desperation of the Indian nature are known to all who are familiar with our history. In addition to this it was well known and Colonel Forsyth had been warned that this particular band contained many of the most desperate and deceitful characters in the Sioux nation, and that a religious excitement nearly approaching frenzy had made them peculiarly dangerous. Under these circumstances the apparent indifference and security of the officer in command of the troops at Wounded Knee Creek is incomprehensive and inexcusable.

Thirdly. An examination of the accompanying map and testimony shows conclusively that at the beginning of the outbreak not a single company of the troops was so disposed as to deliver its fire upon the warriors without endangering the lives of some of their own comrades. It is in fact difficult to conceive how a worse disposition of the troops could have been made. It will be noticed that it would have been perfectly practicable for the entire command of upwards of four hundred and fifty men to have been placed between the warriors and the women and children, with their backs toward the latter and their faces toward the warriors, where they might have used their weapons effectively if required. The testimony goes to show that most of the troops were forced to withhold their fire, leaving the brunt of the affair to fall upon two companies until such warriors as had not been killed broke through or overpowered the small force directly about them and reached the camp occupied by their women and children. The battery of four Hotchkiss guns had until then been useless, the friction primers having been removed from the guns by order of the Captain commanding the battery, lest the gunners might in their excitement discharge the pieces and destroy their own comrades. These guns were now opened upon the Indian camp, even at that time placing in peril Troops C and D, 7th Cav., which were obliged to retreat for some distance owing to the fire from these guns and from the small arms of other portions of the command. The fact that a large number of the one hundred and six warriors were without fire arms when the outbreak occurred is shown by the evidence that forty-eight guns had been taken from the tepees and that a personal search of twenty or more warriors resulted in finding them unarmed. This fact taken in connection with the extremely injudicious disposition of the troops, and the large number of casualties among them, constrains the belief that some of these casualties were suffered at the hands of our own men. The fatal disposition of the troops was such as at the outset to counteract in great measure the immense disparity of strength, and would have been inexcusable in the face of an armed and desperate foe, even had no special warnings and orders been received from higher authority. . . .

Nelson A. Miles

DOCUMENT 8 *Eyewitness Reports of Indians Interviewed by the Office of Indian Affairs*

Turning Hawk, Pine Ridge (Mr. Cook, interpreter). . . . In the course of time we heard that the soldiers were moving toward the scene of trouble. After awhile some of the soldiers finally reached our place and we heard that a number of them also reached our friends at Rosebud. Of course, when a large body of soldiers is moving toward a certain direction they inspire a more or less amount of awe, and it is natural that the women and children who see this large moving mass are made afraid of it and be put in a condition to make them run away. At first we thought that Pine Ridge and Rosebud were the only two agencies where soldiers were sent, but finally we heard that the other agencies fared likewise. We heard and saw that about half our friends at Rosebud agency, from fear at seeing the soldiers, began the move of running away from their agency toward ours (Pine Ridge), and when they had gotten inside of our reservation they there learned that right ahead of them at our agency was another large crowd of soldiers, and while the soldiers were there, there was constantly a great deal of false rumor flying back and forth. The special rumor I have in mind is the threat that the soldiers had come there to disarm the Indians entirely and to take away all their horses from them. That was the oft-repeated story. . . .

They were met by the soldiers and surrounded and finally taken to the Wounded Knee creek, and there at a given time their guns were demanded. When they had delivered them up, the men were separated from their families, from their tipis, and taken to a certain spot. When the guns were thus taken and the men thus separated, there was a crazy man, a young man of very bad influence and in fact a nobody, among that bunch of Indians fired his gun, and of course the firing of a gun must have been the breaking of a military rule of some sort, because immediately the soldiers returned fire and indiscriminate killing followed.

Spotted Horse. This man shot an officer in the army; the first shot killed this officer. I was a voluntary scout at that encounter and I saw exactly what was done, and that was what I noticed; that the first shot killed an officer. As soon as this shot was fired the Indians immediately began drawing their knives, and they were exhorted from all sides to desist, but this was not obeyed. Consequently the firing began immediately on the part of the soldiers.

Turning Hawk. All the men who were in a bunch were killed right there, and those who escaped that first fire got into the ravine, and as they went along up the ravine for a long distance they were pursued on both sides by the soldiers and shot down, as the dead bodies showed afterwards. The women were standing off at a different place from where the men were stationed, and when the firing began, those of the men who escaped the first onslaught went in one direction up the ravine, and then the women, who were bunched together at another place, went entirely in a different direction through an open field, and the women fared the same fate as the men who went up the deep ravine.

American Horse. The men were separated, as has already been said, from the women, and they were surrounded by the soldiers. Then came next the village of the Indians and that was entirely surrounded by the soldiers also. When the firing began, of course the people who were standing immediately around the young man who fired the first shot were killed right together, and then they turned their guns, Hotchkiss guns, etc., upon the women who were in the lodges standing there under a flag of truce, and of course as soon as they were fired upon they fled, the men fleeing in one direction and the women running in two different directions. So that there were three general directions in which they took flight.

There was a woman with an infant in her arms who was killed as she almost touched the flag of truce, and the women and children of course were strewn all along the circular village until they were dispatched. Right near the flag of truce a mother was shot down with her infant; the child not knowing that its mother was dead was still nursing, and that especially was a very sad sight. The women as they were fleeing with their babes were killed together, shot right through, and the women who were very heavy with child were also killed. All the Indians fled in these three directions, and after most all of them had been killed a cry was made that all those who were not killed or wounded should come forth and they would be safe. Little boys who were not wounded came out of their places of refuge, and as soon as they came in sight a number of soldiers surrounded them and butchered them there. . . .

Introduction to Document 9

The following two reports try to assess what happened at Wounded Knee Creek and why. Dr. V. T. McGillycuddy had been the agent at the Pine Ridge reservation but had left months before the bloodshed. He wrote his report two weeks after the incident as a letter to General L. W. Colby. General Nelson A. Miles was in charge of the overall military operation on the plains. His report was printed in the Annual Report of the Secretary of War for 1891. How do the two reports agree or disagree on what happened and why?

DOCUMENT 9 *Government and Military Statements on Wounded Knee*

Ex-Agent McGillycuddy's Statement

Sir:

In answer to your inquiry of a recent date, I would state that in my opinion to no one cause can be attributed the recent so-called outbreak on the part of the Sioux, but rather to a combination of causes gradully cumulative in their effect and dating back through many years—in fact to the inauguration of our practically demonstrated faulty Indian policy.

There can be no question but that many of the treaties, agreements, or solemn promises made by our government with these Indians have been broken. Many of them have been kept by us technically, but as far as the Indian is concerned have been misunderstood by him through a lack of proper explanation at time of signing, and hence considered by him as broken.

It must also be remembered that in all of the treaties made by the government with the Indians, a large portion of them have not agreed to or signed the same. Noticeably was this so in the agreement secured by us with them the summer before last, by which we secured one-half of the remainder of the Sioux reserve, amounting to about 16,000 square miles. This agreement barely carried with the Sioux nation as a whole, but did not carry at Pine Ridge or Rosebud, where the strong majority were against it; and it must be noted that wherever there was the strongest opposition manifested to the recent treaty, there, during the present trouble, have been found the elements opposed to the government.

The Sioux nation, which at one time, with the confederated bands of Cheyennes and Araphahos, controlled a region of country bounded on the north by the Yellowstone, on the south by the Arkansas, and reaching from the Missouri river to the Rocky mountains, has seen this large domain, under the various treaties, dwindle down to their now limited reserve of less than 16,000 square miles, and with the land has disappeared the buffalo and other game. The memory of this, chargeable by them to the white man, necessarily irritates them.

There is back of all this the natural race antagonism which our dealings with the aborigine in connection with the inevitable onward march of civilization has in no degree lessened. It has been our experience, and the experience of other nations, that defeat in war is soon, not sooner or later, forgotten by the coming generation, and as a result we have a tendency to a constant recurrence of outbreak on the part of the weaker race. It is now sixteen years since our last war with the Sioux in 1876—a time when our present Sioux warriors were mostly children, and therefore have no memory of having felt the power of the government. It is but natural that these young warriors, lacking in experience, should require but little incentive to induce them to test the bravery of the white man on the war path, where the traditions of his people teach him is the only path to glory and a chosen seat in the "happy hunting grounds." For these reasons every precaution should be adopted by the government to guard against trouble with its disastrous results. Have such precautions been adopted? Investigation of the present trouble does not so indicate. . . .

By the fortunes of political war, weak agents were placed in charge of some of the agencies at the very time that trouble was known to be brewing. Noticeably was this so at Pine Ridge, where a notoriously weak and unfit man was placed in charge. His flight, abandonment of his agency, and his call for troops have, with the horrible results of the same, become facts in history.

Now, as for facts in connection with Pine Ridge, which agency has unfortunately become the theater of the present "war," was there necessity for troops? My past experience with those Indians does not so indicate. For seven long years, from 1879 to 1886, I, as agent, managed this agency without the presence of a soldier on the reservation, and none nearer than 60 miles, and in those times the Indians were naturally much wilder than they are to-day. To be sure, during the seven years we occasionally had exciting times, when the only thing lacking to cause an outbreak was the calling for troops by the agent and the presence of the same. As a matter of fact, however, no matter how much disturbed affairs were, no matter how imminent an outbreak, the progressive chiefs, with their following, came to the front enough in the majority, with the fifty Indian policemen, to at once crush out all attempts at rebellion against the authority of the agent and the government.

Why was this? Because in those times we believed in placing confidence in the Indians; in establishing, as far as possible, a home-rule government on the reservation. We established local courts, presided over by the Indians, with Indian juries; in fact, we believed in having the Indians assist in working out their own salvation. We courted and secured the friendship and support of the progressive and orderly element, as against the mob element. Whether the system thus inaugurated was practicable, was successful, comparison with recent events will decide. . . .

As for the ghost dance, too much attention has been paid to it. It was only the symptom or surface indication of deep-rooted, long-existing difficulty: as well treat the eruption of smallpox as the disease and ignore the constitutional disease.

As regards disarming the Sioux, however desirable it may appear, I consider it neither advisable nor practicable. I fear that it will result as the theoretical enforcement of prohibition in Kansas, Iowa, and Dakota; you will succeed in disarming the friendly Indians, because you can, and you will not so succeed with the mob element, because you can not. If I were again to be an Indian agent and had my choice, I would take charge of 10,000 armed Sioux in preference to a like number of disarmed ones: and, furthermore, agree to handle that number, or the whole Sioux nation, without a white soldier.

Respectfully, etc.
V. T. McGillycuddy

Statement of General Miles

Cause of Indian dissatisfaction. The causes that led to the serious disturbance of the peace in the northwest last autumn and winter were so remarkable that an explanation of them is necessary in order to comprehend the seriousness of the situation. The Indians assuming the most threatening attitude of hostility were the Cheyennes and Sioux. . . .

The commanding officer at Fort Yates, North Dakota, under date of December 7, 1890, at the time the Messiah delusion was approaching a climax, says, in reference to the disaffection of the Sioux Indians at Standing Rock agency, that it is due to the following causes:

1. Failure of the government to establish an equitable southern boundary of the Standing Rock agency reservation.
2. Failure of the government to expend a just proportion of the money received from the Chicago, Milwaukee and St. Paul railroad company, for right of way privileges, for the benefit of the Indians of said agency. Official notice was received October 18, 1881, by the Indian agent at the Standing Rock agency, that the said railroad company had paid the government under its agreement with the Sioux Indians, for right of way privileges, the sum of $13,911. . . . No portion of the money had been expended up to that time (December, 1890) for the benefit of the Indians of the agency, and frequent complaints had been made to the agent by the Indians because they had received no benefits from their concessions to the said railroad companies.
3. Failure of the government to issue the certificates of title to allotments, as required by article 6 of the treaty of 1868.
4. Failure of the government to provide the full allowance of seeds and agricultural implements to Indians engaged in farming, as required in article 8, treaty of 1868.
5. Failure of the government to issue to such Indians the full number of cows and oxen provided in article 10, treaty of 1876.
6. Failure of the government to issue to the Indians the full ration stipulated in article 5, treaty of 1876. (For the fiscal year beginning July 1, 1890, the following shortages in the rations were found to exist: 485,275 pounds of beef [gross], 761,212 pounds of corn, 11,937 pounds of coffee, 281,712 pounds of flour, 26,234 pounds of sugar, and 39,852 pounds of beans.) . . .
7. Failure of the government to issue to the Indians the full amount of annuity supplies to which they were entitled under the provisions of article 10, treaty of 1868.
8. Failure of the government to have the clothing and other annuity supplies ready for issue on the first day of August of each year. Such supplies have not been ready for issue to the Indians, as a rule, until the winter season is well advanced. . . . Such supplies for the present fiscal year, beginning July 1, 1890, had not yet reached

(December, 1890) the nearest railway station, about 60 miles distant, from which point they must, at this season of the year, be freighted to this agency in wagons. It is now certain that the winter will be well advanced before the Indians at this agency receive their annual allowance of clothing and other annuity supplies.)

9. Failure of the government to appropriate money for the payment of the Indians for the ponies taken from them, by the authority of the government, in 1876.

In conclusion, the commanding officer says: "It, however, appears from the foregoing, that the government has failed to fulfill its obligations, and in order to render the Indians law-abiding, peaceful, contented, and prosperous it is strongly recommended that the treaties be promptly and fully carried out, and that the promises made by the commission in 1889 be faithfully kept."

POSTSCRIPT

Ten days before the bloodletting at Wounded Knee, an editorial appeared in the Aberdeen, South Dakota, *Pioneer.* The author declared that Sitting Bull's death marked the final passing of the "proud spirit" of these "wild" and "untamed" people. The best thing for whites to do now was to exterminate the remaining thousands:

> . . . The nobility of the Redskin is extinguished, and what few are left are a pack of whining curs who lick the hand that smites them. The Whites, by law of conquest, by justice of civilization, are masters of the American continent, and the best safety of the frontier settlements will be secured by the total annihilation of the few remaining Indians. Why not annihilation? Their glory has fled, their spirit broken, their manhood effaced; better that they should die than live the miserable wretches that they are. History would forget these latter despicable beings, and speak, in latter ages of the glory of these grand Kings of the forest and plain. . . .

The author's belief in the Indians' former nobility was no bar to his calling for their elimination. Rather, by romanticizing their past, he was able to condemn them in the present. Two weeks after the editorial appeared, just four days after Wounded Knee, the editor concluded: "Having wronged them for centuries we had better, in order to protect our civilization, follow it up by one more wrong and wipe these untamed and untamable creatures from the face of the earth. . . . Otherwise, we may expect future years to be as full of trouble with the redskins as those have been in the past." The author of these editorials was L. Frank Baum, who in 1900 became famous for writing *The Wizard of Oz.*

QUESTIONS

Defining Terms

Identify in the context of the chapter each of the following:

George Custer	Messiah Craze
Wavoka	Sioux
Ghost Dance	revitalization movements
Pine Ridge Agency	William T. Selwyn
Sitting Bull	Wounded Knee Creek

Probing the Sources

1. Describe the "Messiah Craze" and the Ghost Dance.
2. What evidence is there that the Sioux were armed and preparing to attack? Do you think that they were purely victims?
3. Give a sense of the range of feelings that agents, military officials, and government employees felt toward the Sioux.
4. How do you think whites and Native Americans differed in their ideas about progress?
5. Recount the story of Wounded Knee.

Interpreting the Sources

1. Why do you think so many Indians became interested in the Ghost Dance?
2. How did various whites react to the new religion? Many whites feared that the new religion was a cover for a Sioux uprising. What do you think?
3. Could Wounded Knee have been avoided? How?
4. Can you identify revitalization movements among Euro-Americans in the nineteenth and twentieth centuries?
5. Was Wounded Knee a battle or a massacre?

ADDITIONAL READING

For the Plains wars, see Dee Brown, *Bury My Heart at Wounded Knee* (1971). A Native American perspective is provided in John G. Neihardt, *Black Elk Speaks* (1932). On the history of white-Indian relations, see Wilcomb Washburn, *The Indian in America* (1975); and Robert M. Utley, *The Indian Frontier of the American West, 1846–1890* (1984). For the myths that whites constructed about their confrontations with the Indians, see Richard Slotkin, *Regeneration Through Violence: The Mythology of the American Frontier, 1600–1860* (1973); and Slotkin, *The Fatal Environment: The Myth of the Frontier in the Age of Industrialization, 1800–1890* (1985). Also see Richard White, *"It's your Misfortune and None of My Own" A New History of the American West* (1991); Donald Worster, *Under Western Skies* (1992); Janet A. McDowell, *The Dispossession of the American Indian* (1991); and Patricia Limerick, *The Legacy of Conquest* (1987). For the Sioux, see Catherine Price, *The Oglala People* (1996); on armed conflict, see John McDermott, *A Guide to the Indian Wars of the West* (1998); on gender, see Theda Perdue, ed. *Sisters: Native American Women's Lives* (2001). For more primary sources, try William S.E. Coleman, *Voices of Wounded Knee* (2000).

4

New Americans

The Immigrants

Historical Context

One day in August 1921, the artist Joseph Pennell was walking in the Lower East Side of New York City. He wandered into a street of houses that were trimmed with ornate carvings, mouldings, and ironwork, all products of old craft traditions. Pennell was at once taken with the beauty of the architecture and disturbed by the people in the neighborhood. He wrote to his friend Cass Gilbert, a renowned architect, that the beauty of the buildings was "destroyed by the tribe of mongrels, the spewings out of niggers, dagoes, Chinese, and Greeks who herd in them and make by millions the new Americans." Nonetheless, Pennell advised Gilbert to go there: "If you can stand the stink and sight of your fellow countrymen and women though they aren't mostly naturalized and can get a police permit to see the dens where they herd and breed, *you might get some marble pieces."* An architect like Gilbert, in other words, could extract artwork from these people's homes and reuse it in buildings located in more respectable neighborhoods. Pennell added as an afterthought that there was no danger that anyone in the neighborhood might object; "as there are no Jews there, these people don't know the things have any value."

It was not uncommon for Americans around the turn of the century to think of those from other lands as "spewings," to comment on how they smelled, or to mention their herding and breeding, terms usually reserved for animals. The inscription on the newly erected Statue of Liberty, after all, referred to immigrants as "wretched refuse," hardly a compliment to the parents, grandparents, and great–grandparents of so many of us. Nativism, racism, and xenophobia have been long and enduring in American culture. Pennell's letter merely tapped into the pervasive prejudices.

Nevertheless, it would be a mistake to see such attitudes as fixed and immutable. Ethnic stereotypes may range from tasteless jokes to vicious images that are used to justify violence. The intensity of prejudice varies with such circumstances as economic conditions, competition for jobs, the degree of closeness in which people of different groups live to each other, and the amount of contact over time they share with each other. (By 1880, for example, few Americans had encountered Polish people, but nearly everyone was familiar with the racist stereotypes of African Americans that infused popular culture.) Prejudice may be enduring, but its pervasiveness, intensity, and consequences change dramatically across time and place.

To read Pennell's letter as part of an unvarying climate of hatred for strangers is to imply that there were no alternatives. The logic is circular: Everyone harbored ugly prejudices because that was how everyone felt. Such a position absolves individuals from responsibility, for it makes them seem powerless before the ideas that control them. But to say "everybody thought that way back then" simply is not true; the history of ideas is never so clear or uniform. For example, Pennell's last remark derives from the age-old stereotype of Jews' alleged obsession with money, their stinginess, wealth, power, and so forth. In the stereotype, an entire people's history, traditions, and religion are reduced to a simple and pernicious cluster of prejudices.

Not everyone believed such nonsense. To cite an alternative (and history is the study of alternatives, of roads taken and not taken), Hutchins Hapgood, a man from an old American family, wrote an extraordinarily sensitive and complex book about the cultural life of the Jewish neighborhoods of New York City. Hapgood walked on the same streets as Pennell (though he had walked through them twenty years earlier) and saw something very different. "The Jewish quarter of New York," Hapgood wrote in the preface to his *Spirit of the Ghetto* (1902), "is generally supposed to be a place of poverty, dirt, ignorance, and immorality. . . . But the unpleasant aspect is not the subject of the following sketches." Philanthropists, sociologists, and reformers might enter ethnic neighborhoods to document the immigrants' debasement, but Hapgood was attracted by "the charm [he] felt in men and things there." By not reducing Jewish immigrant culture to poverty, depravity, or stereotypes, Hapgood could sensitively and complexly explore the rich cultural life that Jews created in America.

The history of America, of course, might be said to be the history of immigrants. But the half century between about 1880 and 1930—by which date new legal restrictions and economic depression had ended the influx of foreign peoples—witnessed unprecedented immigration. Roughly twenty-seven million newcomers entered the country in those years, sometimes at a rate of over one million per year. They came less from western and northern Europe than from southern and eastern Europe, and they came too from Asia, so that, taken together, Italians, Jews, Poles, Russians, and other Slavic and Mediterranean peoples, as well as Chinese, arrived in numbers far exceeding the numbers of the Irish, Germans, and Scandinavians who had dominated earlier migrations.

The newcomers tended to settle north of the Ohio and east of the Mississippi in burgeoning urban centers like Chicago and New York. Industrialization and the expansion of the worldwide market economy caused massive shifts in the supply of goods and the demand for labor, so that millions found themselves in motion. Italian peasants, for example, might discover that an overproduction of citrus fruit left them without work, but the need for laborers to build roads and subways in New York City offered a chance to survive. If the efficiency of wheat production now drove prices so low that Slavic peasants could not earn enough to eat, the mines and mills of Pennsylvania needed their backs and hands. Some people migrated within their native countries; others moved through Europe or Asia; many went overseas to Latin America, Canada, or especially the United States; but immigration was an international phenomenon rooted in economic dislocations that left millions without the means to make a living.

The majority of the new immigrants were men; they came in search of jobs while their families stayed behind. (Jews, more than other ethnic groups, migrated as whole families because political persecution in eastern Europe gave them little hope of a decent life there; Chinese women, on the other hand, were forbidden to enter the United States, so the men settled in all-male work camps to mine gold or to build the railroads in the West.) Many intended to remain in America—or wherever they found work—only long enough to send money home to secure the survival of their families in the old country. In some years, half as many people returned to Europe as came to America. Moreover, immigrants tended to come in patterns that demographers call *chain migrations.* The decision to go was not made randomly by individuals; rather, extended families, neighbors, or townspeople migrated together, sold their labor together, and settled into new communities together. The Chinatowns, Little Italys, and other ethnic neighborhoods were the result of people's need to help one another economically, to maintain their language and culture, and to defend themselves from prejudice.

Despite occasional recessions, America's economy boomed during this era, providing plenty of work to lure the newcomers. But immigrants were exploitable labor, easily replaced by others if they started to organize and make demands. In New York sweatshops, Jews sewed garments for the ready-to-wear industry; in Pittsburgh mills, Poles poured steel; on California ranches, Mexicans picked the crops; in downtown Chicago, Greeks shined businessmen's shoes—and most worked brutally long hours to make a bit more or less than subsistence wages. All lived with the fear that new workers might undercut their wages, and they labored in horrid conditions that caused tens of thousands to die prematurely every year. Epidemics swept the crowded slums, mines caved in, explosions rocked the mills, construction workers fell from shoddy scaffoldings, and tenements burned to the ground. Prejudice prevented many Americans from recognizing the human tragedy before their eyes. The relative powerlessness of immigrants—their inability to communicate across ethnic boundaries, their need to keep jobs, their sheer exhaustion from overwork—too often kept them from organizing effectively to resist oppression.

All of their hardships notwithstanding, the immigrants made a life for themselves and their children. Perhaps it is more accurate to say that, in order to survive the hardships—the prejudice, poverty, disease, and death—they knew they must stick together and cling to their old ways. In ethnic communities, they sang the songs, played the games, and told the stories of the old country. Extended families reinforced distinctive gender roles, food ways, languages, and other cultural patterns. The new immigrants built churches, especially Catholic churches, since the majority of them were of that faith. They worshiped in their own unique ways; Polish Catholicism differed markedly from Italian Catholicism, as did the Greek Orthodox church from the Russian Orthodox church. Politics engaged many immigrants' attention, and community leaders helped to develop local resources, to accomplish goals for their people, and, in the process, to become powerful individuals. Many groups also came with well-developed traditions of economic protest, so socialist, communist, trade unionist, and anarchist organizations flourished.

But always there were tensions. The children of immigrants were divided in their loyalties between the ways of their parents and those of the American culture. Wealthier foreigners were embarrassed by their poor compatriots, but often not too embarrassed to exploit them. Patriotic feelings toward the new home that fed them vied with hatred of America's prejudice and exploitation. The experiences of migrating to a new land, settling, making a living, establishing communities, and deciding whether to stay or for how long were difficult challenges that individuals negotiated for themselves day by day.

THE DOCUMENTS

Introduction to Documents 1 through 6

The documents in this chapter give a sense of the complexity of the immigrant experience. There are interviews with three immigrants—one Italian, one Chinese, and one Jewish—that appeared in the reform magazine *The Independent* just after the turn of the nineteenth century. While we cannot know what questions were asked by the representative of the magazine or how the interviews were edited, these pieces give us the rare opportunity to hear the immigrants' own voices and to glimpse how they viewed themselves. Preceding each interview is a portion of Jacob Riis's famous book *How the Other Half Lives* (1890). Riis was a Danish immigrant who became a journalist and a social reformer. Before his success and fame in middle age, however, he had suffered severe poverty and alienation shortly after he migrated to America. During the economic depression of the 1870s, when he was in his twenties, Riis wandered around the streets of New York unemployed, homeless, and suicidal. He was saved by a job as a police reporter for the *New York Tribune*. For the rest of the century, he wrote about the city's impoverished lower Manhattan wards.

Despite his own experience of immigration and poverty, Riis was by no means wholly sympathetic to the people he wrote about and photographed. He hated the dirt and the anarchy, the stink and the poverty of lower Manhattan, but he hated these things as a man running from something in himself. He saw mostly the immigrants' degradation, barely the people themselves, so he readily fastened onto ethnic stereotypes to describe them. Compare Riis's characterization of the Chinese with what Lee Chew says about himself and his people. Are there similarities between Riis's description of Italians and the picture we get from Rocco Corresca? Can you square Riis's characterization of Jews as obsessed with money with Rose Schneiderman's commitment to labor organizing?

DOCUMENT 1 *"Little Italy"*

Jacob Riis

Certainly a picturesque, if not very tidy, element has been added to the population in the "assisted" Italian immigrant who claims so large a share of public attention, partly because he keeps coming at such a tremendous rate, but chiefly because he elects to stay in New York, or near enough for it to serve as his base of operations, and here promptly reproduces conditions of destitution and disorder which, set in the frame-work of Mediterranean exuberance, are the delight of the artist, but in a matter-of-fact American community become its danger and reproach. The reproduction is made easier in New York because he finds the material ready to hand in the worst of the slum tenements; but even where it is not he soon reduces what he does find to his own level, if allowed to follow his natural bent. The Italian comes in at the bottom, and in the generation that came over the sea he stays there. In the slums he is welcomed as a tenant who "makes less trouble" than the contentious Irishman or the order-loving German, that is to say: is content to live in a pigsty and submits to robbery at the hands of the rent-collector without murmur. Yet this very tractability makes of him in good hands, when firmly and intelligently managed, a really desirable tenant. But it is not his good fortune often to fall in with other hospitality upon his coming than that which brought him here for its own profit, and has no idea of letting go its grip upon him as long as there is a cent to be made out of him.

Recent Congressional inquiries have shown the nature of the "assistance" he receives from greedy steamship agents and "bankers," who persuade him by false promises to mortgage his home, his few belongings, and his wages for months to come for a ticket to the land where plenty of work is to be had at princely wages. The padrone—the "banker" is nothing else—having made his ten per cent. out of him en route, receives him at the landing and turns him to double account as a wage-earner and a rent-payer. In each of these roles he is made to yield a profit to his unscrupulous countryman, whom he trusts implicitly with the instinct of utter helplessness. The man is so ignorant that, as one of the sharpers who prey upon him put it once, it "would be downright sinful not to take him in." His ignorance and unconquerable suspicion of strangers dig the pit into which he falls. He not only knows no word of English, but he does not know enough to learn. Rarely only can he write his own language. Unlike the German, who begins learning English the day he lands as a matter of duty, or the Polish Jew, who takes it up as soon as he is able as an investment, the Italian learns slowly, if at all. Even his boy, born here, often speaks his native tongue indifferently. He is forced, therefore, to have constant recourse to the middle-man who makes him pay handsomely at every turn. He hires him out to the railroad contractor, receiving a commission from the employer as well as from the laborer, and repeats the performance monthly, or as often as he can have him dismissed. In the city he contracts for his lodging, subletting to him space in the vilest tenements at extortionate rents, and sets an example that does not lack imitators. The "princely wages" have vanished with his coming, and in their place hardships and a dollar a day, [along] with the padrone's merciless mortgage, confront him. Bred to even worse fare, he takes both as a matter of course, and, applying the maxim that it is not what one makes but what he saves that makes him rich, manages to turn the very dirt of the streets into a hoard of gold, with which he either returns to his Southern home, or brings over his family to join in his work and in his fortunes the next season. . . .

Did the Italian always adapt himself as readily to the operation of the civil law as to the manipulation of political "pull" on occasion, he would save himself a good deal of unnecessary trouble. Ordinarily he is easily enough governed by authority—always excepting Sunday, when he settles down to a game of cards and lets loose all his bad passions. Like the Chinese, the Italian is a born gambler. His soul is in the game from the moment the cards are on the table, and very frequently his knife is in it too before the game is ended. No Sunday has passed in New York since "the Bend" became a suburb of Naples without one or more of these murderous affrays coming to the notice of the police. As a rule that happens only when the man the game went against is either dead or so badly wounded as to require instant surgical help. As to the other, unless he be caught red-handed, the chances that the police will ever get him are slim indeed. The wounded man can seldom be persuaded to betray him. He wards off all inquiries with a wicked "I fix him myself," and there the matter rests until he either dies or recovers. If the latter, the community hears after a while of another Italian affray, a man stabbed in a quarrel, dead or dying, and the police know that "he" has been fixed, and the account squared.

With all his conspicuous faults, the swarthy Italian immigrant has his redeeming traits. He is as honest as he is hot-headed. There are no Italian burglars in the Rogues' Gallery; the ex-brigand toils peacefully with pickaxe and shovel on American ground. His boy occasionally shows, as a pick-pocket, the results of his training with the toughs of the Sixth Ward slums. The only criminal business to which the father occasionally lends his hand, outside of murder, is a bunco game, of which his confiding countrymen, returning with their hoard to their native land, are the victims. The women are faithful wives and devoted mothers. Their vivid and picturesque costumes lend a tinge of color to the otherwise dull monotony of the slums they inhabit. The Italian is gay, lighthearted and, if his fur is not stroked the wrong way, inoffensive as a child. His worst offence is that he keeps the stale-beer dives. Where his headquarters is, in the Mulberry Street Bend, these vile dens flourish and gather about them all the wrecks, the utterly wretched, the hopelessly lost, on the lowest slope of depraved humanity. And out of their misery he makes a profit. . . .

DOCUMENT 2 *"The Biography of a Bootblack"*

Rocco Corresca

[The story of Rocco Corresca is presented almost as he told it to a representative of *The Independent*. There are changes of language and some suppressions, but no change of meaning has been made. The ideas and statements of fact are all his, and, astonishing as it may seem to Americans, much of the experience is typical of thousands of Italians who come to this country penniless and make their fortunes, though beginning as low down in the scale as the narrator. Rocco is known to many people as "Joe." He claims that he has always been known as Rocco but that the name Corresca was given him when he went aboard the ship that brought him here. It was entered on the books. He has since kept it for official purposes and proposes to be known by it in the future. —*Editor*.]

When I was a very small boy I lived in Italy in a large house with many other small boys, who were all dressed alike and were taken care of by some nuns. It was a good place, situated on the side of the mountain, where grapes were growing and melons and oranges and plums.

They taught us our letters and how to pray and say the catechism, and we worked in the fields during the middle of the day. We always had enough to eat and good beds to sleep in at night, and sometimes there were feast days, when we marched about wearing flowers.

Those were good times and they lasted till I was nearly eight years of age. Then an old man came and said he was my grandfather. He showed some papers and cried over me and said that the money had come at last and now he could take me to his beautiful home. He seemed very glad to see me and after they looked at his papers he took me away and we went to the big city—Naples. He kept talking about his beautiful house, but when we got there it was a dark cellar that he lived in and I did not like it at all. Very rich people were on the first floor. They had carriages and servants and music and plenty of good things to eat, but we were down below in the cellar and had nothing. There were four other boys in the cellar and the old man said they were all my brothers. All were larger than I and they beat me at first till one day Francisco said that they should not beat me any more, and then Paulo, who was the largest of all, fought him till Francisco drew a knife and gave him a cut. Then Paulo, too, got a knife and said that he would kill Francisco, but the old man knocked them both down with a stick and took their knives away and gave them beatings.

Each morning we boys all went out to beg and we begged all day near the churches and at night near the theatres, running to the carriages and opening the doors and then

In the home of an Italian Ragpicker, Jersey Street, photograph, Museum of the City of New York Jacob A. Riis Collection, #157

getting in the way of the people so that they had to give us money or walk over us. The old man often watched us and at night he took all the money, except when we could hide something. . . .

Then the old man said to me: "If you don't want to be a thief you can be a cripple. That is an easy life and they make a great deal of money."

I was frightened then, and that night I heard him talking to one of the men that came to see him. He asked how much he would charge to make me a good cripple like those that crawl about the church. They had a dispute, but at last they agreed and the man said that I should be made so that people would shudder and give me plenty of money.

I was much frightened, but I did not make a sound and in the morning I went out to beg with Francisco. I said to him: "I am going to run away. I don't believe 'Tony is my grandfather . . . and I don't want to be a cripple, no matter how much money the people may give."

"Where will you go?" Francisco asked me.

"I don't know," I said; "somewhere."

He thought awhile and then he said: "I will go, too."

So we ran away out of the city and begged from the country people as we went along. We came to a village down by the sea and a long way from Naples and there we found some fishermen and they took us aboard their boat. We were with them five years, and tho it was a very hard life we liked it well because there was always plenty to eat. Fish do not keep long and those that we did not sell we ate.

The chief fisherman, whose name was Ciguciano, had a daughter, Teresa, who was very beautiful, and tho she was two years younger than I, she could cook and keep house quite well. She was a kind, good girl and he was a good man. When we told him about the old man who told us he was our grandfather, the fisherman said he was an old rascal who should be in prison for life. Teresa cried much when she heard that he was going to make me a cripple. Ciguciano said that all the old man had taught us was wrong—that it was bad to beg, to steal and to tell lies. He called in the priest and the priest said the same thing and was very angry at the old man in Naples, and he taught us to read and write in the evenings. He also taught us our duties to the church. . . .

We grew large and strong with the fisherman and he told us that we were getting too big for him, that he could not afford to pay us the money that we were worth. He was a fine, honest man—one in a thousand.

Now and then I had heard things about America—that it was a far off country where everybody was rich and that Italians went there and made plenty of money, so that they could return to Italy and live in pleasure ever after. One day I met a young man who pulled out a handful of gold and told me he had made that in America in a few days.

I said I should like to go there, and he told me that if I went he would take care of me and see that I was safe. I told Francisco and he wanted to go, too. So we said good-by to our good friends. Teresa cried and kissed us both and the priest came and shook our hands and told us to be good men, and that no matter where we went God and his saints were always near us and that if we lived well we should all meet again in heaven. We cried, too, for it was our home, that place. Ciguciano gave us money and slapped us on the back and said that we should be great. But he felt bad, too, at seeing us go away after all that time.

The young man took us to a big ship and got us work away down where the fires are. We had to carry coal to the place where it could be thrown on the fires. Francisco and I were very sick from the great heat at first and lay on the coal for a long time, but they threw water on us and made us get up. We could not stand on our feet well, for everything was going around and we had no strength. We said that we wished we had stayed in Italy no matter how much gold there was in America. We could not eat for three days and could not do much work. Then we got better and sometimes we went up above and looked about. There was no land anywhere and we were much surprised. How could the people tell where to go when there was no land to steer by? . . .

We were all landed on an island and the bosses there said that Francisco and I must go back because we had not enough money, but a man named Bartolo came up and told them that we were brothers and he was our uncle and would take care of us. He brought two other men who swore that they knew us in Italy and that Bartolo was our uncle. I had never seen any of them before, but even then Bartolo might be my uncle, so I did not say anything. The bosses of the island let us go out with Bartolo after he had made the oath.

We came to Brooklyn to a wooden house in Adams Street that was full of Italians from Naples. Bartolo had a room on the third floor and there were fifteen men in the room, all boarding with Bartolo. He did the cooking on a stove in the middle of the room and there were beds all around the sides, one bed above another. It was very hot in the room, but we were soon asleep, for we were very tired.

The next morning, early, Bartolo told us to go out and pick rags and get bottles. He gave us bags and hooks and showed us the ash barrels. On the streets where the fine houses are the people are very careless and put out good things, like mattresses and umbrellas, clothes, hats and boots. We brought all these to Bartolo and he made them new again and sold them on the sidewalk; but mostly we brought rags and bones. The rags we had to wash in the back yard and then we hung them to dry on lines under the ceiling in our room. The bones we kept under the beds till Bartolo could find a man to buy them.

Most of the men in our room worked at digging the sewer. Bartolo got them the work and they paid him about one quarter of their wages. Then he charged them for board and he bought the clothes for them, too. So they got little money after all.

Bartolo was always saying that the rent of the room was so high that he could not make anything, but he was really making plenty. He was what they call a padrone and is now a very rich man. The men that were living with him had just come to the country and could not speak English. They had all been sent by the young man we met in Italy. Bartolo told us all that we must work for him and that if we did not the police would come and put us in prison.

He gave us very little money, and our clothes were some of those that were found on the street. Still we had enough to eat and we had meat quite often, which we never had in Italy. Bartolo got it from the butcher—the meat that he could not sell to the other people—but it was quite good meat. Bartolo cooked it in the pan while we all sat on our beds in the evening. Then he cut it into small bits and passed the pan around, saying:

"See what I do for you and yet you are not glad. I am too kind a man, that is why I am so poor."

We were with Bartolo nearly a year, but some of our countrymen who had been in the place a long time said that Bartolo had no right to us and we could get work for a dollar and a half a day, which, when you make it *lire* (reckoned in the Italian currency) is very much. So we went away one day to Newark and got work on the street. Bartolo came after us and made a great noise, but the boss said that if he did not go away soon the police would have him. Then he went, saying that there was no justice in this country.

We paid a man five dollars each for getting us the work and we were with that boss for six months. He was Irish, but a good man and he gave us our money every Saturday night. We lived much better than with Bartolo, and when the work was done we each had nearly $200 saved. Plenty of the men spoke English and they taught us, and we taught them to read and write. That was at night, for we had a lamp in our room, and there were only five other men who lived in that room with us. . . .

When the Newark boss told us that there was no more work Francisco and I talked about what we would do and we went back to Brooklyn to a saloon near Hamilton Ferry, where we got a job cleaning it out and slept in a little room upstairs. There was a bootblack named Michael on the corner and when I had time I helped him and learned the business. Francisco cooked the lunch in the saloon and he, too, worked for the bootblack and we were soon able to make the best polish.

Then we thought we would go into business and we got a basement on Hamilton avenue, near the Ferry, and put four chairs in it. We paid $75 for the chairs and all the other things. We had tables and looking glasses there and curtains. We took the papers that have the pictures in and made the place high toned. Outside we had a big sign that said:

THE BEST SHINE FOR TEN CENTS

Men that did not want to pay ten cents could get a good shine for five cents, but it was not an oil shine. We had two boys helping us and paid each of them fifty cents a day. The rent of the place was $20 a month, so the expenses were very great, but we made money from the beginning. We slept in the basement, but got our meals in the saloon till we could put a stove in our place, and then Francisco cooked for us all. That would not do, tho, because some of our customers said that they did not like to smell garlic and onions and red herrings. I thought that was strange, but we had to do what the customers said. So we got the woman who lived upstairs to give us our meals and paid her $1.50 a week each. She gave the boys soup in the middle of the day—five cents for two plates. . . .

We had said that when we saved $1,000 each we would go back to Italy and buy a farm, but now that the time is coming we are so busy and making so much money that we think we will stay. We have opened another parlor near South Ferry, in New York. We have to pay $30 a month rent, but the business is very good. The boys in this place charge sixty cents a day because there is so much work.

At first we did not know much of this country, but by and by we learned. There are here plenty of Protestants who are heretics, but they have a religion, too. Many of the finest churches are Protestant, but they have no saints and no altars, which seems strange. . . .

There are plenty of rich Italians here, men who a few years ago had nothing and now have so much money that they could not count all their dollars in a week. The richest ones go away from the other Italians and live with the Americans. . . .

I am nineteen years of age now and have $700 saved. Francisco is twenty-one and has about $900. We shall open some more parlors soon. I know an Italian who was a bootblack ten years ago and now bosses bootblacks all over the city, who has so much money that if it was turned into gold it would weight more than himself. . . .

Brooklyn, N.Y.

DOCUMENT 3 *"Chinatown"*

Jacob Riis

Between the tabernacles of Jewry and the shrines of the Bend, Joss has cheekily planted his pagan worship of idols, chief among which are the celestial worshippers' own gain and lusts. Whatever may be said about the Chinaman being a thousand years behind the age on his own shores, here he is distinctly abreast of it in his successful scheming to "make it pay." It is doubtful if there is anything he does not turn to a paying account, from his religion down, or up, as one prefers. At the risk of distressing some well-meaning, but, I fear, too trustful people, I state it in advance as my opinion, based on the steady observation of years, that all attempts to make an effective Christian of John Chinaman will remain abortive in this generation; of the next I have, if anything, less hope. Ages of senseless idolatry, a mere grub-worship, have left him without the essential qualities for appreciating the gentle teachings of a faith whose motive and unselfish spirit are alike beyond his grasp. He lacks the handle of a strong faith in something, anything, however wrong, to catch him by. There is nothing strong about him, except his passions when aroused. I am convinced that he adopts Christianity, when he adopts it at all, as he puts on American clothes, with what the politicans would call an ulterior motive, some sort of gain in the near prospect—washing, a Christian wife perhaps, anything he happens to rate for the moment above his cherished pigtail.

Stealth and secretiveness are as much part of the Chinaman in New York as the cat-like tread of his felt shoes. His business, as his domestic life, shuns the light, less because there is anything to conceal than because that is the way of the man. Perhaps the attitude of American civilization toward the stranger, whom it invited in, has taught him that way. At any rate, the very doorways of his offices and shops are fenced off by queer, forbidding partitions suggestive of a continual state of siege. The stranger who enters through the crooked approach is received with sudden silence, a sullen stare, and an angry "Vat you vant?" that breathes annoyance and distrust.

. . . The average Chinaman, the police will tell you, would rather gamble than eat any day, and they have ample experience to back them. Only the fellow in the bunk smokes away, indifferent to all else but his pipe and his own enjoyment. It is a mistake to assume that Chinatown is honeycombed with opium "joints." There are a good many more outside of it than in it. The celestials do not monopolize the pipe. In Mott Street there is no need of them. Not a Chinese home or burrow there but has its bunk and its lay-out, where they can be enjoyed safe from police interference. The Chinaman smokes opium as Caucasians smoke tobacco, and apparently with little worse effect upon himself. But woe unto the white victim upon which his pitiless drug gets its grip! . . .

From the teeming tenements to the right and left of [Chinatown] come the white slaves of its dens of vice and their infernal drug, that have infused into the "Bloody Sixth" Ward a subtler poison than ever the stale-beer dives knew, or the "sudden death" of the Old Brewery. There are houses, dozens of them, in Mott and Pell Streets, that are literally jammed, from the "joint" in the cellar to the attic, with these hapless victims of a passion which, once acquired, demands the sacrifice of every instinct of decency to its insatiate desire. . . . I came across a company of them [young Caucasian prostitutes] "hitting the pipe" together, on a tour through their dens one night with the police captain of the precinct. The girls knew him, called him by name, offered him a pipe, and chatted with him about the incidents of their acquaintance, how many times he had "sent them up," and their chances of "lasting" much longer. There was no shade of regret in their voices, nothing but utter indifference and surrender.

One thing about them was conspicuous: their scrupulous neatness. It is the distinguishing mark of Chinatown, outwardly and physically. It is not altogether by chance the Chinaman has chosen the laundry as his distinctive field. He is by nature as clean as the cat, which he resembles in his traits of cruel cunning and savage fury when aroused. On this point of cleanliness he insists in his domestic circle, yielding in others with crafty submissiveness to the caprice of the girls, who "boss" him in a very independent manner, fretting vengefully under the yoke they loathe, but which they know right well they can never shake off, once they have put the pipe to their lips and given Mott Street a mortgage upon their souls for all time. . . .

The frequent assertions of the authorities that at least no girls under age are wrecked on this Chinese shoal, are disproved by the observation of those who go frequently among these dens, though the smallest girl will invariably, and usually without being asked, insist that she is sixteen, and so of age to choose the company she keeps. Such assertions are not to be taken seriously. Even while I am writing, the morning returns from one of the precincts that pass through my hands report the arrest of a Chinaman for "inveigling little girls into his laundry," one of the hundred outposts of Chinatown that are scattered all over the city, as the outer threads of the spider's web that holds its prey fast. . . .

Withal the police give the Chinese the name of being the "quietest people down there," meaning in the notoriously turbulent Sixth Ward; and they are. The one thing they desire above all is to be let alone, a very natural wish perhaps, considering all the circumstances. If it were a laudable or even an allowable ambition that prompts it, they might be humored with advantage, probably, to both sides. But the facts show too plainly that it is not, and that in their very exclusiveness and reserve they are a constant and terrible menace to society, wholly regardless of their influence upon the industrial problems which their presence confuses. The severest official scrutiny, the harshest repressive measures are justifiable in Chinatown, orderly as it appears on the surface, even more than in the Bend, and the case is infinitely more urgent. To the peril that threatens there all the senses are alert, whereas the poison that proceeds from Mott Street puts mind and body to sleep, to work out its deadly purpose in the corruption of the soul. . . .

DOCUMENT 4 ***"The Biography of a Chinaman"***

Lee Chew

[Mr. Lee Chew is a representative Chinese business man who expresses with much force views that are generally held by his countrymen throughout America. The interview that

follows *is strictly as he gave it,* except as to detail of arrangement and mere verbiage. Mr. Lee was assisted by the well-known Chinese interpreter, Mr. Joseph M. Singleton, of 24 Pell Street.
—*Editor.*]

The village where I was born is situated in the province of Canton, on one of the banks of the Si-Kiang River. It is called a village, altho it is really as big as a city, for there are about 5,000 men in it over eighteen years of age—women and children and even youths are not counted in our villages.

All in the village belonged to the tribe of Lee. They did not intermarry with one another, but the men went to other villages for their wives and brought them home to their fathers' houses, and men from other villages—Wus and Wings and Sings and Fongs, etc.—chose wives from among our girls. . . .

My father's house is built of fine blue brick, better than the brick in the houses here in the United States. It is only one story high, roofed with red tiles and surrounded by a stone wall which also incloses the yard. There are four rooms in the house, one large living room which serves for a parlor and three private rooms, one occupied by my grandfather, who is very old and very honorable; another by my father and mother, and the third by my oldest brother and his wife and two little children. There are no windows, but the door is left open all day.

All the men of the village have farms, but they don't live on them as the farmers do here; they live in the village, but go out during the day time and work their farms, coming home before dark. My father has a farm of about ten acres, on which he grows a great abundance of things—sweet potatoes, rice, beans, peas, yams, sugar cane, pineapples, bananas, lychee nuts and palms. The palm leaves are useful and can be sold. Men make fans of the lower part of each leaf near the stem, and water proof coats and hats, and awnings for boats, of the parts that are left when the fans are cut out. . . .

We have our own Government, consisting of the elders of our tribe—the honorable men. When a man gets to be sixty years of age he begins to have honor and to become a leader, and then the older he grows the more he is honored. We had some men who were nearly one hundred years, but very few of them.

In spite of the fact that any man may correct them for a fault, Chinese boys have good times and plenty of play. We played games like tag, and other games like shinny and a sort of football called yin. . . . It was not all play for us boys, however. We had to go to school, where we learned to read and write and to recite the precepts of Kong-foo-tsze and the other Sages, and stories about the great Emperors of China, who ruled with the wisdom of gods and gave to the whole world the light of high civilization and the culture of our literature, which is the admiration of all nations.

I went to my parents' house for meals, approaching my grandfather with awe, my father and mother with veneration and my elder brother with respect. I never spoke unless spoken to, but I listened and heard much concerning the red haired, green eyed foreign devils with the hairy faces, who had lately come out of the sea and clustered on our shores. They were wild and fierce and wicked, and paid no regard to the moral precepts of Kong-foo-tsze and the Sages; neither did they worship their ancestors, but pretended to be wiser than their fathers and grandfathers. They loved to beat people and to rob and murder. In the streets of Hong Kong many of them could be seen reeling drunk. Their speech was a savage roar, like the voice of the tiger or the buffalo, and they wanted to take the land away from the Chinese. Their men and women lived together like animals, without any marriage or faithfulness, and even were shameless enough to walk the streets arm in arm in daylight. So the old men said.

All this was very shocking and disgusting, as our women seldom were on the street, except in the evenings, when they went with the water jars to the three wells that supplied all the people. Then if they met a man they stood still, with their faces turned to the

A scene from New York City's Chinatown around the turn of the century. (Museum of the City of New York, Jacob A. Riis Collection, #260)

wall, while he looked the other way when he passed them. A man who spoke to a woman on the street in a Chinese village would be beaten, perhaps killed.

My grandfather told how the English foreign devils had made wicked war on the Emperor, and by means of their enchantments and spells had defeated his armies and forced him to admit their opium, so that the Chinese might smoke and become weakened and the foreign devils might rob them of their land.

My grandfather said that it was well known that the Chinese were always the greatest and wisest among men. They had invented and discovered everything that was good. Therefore the things which the foreign devils had and the Chinese had not must be evil. Some of these things were very wonderful, enabling the red haired savages to talk with one another, tho they might be thousands of miles apart. They had suns that made darkness like day, their ships carried earthquakes and volcanoes to fight for them, and thousands of demons that lived in iron and steel houses spun their cotton and silk, pushed their boats, pulled their cars, printed their newspapers and did other work for them. They were constantly showing disrespect for their ancestors by getting new things to take the place of the old.

I heard about the American foreign devils, that they were false, having made a treaty by which it was agreed that they could freely come to China, and the Chinese as freely go to their country. After this treaty was made China opened its doors to them and then they broke the treaty that they had asked for by shutting the Chinese out of their country. . . .

I worked on my father's farm till I was about sixteen years of age, when a man of our tribe came back from America and took ground as large as four city blocks and made a paradise of it. He put a large stone wall around and led some streams through and built a palace and summer house and about twenty other structures, with beautiful bridges over the streams and walks and roads. Trees and flowers, singing birds, water fowl and curious animals were within the walls.

The man had gone away from our village a poor boy. Now he returned with unlimited wealth, which he had obtained in the country of the American wizards. After many amazing adventures he had become a merchant in a city called Mott Street, so it was said.

When his palace and grounds were completed he gave a dinner to all the people who assembled to be his guests. One hundred pigs roasted whole were served on the tables, with chickens, ducks, geese and such an abundance of dainties that our villagers even now lick their fingers when they think of it. He had the best actors from Hong Kong performing, and every musician for miles around was playing and singing. At night the blaze of the lanterns could be seen for many miles.

Having made his wealth among the barbarians this man had faithfully returned to pour it out among his tribesmen, and he is living in our village now very happy, and a pillar of strength to the poor.

The wealth of this man filled my mind with the idea that I, too, would like to go to the country of the wizards and gain some of their wealth, and after a long time my father consented, and gave me his blessing, and my mother took leave of me with tears, while my grandfather laid his hand upon my head and told me to remember and live up to the admonitions of the Sages, to avoid gambling, bad women and men of evil minds, and so to govern my conduct that when I died my ancestors might rejoice to welcome me as a guest on high.

My father gave me $100, and I went to Hong Kong with five other boys from our place and we got steerage passage on a steamer, paying $50 each. Everything was new to me. All my life I had been used to sleeping on a board bed with a wooden pillow, and I found the steamer's bunk very uncomfortable, because it was so soft. The food was different from that which I had been used to, and I did not like it at all. I was afraid of the stews, for the thought of what they might be made of by the wicked wizards of the ship made me ill. Of the great power of these people I saw many signs. The engines that moved the ship were wonderful monsters, strong enough to lift mountains. When I got to San Francisco, which was before the passage of the Exclusion act, I was half starved, because I was afraid to eat the provisions of the barbarians, but a few days' living in the Chinese quarter made me happy again. A man got me work as a house servant in an American family, and my start was the same as that of almost all the Chinese in this country.

The Chinese laundryman does not learn his trade in China; there are no laundries in China. The women there do the washing in tubs and have no washboards or flat irons. All the Chinese laundrymen here were taught in the first place by American women just as I was taught.

When I went to work for that American family I could not speak a word of English, and I did not know anything about housework. The family consisted of husband, wife and two children. They were very good to me and paid me $3.50 a week, of which I could save $3.

I did not know how to do anything, and I did not understand what the lady said to me, but she showed me how to cook, wash, iron, sweep, dust, make beds, wash dishes, clean windows, paint and brass, polish the knives and forks, etc., by doing the things herself and then overseeing my efforts to imitate her. She would take my hands and show them how to do things. She and her husband and children laughed at me a great deal, but it was all good natured. I was not confined to the house in the way servants are confined here, but when my work was done in the morning I was allowed to go out till lunch time. People in California are more generous than they are here.

In six months I had learned how to do the work of our house quite well, and I was getting $5 a week and board, and putting away about $4.25 a week. I had also learned some English, and by going to a Sunday school I learned more English and something about Jesus, who was a great Sage, and whose precepts are like those of Kong-foo-tsze.

It was twenty years ago when I came to this country, and I worked for two years as a servant, getting at the last $35 a month. I sent money home to comfort my parents, but tho I dressed well and lived well and had pleasure, going quite often to the Chinese theater and to dinner parties in Chinatown, I saved $50 in the first six months, $90 in the second, $120 in the third and $150 in the fourth. So I had $410 at the end of two years, and I was now ready to start in business.

When I first opened a laundry it was in company with a partner, who had been in the business for some years. We went to a town about 500 miles inland, where a railroad was building. We got a board shanty and worked for the men employed by the railroads. Our rent cost us $10 a month and food nearly $5 a week each, for all food was dear and we wanted the best of everything—we lived principally on rice, chickens, ducks and pork, and did our own cooking. The Chinese take naturally to cooking. It cost us about $50 for our furniture and apparatus, and we made close upon $60 a week, which we divided between us. We had to put up with many insults and some frauds, as men would come in and claim parcels that did not belong to them, saying they had lost their tickets, and would fight if they did not get what they asked for. Sometimes we were taken before Magistrates and fined for losing shirts that we had never seen. On the other hand, we were making money, and even after sending home $3 a week I was able to save about $15. When the railroad construction gang moved on we went with them. The men were rough and prejudiced against us, but not more so than in the big Eastern cities. It is only lately in New York that the Chinese have been able to discontinue putting wire screens in front of their windows, and at the present time the street boys are still breaking the windows of Chinese laundries all over the city, while the police seem to think it a joke.

We were three years with the railroad, and then went to the mines, where we made plenty of money in gold dust, but had a hard time, for many of the miners were wild men who carried revolvers and after drinking would come into our place to shoot and steal shirts, for which we had to pay. One of these men hit his head hard against a flat iron and all the miners came and broke up our laundry, chasing us out of town. They were going to hang us. We lost all our property and $365 in money, which members of the mob must have found.

Luckily most of our money was in the hands of Chinese bankers in San Francisco. I drew $500 and went East to Chicago, where I had a laundry for three years, during which I increased my capital to $2,500. After that I was four years in Detroit. I went home to China in 1897, but returned in 1898, and began a laundry business in Buffalo. But Chinese laundry business now is not as good as it was ten years ago. American cheap labor in the steam laundries had hurt it. So I determined to become a general merchant, and with this idea I came to New York and opened a shop in the Chinese quarter. . . .

The ordinary laundry shop is generally divided into three rooms. In front is the room where the customers are received, behind that a bedroom and in the back the work shop, which is also the dining room and kitchen. The stove and cooking utensils are the same as those of the Americans.

Work in a laundry begins early on Monday morning—about seven o'clock. There are generally two men, one of whom washes while the other does the ironing. The man who irons does not start in till Tuesday, as the clothes are not ready for him to begin till that time. So he has Sundays and Mondays as holidays. The man who does the washing finishes up on Friday night, and so he has Saturday and Sunday. Each works only five days a week, but those are long days—from seven o'clock in the morning till midnight.

During his holidays the Chinaman gets a good deal of fun out of life. There's a good deal of gambling and some opium smoking, but not so much as Americans imagine. Only a few of New York's Chinamen smoke opium. The habit is very general among rich men and the officials in China, but not so much among poor men. I don't think it does as much harm as the liquor that the Americans drink. There's nothing so bad as a drunken man. Opium doesn't make people crazy. . . .

The fights among the Chinese and the operations of the hatchet men are all due to gambling. Newspapers often say that there are feuds between the six companies, but that is a mistake. The six companies are purely benevolent societies, which look after the Chinaman when he first lands here. They represent the six southern provinces of China, where most of our people are from, and they are like the German, Swedish, English, Irish and Italian societies which assist emigrants. When the Chinese keep clear of gambling and opium they are not blackmailed, and they have no trouble with hatchet men or any others.

About 500 of New York's Chinese are Christians, the others are Buddhists, Taoists, etc., all mixed up. These haven't any Sunday of their own, but keep New Year's Day and the first and fifteenth days of each month, when they go to the temple in Mott Street.

In all New York there are only thirty-four Chinese women, and it is impossible to get a Chinese woman out here unless one goes to China and marries her there, and then he must collect affidavits to prove that she really is his wife. That is in case of a merchant. A laundryman can't bring his wife here under any circumstances, and even the women of the Chinese Ambassador's family had trouble getting in lately.

Is it any wonder, therefore, or any proof of the demoralization of our people if some of the white women in Chinatown are not of good character? What other set of men so isolated and so surrounded by alien and prejudiced people are more moral? Men, wherever they may be, need the society of women, and among the white women of Chinatown are many excellent and faithful wives and mothers. . . .

I have found out, during my residence in this country, that much of the Chinese prejudice against Americans is unfounded, and I no longer put faith in the wild tales that were told about them in our village, tho some of the Chinese, who have been here twenty years and who are learned men, still believe that there is no marriage in this country, that the land is infested with demons and that all the people are given over to general wickedness.

I know better. Americans are not all bad, nor are they wicked wizards. Still, they have their faults, and their treatment of us is outrageous.

The reason why so many Chinese go into the laundry business in this country is because it requires little capital and is one of the few opportunities that are open. Men of other nationalities who are jealous of the Chinese, because he is a more faithful worker than one of their people, have raised such a great outcry about Chinese cheap labor that they have shut him out of working on farms or in factories or building railroads or making streets or digging sewers. He cannot practice any trade, and his opportunities to do business are limited to his own countrymen. So he opens a laundry when he quits domestic service.

The treatment of the Chinese in this country is all wrong and mean. It is persisted in merely because China is not a fighting nation. The Americans would not dare to treat Germans, English, Italians or even Japanese as they treat the Chinese, because if they did there would be a war.

There is no reason for the prejudice against the Chinese. The cheap labor cry was always a falsehood. Their labor was never cheap, and is not cheap now. It has always commanded the highest market price. But the trouble is that the Chinese are such excellent and faithful workers that bosses will have no others when they can get them. If you look at men working on the street you will find an overseer for every four or five of them. That watching is not necessary for Chinese. They work as well when left to themselves as they do when some one is looking at them.

It was the jealousy of laboring men of other nationalities—especially the Irish—that raised all the outcry against the Chinese. No one would hire an Irishman, German, Englishman or Italian when he could get a Chinese, because our countrymen are so much more honest, industrious, steady, sober and painstaking. Chinese were persecuted, not for their vices, but for their virtues. There never was any honesty in the pretended fear of leprosy or in the cheap labor scare, and the persecution continues still, because Americans make a mere practice of loving justice. They are all for money making, and they want to be on the strongest side always. They treat you as a friend while you are prosperous, but if you have a misfortune they don't know you. There is nothing substantial in their friendship. . . .

Irish fill the almshouses and prisons and orphan asylums, Italians are among the most dangerous of men, Jews are unclean and ignorant. Yet they are all let in, while Chinese, who are sober, or duly law abiding, clean, educated and industrious, are shut out. There are few Chinamen in jails and none in the poor houses. There are no Chinese tramps or drunkards. Many Chinese here have become sincere Christians, in spite of the persecution which they have to endure from their heathen countrymen. More than half the Chinese in this country would become citizens if allowed to do so, and would be patriotic Americans. But how can they make this country their home as matters now are! They are not allowed to bring wives here from China, and if they marry American women there is a great outcry.

All Congressmen acknowledge the injustice of the treatment of my people, yet they continue it. They have no backbone.

Under the circumstances, how can I call this my home, and how can any one blame me if I take my money and go back to my village in China?

New York

DOCUMENT 5 *"Jewtown"*

Jacob Riis

Thrift is the watchword of Jewtown, as of its people the world over. It is at once its strength and its fatal weakness, its cardinal virtue and its foul disgrace. Become an overmastering passion with these people who come here in droves from Eastern Europe to escape persecution, from which freedom could be bought only with gold, it has enslaved them in bondage worse than that from which they fled. Money is their God. Life itself is of little value compared with even the leanest bank account. In no other spot does life wear so intensely bald and materialistic an aspect as in Ludlow Street. Over and over again I have met with instances of these Polish or Russian Jews deliberately starving themselves to the point of physical exhaustion, while working night and day at a tremendous pressure to save a little money. An avenging Nemesis pursues this headlong hunt for wealth; there is no worse paid class anywhere. . . .

Penury and poverty are wedded everywhere to dirt and disease, and Jewtown is no exception. It could not well be otherwise in such crowds, considering especially their low intellectual status. The managers of the Eastern Dispensary, which is in the very heart of their district, told the whole story when they said: "The diseases these people suffer from are not due to intemperance or immorality, but to ignorance, want of suitable food, and the foul air in which they live and work." The homes of the Hebrew quarter are its workshops also. Reference will be made to the economic conditions under which they work in a succeeding chapter. Here we are concerned simply with the fact. You are made fully aware of it before you have travelled the length of a single block in any of these East Side streets, by the whir of a thousand sewing-machines, worked at high pressure from earliest dawn till mind and muscle give out together. Every member of the family, from the youngest to the oldest, bears a hand, shut in the qualmy rooms, where meals are cooked and clothing washed and dried besides, the live-long day. It is not unusual to find a dozen persons—men, women, and children—at work in a single small room. . . .

Oppression, persecution, have not shorn the Jew of his native combativeness one whit. He is as ready to fight for his rights, or what he considers his rights, in a business transaction—synonymous generally with his advantage—as if he had not been robbed of them for eighteen hundred years. One strong impression survives with him from his days of bondage: the power of the law. On the slightest provocation he rushes off to invoke it for his protection. . . .

In all matters pertaining to their religious life that tinges all their customs, they stand, these East Side Jews, where the new day that dawned on Calvary left them standing, stubbornly refusing to see the light. A visit to a Jewish house of mourning is like bridging the gap of two thousand years. The inexpressibly sad and sorrowful wail for the dead, as it swells and rises in the hush of all sounds of life, comes back from the ages like a mournful echo of the voice of Rachel "weeping for her children and refusing to be comforted, because they are not."

Attached to many of the synagogues, which among the poorest Jews frequently consist of a scantily furnished room in a rear tenement, with a few wooden stools or benches for the congregation, are Talmudic schools that absorb a share of the growing youth. The school-master is not rarely a man of some attainments who has been stranded there, his native instinct for money-making having been smothered in the process that has made of him a learned man. . . . But the majority of the children seek the public schools, where they are received sometimes with some misgivings on the part of the teachers, who find it necessary to inculcate lessons of cleanliness in the worst cases by practical demonstration with wash-bowl and soap. "He took hold of the soap as if it were some animal," said one of these teachers to me after such an experiment upon a new pupil, "and wiped three fingers across his face. He called that washing." . . .

As scholars, the children of the most ignorant Polish Jew keep fairly abreast of their more favored playmates, until it comes to mental arithmetic, when they leave them behind with a bound. It is surprising to see how strong the instinct of dollars and cents is in them. They can count, and correctly, almost before they can talk.

DOCUMENT 6 *"A Cap Maker's Story"*

Rose Schneiderman

[Miss Schneiderman led the women capmakers in their recent successful strike for the union shop. She is a small, quiet, serious, good looking young woman of twenty years, already a member of the National Board, and fast rising in the labor world.

—*Editor.*]

My name is Rose Schneiderman, and I was born in some small city of Russian Poland. I don't know the name of the city, and have no memory of that part of my childhood. When I was about five years of age my parents brought me to this country and we settled in New York.

So my earliest recollections are of living in a crowded street among the East Side Jews, for we also are Jews.

Sweatshop in a Hester Street Tenement, © 1889, photograph, Museum of the City of New York, Jacob A. Riis Collection, #149

My father got work as a tailor, and we lived in two rooms on Eldridge Street, and did very well, though not so well as in Russia, because mother and father both earned money, and here father alone earned the money, while mother attended to the house. There were then two other children besides me, a boy of three and one of five.

I went to school until I was nine years old, enjoying it thoroughly and making great progress, but then my father died of brain fever and mother was left with three children and another one coming. So I had to stay at home to help her and she went out to look for work.

A month later the baby was born, and mother got work in a fur house, earning about $6 a week and afterward $8 a week, for she was clever and steady.

I was the house worker, preparing the meals and looking after the other children—the baby, a little girl of six years, and a boy of nine. I managed very well, tho the meals were not very elaborate. I could cook simple things like porridge, coffee and eggs, and mother used to prepare the meat before she went away in the morning, so that all I had to do was to put it in the pan at night. . . .

I was finally released by my little sister being taken by an aunt, and the two boys going to the Hebrew Orphan Asylum, which is a splendid institution, and turns out good men. One of these brothers is now a student in the City College, and the other is a page in the Stock Exchange.

When the other children were sent away mother was able to send me back to school, and I stayed in this school (Houston Street Grammar) till I had reached the Sixth Grammar Grade.

Then I had to leave in order to help support the family. I got a place in Hearn's as a cash girl, and after working there three weeks changed to Ridley's, where I remained for two and a half years. I finally left because the pay was so very poor and there did not seem to be any chance of advancement, and a friend told me that I could do better making caps.

So I got a place in the factory of Hein & Fox. The hours were from 8 A.M. to 6 P.M., and we made all sorts of linings—or, rather, we stitched in the linings—golf caps, yachting caps, etc. It was piece work, and we received from 3 1/2 cents to 10 cents a dozen, according to the different grades. By working hard we could make an average of about $5 a week. We would have made more but had to provide our own machines, which cost us $45, we paying for them on the installment plan. We paid $5 down and $1 a month after that.

I learned the business in about two months, and then made as much as the others, and was consequently doing quite well when the factory burned down, destroying all our machines—150 of them. This was very hard on the girls who had paid for their machines. It was not so bad for me, as I had only paid a little of what I owed.

The bosses got $500,000 insurance, so I heard, but they never gave the girls a cent to help them bear their losses. I think they might have given them $10, anyway.

Soon work went on again in four lofts, and a little later I became assistant sample maker. This is a position which, tho coveted by many, pays better in glory than in cash. It was still piece work, and tho the pay per dozen was better the work demanded was of a higher quality, and one could not rush through samples as through the other caps. So I still could average only about $5 per week.

After I had been working as a cap maker for three years it began to dawn on me that we girls needed an organization. The men had organized already, and had gained some advantages, but the bosses had lost nothing, as they took it out of us.

We were helpless; no one girl dare stand up for anything alone. Matters kept getting worse. The bosses kept making reductions in our pay, half a cent a dozen at a time. It did not sound important, but at the end of the week we found a difference.

We didn't complain to the bosses; we didn't say anything except to each other. There was no use. The bosses would not pay any attention unless we were like the men and could make them attend.

One girl would say that she didn't think she could make caps for the new price, but another would say that she thought she could make up for the reduction by working a little harder, and then the first would tell herself:

"If she can do it, why can't I?"

They didn't think how they were wasting their strength.

A new girl from another shop got in among us. She was Miss Bessie Brout, and she talked organization as a remedy for our ills. She was radical and progressive, and she stimulated thoughts which were already in our minds before she came.

Finally Miss Brout and I and another girl went to the National Board of United Cloth Hat and Cap Makers when it was in session, and asked them to organize the girls.

They asked us:

"How many of you are there willing to be organized?"

"In the first place about twelve," we said. We argued that the union label would force the bosses to organize their girls, and if there was a girls' union in existence the bosses could not use the union label unless their girls belonged to the union.

We were told to come to the next meeting of the National Board, which we did, and then received a favorable answer, and were asked to bring all the girls who were willing to be organized to the next meeting, and at the next meeting, accordingly, we were there twelve strong and were organized.

When Fox found out what had happened he discharged Miss Brout, and probably would have discharged me but that I was a sample maker and not so easy to replace. In a few weeks we had all the girls in the organization, because the men told the girls that they must enter the union or they would not be allowed to work in the shop.

Then came a big strike. Price lists for the coming season were given in to the bosses, to which they did not agree. After some wrangling a strike was declared in five of the biggest factories. There are 30 factories in the city. About 100 girls went out.

The result was a victory, which netted us—I mean the girls—$2 increase in our wages on the average.

All the time our union was progressing very nicely. There were lectures to make us understand what trades unionism is and our real position in the labor movement. I read upon the subject and grew more and more interested, and after a time I became a member of the National Board, and had duties and responsibilities that kept me busy after my day's work was done.

But all was not lovely by any means, for the bosses were not at all pleased with their beating and had determined to fight us again.

They agreed among themselves that after the 26th of December, 1904, they would run their shops on the "open" system.

This agreement was reached last fall, and soon notices, reading as follows, were hung in the various shops:

> *Notice*
>
> After the 26th of December, 1904, this shop will be run on the open shop system, the bosses having the right to engage and discharge employees as they see fit, whether the latter are union or nonunion.

Of course, we knew that this meant an attack on the union. The bosses intended gradually to get rid of us, employing in our place child labor and raw immigrant girls who would work for next to nothing.

On December 22d the above notice appeared, and the National Board, which had known about it all along, went into session prepared for action.

Our people were very restive, saying that they could not sit under that notice, and that if the National Board did not call them out soon they would go out of themselves.

At last word was sent out, and at 2:30 o'clock all the workers stopped, and, laying down their scissors and other tools, marched out, some of them singing the "Marseillaise."

We were out for thirteen weeks, and the girls established their reputation. They were on picket duty from seven o'clock in the morning till six o'clock in the evening, and gained over many of the nonunion workers by appeals to them to quit working against us.

Our theory was that if properly approached and talked to few would be found who would resist our offer to take them into our organization. No right thinking person desires to injure another. We did not believe in violence and never employed it.

During this strike period we girls each received $3 a week; single men $3 a week, and married men $5 a week. This was paid us by the National Board.

We were greatly helped by the other unions, because the open shop issue was a tremendous one, and this was the second fight which the bosses had conducted for it.

Their first was with the tailors, whom they beat. If they now could beat us the outlook for unionism would be bad.

Some were aided and we stuck out, and won a glorious victory all along the line. That was only last week. The shops are open now for all union hands and for them only. . . .

The bosses try to represent this open shop issue as tho they were fighting a battle for the public, but really it is nothing of the sort. The open shop is a weapon to break the unions and set men once more cutting each other's throats by individual competition.

Why, there was a time in the cap trade when men worked fourteen hours a day, and then took the heads of their machines home in bags and setting them up on stands, put mattresses underneath to deaden the sound and worked away till far into the morning.

We don't want such slavery as that to come back.

The shops are open now for all union people, and all nonunion people can join the union. In order to take in newcomer foreigners we have for them cut the initiation fees down to one-half what we Americans have to pay, and we trust them till they get work and their wages.

In order to give the newcomers a chance we have stopped night work, which doesn't suit the bosses, because it causes them to pay more rent when they can't use their buildings night and day. It costs them the price of another loft instead of costing the workers their health and lives as in the old days.

Our trade is well organized, we have won two victories and are not going backward.

But there is much to be done in other directions. The shop girls certainly need organization, and I think that they ought to be easy to organize, as their duties are simple and regular and they have a regular scale of wages.

Many saleswomen on Grand and Division streets, and, in fact, all over the East Side, work from 8 A.M. till 9 P.M. week days, and one-half a day on Sundays for $5 and $6 a week; so they certainly need organization.

The waitresses also could easily be organized, and perhaps the domestic servants. I don't know about stenographers. I have not come in contact with them.

Women have proved in the late strike that they can be faithful to an organization and to each other. The men give us the credit of winning the strike.

Certainly our organization constantly grows stronger, and the Woman's Trade Union League makes progress.

The girls and women by their meetings and discussions come to understand and sympathize with each other, and more and more easily they act together.

It is the only way in which they can hope to hold what they now have or better present conditions.

Certainly there is no hope from the mercy of the bosses.

Each boss does the best he can for himself with no thought of the other bosses, and that compels each to gouge and squeeze his hands to the last penny in order to make a profit.

So we must stand together to resist, for we will get what we can take—just that and no more.

New York

POSTSCRIPT

In 1921, 1924, and 1927, Congress passed a series of laws to restrict the flow of immigrants. The legislation targeted southern and eastern Europeans, as well as Asians. These laws were woven out of several ideological strands: resurgent fundamentalist Protestantism perceived Catholics as a major threat; immigrants were associated with important strikes and radical movements of the post-World War I period and so were targeted as un-American; and citizens from old families grew increasingly concerned about the so-called dilution of American stock, upholding their Anglo-Saxon ancestry as the key to national greatness. This last was a particularly insidious form of racism and was uppermost in Joseph Pennell's thinking. Whereas Jacob Riis would reform the immigrants into Americans, the new trend was toward exclusion. By the late 1920s, total immigration was capped at about one-quarter million per year, with western and northern Europe receiving much higher quotas than countries from the east or the south. Immigration did not reemerge as a vital factor in American life until the last decades of the twentieth century, when new migrants, especially from Latin America and Asia, poured in in numbers comparable to those of the late nineteenth and early twentieth centuries.

QUESTIONS

Defining Terms

Identify in the context of the chapter each of the following:

chain migrations	*How the Other Half Lives*
Little Italy	bootblack
padrone	Chinatown
Kong-foo-tsze	Rose Schneiderman
East Side Jews	Joseph Pennell

Probing the Sources

1. What was daily work like for the immigrants you have read about? Give details.
2. How did Riis describe the various immigrant groups? Did he use stereotypes that are still current today?
3. How did Corresca, Lee, and Schneiderman differ in their memories of their homelands? In their attitudes toward America? What do you think accounted for the differences?
4. What role did the family play in the lives of these people?
5. Compare Riis's depictions of immigrant groups with the interviews.

Interpreting the Sources

1. How do you think these three immigrants would have defined success? Had they achieved it by their own standards? By the standards of the larger society?
2. To what extent did the immigrants consider themselves American? To what extent Chinese, Italian, or Jewish?
3. How were the three immigrants whose life stories you read typical or atypical?
4. How and why did the lives of immigrant men and women differ?

ADDITIONAL READING

The classic work on nativism is John Higham's *Strangers in the Land: Patterns of American Nativism, 1860–1925* (1955). Oscar Handlin's *The Uprooted: The Epic Story of the Great Migration That Made the American People* (1951) remains a moving study of the pressures immigrants felt to abandon their native cultures. More recent studies, however, have emphasized ethnic groups' success in community building. For examples, see Irving Howe, *World of Our Fathers* (1976); and Ronald Takaki, *Strangers from a Different Shore: A History of Asian Americans* (1989). For a marvelous immigrant autobiography, try Marie Hall Ets, ed., *Rosa: The Life of an Italian Immigrant* (1970). For a survey of the diverse peoples' experiences, see Stephan Thernstrom, ed., *The Harvard Encyclopedia of American Ethnic Groups* (1980). For a fine anthology of women's writings, see Ellen Dubois and Vicki Ruiz, eds., *Unequal Sisters* (1990). A synthesis of multiculturalism is Ronald Takaki, *A Different Mirror* (1993). Also, see Matthew Frye Jacobson, *Special Sorrows* (1992), and Jacobson, *Whiteness of a Different Color* (1999). On recent immigration, try David Reimers, *Still The Golden Door* (1992) and especially Mae Ngai, *Impossible Subjects* (2005).

5

Building an Empire

America and the Philippines

Historical Context

Woodrow Wilson once declared Theodore Roosevelt "the most dangerous man of the age." Mark Twain called him "clearly insane," and added that Roosevelt was "insanest upon war and its supreme glories." Yet Roosevelt exercised an almost magical pull on the imagination of Americans. He was the very embodiment of energy. Even as president, he boxed and wrestled in the White House, took grueling cross-country hikes, and, after he stepped down from the presidency in 1909, went on a long hunting safari in Africa. Small and anemic as a child, he had whipped his body into shape with strenuous rounds of swimming, calisthenics, and gymnastics. At Harvard in the 1870s he was known for his sheer doggedness, if not his raw talent, as an athlete. Descriptions of his speeches as governor of New York in the 1890s refer endlessly to how his hands chopped the air, his body danced, his voice bristled, and his eyeglasses flashed. If, as the historian John Higham claims, there was a vigorous new spirit and an upbeat tempo in turn-of-the-century America, then Theodore Roosevelt was its embodiment.

One thing Roosevelt was not, however, was an example of the rags-to-riches mythology of American culture. He was born in 1858 to one of the wealthiest families in New York City, heirs to a Dutch fortune as old as the colony itself. Yet wealth did not confer ease. Like many men and women born to elite, or Brahmin, families, as they were known, privilege meant responsibility, a Calvinist sense of stewardship in which the "elect" must help take care of the less fortunate. Roosevelt grew up in a family of jurists, public servants, and philanthropists, and he was imbued early with a powerful sense of social duty.

The selections by Roosevelt in this chapter are from essays that he wrote in the years just before he became president. Read carefully, they give a sense of many of his underlying assumptions and values, what we might call his *ideology.* Ideology includes a person's or a society's fundamental beliefs about how the world is structured and what the relationship of individuals or nations to each other should be; it also includes their beliefs about the uses of power and the very nature of the social order.

For example, a simple statement such as "In America, any man can become president" is ideological. In the most literal sense, it is a true statement, for any native-born male who is not a felon and is over the age of thirty-five *can* run for the office of president; no legal barriers stand in his way. But usually when people use this phrase, they mean something more. They are expressing an ideal of equality, the faith that a person's own drive and talent are the keys to advancement in this society. To say that any man can become president is shorthand for the American dream, the belief that this nation offers equal and virtually unlimited opportunity for all and that such openness is one of the greatest things about our country.

Ideological statements, however, even as they purport to describe reality, tend to confuse the way things are with the way we would like them to be. For example, the phrase "any *man* can become president" already has inequality built into it, for it excludes women, over half of the population. This raises a question: Is the statement that any man can become president intended to be an expression of fact or of a hoped-for condition? Presidents have historically tended to be white males from upper-middle-class or wealthy families whose ethnic backgrounds were British and Protestant.

While America has provided considerable opportunity for social and economic mobility, that opportunity has never been equally distributed among all groups of citizens. Over the decades, some individuals have made dramatic leaps up and down in power and wealth, but recent research in social history shows that most Americans make only modest gains or losses in their class status across the generations. To put it concretely, the son of a small-town banker has a much better chance of becoming wealthy than the son of an Appalachian coal miner or the daughter of a black inner-city mail carrier. So the statement that any man can become president is an ideological one; behind its literal truth there is an *idealized* picture of the way American society works and a very loud silence about excluded groups. Ideological statements like this one invite us to question how closely historical reality approaches the social ideal.

American foreign policy at the end of the nineteenth century became a focus of deep ideological tensions. As the country grew increasingly involved in overseas business and military ventures, Americans debated the proper place of a democracy in a world divided between imperial powers and their colonies. Just as in the Mexican War a half century earlier, the conflicts at the end of the nineteenth century had grown out of the presence of the old Spanish Empire in the Western Hemisphere.

Cuba lies less than one hundred miles off the Florida coast. Before the Civil War, southerners coveted the island as an extension of the slave empire. For decades, the Cuban people had sought their independence from Spain in a series of rebellions, and a new round of insurgency and repression beginning in 1895 brought a wave of American sympathy for the rebels. American newspapers whipped up sentiment for the underdog Cubans, as Spain moved to crush the uprising. Moreover, large American companies had invested millions of dollars in Cuban sugar plantations, and these companies wanted to secure stable markets against political upheaval. President William McKinley resisted calls for American intervention until 1898. The revelation of a secret cable by the Spanish minister to the United States calling McKinley weak and hypocritical, followed by the mysterious blowing up of the United States battleship *Maine,* docked in Havana harbor (262 sailors perished on the ship sent to Cuba to protect Americans), made the pressure for American intervention irresistible. McKinley asked Congress for a declaration of war.

The war was popular, quick, and glorious. The Spanish colonies of Cuba, Guam, Puerto Rico, and the Philippines all fell with only a few hundred American battle deaths (though over five thousand died of tropical diseases). Naval confrontations in Santiago Bay and Manila Bay were even more decisive, as American ships destroyed the Spanish fleet while sustaining minimal damage and casualties.

With victory came controversy. By August 1898, an armistice had ended hostilities, but within half a year, Filipinos and Americans—former allies—were locked in war with each other. The Treaty of Paris between Spain and the United States ceded all seven thousand islands of the Philippine archipelago to the United States, in exchange for $20 million. Philippine rebels were not willing to trade Spain's domination for America's. By February 1899, Congress had approved the treaty with Spain, McKinley was on the verge of calling for Philippine annexation, and a bloody two-year struggle had begun. Before it was over, more than 100,000 Americans served in the Philippines; over 4,000 of them were killed, and another 3,000 were wounded. Nearly 20,000 Filipinos were killed in combat, and ten times that number died of starvation and disease, as the American military pursued a policy of burning villages and destroying farms.

Those Americans who opposed annexation were never a majority, but they were very vocal and included such diverse people as Andrew Carnegie, Jane Addams, William Jennings Bryan, Mark Twain, Samuel Gompers, and former presidents Harrison and Cleveland. Their arguments ranged widely. Friends of unions worried that new territories would only supply a cheap source of labor that would undercut American workers. Racists like Senator Ben Tillman of South Carolina argued that freeing Spain's colonies was a patriotic act, but that annexing those territories to the United States would not only defy our democratic principles but contaminate American blood with inferior racial stock. Still others argued that an empire would overextend an already troubled American economy, or that it would dangerously expand the powers of the presidency, or that a colonial empire simply could not be reconciled with deep American principles of freedom and self-determination. Proponents of overseas expansion argued that other imperial powers would seize the islands if we failed to, that America was obliged to civilize and Christianize "inferior" peoples, that an empire would open new markets and bring prosperity to all, and that overseas expansion would bring glory and honor to the military.

THE DOCUMENTS

The following documents are filled with ideological positions on politics, foreign policy, labor, gender, race, and ethnicity. As you read these selections, try to uncover their authors' underlying ideological assumptions. What were their social ideals? How did they believe groups interacted or ought to interact? With what tone did they address their audience, and who was that audience?

Introduction to Documents 1 and 2

Albert J. Beveridge was elected Republican senator from Indiana in 1898, when he was just thirty-six years old. The following speech, "The March of the Flag," was delivered first in Indianapolis in September 1898, after the victory over Spain but before the Treaty of Paris ceding the Philippines to the United States. Beveridge's speech became a kind of manifesto of American expansionism during this era; it was widely reprinted. Note how seamlessly he merged America's God-given mission in the world to elevate those less "civilized" than ourselves, the almost mystical spread of freedom wherever the American flag waved, the need for the United States to compete with other imperial powers, and the benefits (moral as well as economic) of opening up new overseas markets. And all were part of a historical pageant of progress from Bunker Hill to Manila Bay. Beveridge gave this speech countless times.

William Graham Sumner, on the contrary, viewed recent events as a betrayal of all that America stood for. Sumner was a professor of sociology at Yale and one of the best-known intellectuals of his day. He had popularized the concept of social Darwinism in America, which held that social groups—nations, classes, businesses—competed for resources, and that, on balance, the most fit among them lived and the weakest perished, ensuring progress through the survival of the strong. Sumner's assumption was that social evolution, like natural selection, created the greatest good for the greatest number, cruel as that process might appear.

Sumner's was an austere view of history's unfolding, but since he assumed that people would wield force in hurtful ways, he advocated limiting the power of institutions. He believed that different peoples had their own values, beliefs, and patterns of interacting—their own folkways, as he called them—and that social life ran as smoothly as possible when these local ways were respected and kept uncontaminated by others. Sumner's ideas could lead in two directions: to an acceptance of provincialism, and even racism and nativism, but also to a hands off policy toward foreign lands. We are not like other people, he declared; we do not understand them and cannot improve them; colonization could only contaminate both cultures and bring on the hatred of those whom we subjugate. Sumner was deeply suspicious of government's tendency to acquire more and more power, and many conservative politicians, especially in the South and the West, agreed with him. The speech "The Conquest of the United States by Spain" was a Phi Beta Kappa address at Yale given in 1898, almost simultaneously with Beveridge's address. What might these two men have said to each other in a debate?

DOCUMENT 1 ***"The March of the Flag"***

Albert J. Beveridge

It is a noble land that God has given us; a land that can feed and clothe the world; a land whose coastlines would inclose half the countries of Europe; a land set like a sentinel between the two imperial oceans of the globe, a greater England with a nobler destiny.

It is a mighty people that He has planted on this soil; a people sprung from the most masterful blood of history; a people perpetually revitalized by the virile, man-producing working-folk of all the earth; a people imperial by virtue of their power, by right of their institutions, by authority of their Heaven-directed purposes—the propagandists and not the misers of liberty.

It is a glorious history our God has bestowed upon His chosen people; a history heroic with faith in our mission and our future. . . .

. . . Shall the American people continue their march toward the commercial supremacy of the world? Shall free institutions broaden their blessed reign as the children of liberty wax in strength, until the empire of our principles is established over the hearts of all mankind?

Have we no mission to perform, no duty to discharge to our fellow-man? Has God endowed us with gifts beyond our deserts and marked us as the people of His peculiar favor, merely to rot in our own selfishness, as men and nations must, who take cowardice for their companion and self for their deity—as China has, as India has, as Egypt has? . . .

The Opposition tells us that we ought not to govern a people without their consent. I answer, The rule of liberty that all just government derives its authority from the consent of the governed, applies only to those who are capable of self-government. We govern the Indians without their consent, we govern our territories without their consent, we govern our children without their consent. How do they know that our government would be without their consent? Would not the people of the Philippines prefer the just, humane, civilizing government of this Republic to the savage, bloody rule of pillage and extortion from which we have rescued them?

And, regardless of this formula of words made only for enlightened, self-governing people, do we owe no duty to the world? Shall we turn these peoples back to the reeking hands from which we have taken them? Shall we abandon them, with Germany, England, Japan, hungering for them? Shall we save them from those nations, to give them a self-rule of tragedy? . . .

The march of the flag! In 1789 the flag of the Republic waved over 4,000,000 souls in thirteen states, and their savage territory which stretched to the Mississippi, to Canada, to the Floridas. The timid minds of that day said that no new territory was needed, and, for the hour, they were right. But Jefferson, through whose intellect the centuries marched; Jefferson, who dreamed of Cuba as an American state; Jefferson, the first Imperialist of the Republic—Jefferson acquired that imperial territory which swept from the Mississippi to the mountains, from Texas to the British possessions, and the march of the flag began!

The infidels to the gospel of liberty raved, but the flag swept on! The title to that noble land out of which Oregon, Washington, Idaho and Montana have been carved was uncertain; Jefferson, strict constructionist of constitutional power though he was, obeyed the Anglo-Saxon impulse within him, whose watchword then and whose watchword throughout the world to-day is, "Forward!": another empire was added to the Republic, and the march of the flag went on!

Those who deny the power of free institutions to expand urged every argument, and more, that we hear, to-day; but the people's judgment approved the command of their blood, and the march of the flag went on!

A screen of land from New Orleans to Florida shut us from the Gulf, and over this and the Everglade Peninsula waved the saffron flag of Spain; Andrew Jackson seized both, the American people stood at his back, and, under Monroe, the Floridas came under the dominion of the Republic, and the march of the flag went on! The Cassandras prophesied every prophecy of despair we hear, to-day, but the march of the flag went on!

Then Texas responded to the bugle calls of liberty, and the march of the flag went on! And, at last, we waged war with Mexico, and the flag swept over the southwest, over peerless California, past the Gate of Gold to Oregon on the north, and from ocean to ocean its folds of glory blazed.

And, now, obeying the same voice that Jefferson heard and obeyed, that Jackson heard and obeyed, that Monroe heard and obeyed, that Seward heard and obeyed, that Grant heard and obeyed, that Harrison heard and obeyed, our President to-day plants the flag over the islands of the seas, outposts of commerce, citadels of national security, and the march of the flag goes on! . . .

But the Opposition is right—there is a difference. We did not need the western Mississippi Valley when we acquired it, nor Florida, nor Texas, nor California, nor the royal provinces of the far northwest. We had no emigrants to people this imperial wilderness, no money to develop it, even no highways to cover it. No trade awaited us in its savage fastnesses. Our productions were not greater than our trade. There was not one reason for the land-lust of our statesmen from Jefferson to Grant, other than the prophet and the

Saxon within them. But, to-day, we are raising more than we can consume, making more than we can use. Therefore we must find new markets for our produce.

And so, while we did not need the territory taken during the past century at the time it was acquired, we do need what we have taken in 1898, and we need it now. The resources and the commerce of these immensely rich dominions will be increased as much as American energy is greater than Spanish sloth. In Cuba, alone, there are 15,000,000 acres of forest unacquainted with the ax, exhaustless mines of iron, priceless deposits of manganese, millions of dollars' worth of which we must buy, to-day, from the Black Sea districts. There are millions of acres yet unexplored.

The resources of Porto Rico have only been trifled with. The riches of the Philippines have hardly been touched by the finger-tips of modern methods. And they produce what we consume, and consume what we produce—the very predestination of reciprocity—a reciprocity "not made with hands, eternal in the heavens." They sell hemp, sugar, cocoanuts, fruits of the tropics, timber of price like mahogany; they buy flour, clothing, tools, implements, machinery and all that we can raise and make. Their trade will be ours in time. Do you endorse that policy with your vote?

Cuba is as large as Pennsylvania, and is the richest spot on the globe. Hawaii is as large as New Jersey; Porto Rico half as large as Hawaii; the Philippines larger than all New England, New York, New Jersey and Delaware combined. Together they are larger than the British Isles, larger than France, larger than Germany, larger than Japan. . . .

So Hawaii furnishes us a naval base in the heart of the Pacific; the Ladrones another, a voyage further on; Manila another, at the gates of Asia—Asia, to the trade of whose hundreds of millions American merchants, manufacturers, farmers, have as good right as those of Germany or France or Russia or England; Asia, whose commerce with the United Kingdom alone amounts to hundreds of millions of dollars every year; Asia, to whom Germany looks to take her surplus products; Asia, whose doors must not be shut against American trade. Within five decades the bulk of Oriental commerce will be ours. . . .

Wonderfully has God guided us. Yonder at Bunker Hill and Yorktown His providence was above us. At New Orleans and on ensanguined seas His hand sustained us. Abraham Lincoln was His minister and His was the altar of freedom the Nation's soldiers set up on a hundred battle-fields. His power directed Dewey in the East and delivered the Spanish fleet into our hands, as He delivered the elder Armada into the hands of our English sires two centuries ago. . . . We can not fly from our world duties; it is ours to execute the purpose of a fate that has driven us to be greater than our small intentions. We can not retreat from any soil where Providence has unfurled our banner; it is ours to save that soil for liberty and civilization.

DOCUMENT 2 ***"The Conquest of the United States by Spain"***

William Graham Sumner

. . . Spain was the first, for a long time the greatest, of the modern imperialistic states. The United States, by its historical origin, its traditions, and its principles, is the chief representative of the revolt and reaction against that kind of state. I intend to show that, by the line of action now proposed to us, which we call expansion and imperialism, we are throwing away some of the most important elements of the American symbol and are adopting some of the most important elements of the Spanish symbol. We have beaten Spain in a military conflict, but we are submitting to be conquered by her on the field of ideas and policies. Expansionism and imperialism are nothing but the old philosophies of national prosperity which have brought Spain to where she now is. Those philosophies appeal to national vanity and national cupidity. They are seductive, especially upon the first view and the most superficial judgment, and therefore it cannot be denied that they are very strong for popular effect. They are delusions, and they will lead us to ruin unless we are hard-headed enough to resist them. . . .

There is not a civilized nation which does not talk about its civilizing mission just as grandly as we do. The English, who really have more to boast of in this respect than anybody else, talk least about it, but the Phariseeism with which they correct and instruct other people has made them hated all over the globe. The French believe themselves the guardians of the highest and purest culture, and that the eyes of all mankind are fixed on Paris, whence they expect oracles of thought and taste. The Germans regard themselves as charged with a mission, especially to us Americans, to save us from egoism and materialism. . . . Now each nation laughs at all the others when it observes these manifestations of national vanity. You may rely upon it that they are all ridiculous by virtue of these pretensions, including ourselves. The point is that each of them repudiates the standards of the others, and the outlying nations, which are to be civilized, hate all the standards of civilized men. We assume that what we like and practice, and what we think better, must come as a welcome blessing to Spanish-Americans and Filipinos. This is grossly and obviously untrue. They hate our ways. They are hostile to our ideas. Our religion, language, institutions, and manners offend them. They like their own ways, and if we appear amongst them as rulers, there will be social discord in all the great departments of social interest. The most important thing which we shall inherit from the Spaniards will be the task of suppressing rebellions. If the United States takes out of the hands of Spain her mission, on the ground that Spain is not executing it well, and if this nation in its turn attempts to be school-mistress to others, it will shrivel up into the same vanity and self-conceit of which Spain now presents an example. To read our current literature one would think that we were already well on the way to it. Now, the great reason why all these enterprises which begin by saying to somebody else, "We know what is good for you better than you know yourself and we are going to make you do it," are false and wrong is that they violate liberty; or, to turn the same statement into other words, the reason why liberty, of which we Americans talk so much, is a good thing is that it means leaving people to live out their own lives in their own way, while we do the same. If we believe in liberty, as an American principle, why do we not stand by it? Why are we going to throw it away to enter upon a Spanish policy of dominion and regulation? . . .

There are plenty of people in the United States to-day who regard negroes as human beings, perhaps, but of a different order from white men, so that the ideas and social arrangements of white men cannot be applied to them with propriety. Others feel the same way about Indians. This attitude of mind, wherever you meet with it, is what causes tyranny and cruelty. . . . The doctrine that all men are equal has come to stand as one of the corner-stones of the temple of justice and truth. It was set up as a bar to just this notion that we are so much better than others that it is liberty for them to be governed by us.

The Americans have been committed from the outset to the doctrine that all men are equal. We have elevated it into an absolute doctrine as a part of the theory of our social and political fabric. It has always been a domestic dogma in spite of its absolute form, and as a domestic dogma it has always stood in glaring contradiction to the facts about Indians and negroes and to our legislation about Chinamen. In its absolute form it must, of course, apply to Kanakas, Malays, Tagals, and Chinese just as much as to Yankees, Germans, and Irish. It is an astonishing event that we have lived to see American arms carry this domestic dogma out where it must be tested in its application to uncivilized and half-civilized peoples. At the first touch of the test we throw the doctrine away and adopt the Spanish doctrine. We are told by all the imperialists that these people are not fit for liberty and self-government; that it is rebellion for them to resist our beneficence; that we must send fleets and armies to kill them if they do it; that we must devise a government for them and administer it ourselves; that we may buy them or sell them as we please, and dispose of their "trade" for our own advantage. What is that but the policy of Spain to her dependencies? What can we expect as a consequence of it? Nothing but that it will bring us where Spain is now.

But then, if it is not right for us to hold these islands as dependencies, you may ask me whether I think that we ought to take them into our Union, at least some of them, and let them help to govern us. Certainly not. . . . It is unwisdom to take into a State like this any foreign element which is not congenial to it. Any such element will act as a solvent upon it. Consequently we are brought by our new conquests face to face with this dilemma: we must either hold them as inferior possessions, to be ruled and exploited by us after the fashion of the old colonial system, or we must take them in on an equality with ourselves, where they will help to govern us and to corrupt a political system which they do not understand and in which they cannot participate. From that dilemma there is no escape except to give them independence and to let them work out their own salvation or go without it. . . .

Everywhere you go on the continent of Europe at this hour you see the conflict between militarism and industrialism. You see the expansion of industrial power pushed forward by the energy, hope, and thrift of men, and you see the development arrested, diverted, crippled, and defeated by measures which are dictated by military considerations. . . . It is militarism which is eating up all the products of science and art, defeating the energy of the population and wasting its savings. It is militarism which forbids the people to give their attention to the problems of their own welfare and to give their strength to the education and comfort of their children. It is militarism which is combating the grand efforts of science and art to ameliorate the struggle for existence. . . .

Now what will hasten the day when our present advantages will wear out and when we shall come down to the conditions of the older and densely populated nations? The answer is: war, debt, taxation, diplomacy, a grand governmental system, pomp, glory, a big army and navy, lavish expenditures, political jobbery—in a word, imperialism. . . .

Expansion and imperialism are at war with the best traditions, principles, and interests of the American people. . . . They will plunge us into a network of difficult problems and political perils, which we might have avoided, while they offer us no corresponding advantage in return. . . . Three years ago we were on the verge of a law to keep immigrants out who were not good enough to be in with us. Now we are going to take in eight million barbarians and semi-barbarians, and we are paying twenty million dollars to get them. . . . That is the great fundamental cause of what I have tried to show throughout this lecture, that we cannot govern dependencies consistently with our political system, and that, if we try it, the State which our fathers founded will suffer a reaction which will transform it into another empire just after the fashion of all the old ones. That is what imperialism means. That is what it will be; and the democratic republic, which has been, will stand in history, like the colonial organization of earlier days, as a mere transition form. . . .

My patriotism is of the kind which is outraged by the notion that the United States never was a great nation until in a petty three months' campaign it knocked to pieces a poor, decrepit, bankrupt old state like Spain. To hold such an opinion as that is to abandon all American standards, to put shame and scorn on all that our ancestors tried to build up here, and to go over to the standards of which Spain is a representative.

Introduction to Document 3

Theodore Roosevelt was one of the most aggressive advocates of overseas empire. He was part of a group of like-minded men who pushed for expansion, men such as Senator Henry Cabot Lodge, Admiral Alfred Thayer Mahan, and Brooks Adams,

all from powerful and wealthy families. Not only did Roosevelt become the most prominent spokesman for freeing Cuba and the Philippines from Spanish rule, annexing Hawaii, and asserting American military might around the world, but as assistant secretary of the Navy in the late 1890s, he was in a position to build up American sea power and beat the drums of war from inside the government. When the Spanish-American War began, Roosevelt resigned his job, obtained a commission as colonel, raised a regiment known as the Rough Riders, and led his men in a bloody charge up San Juan Hill in Cuba. Document 3 is taken from Roosevelt's speech "The Strenuous Life," given to an audience of businessmen and local leaders at the Hamilton Club in Chicago on April 10, 1899. The very phrase "the strenuous life" became an emblem for the age of Roosevelt.

DOCUMENT 3 *"The Strenuous Life"*

Theodore Roosevelt

In speaking to you, men of the greatest city of the West, men of the State which gave to the country Lincoln and Grant, men who preeminently and distinctly embody all that is most American in the American character, I wish to preach, not the doctrine of ignoble ease, but the doctrine of the strenuous life, the life of toil and effort, of labor and strife; to preach that highest form of success which comes, not to the man who desires mere easy peace, but to the man who does not shrink from danger, from hardship, or from bitter toil, and who out of these wins the splendid ultimate triumph.

A life of slothful ease, a life of that peace which springs merely from lack either of desire or of power to strive after great things, is as little worthy of a nation as of an individual. I ask only that what every self-respecting American demands from himself and from his sons shall be demanded of the American nation as a whole. Who among you would teach your boys that ease, that peace, is to be the first consideration in their eyes—to be the ultimate goal after which they strive? . . . We do not admire the man of timid peace. We admire the man who embodies victorious effort; the man who never wrongs his neighbor, who is prompt to help a friend, but who has those virile qualities necessary to win the stern strife of actual life. . . . A mere life of ease is not in the end a very satisfactory life, and, above all, it is a life which ultimately unfits those who follow it for serious work in the world.

In the last analysis a healthy state can exist only when the men and women who make it up lead clean, vigorous, healthy lives; when the children are so trained that they shall endeavor, not to shirk difficulties, but to overcome them; not to seek ease, but to know how to wrest triumph from toil and risk. The man must be glad to do a man's work, to dare and endure and to labor; to keep himself, and to keep those dependent upon him. The woman must be the housewife, the helpmeet of the homemaker, the wise and fearless mother of many healthy children. . . . When men fear work or fear righteous war, when women fear motherhood, they tremble on the brink of doom; and well it is that they should vanish from the earth, where they are fit subjects for the scorn of all men and women who are themselves strong and brave and high-minded.

As it is with the individual, so it is with the nation. It is a base untruth to say that happy is the nation that has no history. Thrice happy is the nation that has a glorious history. Far better it is to dare mighty things, to win glorious triumphs, even though checkered by failure, than to take rank with those poor spirits who neither enjoy much nor suffer much, because they live in the gray twilight that knows not victory nor defeat. If in 1861 the men who loved the Union had believed that peace was the end of all things, and war and strife the worst of all things, and had acted up to their belief, we would have saved hundreds of thousands of lives, we would have saved hundreds of millions of dollars. Moreover, besides saving all the blood and treasure we then lavished, we would have prevented the heartbreak of many women, the dissolution of many homes, and we would have spared the country those months of gloom and shame when it seemed as if our armies marched only to defeat. We could have avoided all this suffering simply by shrinking from strife. And if we had thus avoided it, we would have shown that we were weaklings, and that we were unfit to stand among the great nations of the earth. Thank God for the iron in the blood of our fathers, the men who upheld the wisdom of Lincoln, and bore sword or rifle in the armies of Grant! Let us, the children of the men who proved themselves equal to the mighty days, let us, the children of the men who carried the great Civil War to a triumphant conclusion, praise the God of our fathers that the ignoble counsels of peace were rejected; that the suffering and loss, the blackness of sorrow and despair, were unflinchingly faced, and the years of strife endured; for in the end the slave was freed, the Union restored, and the mighty American republic placed once more as a helmeted queen among nations.

We of this generation do not have to face a task such as that our fathers faced, but we have our tasks, and woe to us if we fail to perform them! We cannot, if we would, play the part of China, and be content to rot by inches in ignoble ease within our borders, taking no interest in what goes on beyond them, sunk in a scrambling commercialism; heedless of the higher life, the life of aspiration, of toil and risk, busying ourselves only with the wants of our bodies for the day, until suddenly we should find, beyond a shadow of question, what China has already found, that in this world the nation that has trained itself to a career of unwarlike and isolated ease is bound, in the end, to go down before other nations which have not lost the manly and adventurous qualities. If we are to be a really great people, we must strive in good faith to play a great part in the world. We cannot avoid meeting great issues. All that we can determine for ourselves is whether we shall meet them well or ill. In 1898 we could not help being brought face to face with the problem of war with Spain. All we could decide was whether we should shrink like cowards from the contest, or enter into it as beseemed a brave and high-spirited people; and, once in, whether failure or success should crown our banners. So it is now. We cannot avoid the responsibilities that confront us in Hawaii, Cuba, Porto Rico, and the Philippines. All we can decide is whether we shall meet them in a way that will redound to the national credit, or whether we shall make of our dealings with these new problems a dark and shameful page in our history. To refuse to deal with them at all merely amounts to dealing with them badly. We have a given problem to solve. If we undertake the solution, there is, of course, always danger that we may not solve it aright; but to refuse to undertake the solution simply renders it certain that we cannot possibly solve it aright. The timid man, the lazy man, the man who distrusts his country, the over-civilized man, who has lost the great fighting, masterful virtues, the ignorant man, and the man of dull mind, whose soul is incapable of feeling the mighty lift that thrills "stern men with empires in their brains"—all these, of course, shrink from seeing the nation undertake its new duties; shrink from seeing us build a navy and an army adequate to our needs; shrink from seeing us do our share of the world's work, by bringing order out of chaos in the great, fair tropic islands from which the valor of our soldiers and sailors has driven the Spanish flag. These are the men who fear the strenuous life, who fear the only national life which is really worth leading. They believe in that cloistered life which saps the hardy virtues in a nation, as it saps them in the individual; or else they are wedded to that base spirit of gain and greed which recognizes in commercialism the be-all and end-all of national life, instead of realizing that, though an indispensable element, it is, after all, but one of the many elements that go to make up true national greatness. No country can long endure if its foundations are not laid deep in the material prosperity which comes from thrift, from business energy and enterprise, from hard, unsparing effort in the fields of industrial activity; but neither was any nation ever yet truly great if it relied upon material prosperity alone. All honor must be paid to the architects of our material prosperity, to the great captains of industry who have built our factories and our railroads, to the strong men who toil for wealth with brain or hand; for great is the debt of the nation to these and their kind. But our debt is yet greater to the men whose highest type is to be found in a statesman like Lincoln, a soldier like Grant. They showed by their lives that they recognized the law of work, the law of strife; they toiled to win a competence for themselves and those dependent upon them; but they recognized that there were yet other and even loftier duties—duties to the nation and duties to the race.

We cannot sit huddled within our own borders and avow ourselves merely an assemblage of well-to-do hucksters who care nothing for what happens beyond. Such a policy would defeat even its own end; for as the nations grow to have ever wider and wider interests, and are brought into closer and closer contact, if we are to hold our own in the struggle for naval and commercial supremacy, we must build up our power without our own borders. We must build the isthmian canal, and we must grasp the points of vantage which will enable us to have our say in deciding the destiny of the oceans of the East and the West.

So much for the commercial side. From the standpoint of international honor the argument is even stronger. The guns that thundered off Manila and Santiago left us echoes of glory, but they also left us a legacy of duty. If we drove out a mediæval tyranny only to make room for savage anarchy, we had better not have begun the task at all. It is worse than idle to say that we have no duty to perform, and can leave to their fates the islands we have conquered. Such a course would be the course of infamy. It would be followed at once by utter chaos in the wretched islands themselves. Some stronger, manlier power would have to step in and do the work, and we would have shown ourselves weaklings, unable to carry to successful completion the labors that great and high-spirited nations are eager to undertake. . . .

The problems are different for the different islands. Porto Rico is not large enough to stand alone. We must govern it wisely and well, primarily in the interest of its own people. Cuba is, in my judgment, entitled ultimately to settle for itself whether it shall be an independent state or an integral portion of the mightiest of republics. But until order and stable liberty are secured, we must remain in the island to insure them, and infinite tact, judgment, moderation, and courage must be shown by our military and civil representatives in keeping the island pacified, in relentlessly stamping out brigandage, in protecting all alike, and yet in showing proper recognition to the men who have fought for Cuban liberty. The Philippines offer a yet graver problem. Their population includes half-caste and native Christians, warlike Moslems, and wild pagans. Many of their people are utterly unfit for self-government, and show no signs of becoming fit. Others may in time become fit but at present can only take part in self-government under a wise supervision, at once firm and beneficent. We have driven Spanish tyranny from the islands. If we now let it be replaced by savage anarchy, our work has been for harm and not for good. I have scant patience with those who fear to undertake the task of governing the Philippines, and who openly avow that they do fear to undertake it, or that they shrink from it because of the expense and trouble; but I have even scanter patience with those who make a pretense of humanitarianism to hide and cover their timidity, and who cant about "liberty" and the "consent of the governed," in order to excuse themselves for their unwillingness to play the part of men. Their doctrines, if carried out, would make it incumbent upon us to leave the Apaches of Arizona to work out their own salvation, and to decline to interfere in a single Indian reservation. Their doctrines condemn your forefathers and mine for ever having settled in these United States.

England's rule in India and Egypt has been of great benefit to England, for it has trained up generations of men accustomed to look at the larger and loftier side of public life. It has been of even greater benefit to India and Egypt. And finally, and most of all, it has advanced the cause of civilization. So, if we do our duty aright in the Philippines, we will add to that national renown which is the highest and finest part of national life, will greatly benefit the people of the Philippine Islands, and, above all, we will play our part well in the great work of uplifting mankind. But to do this work, keep ever in mind that we must show in a very high degree the qualities of courage, of honesty, and of good judgment. Resistance must be stamped out. The first and all-important work to be done is to establish the supremacy of our flag. We must put down armed resistance before we can accomplish anything else, and there should be no parleying, no faltering, in dealing with our foe. As for those in our own country who encourage the foe, we can afford contemptuously to disregard them; but it must be remembered that their utterances are not saved from being treasonable merely by the fact that they are despicable. . . .

I preach to you, then, my countrymen, that our country calls not for the life of ease but for the life of strenuous endeavor. The twentieth century looms before us big with the fate of many nations. If we stand idly by, if we seek merely swollen, slothful ease and ignoble peace, if we shrink from the hard contests where men must win at hazard of their lives and at the risk of all they hold dear, then the bolder and stronger peoples will pass us by, and will win for themselves the domination of the world. Let us therefore boldly face the life of strife, resolute to do our duty well and manfully; resolute to uphold righteousness by deed and by word; resolute to be both honest and brave, to serve high ideals, yet to use practical methods. Above all, let us shrink from no strife, moral or physical, within or without the nation, provided we are certain that the strife is justified, for it is only through strife, through hard and dangerous endeavor, that we shall ultimately win the goal of true national greatness.

Introduction to Document 4

Although most newspapers supported government policy, there was dissent. Document 4 consists of five newspaper articles that appeared in the summer of 1899, shortly after Roosevelt's "Strenuous Life" speech, during the height of the controversy following President McKinley's decision to annex the Philippines. The first, an editorial from the *New York Evening Post,* directly challenged Roosevelt's ideas. The second piece is from the *New Orleans Times Democrat,* and it suggested that the war threatened to become more costly and difficult than its supporters had admitted.

The article from the *Baltimore Sun* contains an interview with an American naval commander newly returned from the Philippines who denied that the Filipinos were either "barbaric" or "uncivilized." "The True American," which appeared in the *Springfield Republican,* again challenged Roosevelt and condemned expansion as a violation of American democratic ideals. The last article is actually an anonymous letter from a black soldier to the editor of the *New York Age*—an African-American newspaper—which expressed anger at the racism of white American troops toward the Filipinos. Taken together, these pieces give a good sense of how controversial the question of empire had become.

DOCUMENT 4 *Press Opposition to the War*

New York Evening Post

. . . Governor Roosevelt's recent speech in Chicago . . . glorified war and fighting as the only remedies of a nation against what he is fond of calling on all occasions "ignoble peace." . . . This is the gospel of war for the sake of war, of fighting, not merely or necessarily for a just and righteous and inevitable cause, but for the effect upon your own virility. Whatever you do, you must fight. The worst thing that can happen to a man or a nation is to remain long in peace. That is to become "despicable," "ignoble," "slothful," an object of contempt to yourself and to the world. This is the view of the savage, the barbarian. . . .

The Roosevelt view of life is essentially a boy's view, and if it were to become the permanent basis of a national policy would make us the most turbulent people the world has ever seen. Our national life would become one perpetual Donnybrook fair, with "rows" with every power that got within range of us, for no other purpose than the development of our "virile strength," lest we become a nation of sloths.

Happily there is no danger of such a future for us. Our governor is not taken seriously by anybody except himself when he talks "war." . . . So long as he insists upon favoring war as the chief end of man, without which the human race can make no progress towards what Admiral Sampson so well calls the "true living which we all long for," the people of this country will never trust him in a station in which he can carry out his views. . . .

New Orleans Times-Democrat

We are beginning to realize the fact—even the imperialists—that we have bought from Spain a very disagreeable guerilla war, in which there are no honors to win, but much loss, expense, and vexation of spirit. . . . As [the Philippines] is a land of swamps and mountains, an ideal country for guerilla warfare, with a malarial tropical climate disastrous to Americans, we can realize the bargain we bought from Spain. . . . It is time for us to count up the cost and see whether our Philippine bargain is worth what we are likely to pay for it before we get through, and then determine whether it would not be better to cease this war of McKinley's, which has accomplished so very little beyond showing the courage and fighting quality of our soldiers, and restore peace in the islands so as to allow their development, retaining such control over them that the United States would share in the prosperity and commerce that would come with peace and order.

Baltimore Sun

Commander John D. Ford, fleet engineer of the Asiatic station, reached his home, No. 1522 West Lanvale street, on Saturday morning before noon, after an absence of a year and a half, most of which period he spent on board the cruiser "Baltimore," in the bay of Manila. . . .

"The Filipinos pictured in the sensational papers are not the men we are fighting. They are entirely distinct and separate. The fellows we deal with out there are not ignorant savages, fighting with bows and arrows, but an intelligent, liberty-loving people, full of courage and determination. The idea that the Filipino is an uncivilized being is a mistaken one. Originally the natives of those islands sprang from Japanese stock, and are identically the same race, with a change of language and customs. There was a time when the feudal system prevailed in Manila, but no vestige now remains, and the savagery of the people is found only in the very lowest class. . . .

"What they are fighting for now is absolute and entire liberty. They don't want us there or over them, and in the course of time might wear out our patience entirely. An excellent postal and telegraph system is in existence, which we wish very much we could get hold of. While they fight for entire freedom, all they ask is a chance for life, liberty, and the pursuit of happiness, and they care not whether it be a republic of their own or some form devised for them by the great United States of North America. I see nothing promising in the struggle now or any hope of speedy success on our part, unless many more troops are sent out. . . .

Springfield [Massachusetts] Republican

What is an American—a true American? It is to be first of all, we conceive, a friend of liberty and self-government at home and abroad. . . . There is not only open and brazen renunciation of the fundamental doctrines which make a republic, but there is the assertion, no longer thinly disguised, that our democracy is called of God to police the world—and that in order to do this we must doff the garments of peaceful republicanism, put on an old-world uniform, and, in the graphic language of Governor Roosevelt, "see that the outburst of savagery" (that we have stirred up by outraging the spirit of liberty) "is repressed once for all." It is a relentless programme, and one impossible of execution. Repression of that sort never represses—but we need not discuss that now.

Our firm belief and expectation is that the people of the United States will, soon or late, stand where they always have stood—with Lincoln and not with Roosevelt. The one is an American and the other represents Anglo-Americanism, and there is not room here for both. We shall stick to the new-world type. As it was in 1776, it must be now, else we shall recant and fall away from the simple yet prophetic and sufficient faith of Washington and Lincoln. Shall we exalt militarism more than struggling freedom, power more than principle, and hold physical dominion higher than the moral sway and helpfulness that has made liberty, as we have practised it with all our imperfections, the light of the world?

New York Age

Letter to the Editor

I have mingled freely with the natives and have had talks with American colored men here in business and who have lived here for years, in order to learn of them the cause of their (Filipino) dissatisfaction and the reason for this insurrection, and I must confess they have a just grievance. All this never would have occurred if the army of occupation would have treated them as people. The Spaniards, even if their laws were hard, were polite and treated them with some consideration; but the Americans, as soon as they saw that the native troops were desirous of sharing in the glories as well as the hardships of the hard-won battles with the Americans, began to apply home treatment for colored peoples: curse them as damned niggers, steal [from] and ravish them, rob them on the street of their small change, take from the fruit vendors whatever suited their fancy, and kick the poor unfortunate if he complained, desecrate their church property, and after fighting began, looted everything in sight, burning, robbing the graves.

This may seem a little tall—but I have seen with my own eyes carcasses lying bare in the boiling sun, the results of raids on receptacles for the dead in search of diamonds. The [white] troops, thinking we would be proud to emulate their conduct, have made bold of telling their exploits to us. One fellow, member of the 13th Minnesota, told me how some fellows he knew had cut off a native woman's arm in order to get a fine inlaid bracelet. On upbraiding some fellows one morning, whom I met while out for a walk (I think they belong to a Nebraska or Minnesota regiment, and they were stationed on the Malabon road) for the conduct of the American troops toward the natives and especially as to raiding, etc., the reply was: "Do you think we could stay over here and fight these damn niggers without making it pay all it's worth? The government only pays us $13 per month: that's starvation wages. White men can't stand it." Meaning they could not live on such small pay. In saying this they never dreamed that Negro soldiers would never countenance such conduct. They talked with impunity of "niggers" to our soldiers, never once thinking that they were talking to home "niggers" and should they be brought to remember that at home this is the same vile epithet they hurl at us, they beg pardon and make some effeminate excuse about what the Filipino is called.

I want to say right here that if it were not for the sake of the 10,000,000 black people in the United States, God alone knows on which side of the subject I would be. And

Wounded Filipinos in a U.S. army camp. (Library of Congress)

for the sake of the black men who carry arms and pioneer for them as their representatives, ask them to not forget the present administration at the next election. Party be damned! We don't want these islands, not in the way we are to get them, and for Heaven's sake, put the party [Democratic] in power that pledged itself against this highway robbery. Expansion is too clean a name for it.

[Unsigned]

Introduction to Document 5

Document 5 is an address called "National Duties" given by Theodore Roosevelt at the Minnesota State Fair on September 2, 1901. Four days later, just six months after Roosevelt had assumed the vice presidency, President William McKinley was assassinated. In this speech, Roosevelt asserted America's obligation as a powerful democratic nation to bring civilization to others. What were Roosevelt's views on the role of war, the responsibilities of wealthy and powerful people like himself, and the limits of acceptable dissent?

DOCUMENT 5 ***"National Duties"***

Theodore Roosevelt

. . . Our country had been populated by pioneers, and therefore it has in it more energy, more enterprise, more expansive power than any other in the wide world. . . . The men who with ax in the forests and pick in the mountains and plow on the prairies pushed to completion the dominion of our people over the American wilderness have given the definite shape to our nation. They have shown the qualities of daring, endurance, and far-sightedness, of eager desire for victory and stubborn refusal to accept defeat, which go to make up the essential manliness of the American character. Above all, they have recognized in practical form the fundamental law of success in American life—the law of worthy work, the law of high, resolute endeavor. . . .

In the Philippines we have brought peace, and we are at this moment giving them such freedom and self-government as they could never under any conceivable conditions have obtained had we turned them loose to sink into a welter of blood and confusion, or to become the prey of some strong tyranny without or within. The bare recital of the facts is sufficient to show that we did our duty; and what prouder title to honor can a nation have than to have done its duty? We have done our duty to ourselves, and we have done the higher duty of promoting the civilization of mankind. The first essential of civilization is law. Anarchy is simply the handmaiden and forerunner of tyranny and despotism. Law and order enforced with justice and by strength lie at the foundations of civilization. . . . There can be no weakening of the law-abiding spirit here at home, if we are permanently to succeed; and just as little can we afford to show weakness abroad. Lawlessness and anarchy were put down in the Philippines as a prerequisite to introducing the reign of justice.

Barbarism has, and can have, no place in a civilized world. It is our duty toward the people living in barbarism to see that they are freed from their chains, and we can free them only by destroying barbarism itself. The missionary, the merchant, and the soldier may each have to play a part in this destruction, and in the consequent uplifting of the people. Exactly as it is the duty of a civilized power scrupulously to respect the rights of all weaker civilized powers and gladly to help those who are struggling toward civilization, so it is its duty to put down savagery and barbarism. . . . Not only in our own land, but throughout the world, throughout all history, the advance of civilization has been of incalculable benefit to mankind, and those through whom it has advanced deserve the highest honor. All honor to the missionary, all honor to the soldier, all honor to the merchant who now in our own day have done so much to bring light into the world's dark places.

Let me insist again, for fear of possible misconstruction, upon the fact that our duty is twofold, and that we must raise others while we are benefiting ourselves. In bringing order to the Philippines, our soldiers added a new page to the honor-roll of American history, and they incalculably benefited the islanders themselves. Under the wise administration of Governor Taft the islands now enjoy a peace and liberty of which they have hitherto never even dreamed. But this peace and liberty under the law must be supplemented by material, by industrial development. Every encouragement should be given to their commercial development, to the introduction of American industries and products; not merely because this will be a good thing for our people, but infinitely more because it will be of incalculable benefit to the people in the Philippines.

We shall make mistakes; and if we let these mistakes frighten us from our work we shall show ourselves weaklings. Half a century ago Minnesota and the two Dakotas were Indian hunting-grounds. We committed plenty of blunders, and now and then worse than blunders, in our dealings with the Indians. But who does not admit at the present day that we were right in wresting from barbarism and adding to civilization the territory out of which we have made these beautiful States? And now we are civilizing the Indian and putting him on a level to which he could never have attained under the old conditions.

In the Philippines let us remember that the spirit and not the mere form of government is the essential matter. The Tagalogs have a hundredfold the freedom under us that they would have if we had abandoned the islands. We are not trying to subjugate a people; we are trying to develop them and make them a law-abiding, industrious, and educated people, and we hope ultimately a self-governing people. In short, in the work we have done we are but carrying out the true principles of our democracy. . . . We gird up our loins as a nation, with the stern purpose to play our part manfully in winning the ultimate triumph; and therefore we turn scornfully aside from the paths of mere ease and idleness, and with unfaltering steps tread the rough road of endeavor, smiting down the wrong and battling for the right, as Greatheart smote and battled in Bunyan's immortal story.

Introduction to Document 6

The public debate over American annexation of the Philippines proved so heated that a special congressional committee was appointed to investigate the conduct of the war. Although the Committee on the Philippines (chaired by Senator Henry Cabot Lodge) was established in January 1900, hearings did not begin until two years later. The following two interviews, part of the investigation, give a sense of the conduct of the war, and of why it was so controversial. Robert P. Hughes was a brigadier general who commanded American troops in the Philippines at the turn of the century. Charles S. Riley had risen from private to first sergeant; he had served in the Philippines from October 1899 through March 1901.

DOCUMENT 6 *Proceedings of the Congressional Committee on the Philippines*

Testimony of Robert P. Hughes

Sen. Rawlins: In burning towns, what would you do? Would the entire town be destroyed by fire or would only offending portions of the town be burned?

Gen. Hughes: I do not know that we ever had a case of burning what you would call a town in this country, but probably a barrio or a sitio; probably a half a dozen houses, native shacks, where the insurrectos would go in and be concealed, and if they caught a detachment passing they would kill some of them.

Sen. Rawlins: What did I understand you to say would be the consequences of that?

Gen. Hughes: They usually burned the village.

Sen. Rawlins: All of the houses in the village?

Gen. Hughes: Yes; every one of them.

Sen. Rawlins: What would become of the inhabitants?

Gen. Hughes: That was their lookout. . . . The destruction was as a punishment. . . .

Sen. Rawlins: The punishment in that case would fall, not upon the men, who could go elsewhere, but mainly upon the women and little children.

Gen. Hughes: The women and children are part of the family, and where you wish to inflict a punishment you can punish the man probably worse in that way than in any other.

Sen. Rawlins: But is that within the ordinary rules of civilized warfare? Of course you could exterminate the family, which would be still worse punishment.

Gen. Hughes: These people are not civilized.

Sen. Rawlins: But is that within the ordinary rules of civilized warfare?

Gen. Hughes: No; I think it is not.

Sen. Rawlins: You think it is not?

Sen. Dietrich: In order to carry on civilized warfare both sides have to engage in such warfare. . .

Testimony of Charles S. Riley

Q. During your service there [in the Philippine Islands] did you witness what is generally known as the water cure?—A. I did.

Q. When and where?—A. On November 27, 1900, in the town of Igbaras, Iloilo Province, Panay Island. . . .

Q. You may state what you saw.—A. I saw the *presidente* standing in the—

Q. Whom do you mean by the presidente?—A. The head official of the town.

The burning of civilian homes in Manila, 1899. (Library of Congress)

Q. The town of Igbaras?—A. Yes, sir.
Q. A Filipino?—A. Yes, sir.
Q. How old was he?—A. I should judge that he was a man of about forty or forty-five years.
Q. When you saw him, what was his condition?—A. He was stripped to the waist; he had nothing on but a pair of white trousers, and his hands were tied behind him. . . . He was then taken and placed under the tank, and the faucet was opened and a stream of water was forced down or allowed to run down his throat; his throat was held so he could not prevent swallowing the water, so that he had to allow the water to run into his stomach. . . .
Q. Was anything done besides forcing his mouth open and allowing the water to run down?—A. When he was filled with water it was forced out of him by pressing a foot on his stomach or else with their hands. . . .
Q. What had been his crime?—A. Information had been obtained from a native source as to his being an insurgent officer. After the treatment he admitted that he held the rank of captain in the insurgent army—an active captain. His police force, numbering twenty-five, were sworn insurgent soldiers. He was the *presidente* of the town and had been for a year, and he always showed himself to be friendly on the outside to the officers, and the men the same way.

Sen. Beveridge: But in reality—

The Witness: He was an insurgent officer and his men were insurgent soldiers. He acknowledged that, and his police acknowledged the same thing. When they took the oath as police they took the oath of an insurgent soldier.

The Chairman: Were they supposed to be friendly to the United States?

The Witness: They were; yes, sir.

Sen. Beveridge: That was a pretense?—A. Yes, sir.

Q. And this was during the time of active warfare?—A. Yes, sir; during the entire time he held the place as the *presidente* in that town.

Sen. Burrows: His offense was treachery to the American cause?—A. Yes, sir. . . .

POSTSCRIPT

Mark Twain returned to the United States in October 1900, after nearly a decade overseas. He had supported American intervention in Cuba, for he believed the war against Spain to be a selfless act of a free people intent on helping a neighbor gain its liberty. Yet as the new century approached, he looked with growing horror on America's ongoing presence in Cuba and its ugly war in the Philippines. Twain became an outspoken anti-imperialist.

The cause elicited some of the most scathing words from his "pen warmed-up in hell," for Twain viewed imperial expansion, especially by America, as a betrayal of Christian and democratic ideals. On December 30, 1900, in the pages of the New York *Herald,* he greeted the new century with an attack on the role of churches and missionaries: "I bring you the stately matron named Christendom, returning bedraggled, besmirched and dishonored from pirate raids in Kiao-Chow, Manchuria, South Africa and the Philippines, with her soul full of meanness, her pockets full of boodle, and her mouth full of pious hypocrisies. Give her soap and a towel, but hide the looking glass."

For the next several years, Twain wrote a series of articles, open letters, and reviews condemning American overseas expansion. He turned away from his original notion of the Spanish-American War as a good cause gone bad and came to see expansionist rhetoric as a cynical cover for avarice. Soon imperialist spokesmen accused Twain of treason, a charge that redoubled his activities. Patriotism, he argued, consisted of following one's own conscience; Filipinos resisting the American invasion were patriots, while American jingoists were traitors to their own ideals.

One of Twain's angriest attacks on American policy in the Philippines came in the article, "To the Person Sitting in Darkness" (*North American Review,* February 1901):

> . . . We have crushed a deceived and confiding people; we have turned against the weak and the friendless who trusted us; we have stamped out a just and intelligent and well-ordered republic; we have stabbed an ally in the back and slapped the face of a guest . . . we have robbed a trusting friend of his land and his liberty; we have invited our clean young men to shoulder a discredited musket and do bandit's work under a flag which bandits have been accustomed to fear, not to follow; we have debauched America's honor and blackened her face before the world. . . .

Perhaps Twain's most despairing antiwar statement was published posthumously. "I have told the whole truth," he declared, "and only dead men can tell the truth in this world. It can be published after I am dead." "The War-Prayer" appeared six years after he died, in the November 1916 issue of *Harper's Monthly.* Twain describes a community preparing for war, with bands and parades swelling the patriotic fervor. On Sunday before the troops leave for the front, the church is filled, and the preacher offers a prayer asking the Lord to bless the soldiers' efforts with victory.

Just as the minister finishes his supplication, an aged stranger with long white hair and robes that reach to the floor ascends the pulpit. He motions the preacher aside and addresses the congregation. He bears a message from the Almighty. God has heard their words and will grant their wishes, but they must know that with their spoken prayer has gone an unspoken one. ". . . O Lord, our God," he prays,

> "help us to tear their soldiers to bloody shreds with our shells; help us to cover their smiling fields with the pale forms of their patriot dead; help us to drown the thunder of the guns with shrieks of their wounded, writhing in pain; help us to lay waste their humble homes with a hurricane of fire; help us to wring the hearts of their unoffending widows with unavailing grief; help us to turn them out roofless with their little children to wander unfriended the wastes of their desolated land. . . . For our sakes who adore Thee, Lord, blast their hopes, blight their lives, protract their bitter pilgrimage, make heavy their steps, water their way with their tears, stain the white snow with the blood of their wounded feet! We ask it in the spirit of love, of Him Who is the Source of Love, . . . Amen.
>
> "[*After a Pause.*] Ye have prayed it; if ye still desire it, speak!—The messenger of the Most High waits."
>
> It was believed afterwards, that the man was a lunatic, because there was no sense in what he said.

QUESTIONS

Defining Terms

Identify in the context of the chapter each of the following:

rags to riches	"the most dangerous man of the age"
ideology	Albert Beveridge
social Darwinism	folkways
imperialism	Henry Cabot Lodge
"The Strenuous Life"	water cure

Probing the Sources

1. What was the fighting like in the Philippines? How did the nature of the war itself relate to people's characterization of the Philippine people?
2. What ideas about racial groups do you find in Beveridge, Sumner, and Roosevelt? What was the relationship of those ideas to their views on overseas expansion?
3. What did Sumner mean by Spain's conquest of the United States? Why did he believe an overseas empire would make America weaker?
4. Why did Roosevelt believe foreign territories would make America stronger? How did his ideas about citizenship relate to foreign policy?
5. How did ideas about "manhood" enter the debates on overseas expansion?
6. Describe Beveridge's belief about America's special mission to the world.

Interpreting the Sources

1. The selections by Roosevelt, Beveridge, and Sumner all contain a sense that American life was threatened at the turn of the century. What did they fear in the future, and why?
2. What was meant by phrases like "true Americanism," "national duties," and the "strenuous life"? In what ways did the anti-imperialists express alternatives to these concepts?
3. How did assumptions about gender influence ideology in these selections? What about race?
4. Do you think that ideologies operate more as a system of lies or as a system of metaphors? Select passages from this chapter to argue your case.
5. How did the various participants in this debate view the role of business, government, and the military in American foreign policy?

ADDITIONAL READING

On America's emergence as a world power in the late nineteenth century, see Walter La Feber, *The New Empire: An Interpretation of American Expansion, 1860–1898* (1963); and Anders Stephanson, *Manifest Destiny* (1995). The role of racial beliefs in foreign policy is discussed in Rubin Weston, *Racism in U.S. Imperialism: The Influence of Racial Assumptions on American Foreign Policy, 1893–1946* (1972); and Tunde Adeleke, *UnAfrican Americans* (1998). For the ideological bases of the new foreign policy, see Emily Rosenberg, *Spreading the American Dream: American Economic and Cultural Expansion, 1890–1945* (1982). On Roosevelt, see Frederick Marks II, *Velvet on Iron: The Diplomacy of Theodore Roosevelt* (1979). For those who opposed the aggressive new tone in late-nineteenth-century foreign policy, see Robert Beisner, *Twelve Against Empire: The Anti-Imperialists, 1898–1900* (1975). For interpretations of American diplomatic history, see Walter La Feber, *The American Age: United States Policy at Home and Abroad Since 1750* (1989); Harvey Rosenfeld, *Diary of a Dirty Little War* (2000); and Ivan Musicant, *Empire by Default* (1998). For American relations with the Philippines, see Stanley Karnow, *In Our Image: America's Empire in the Philippines* (1989). For geographers' perspectives, try Neil Smith, *American Empire* (2003). Finally, see Kristin L. Hoganson, *Fighting for American Manhood* (1998). Gail Bederman, *Manliness and Civilization* (1996) and Matthew Frye Jacobson, *Barbarian Virtues* (2000).

6

The Progressive Era

Chicago's growth during the nineteenth century was nothing short of astonishing. It was a backwoods settlement in 1830, and in the 1840s, a provincial berg dwarfed by the likes of Cincinnati and St Louis. With their domination over commerce on the Ohio and Mississippi Rivers, the supremacy of those two cities over the American heartland seemed assured. But when Chicago established itself as the main western hub for railroad traffic, it began to grow at an astonishing rate, easily overtaking its Midwestern rivals in just a few years. Over 100,000 Chicagoans in 1860 became a quarter million a decade later, a number that kept doubling every ten years until at the turn of the century, Chicago's population approached two million people. Here the goods flowed in–timber from the northwest, wheat and corn from prairie states, coal from mines scattered cross the middle west, cattle from out on the plains–and were processed into things like lumber, meat, and steel, then shipped back out, not just to the far corners of America but into the world aboard ships that sailed out of the Great Lakes to international ports. People were part of this flow of commodities. All American cities contained enormous numbers of immigrants but Chicago was at the high end of the trend. Roughly two thirds of turn-of-the-century Chicago's citizens were either born overseas or had a parent who started life outside America. Along with enormous growth came horrifying social problems of poverty, illness, and social alienation. The "muckraking" journalist Lincoln Steffens described Chicago as "first in violence, deepest in dirt, lawless, unlovely, ill-smelling, irreverent, new; an overgrown gawk of a village, the 'tough' among cities, a spectacle for the nation."

Chicago was emblematic of the difficulties facing America in the new century. The Progressive Era, which lasted roughly from 1900 through World War I, was a set of responses to these problems. The Gilded Age unleashed the incredible productive capacity of American business. With new technologies such as the telephone, massive infrastructure including tens of thousands of miles of railroad track, enormous amounts of capital invested in new corporations, and a young and ambitious labor force, the national economy grew at an astonishing rate. But rapid urbanization and industrialization had their costs. While enormous fortunes were built up (and displayed in new playgrounds for the rich like Newport, Rhode Island), a disconcerting number of Americans went to bed hungry at night. Workers often put in 10 and 12 hour days, 6 days a week, and many families barely made ends meet on a "family wage," the combined income of husband, wife, and children, all going out to work. Equally important, to the extent that government intervened in daily life, it was to assist the productive capacity of business—granting corporations limited liability, giving away public lands to encourage the development of new markets, sending in troops to break strikes. Problems like garbage piling up in the streets, drinking water contaminated by sewage, and deadly streetcar crossings in every American town all contributed to a grudging reconsideration of the role of government in the lives of citizens.

Not everyone agreed on what reforms were needed, and historians have differed for decades on what to include or exclude within the category of "progressivism," but reformers generally believed that the sheer size of business created problems. America was more organized, centralized, and bureaucratic than ever before. For example, at the turn of the century, banker J. P. Morgan purchased Andrew Carnegie's steel plants and folded them into a new company called United States Steel, capitalized at an unheard of one billion dollars. The old fears of massive agglomerations of wealth and power crushing economic opportunity, destroying workers' chance for a decent life, polluting democracy, and undermining the citizens' republic grew more intense than ever. In the late nineteenth century, labor unions proliferated among the working class, and by the 1890s, farmers organized against the incorporation of America. At the beginning of the twentieth century, the Progressive Era was a middle class response to the situation. Crusading journalists, reform-minded women, college professors, preachers of the new "social gospel," liberal politicians, and even forward-thinking businessmen joined together in shifting coalitions to expose problems and seek solutions.

For many, the answer to growing corporate power was the countervailing force of government. To make democracy less vulnerable to corruption, cities reconfigured themselves, holding "at-large" elections for local offices, vesting power in "expert" managers, and assuring fair elections with the "Australian" ballot, all designed, it was said, to reduce the power of corrupt aldermen. States instituted the initiative, referendum, and recall to revitalize citizen participation in the political process. And in countless ways, the federal government weighed in, from the "trust-busting" of President Theodore Roosevelt (which broke up only a handful of businesses) to such regulatory legislation as the Federal Reserve Act of 1913 and the Clayton Antitrust Act of 1914 under Woodrow Wilson. Progressive reforms, however, were not always as progressive as their proponents claimed. "At-large" elections disenfranchised many neighborhoods, and state electoral reforms often became new tools for the powerful. Moreover, laws reigning in business frequently were written with the help of the very companies they were designed to regulate, and the results often reduced competition and encouraged bigness.

The progressives' style was as notable as their substance. As a middle class movement led largely by well-educated people, progressives valued facts and figures, expert knowledge, and bureaucratic efficiency. The attorney Louis Brandeis, who became a Supreme Court Justice appointed by Woodrow Wilson, pioneered the use of sociological knowledge in legal briefs—precedent and case-law were not enough to win the day, "scientifically" gathered data mattered too. The progressive style was fact-laden, logical, and systematic. Progressives placed great faith in the wisdom of "experts," those with the training and knowledge to address social problems in methodical ways. This emphasis on expertise gave a distinctly elitist cast to much of their thinking and writing, even as they professed reforms in the name of "the people" against special interests. But parallel to the rhetoric of disinterested expertise was another language, often quite emotional, filled with moral and even religious fervor. One need only picture the Progressive (or Bull Moose) Party convention in Chicago in 1912. Having nominated former president Theodore Roosevelt to run as a third-party candidate for president, the delegates concluded their meetings by rising and singing in unison "Onward Christian Soldiers." One might even argue that the old revulsion against drinking, so common in Protestant churches throughout the nineteenth century, became the culmination of progressive reform when in 1920 Congress passed the eighteenth amendment to the constitution, banning the sale of alcohol entirely.

In this chapter, we will examine two examples of the Progressive Era's reform impulse, the first involving workers in the meatpacking industry, the second women and the birth-control movement. As distinct as these stories were, think about their commonalities—who wanted to do the reforming, whom did they seek to help, what methods did they use, how did they conceptualize their goals, what results did they achieve, to what extent were they successful?

PART I: UPTON SINCLAIR AND THE MEATPACKING INDUSTRY

HISTORICAL CONTEXT

A cow grazes in Texas. A month later, part of it is being eaten by a family in New Jersey. This would not have happened before the Civil War, yet it was commonplace by 1900. What happened? Technology was important—the railroad connected the Great Plains with the East, so that shipping goods over hundreds, even thousands of miles now took but a few days. Also refrigeration allowed freshly butchered beef to be preserved. But equally important was the mental leap of thinking of meat as just one more product in the marketplace.

The key was keeping goods cheap through mass production, and using every part of an animal—bone for buttons, gut for sporting goods, hides for outerwear. If thousands of cattle—which required a lot of space to raise—could be brought together and slaughtered systematically, and every part of each animal made into a commodity with a market value, then costs would come down, manufacturers might ship dressed meat to distant places for less money than local butchers could produce it, and beef would be consumed by more and more new customers. Butchers—skilled tradesmen whose labor was expensive—could be replaced by countless unskilled workers who performed but one task over and over, such as cutting off a particular part of the cow as it came down the "disassembly line." These ideas did not occur all at once, but slowly a handful of Chicago entrepreneurs in competition with each other turned what had been a locally based business into a national industry. The result was the famous Packingtown on Chicago's South Side, roughly a mile-and-a-half square bordered by Thirty-Ninth and Fifty-First Streets, and by Halsted and Western, filled with meatpacking plants and slaughterhouses.

Packingtown stank. It was ugly, dangerous, and unhealthy. Entering Packingtown from the north, a visitor was greeted—or perhaps insulted—by two prominent landmarks. The main entrance to the Union Stockyards was an imposing stone and iron gate that dwarfed humans and served as a grim portent of the serious and difficult work inside. Snaking its way to the west of the stockyards was Bubbly Creek, a branch of the Chicago River named for the carbolic acid gas that rose to the surface from the decaying wastes. The gasses of Bubbly Creek mixed with the odors of dying animals and decaying meat, and a series of uncovered dumps gave Packingtown its unforgettable smell.

Forty thousand people lived and worked in Packingtown. Most resided in poorly constructed frame houses that were often firetraps. Unlike better South Side neighborhoods, Packingtown's roads were largely unpaved and its sewage facilities were inadequate. The uncollected garbage, open sewers, and accumulated filth lowered health standards as well as human morale. Tuberculosis was the major scourge, but bronchitis, diphtheria, and other contagious diseases also claimed their victims. Children were especially vulnerable; one out of every three infants did not live to a second birthday.

The residents of Packingtown, mostly immigrants from central Europe and Scandinavia at the turn of the century, tolerated these dreadful conditions for a chance to work in the packinghouses. The jobs they acquired were difficult and dangerous—very dangerous. And for risking lives and limbs, unskilled workers were paid between fifteen and eighteen cents per hour, barely enough to starve by inches. Seasoned or cynical immigrants might take refuge in the old Yiddish proverb: "If the rich could pay people to die for them, the poor would make a wonderful living."

Historian James R. Barrett, in his study of Chicago's packinghouse workers, has written, "Each job had its own dangers: the dampness and cold of the packing rooms and hide cellar; the sharp blade of the beef boner's knife; the noxious dust of the wool department and fertilizer plant; the wild charge of a half-crazed steer on the killing floor." And the frantic pace forced on the workers increased the chances of serious injury. Often the results read more like battlefield casualty reports than worker accidents. During the first six months of 1910, Swift and Company reported 3,500 injuries serious enough to require a physician's care. And in 1917 Armour workers became ill or injured over 22,000 times.

A man named Upton Sinclair came to Packingtown in 1904. He did not come as a worker looking for a job but as a writer in pursuit of a subject. Workers had just lost a major strike, and Sinclair went to the stockyards to observe their lives. Thirty-five years old, he had been a novelist for many years. The literary marketplace rewarded sensational writing, and the ambitious young Sinclair had been successful with tales of love and blood and revenge. But he was also ambitious to produce "art." Writing dime novels, even though it paid the bills, failed to satisfy his soul. Sinclair's early efforts at serious fiction were commercial and artistic failures. His characters, like the author himself, were consumed with the idea of individual genius, with the rather romantic notion of the suffering and misunderstood artist dedicated to the singularity of his private vision. But then Upton Sinclair had what amounted to a religious conversion—he discovered socialism.

Various ideas for bringing the enormous new corporations under public control were advanced after 1900, but socialism was a radical solution. Socialists wanted to nationalize the means of production—factories, mills, and mines must be owned by the state; no more private profits for capitalists and low wages for workers. The socialists proposed to remake America through the electoral system, and they saw their cause as a patriotic calling. The Socialist Party never threatened to displace the Democrats or Republicans, but before World War I, dozens of socialists became legislators, mayors, and councilmen, while Eugene Debs of Terre Haute, Indiana, garnered six percent of the vote for president in 1912.

Sinclair remained an ambitious writer, but by 1904, his faith in the socialist cause led his work away from depicting suffering artists toward analyzing the plight of American workers. New magazines like *McClure's* had published so-called muckraking journalists such as Ida Tarbell and Lincoln Steffens, who wrote exposés of civic and corporate corruption, but Sinclair was much more radical than them. He went to Packingtown, studied the factories, the workers, and the "Back-of-the-Yards" neighborhoods. He wrote rapidly and intensely. His novel, *The Jungle,* was first published in serial form in 1905, not in the mainstream press but in the *Appeal to Reason,* a popular socialist newspaper based in Girard, Kansas.

The Jungle came out in book form in 1906 and was an instant success. Sinclair told the story of the Rudkus family, Lithuanian immigrants who came to America only to be used and discarded by the companies that owned Packingtown. The human and sanitary abuses Sinclair catalogued shocked Americans in 1906, and they continue to shock us today. Although *The Jungle* followed the style of literary realism, the conventions of the early twentieth century forced Sinclair to use euphemisms to discuss certain problems in the workplace. For example, he often remarks that there were no places in the packinghouses for the workers to wash their hands. The early twentieth century reader would understand that Sinclair meant that no toilet facilities were provided and that human urine and feces accumulated on the floors of the packinghouses. Despite his attempts to preserve literary delicacy, some reviewers were scandalized by Sinclair's violations of good taste. A reviewer for *The Outlook* declared, "to disgust the reader by dragging him through every conceivable horror, physical and moral, and to depict with lurid excitement and with offensive minuteness the life in jail and brothel—all is to overstep the object."

The Documents

Introduction to Document 1

The publication of *The Jungle* and the wide readership it attracted gave ammunition to the politicians who were seeking reforms in the meatpacking industry. Even President Roosevelt entered the fight to demand change. The result of the ferment was the Meat Inspection Act of 1906. Far from a perfect piece of legislation, it represented a compromise between the meatpacking companies and the reformers. It helped to restore confidence in the American packing industry, however, it did little for the residents of Packingtown. As Sinclair later remarked, "I aimed at the public's heart, and by accident I hit it in the stomach." In the following scene, Sinclair's main character, Jurgis Rudkis, looks for work.

DOCUMENT 1 *From* The Jungle

Upton Sinclair

. . . There was another interesting set of statistics that a person might have gathered in Packingtown—those of the various afflictions of the workers. . . . There were the men in the pickle-rooms, for instance, where old Antanas had gotten his death; scarce a one of these that had not some spot of horror on his person. Let a man so much as scrape his finger pushing a truck in the pickle-rooms, and he might have a sore that would put him out of the world; all the joints in his fingers might be eaten by the acid, one by one. Of the butchers and floorsmen, the beef-boners and trimmers, and all those who used knives, you could scarcely find a person who had the use of his thumb; time and time again the base of it had been slashed, till it was a mere lump of flesh against which the man pressed the knife to hold it. The hands of these men would be criss-crossed with cuts, until you could no longer pretend to count them or to trace them. They would have no nails,—they had worn them off pulling hides; their knuckles were swollen so that their fingers spread out like a fan. There were men who worked in the cooking-rooms, in the midst of steam and sickening odors, by artificial light; in these rooms the germs of tuberculosis might live for two years, but the supply was renewed every hour. There were the beef-luggers, who carried two-hundred-pound quarters into the refrigerator-cars; a fearful kind of work, that began at four o'clock in the morning, and that wore out the most powerful men in a few years. There were those who worked in the chilling-rooms, and whose special disease was rheumatism; the time-limit that a man could work in the chilling-rooms was said to be five years. There were the wool-pluckers, whose hands went to pieces even sooner than the hands of the pickle-men; for the pelts of the sheep had to be painted with acid to loosen the wool, and then the pluckers had to pull out this wool with their bare hands, till the acid had eaten their fingers off. There were those who made the tins for the canned-meat; and their hands, too, were a maze of cuts, and each cut represented a chance for blood-poisoning. Some worked at the stamping-machines, and it was very seldom that one could work long there at the pace that was set, and not give out and forget himself, and have a part of his hand chopped off. . . . As for the other men, who worked in tank-rooms full of steam, and in some of which there were open vats near the level of the floor, their peculiar trouble was that they fell into the vats; and when they were fished out, there was never enough of them left to be worth exhibiting,—sometimes they would be overlooked for days, till all but the bones of them had gone out to the world as Durham's Pure Leaf Lard! . . .

All this while that he was seeking for work, there was a dark shadow hanging over Jurgis; as if a savage beast were lurking somewhere in the pathway of his life, and he knew it, and yet could not help approaching the place. There were all stages of being out of work in Packingtown, and he faced in dread the prospect of reaching the lowest. There is a place that waits for the lowest man—the fertilizer-plant!

The men would talk about it in awe-stricken whispers. Not more than one in ten had ever really tried it; the other nine had contented themselves with hearsay evidence and a peep through the door. There were some things worse than even starving to death. They would ask Jurgis if he had worked there yet, and if he meant to; and Jurgis would debate the matter with himself. As poor as they were, and making all the sacrifices that they were, would he dare to refuse any sort of work that was offered to him, be it as horrible as ever it could? Would he dare to go home and eat bread that had been earned by Ona, weak and complaining as she was, knowing that he had been given a chance, and had not had the nerve to take it?—And yet he might argue that way with himself all day, and one glimpse into the fertilizer-works would send him away again shuddering. He was a man, and he would do his duty; he went and made application—but surely he was not also required to hope for success! . . .

The boss of the grinding room had come to know Jurgis by this time, and had marked him for a likely man; and so when he came to the door about two o'clock this breathless hot day, he felt a sudden spasm of pain shoot through him—the boss beckoned to him! In ten minutes more Jurgis had pulled off his coat and overshirt, and set his teeth together and gone to work. Here was one more difficulty for him to meet and conquer!

His labor took him about one minute to learn. Before him was one of the vents of the mill in which the fertilizer was being ground-rushing forth in a great brown river, with a spray of the finest dust flung forth in clouds. Jurgis was given a shovel, and along with half a dozen others it was his task to shovel this fertilizer into carts. That others were at work he knew by the sound, and by the fact that he sometimes collided with them; otherwise they might as well not have been there, for in the blinding dust-storm a man could not see six feet in front of his face. When he had filled one cart he had to grope around him until another came, and if there was none on hand he continued to grope till one arrived. In five minutes he was, of course, a mass of fertilizer from head to feet; they gave him a sponge to tie over his mouth, so that he could breathe, but the sponge did not prevent his lips and eyelids from caking up with it and his ears from filling solid. He looked like a brown ghost at twilight—from hair to shoes he became the color of the building and of everything in it, and for that matter a hundred yards outside it. The building had to be left open, and when the wind blew Durham and Company lost a great deal of fertilizer.

Working in his shirt-sleeves, and with the thermometer at over a hundred, the phosphates soaked in through every pore of Jurgis's skin, and in five minutes he had a headache, and in fifteen was almost dazed. The blood was pounding his brain like an engine's throbbing; there was a frightful pain in the top of his skull, and he could hardly control his hands. Still, with the memory of his four months' siege [of illness and unemployment] behind him, he fought on, in a frenzy of determination; and half an hour later he began to vomit—he vomited until it seemed as if his inwards must be torn to shreds. A man could get used to the fertilizer-mill, the boss had said, if he would only make up his mind to it; but Jurgis now began to see that it was a question of making up his stomach.

At the end of that day of horror, he could scarcely stand. He had to catch himself now and then, and lean against a building and get his bearings. Most of the men, when they came out, made straight for a saloon—they seemed to place fertilizer and rattlesnake poison in one class. But Jurgis was too ill to think of drinking—he could only make his way to the street and stagger on to a car. He had a sense of humor, and later on, when he became an old hand, he used to think it fun to board a street-car and see what happened. Now, however, he was too ill to notice it—how the people in the car began to gasp and sputter, to put their handkerchiefs to their noses, and transfix him with furious glances. Jurgis only knew that a man in front of him immediately got up and gave him a seat; and that half a minute later the two people on each side of him got up; and that in a full minute the crowded car was nearly empty—those passengers who could not get room on the platform having gotten out to walk.

Of course Jurgis had made his home a miniature fertilizer-mill a minute after entering. The stuff was half an inch deep in his skin—his whole system was full of it, and it would have taken a week not merely of scrubbing, but of vigorous exercise, to get it out of him. As it was, he could be compared with nothing known to men, save that newest discovery of the savants, a substance which emits energy for an unlimited time, without being itself in the least diminished in power. He smelt so that he made all the food at the table taste, and set the whole family to vomiting; for himself it was three days before he could keep anything upon his stomach—he might wash his hands, and use a knife and fork, but were not his mouth and throat filled with the poison? . . .

With one member trimming beef in a cannery, and another working in a sausage factory, the family had a first-hand knowledge of the great majority of Packingtown swindles. For it was the custom, as they found, whenever meat was so spoiled that it could not be used for anything else, either to can it or else to chop it up into sausage. With what had been told them by Jonas, who had worked in the pickle-rooms, they could now study the whole of the spoiled-meat industry on the inside, and read a new and grim meaning into that old Packingtown jest—that they use everything of the pig except the squeal.

Jonas had told them how the meat that was taken out of pickle would often be found sour, and how they would rub it up with soda to take away the smell, and sell it to be eaten on free-lunch counters; also of all the miracles of chemistry which they performed, giving to any sort of meat, fresh or salted, whole or chopped, any color and any flavor and any odor they chose. In the pickling of hams they had an ingenious apparatus, by which they saved time and increased the capacity of the plant—a machine consisting of a hollow needle attached to a pump; by plunging this needle into the meat and working with his foot, a man could fill a ham with pickle in a few seconds. And yet, in spite of this, there would be hams found spoiled, some of them with an odor so bad that a man could hardly bear to be in the room with them. To pump into these the packers had a second and much stronger pickle which destroyed the odor—a process known to the workers as "giving them thirty per cent." Also, after the hams had been smoked, there would be found some that had gone to the bad. Formerly these had been sold as "Number Three Grade," but later on some ingenious person had hit upon a new device, and now they would extract the bone, about which the bad part generally lay, and insert in the hole a white-hot iron. After this invention there was no longer Number One, Two, and Three Grade—there was only Number One Grade. The packers were always originating such schemes—they had what they called "boneless hams," which were all the odds and ends of pork stuffed into casings; and "California hams," which were the shoulders, with big knuckle-joints, and nearly all the meat cut out; and fancy "skinned hams," which were made of the oldest hogs, whose skins were so heavy and coarse that no one would buy them—that is, until they had been cooked and chopped fine and labelled "head cheese"!

It was only when the whole ham was spoiled that it came into the department of Elzbieta. Cut up by the two-thousand-revolutions-a-minute flyers, and mixed with half a ton of other meat, no odor that ever was in a ham could make any difference. There was never the least attention paid to what was cut up for sausage; there would come all the way back from Europe old sausage that had been rejected, and that was mouldy and white—it would be dosed with borax and glycerine, and dumped into the hoppers, and made over again for home consumption. There would be meat that had tumbled out on the floor, in the dirt and sawdust, where the workers had tramped and spit uncounted billions of consumption germs. There would be meat stored in great piles in rooms; and the water from leaky roofs would drip over it, and thousands of rats would race about on it. It was too dark in these storage places to see well, but a man could run his hand over these piles of meat and sweep off handfuls of the dried dung of rats. These rats were nuisances, and the packers would put poisoned bread out for them; they would die, and then rats, bread and meat would go into the hoppers together. This is no fairy story and no joke; the meat would be shovelled into carts, and the man who did the shovelling would not trouble to lift out a rat even when he saw one—there were things that went into the sausage in comparison with which a poisoned rat was a tidbit. . . .

Such were the new surroundings in which Elzbieta was placed, and such was the work she was compelled to do. It was stupefying, brutalizing work; it left her no time to think, no strength for anything. She was part of the machine she tended, and every faculty that was not needed for the machine was doomed to be crushed out of existence. There was only one mercy about the cruel grind—that it gave her the gift of insensibility. Little by little she sank into a torpor—she fell silent. She would meet Jurgis and Ona in the evening, and the three would walk home together, often without saying a word. Ona, too, was falling into a habit of silence—Ona, who had once gone about singing like a bird. She was sick and miserable, and often she would barely have strength enough to drag herself home. And there they would eat what they had to eat, and afterwards, because there was only their misery to talk of, they would crawl into bed and fall into a stupor and never stir until it was time to get up again, and dress by candle-light, and go back to the machines. They were so numbed that they did not even suffer much from hunger, now; only the children continued to fret when the food ran short.

Yet the soul of Ona was not dead—the souls of none of them were dead, but only sleeping; and now and then they would waken, and these were cruel times. The gates of memory would roll open—old joys would stretch out their arms to them, old hopes and dreams would call to them, and they would stir beneath the burden that lay upon them, and feel its forever immeasurable weight. They could not even cry out beneath it; but anguish would seize them, more dreadful than the agony of death. It was a thing scarcely to be spoken—a thing never spoken by all the world, that will not know its own defeat. . . .

Introduction to Document 2

Was *The Jungle* an accurate depiction of life in Packingtown? Historians have differed on this point. Certainly Sinclair exaggerated the plight that any one family might endure. Moreover, some have questioned how well he knew the packing industry; he spent only a few weeks in Packingtown, did not go into the factories very much, and gathered most of his information through interviews. Ralph Chaplin, also a writer and a political radical, declared in his autobiography *Wobbly,* "I thought it a very inaccurate picture of the stockyards district which I knew so well, but I waited for each installment eagerly and read it with great interest." Above all, Sinclair minimized the resources of workers to improve their own lives even when they were feeling the brunt of an economic system that sought to buy their labor as cheaply as possible. For example, like many other middle-class Protestants of his day, Sinclair was appalled by drinking, so he interpreted workers' saloons as places of evil rather than community institutions. Read the following autobiography of Antanas Kaztauskis, a Lithuanian immigrant who lived and worked in Packingtown. Kaztauskis's story was published in the magazine *The Independent* three months before Sinclair began his research for *The Jungle.* As you read, think about how this autobiography confirms or contradicts Sinclair's depiction of the lives of immigrant workers. Ask yourself about the role of unions, political organizations, churches, schools, and ethnic communities in daily life. How did working-class people adjust to their lives in America, what values and institutions did they cling to, how did they reinterpret the American dream for themselves?

DOCUMENT 2 *Antanas Kaztauskis's Story*

. . . In our house my room was in the basement. I lay down on the floor with three other men and the air was rotten. I did not go to sleep for a long time. I knew then that money was everything I needed. My money was almost gone and I thought that I would soon die unless I got a job, for this was not like home. Here money was everything and a man without money must die.

The next morning my friends woke me up at five o'clock and said, "Now, if you want life, liberty and happiness," they laughed, "you must push for yourself. You must get a job. Come with us." And we went to the yards. Men and women were walking in by thousands as far as we could see. We went to the doors of one big slaughter house. There was a crowd of about 200 men waiting there for a job. They looked hungry and kept watching the door. At last a special policeman came out and began pointing to men, one by one. Each one jumped forward. Twenty-three were taken. Then they all went inside, and all the others turned their faces away and looked tired. I remember one boy sat down and cried, just next to me, on a pile of boards. Some policemen waved their clubs and we all walked on. I found some Lithuanians to talk with, who told me they had come every morning for three weeks. Soon we met other crowds coming away from other slaughter houses, and we all walked around and felt bad and tired and hungry.

That night I told my friends that I would not do this many days, but would go some place else. "Where?" they asked me, and I began to see then that I was in bad trouble, because I spoke no English. Then one man told me to give him $5 to give the special policeman. I did this and the next morning the policeman pointed me out, so I had a job. I have heard some big talk since then about my American freedom of contract, but I do not think I had much freedom in bargaining for this job with the Meat Trust. My job was in the cattle killing room. I pushed the blood along the gutter. . . . One Lithuanian, who worked with me, said, "They get all the blood out of those cattle and all the work out of us men." This was true, for we worked that first day from six in the morning till seven at night. The next day we worked from six in the morning till eight at night. The next day we had no work. So we had no good, regular hours. It was hot in the room that summer, and the hot blood made it worse.

I held this job six weeks and then I was turned off. I think some other man had paid for my job, or perhaps I was too slow. The foreman in that room wanted quick men to make the work rush, because he was paid more if the work was done cheaper and quicker. I saw now that every man was helping himself, always trying to get all the money he could. At that time I believed that all men in Chicago were grafters when they had to be. They only wanted to push themselves. Now, when I was idle I began to look about, and everywhere I saw sharp men beating out slow men like me. Even if we worked hard it did us no good. I had saved $13—$5 a week for six weeks makes $30, and take off $15 for six weeks' board and lodging and $2 for other things. I showed this to a Lithuanian, who had been here two years, and he laughed. "It will be taken from you," he said. He had saved a hundred dollars once and had begun to buy a house on the instalment plan, but something had happened that he did not know about and his landlord put him out and kept the hundred dollars. I found that many Lithuanians had been beaten this way. At home we never made a man sign contract papers. We only had him make the sign of a cross and promise he would do what he said. But this was no good in Chicago. So these sharp men were beating us.

. . . I kept walking around with many other Lithuanians who had no job. Our money was going and we could find nothing to do. At night we got homesick for our fine green mountains. We read all the news about home in our Lithuanian Chicago newspaper, *The Katalikas*. It is a good paper and gives all the news. In the same office we bought this song, which was written in Brooklyn by P. Brandukas. He, too, was homesick. It is sung all over Chicago now and you can hear it in the summer evenings through the open windows. In English it is something like this:

> Oh, Lithuania, so dear to me,
> Good-by to you, my Fatherland.
> Sorrowful in my heart I leave you,
> I know not who will stay to guard you. . . .

Those were bad days and nights. At last I had a chance to help myself. Summer was over and Election Day was coming. The Republican boss in our district, Jonidas, was a saloonkeeper. A friend took me there. Jonidas shook hands and treated me fine. He taught me to sign my name, and the next week I went with him to an office and signed some paper, and then I could vote. I voted as I was told, and then they got me back into the yards to work, because one big politician owns stock in one of those houses. Then I felt that I was getting in beside the game. I was in a combine like other sharp men. Even when work was slack I was all right, because they got me a job in the street cleaning department.

I felt proud, and I went to the back room in Jonidas's saloon and got him to write a letter to Alexandria to tell her she must come soon and be my wife.

But this was just the trouble. All of us were telling our friends to come soon. Soon they came—even thousands. The employers in the yard liked this, because those sharp foremen are inventing new machines and the work is easier to learn, and so these slow Lithuanians and even green girls can learn to do it, and then the Americans and Germans and Irish are put out and the employer saves money, because the Lithuanians work cheaper. This was why the American labor unions began to organize us all just the same as they had organized the Bohemians and Poles before us.

Well, we were glad to be organized. We had learned that in Chicago every man must push himself always, and Jonidas had taught us how much better we could push ourselves by getting into a combine. Now, we saw that this union was the best combine for us, because it was the only combine that could say, "It is our business to raise your wages." . . . I joined the Cattle Butchers' Union. This union is honest and it has done me a great deal of good. It has raised my wages. The man who worked at my job before the union came was getting through the year an average of $9 a week. I am getting $11. In my first job I got $5 a week. The man who works there now gets $5.75.

It has given me more time to learn to read and speak and enjoy life like an American. I never work now from 6 A.M. to 9 P.M. and then be idle the next day. I work now from 7 A.M. to 5.30 P.M., and there are not so many idle days. The work is evened up.

With more time and more money I live much better and I am very happy. So is Alexandria. She came a year ago and has learned to speak English already. Some of the women go to the big store the day they get here, when they have not enough sense to pick out the clothes that look right, but Alexandria waited three weeks till she knew, and so now she looks the finest of any woman in the district. We have four nice rooms, which she keeps very clean, and she has flowers growing in boxes in the two front windows. We do not go much to church, because the church seems to be too slow. But we belong to a Lithuanian society that gives two picnics in summer and two big balls in winter, where we have a fine time. I go one night a week to the Lithuanian Concertina Club. On Sundays we go on the trolley out into the country.

But we like to stay at home more now because we have a baby. When he grows up I will not send him to the Lithuanian Catholic school. They have only two bad rooms and two priests, who teach only in Lithuanian from prayer books. I will send him to the American school, which is very big and good. The teachers there are Americans and they belong to the Teachers' Labor Union, which has three thousand teachers and belongs to our Chicago Federation of Labor. I am sure that such teachers will give him a good chance. . . .

The union is doing another good thing. It is combining all the nationalities. The night I joined the Cattle Butchers' Union I was led into the room by a negro member. With me were Bohemians, Germans and Poles, and Mike Donnelly, the President, is an Irishman. He spoke to us in English and then three interpreters told us what he said. We swore to be loyal to our union above everything else except the country, the city and the State—to be faithful to each other—to protect the women workers—to do our best to understand the history of the labor movement, and to do all we could to help it on. Since then I have gone there every two weeks and I help the movement by being an interpreter for the other Lithuanians who come in. That is why I have learned to speak and write good English. The others do not need me long. They soon learn English, too, and when they have done that they are quickly becoming Americans.

But the best thing the union does is to make me feel more independent. I do not have to pay to get a job and I cannot be discharged unless I am no good. For almost the whole 30,000 men and women are organized now in some one of our unions and they all are directed by our central council. No man knows what it means to be sure of his job unless he has been fired like I was once without any reason being given.

So this is why I joined the labor union. There are many better stories than mine, for my story is very common. There are thousands of immigrants like me. Over 300,000 immigrants have been organized in the last three years by the American Federation of Labor. The immigrants are glad to be organized if the leaders are as honest as Mike Donnelly is. You must get money to live well, and to get money you must combine. I cannot bargain alone with the Meat Trust. I tried it and it does not work. . . .

Introduction to Document 3

The Jungle **stirred up a storm of criticism. President Theodore Roosevelt obtained an advance copy of the book and appointed a committee to investigate the Chicago stockyards. The committee's report was detailed but mixed—there were breaches of cleanliness, but also many plants that were quite hygienic. The passage reprinted here describes a plant that seemed to confirm many of *The Jungle's* accusations. Remember, however, that Sinclair wrote an indictment of capitalism—his point was that the power of the packinghouses and their desire for profit necessarily caused them to cut corners, to cheat workers, and sell adulterated meat. The following report went to Congress and became evidence that helped pass Senator Albert Beveridge's bill to regulate the packing industry. Even in this most critical part of the investigators' report, note that they slight Sinclair's main concern, the working conditions of the employees in Packingtown.**

DOCUMENT 3 *House Congressional Record, June 4, 1906*

The Senate and House of Representatives:

I transmit herewith the report of Mr. James Bronson Reynolds and Commissioner Charles P. Neill, the special committee whom I appointed to investigate into the conditions in the stock yards of Chicago and report thereon to me. . . . The conditions shown by even this short inspection to exist in the Chicago stock yards are revolting. It is imperatively necessary in the interest of health and of decency that they should be radically changed. Under the existing law it is wholly impossible to secure satisfactory results. . . . I urge the immediate enactment into law of provisions which will enable the Department of Agriculture adequately to inspect the meat and meat food products entering into interstate commerce and to supervise the methods of preparing the same, and to prescribe the sanitary conditions under which the work shall be performed. . . .

Theodore Roosevelt
The White House, June 4, 1906

Condition of the Yards

Before entering the buildings we noted the condition of the yards themselves as shown in the pavement, pens, viaducts, and platforms. The pavement is mostly of brick, the bricks laid with deep grooves between them, which inevitably fill with manure and refuse. Such pavement can not be properly cleaned and is slimy and malodorous when wet, yielding clouds of ill-smelling dust when dry. The pens are generally uncovered except those for sheep; these latter are paved and covered. The viaducts and platforms are of wood. Calves, sheep, and hogs that have died en route are thrown out upon the platforms where cars are unloaded. On a single platform on one occasion we counted fifteen dead hogs, on the next ten dead hogs. The only excuse given for delay in removal was that so often heard—the expense.

Buildings

Ventilation—Systematic ventilation of the workrooms is not found in any of the establishments we visited. In a few instances electric fans mitigate the stifling air, but usually the workers toil without relief in a humid atmosphere heavy with the odors of rotten wood, decayed meats, stinking offal, and entrails.

Equipment—The work tables upon which the meat is handled, the floor carts on which it is carried about, and the tubs and other receptacles into which it is thrown are generally of wood. In all the places visited but a single porcelain-lined receptacle was seen. Tables covered with sheet iron, iron carts, and iron tubs are being introduced into the better establishments, but no establishment visited has as yet abandoned the extensive use of wooden tables and wooden receptacles. These wooden receptacles are frequently found water soaked, only half cleansed, and with meat scraps and grease accumulations adhering to their sides, and collecting dirt. . . .

Sanitary conveniences—Abominable as the above-named conditions are, the one that affects most directly and seriously the cleanliness of the food products is the frequent absence of any lavatory provisions in the privies. Washing sinks are either not furnished at all or are small and dirty. Neither are towels, soap, or toilet paper provided. Men and women return directly from these places to plunge their unwashed hands into the meat to be converted into such food products as sausages, dried beef, and other compounds. Some of the privies are situated at a long distance from the workrooms, and men relieve themselves on the killing floors or in a corner of the workrooms. Hence, in some cases the fumes of the urine swell the sum of nauseating odors arising from the dirty, blood-soaked, rotting, wooden floors—fruitful culture beds for the disease germs of men and animals. . . .

Treatment of Meats and Prepared Food Products

A particularly glaring instance of uncleanliness was found in a room where the best grade of sausage was being prepared for export. It was made from carefully selected meats, and was being prepared to be eaten uncooked. In this case the employee carted the chopped-up meat across a room in a barrow, the handles of which were filthy with grease. The meat was then thrown out upon tables, and the employee climbed upon the table, handled the meat with his unwashed hands, knelt with his dirty apron and trousers in contact with the meat he was spreading out, and, after he had finished his operation, again took hold of the dirty handles of the wheelbarrow, went back for another load, and repeated this process indefinitely. Inquiry developed the fact that there was no water in this room at all, and the only method the man adopted for cleaning his hands was to rub them against his dirty apton or on his still filthier trousers.

As an extreme example of the entire disregard on the part of employees of any notion of cleanliness in handling dressed meat, we saw a hog that had just been killed, cleaned, washed, and started on its way to the cooling room fall from the sliding rail to a dirty wooden floor and slide part way into a filthy men's privy. It was picked up by two employees, placed upon a truck, carried into the cooling room and hung up with other carcasses, no effort being made to clean it. . . .

All of [the] canned products bear labels, of which the following is a sample: "The contents of this package have been inspected according to the act of Congress of March 3, 1891. QUALITY GUARANTEED."

The phraseology of these labels is wholly unwarranted. The Government inspectors pass only upon the healthfulness of the animal at the time of killing. They know nothing of the process through which the meat has passed since this inspection. They do not know what else may have been placed in the cans in addition to "inspected meat." As a matter of fact, they know nothing about the "contents" of the can upon which the packers place these labels—do not even know that it contains what it purports to contain. The legend

"Quality guaranteed" immediately following the statement as to Government inspection is wholly unjustifiable. It deceives and is plainly designed to deceive the average purchaser, who naturally infers from the label that the Government guarantees the contents of the can to be what it purports to be. . . .

Treatment of Employees

The lack of consideration for the health and comfort of the laborers in the Chicago stock yards seem to be a direct consequence of the system of administration that prevails. The various departments are under the direct control of superintendents who claim to use full authority in dealing with the employees and who seem to ignore all considerations except those of the account book. Under this system proper care of the products and of the health and comfort of the employees is impossible, and the consumer suffers in consequence. The insanitary conditions in which the laborers work and the feverish pace which they are forced to maintain inevitably affect their health. Physicians state that tuberculosis is disproportionately prevalent in the stock yards, and the victims of this disease expectorate on the spongy wooden floors of the dark workrooms, from which falling scraps of meat are later shoveled up to be converted into food products.

Even the ordinary decencies of life are completely ignored. In practically all cases the doors of the toilet rooms open directly into the working rooms, the privies of men and women frequently adjoin, and the entrances are sometimes no more than a foot or two apart. In other cases there are no privies for women in the rooms in which they work, and to reach the nearest it is necessary to go up or down a couple of flights of stairs. In one noticeable instance the privy for the women working in several adjoining rooms was in a room in which men chiefly were employed, and every girl going to use this had to pass by the working places of dozens of male operatives and enter the privy, the door of which was not 6 feet from the working place of one of the men operatives. As previously noted, in the privies for men and women alike there are no partitions, but simply a long row of open seats. . . .

Much of the work in connection with the handling of meat has to be carried on in rooms of a low temperature, but even here a callous disregard was everywhere seen for the comfort of those who work in these rooms. Girls and women were found in rooms registering a temperature of 38° F without any ventilation whatever, depending entirely upon artificial light. The floors were wet and soggy, and in some cases covered with water, so that the girls had to stand in boxes of sawdust as a protection for their feet. In a few cases even drippings from the refrigerator rooms above trickled through the ceiling upon the heads of the workers and upon the food products being prepared. . . .

The neglect on the part of their employers to recognize or provide for the requirements of cleanliness and decency of the employees must have an influence that can not be exaggerated in lowering the morals and discouraging cleanliness on the part of the workers employed in the packing houses. The whole situation as we saw it in these huge establishments tends necessarily and inevitably to the moral degradation of thousands of workers, who are forced to spend their working hours under conditions that are entirely unnecessary and unpardonable, and which are a constant menace not only to their own health, but to the health of those who use the food products prepared by them. . . .

Introduction to Document 4

The meatpacking industry had been very resistant to federal regulation, but the public had been so stirred up by *The Jungle* and subsequent publicity that some sort of federal regulation was all but inevitable. Packinghouses quickly turned to damage control—the industry must win back public confidence by seeming to be out front on reform. Even advertising shifted toward issues of cleanliness. "The Massachusetts State Board of Health Endorses William Underwood Company's

Products," an advertisement in a 1906 issue of *Outlook* magazine declared; "The report shows their ABSOLUTE PURITY and freedom from improper adulterants and preservatives. . . . [and] recommends the Wm. Underwood Co.'s CANNING PLANTS as MODELS to be copied by others in the same business." Louis F. Swift, president of one of the largest packing houses in Chicago, published the following open letter, also in *The Outlook,* on June 23, 1906.

DOCUMENT 4 *Letter from Louis F. Swift*

SWIFT & COMPANY,

Union Stock Yards.
Office of the President.
Chicago, June 14, 1906.

Government Supervision of the Meat Industry

No. 1. All cattle, sheep, and hogs purchased by Swift & Company are U.S. Government inspected, both before and after dressing. Those condemned in the ante-mortem inspection are refused and disposed of under local health authorities' supervision.

No. 2. The animals condemned by the Federal inspectors after dressing are destroyed under the inspector's supervision. Ante-mortem and post-mortem inspection is now furnished by the Government only when requested and not compulsory under present law. Swift & Company have always been strong advocates of thorough Government inspection both before and after slaughter, and we desire an extension of these regulations to cover all packing and slaughtering establishments, in order that uniform regulations may govern the entire industry; and to be compulsory.

No. 3. All processes in the preparation of meats to be under Federal inspection, which should require (*a*) that the meats are from healthy animals proper for food; (*b*) that the conditions under which the work is conducted are sanitary.

No. 4. The Government should pay the cost of inspection, thus affording the packer the same protection given the consumer. The packer does not produce any animals, and under Government inspection will not accept any showing traces of disease in the live examination. The packer now stands the loss of any animals condemned in the post-mortem examination, and to add an inspection fee is unfair.

Swift & Company want to be fully understood when they say that the same *open-door policy* which has prevailed in their plants will continue, the public being welcome to inspect the conditions under which the work is conducted, Further, we desire the continuance of Government inspection for all of our own plants and its strict compulsory enforcement in all other plants, regulating both the inspection of dressed meats and all food products, and the conditions under which the work is performed.

I desire to fix firmly in the minds of the readers of The Outlook the aim for integrity governing our purpose to supply the world with wholesome meats, and to decry the promiscuous attacks upon the industry in general.

We are obliged to The Outlook for the courtesy of its columns to dissipate any suspicion which may exist (through the wholesale, condemnation of the industry), and to maintain the confidence that has been enjoyed in the past, and made possible the progress accomplished in twenty years in the preparation of the world's supply of meat.

Louis F. Swift, President.

POSTSCRIPT

Louis Swift endorsed in almost every detail Senator Albert Beveridge's bill, which became the Meat Inspection Act of 1906. One reason that the large meat packers supported the bill can be found in a single sentence in Swift's letter: "we desire the continuance of Government inspection for all of our own plants and its strict compulsory enforcement in all other plants, regulating both the inspection of dressed meats and all food products, and the conditions under which the work is performed." Many small independent butchers objected to the Meat Inspection Act because they simply would not be able to afford the equipment and labor to comply with its provisions. The large packers saw this as an opportunity to drive out some small competitors and increase their markets. Moreover, with the federal government acting as an impartial guarantor of cleanliness, the public at home and abroad would be reassured and would return to buying meat from the packing companies. In exchange for a bit of federal interference, the large packers would operate in a much more stable marketplace.

PART II: MARGARET SANGER AND THE BIRTH CONTROL MOVEMENT

HISTORICAL CONTEXT

Upton Sinclair aimed his arrows at the "meat trust," and his rhetoric attacking the greed of consolidated capital was very much in the Progressive tradition. But *The Jungle* found its moral center in the family, in the need to stop modern business from destroying families. The concern for home was central to Progressives, and the impetus for reform came especially from women, traditionally seen as defenders of the family. While the phrase "the personal *is* political" did not arise until half a century after the Progressive Era, it might well have described those years. Educated women such as Jane Addams, Florence Kelly, and Margaret Sanger—who all came of age in an era that still shunted women into the home and away from leadership roles in the public sphere—publicized women's and children's issues; raised public awareness of matters such as day care, playgrounds, and child labor; and turned the nation's attention to topics where public policy and home life met.

The use of contraceptive devices for family planning has become so common that it is difficult to imagine a time when it was controversial. Yet in 1914, when Margaret Sanger began to speak and write openly in behalf of birth control, she put herself in jeopardy of prosecution under the so-called Comstock Law of 1873, which prohibited mailing, importing, or selling materials of an "obscene, lewd, or lascivious" nature. Indeed, both she and her husband, William Sanger, were indicted under the law for distributing birth control information.

The irony is that family planning had been practiced in America for a century. (Indeed, ancient Greek and Roman doctors had prescribed a variety of contraceptive methods.) Couples limited their offspring by simply abstaining from sexual contact and by practicing coitus interruptus. Equally important, a variety of contraceptive devices, including forerunners of modern condoms, diaphragms, and douches, had been available since at least the early nineteenth century. Not only were such items occasionally advertised in popular magazines, but retailers of contraceptive paraphernalia mailed printed circulars advertising their wares to couples whose wedding announcements appeared in the newspapers. One bit of indirect evidence that the use of such devices was widespread is to be found in declining birthrates: in 1800, families averaged slightly over 7 children, under 6 by 1825, 5.4 in 1850, 4.24 by 1880, and 3.54 in 1900. In other words, the overall fertility rate declined by half in a century, with most urban middle-class families having no more than two children.

The declining birthrate was not simply a matter of new technology changing peoples' lives. Couples' willingness to use contraceptive devices or to otherwise limit the size of their families had social, economic, and cultural origins. As Americans left the countryside for the city, and as the old artisan system of manufacture declined, large numbers of children usually became a hindrance rather than an aid to a family's economic well-being; in a modern urban setting, children entered a family more as mouths to feed than as hands to labor. A cash-based economy (in which people exchanged goods and labor for money) rather than a subsistence one (where work produced items for home consumption) made raising a child very costly and made the "return" on parents' "investment" in their children very slow.

Other important social changes encouraged the use of birth control. The turn of the century witnessed a new emphasis on sexuality as an expression of passion, love, and intimacy. Contraception liberated these feelings from the fear of unwanted pregnancy. This was especially true for women, who had always borne the burden of child rearing. Birth control was part of a larger transformation of women's position in society. Important female voices were raised during the nineteenth and early twentieth century demanding new roles for women, roles apart from the home-centered ones of wife and mother, roles that placed women in the practical worlds of politics, business, and reform. Needless to say, the average of seven children per family in 1800, had it continued, would have made education and careers impossible for most women.

Even though contraception had been practiced for a century when Margaret Sanger began to champion the cause in the years straddling World War I, her crusade generated great controversy. Part of the reason was that she was so open in her advocacy. The genteel Victorian code still held sway sufficiently so that sex remained a subject most people preferred not to talk about in public; even couples who practiced birth control—a criminal act, after all—were silent. Their open discussion of sexuality made birth control advocates harbingers of the freer, less morally rigid styles of living and speaking that we associate with the 1920s.

But it was more than a matter of style alone. At the beginning of her crusade, Sanger allied herself with a variety of radical thinkers—feminists, socialists, labor militants (such as the Industrial Workers of the World), and others—and it was out of the creative, avant-garde ferment of New York City in the prewar era that she forged her ideas. Birth control was not merely a technique; it grew out of a radical political ideology, and Sanger believed it would contribute to the liberation of women, especially working-class women. She did not argue for the open distribution of contraceptive information and devices in order simply to expand the realm of personal freedom. She believed that limitation of family size was the key to freeing women from the physical dangers of continual childbearing and to giving them the opportunity to become active outside the home.

Nineteenth-century feminists often opposed the use of contraception, believing that birth control would make women more vulnerable to male sexual aggressiveness. In this way of thinking, abstinence and self-control became a form of sexual liberation because women rejected male desires.

Contraceptive devices and literature were illegal in most states for years after Sanger began her crusade. They remained a delicate subject until birth control pills became widely available in the 1960s; the Catholic Church prohibits their use today. Feminists point out that the burden of contraception still falls on women. Nonetheless, Margaret Sanger succeeded in opening the *public* debate that led to eventual legalization. Although she was forced to flee the country in 1914 for distributing literature about family limitation, she returned a few years later and founded the National Birth Control League, an organization supported by doctors, social workers, and other professionals from the mainstream of American life.

There were ironies on the road to victory. Those who believed contraception to be against the laws of God and nature were eventually marginalized and often dismissed as prudes or fanatics. But Margaret Sanger's morally earnest campaign to uplift the downtrodden through family planning moved onto a siderail of history, too. The birth control campaign succeeded when it became a movement by and for the middle class; family planning grew acceptable not because of some new passion for the plight of the poor, but because it was indispensable to middle-class families balancing growing expenses, careers for both parents, sexual pleasure within marriage, the allures of consumer life, and the difficulties of raising children in urban or suburban nuclear families.

THE DOCUMENTS

The debate over birth control takes us into a variety of important issues. These include the right of individuals to privacy versus the right of a community to regulate moral behavior; the ethnic makeup of the American people; the ability of women to control their own physical destinies by limiting family size; and the feeling of many people that opportunities for advancement were shrinking and that small families were one way to keep the American dream alive.

As you read these documents, ask yourself about the connections between personal issues and political ones. Was birth control merely a matter of individual choice, or was it about power, wealth, opportunity, and similar issues? How did gender, ethnicity, and social class figure in the debate?

Introduction to Document 1

Margaret Sanger burst on the scene in 1914 with the publication of the first issue of *The Woman Rebel.* The tabloid described itself as "A Monthly Paper of Militant Thought." Testimony to the editor's radical political commitments was the reprinting of the Preamble to the Charter of the Industrial Workers of the World: "The working class and the employing class have nothing in common. . . . Between these two classes a struggle must go on until the workers of the world organize as a class, take possession of the earth and the machinery of production, and abolish the wage system. . . . It is the historic mission of the working class to do away with capitalism." Making contraceptive devices available, then, was part of a much larger project of radical social change, embracing the liberation of women and of the working class. In the very first issue, Sanger explained herself in an essay entitled "Why the Woman Rebel?" Later on the same page, in an article entitled "The

Margaret Sanger with her son Stuart in 1904. (Sophia Smith Collection, Smith College, Northampton, MA)

Prevention of Conception," Sanger made it clear that she would defy the laws against distributing birth control information.

DOCUMENT 1 *From* The Woman Rebel

Margaret Sanger

Why the Woman Rebel?

Because I believe that deep down in woman's nature lies slumbering the spirit of revolt.

Because I believe that woman is enslaved by the world machine, by sex conventions, by motherhood and its present necessary child-rearing, by wage slavery, by middle-class morality, by customs, laws and superstitions.

Because I believe that woman's freedom depends upon awakening that spirit of revolt within her against these things which enslave her.

Because I believe that these things which enslave woman must be fought openly, fearlessly, consciously.

Because I believe she must consciously disturb and destroy and be fearless in its accomplishment.

Because I believe in freedom, created through individual action.

Because I believe in the offspring of the immigrant, the great majority of whom make up the unorganized working class to-day. . . .

Because I believe that through the efforts of the industrial revolution will woman's freedom emerge.

Because I believe that not until wage slavery is abolished can either woman's or man's freedom be fully attained.

Introduction to Document 2

The second issue of *The Woman Rebel* announced that the United States postmaster had declared the newspaper unmailable under section 211 of the United States Criminal Code. Copies of that issue and subsequent ones were confiscated. The man most responsible for marshaling support for such legislation, then seeing it enforced, was Anthony Comstock, who had a long career during the late nineteenth and early twentieth centuries as a crusader against vice. Violation of the law carried a maximum five-year prison sentence or a $5,000 fine. Comstock founded the Society for the Suppression of Vice in 1873, which drew financial backing from some of America's wealthiest men, and he was appointed special agent of the U.S. Post Office Department. In an interview with Mary Alden Hopkins, who wrote a series of articles on the birth control controversy for *Harper's Weekly* in Spring 1915, Comstock justified the laws against publicizing contraception:

DOCUMENT 2 *Anthony Comstock's Views on Birth Control*

The three great crime-breeders of today are intemperance, gambling, and evil reading. The devil is sowing his seed for his future harvest. There is no foe so much to be dreaded as that which perverts the imagination, sears the conscience, hardens the heart, and damns the soul.

If you allow the devil to decorate the Chamber of Imagery in your heart with licentious and sensual things, you will find that he has practically thrown a noose about your neck and will forever after exert himself to draw you away from the "Lamb of God which taketh away sins of the world." You have practically put rope on memory's bell and placed the other end of the rope in the devil's hands, and, though you may will out your mind, the memory of some vile story or picture that you may have looked upon, be assured that even in your most solitary moments the devil will ring memory's bell and call up the hateful thing to turn your thoughts away from God and undermine all aspirations for holy things.

. . . My experience leads me to the conviction that once these matters enter through the eye and ear into the chamber of imagery in the heart of the child, nothing but the grace of God can ever erase or blot it out. . . .

Brethren, "let us not be weary in well doing, for in due season we shall reap if we faint not." Raise over each of your heads the banner of the Lord Jesus Christ. Look to Him as your Commander and Leader. . . .

"Do the laws never thwart the doctor's work; in cases, for instance, where pregnancy would endanger a woman's life?"

Mr. Comstock replied with the strongest emphasis:

"A doctor is allowed to bring on an abortion in cases where a woman's life is in danger. And is there anything in these laws that forbids a doctor's telling a woman that preg-

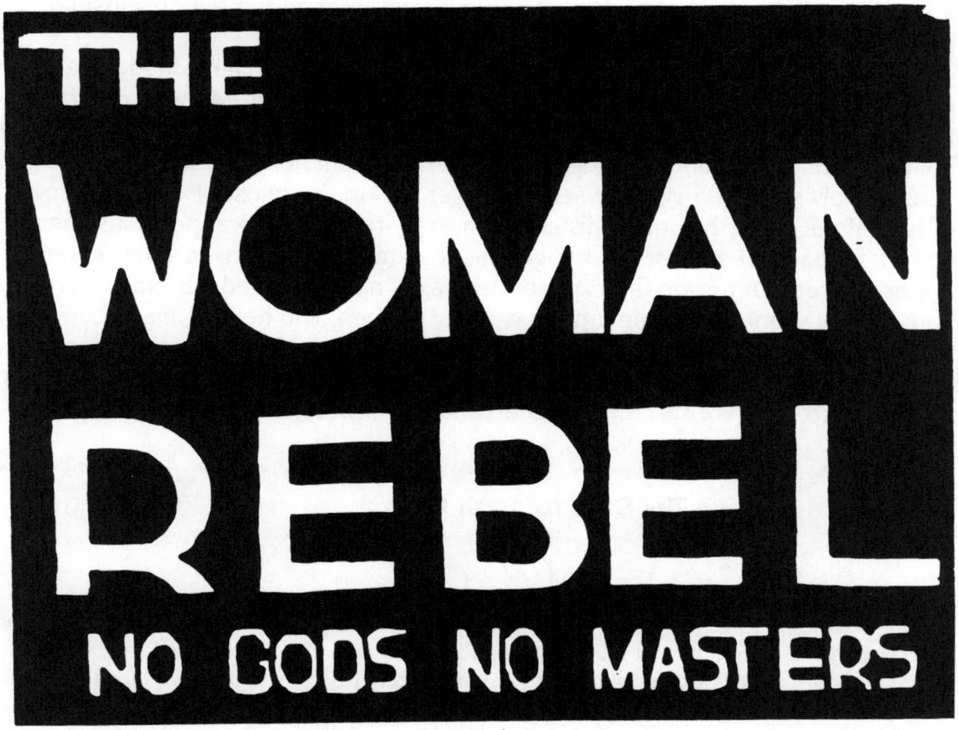

The masthead of Margaret Sanger's radical newspaper.

nancy must not occur for a certain length of time or at all? Can they not use self-control? Or must they sink to the level of the beast?"

"But," I protested, . . . "if the parents lack that self-control the punishment falls upon the child."

"It does not," replied Mr. Comstock. "The punishment falls upon the parents. When a man and woman marry they are responsible for their children. You can't reform a family in any of these superficial ways. You have to go deep down into their minds and souls. The prevention of conception would work the greatest demoralization. God has set certain natural barriers. If you turn loose the passions and break down the fear you bring worse disaster than the war. It would debase sacred things, break down the health of women and disseminate a greater curse than the plagues and diseases of Europe."

Introduction to Document 3

Just before she was to be arrested for distributing contraceptive information, Sanger fled America for England, where she spent her time among European radicals, reformers, and family-planning professionals. But a few months later, her husband, William Sanger, was arrested by Anthony Comstock in New York City, then imprisoned for purveying lewd materials (he gave a copy of his wife's little book, *Family Limitation,* to one of Comstock's undercover agents). Margaret Sanger returned to New York, where she knew she would face trial. She was eventually acquitted, but

in the meantime, she lectured, wrote essays, and opened the nation's first family-planning clinic.

Document 3 comes from the introduction to a book Sanger edited called *The Case for Birth Control* (1917). In this brief essay, she summarized much of the argument she had been promulgating since returning to the United States. While her commitment to poor and working women is still evident here, her style had changed considerably since *The Woman Rebel.* Sanger was in the midst of concentrating all of her efforts on birth control, distancing herself from the radical positions she had staked out earlier. Perhaps she thought this was the practical way to achieve her one important goal. Or maybe the experience of exile had tempered her ardor. Certainly Sanger now spent more time among wealthy women who helped finance both her trial defense and the birth control movement. Note how the tone of this essay differs from that of *The Woman Rebel;* the radical passion is now obscured somewhat by the Progressive Era style of fact-laden analysis in the name of practical reform.

DOCUMENT 3 ***From* The Case for Birth Control**

Margaret Sanger

Before I attempt to refute the arguments against birth control, I should like to tell you something of the conditions I met with as a trained nurse and of the experience that convinced me of its necessity and led me to jeopardize my liberty in order to place this information in the hands of the women who need it.

My first clear impression of life was that large families and poverty went hand in hand. I was born and brought up in a glass factory town in the western part of New York State. I was one of eleven children—so I had some personal experience of the struggles and hardships a large family endures.

When I was seventeen years old my mother died from overwork and the strain of too frequent child bearing. I was left to care for the younger children and share the burdens of all. When I was old enough I entered a hospital to take up the profession of nursing.

In the hospital I found that seventy-five percent of the diseases of men and women are the result of ignorance of their sex functions. I found that every department of life was open to investigation and discussion except that shaded valley of sex. . . .

So great was the ignorance of the women and girls I met concerning their own bodies that I decided to specialize in woman's diseases and took up gynecological and obstetrical nursing.

A few years of this work brought me to a shocking discovery—that knowledge of the methods of controlling birth was accessible to the women of wealth while the working women were deliberately kept in ignorance of this knowledge!

I found that the women of the working class were as anxious to obtain this knowledge as their sisters of wealth, but that they were told that there are laws on the statute books against imparting it to them. And the medical profession was most religious in obeying these laws when the patient was a poor woman.

For the laws against imparting this knowledge force these women into the hands of the filthiest midwives and the quack abortionists—unless they bear unwanted children—with the consequence that the deaths from abortions are almost wholly among the working-class women.

No other country in the world has so large a number of abortions nor so large a number of deaths of women resulting therefrom as the United States of America. Our law makers close their virtuous eyes. A most conservative estimate is that there are 250,000 abortions performed in this country every year.

How often have I stood at the bedside of a woman in childbirth and seen the tears flowing in gladness and heard the sigh of "Thank God" when told that her child was born dead! What can man know of the fear and dread of unwanted pregnancy? What can man know of the agony of carrying beneath one's heart a little life which tells the mother every instant that it cannot survive? Even were it born alive the chances are that it would perish within a year.

Do you know that three hundred thousand babies under one year of age die in the United States every year from poverty and neglect, while six hundred thousand parents remain in ignorance of how to prevent three hundred thousand more babies from coming into the world the next year to die of poverty and neglect?

I found from records concerning women of the underworld that eighty-five percent of them come from parents averaging nine living children. And that fifty percent of these are mentally defective.

We know, too, that among mentally defective parents the birth rate is four times as great as that of the normal parent. Is this not cause for alarm? Is it not time for our physicians, social workers and scientists to face this array of facts and stop quibbling about woman's morality? I say this because it is these same people who raise objection to birth control on the ground that it *may* cause women to be immoral.

Solicitude for woman's morals has ever been the cloak Authority has worn in its age-long conspiracy to keep woman in bondage. . . .

Is woman's health not to be considered? Is she to remain a producing machine? Is she to have time to think, to study, to care for herself? Man cannot travel to his goal alone. And until woman has knowledge to control birth she cannot get the time to think and develop. Until she has the time to think, neither the suffrage question nor the social question nor the labor question will interest her, and she will remain the drudge that she is and her husband the slave that he is just as long as they continue to supply the market with cheap labor. . . .

Am I to be classed as immoral because I advocate small families for the working class while Mr. [Theodore] Roosevelt can go up and down the length of the land shouting and urging these women to have large families and is neither arrested nor molested but considered by all society as highly moral?

But I ask you which is the more moral—to urge this class of women to have only those children she desires and can care for, or to delude her into breeding thoughtlessly. Which is America's definition of morality?

You will agree with me that a woman should be free.

Yet no adult woman who is ignorant of the means to prevent conception can call herself free.

No woman can call herself free who cannot choose the time to be a mother or not as she sees fit. This should be woman's first demand. . . .

Introduction to Document 4

Michael P. Dowling was a member of the Society of Jesus, and as a Jesuit, he articulated a position familiar to the Catholic Church and its followers. Document 4 is excerpted from his pamphlet *Race-Suicide* (1915), which couched arguments against birth control in the language of duty, self-sacrifice, religious obligation, and family values. Whereas Sanger argued for the right of women and the poor to make individual decisions about contraception, Dowling appealed to the good of the community, which he asserted took precedence over personal needs or desires. Note that the phrase "race-suicide" was highly charged. These could become code words meaning that the white race—and therefore civilization itself—was in jeopardy.

DOCUMENT 4 *From* Race-Suicide

Michael P. Dowling

. . . At three different epochs in human history, the Creator made known His will. Just as to the first man, He said: "Increase and multiply," so a thousand years later to the second father of humanity, to Noe [Noah], and to his sons, He spoke a pregnant word, and it bore the same burden, "Increase and multiply and fill the earth"; for so we read in Genesis. Still another thousand years rolled on and the same blessing was repeated, for the word of the Lord came to Abraham: "Fear not; I am thy protector and thy reward exceeding great." The patriarch answered: "What wilt Thou give me; behold, I have no child." Then God brought him forth out of the tent, saying: "Look up to the heavens and number the stars, if thou canst; so shall thy seed be." The reward of Abraham's faith is paternity.

And after that, from Abraham to the last of the prophets, text on text and example after example, confirm the doctrine that children are the blessing of marriage, no matter what the new gospel of selfishness may proclaim. In the Old Testament curse alternates with blessing: "He who is blessed shall be a father, the cursed shall stand alone." If it is said to the just, "Thy wife shall be like a fruitful vine," to the wicked man and the sinner comes the sentence: "In a single generation his name will be blotted out." . . . .

God said: "Increase and multiply"; man says: "Let us fear to increase and multiply; the earth might become too narrow; the fewer there are to share the good things of life the more there will be for each. . . .

. . . Malthus, in his book entitled "Principles of Population As It Affects the Future Improvement of Society," gave the impetus to the movement. He held that the population of the earth increases more rapidly than the means of subsistence, because population advances almost in a geometrical proportion, as two, four, eight, sixteen, while the fertility of the land increases approximately only in an arithmetical proportion, as one, two, three, four, five and so on. Hence, the continually increasing population must eventually exceed the capacity of the earth to supply food. . . .

But the facts are against the theory that the earth is inadequate to support the growth of population. The United States, even with the wasteful methods of farming now in vogue, could feed hundreds of millions. Under different conditions even little Ireland would be capable of supporting three times its present population. Brazil, Peru, Mexico have room for teeming millions within their borders. Portions of the dark continent of Africa were once densely peopled; so was Asia Minor; and they might become garden spots of the earth once more. There is still plenty of elbow room on the globe. . . .

God makes no mistakes, and for every soul He creates and infuses into a mortal body, He furnishes what is needful for its well-being. History may be reviewed in vain for an instance of any considerable country wherein poverty and want can be fairly traced to the increase of the number of mouths beyond the power of the accompanying hands to fill them. In most cases they can, more properly, be attributed to unjust laws, misgovernment, destructive warfare, decadent commerce, a disregard of the Divine law, vice and crime. . . .

Can it be possible that wealth is the natural enemy of infancy and childhood? And is the instinct of reproduction weaker in the privileged classes, the spirit of self-denial more pronounced? Is it not rather that large families are looked upon with disdain as a plebeian institution, entailing too much sacrifice, debarring the mother from many pleasures she is unwilling to forgo? Is it not because every new birth requires the expense account to be overhauled, several chapters of travel to be blotted out, transfers to be made to the side of the nurse and the governess, balls and parties and receptions to be given up?

People sin today by excessive prudence. If families are growing smaller, it is not because there is less natural fruitfulness; if the births do not keep pace with the deaths, it is not because men and women are attracted by a life of voluntary chastity or are deeply in love with the Evangelical Counsels; but because the designs of God are frustrated by the prosperous classes; and that a period of moral decay is begun. It is because the warm stream of infant life is kept back. It is because instead of guardian spirits parents become the exterminating angels of their offspring. In rigorous simplicity of language, it must be said that too many are engaged in a systematic and deliberate opposition to God, in as far as they can thwart His designs and impede His providential dispensations. Practically, they say to Him: "Let us make a compact; in the law You place before me are certain things which I accept; but the consequences I decline; I will embrace pleasure but reject duty; what agrees with my inclinations and the ideas and decrees of contemporary society, I will obey, but I will carry no cross, make no sacrifices." . . .

We must get back to Christian principles and mold Christian lives, till the humblest sees that life is not all for pleasure, self-ease and enjoyment, that duty and conscience must play a great part and march in the vanguard of true progress.

Introduction to Document 5

In its series of articles by Mary Alden Hopkins on contraception, *Harper's Weekly* published the thoughts of several doctors. While we cannot assume that the following statements represented the opinions of the entire medical profession, they do give a sense of the arguments offered by physicians. The only doctor who spoke unequivocally in favor of contraception to *Harper's* (the first interview here) was Dutch, not American, and a woman, not a man.

DOCUMENT 5 *Physicians' Statements About Birth Control*

Dr. Aletta Jacobs

Very often the mothers in this hospital did not want the babies that were born to them. They were actually glad when the babies were born dead. No, they were not bad women—just ordinary, every-day women. Sometimes it was because they already had enough babies, sometimes because the previous baby was still so little, sometimes because they were so very poor, sometimes for other reasons. But whether the reason was a good one or a bad one, the fact remained that the baby was not desired. Now it seemed to me that a baby should not be a punishment. If a woman does not want a child it is better both for her and for the child that she should not have one.

Moreover, I noticed that many of the sickly children born in the hospital were children that had been born against their mothers' wishes. The mothers' state of mind during pregnancy had affected the baby. Besides this there were many children with very bad heredity—mental sickness and physical sickness in the parents, which would very probably appear in the offspring. These children should never have been born.

Sometimes a mother would say to me. "No wonder the baby is puny and sick. Why, when this child was conceived my husband was as drunk as could be." For reasons like these I decided that mothers should be taught how to prevent conception.

Children should be born not oftener than once in three years. For the first year the mother should devote herself to caring for the child. The second year she should have to get back her vitality and strength. The third year she may again become pregnant.

Dr. Howard A. Kelly

Let me enunciate these fundamental principles which must control my judgment:

1. That the medical profession must continually deal with the moral aspects of a case, and today our great loss is the unwillingness of some doctors to have anything to do with morals, because they have had no moral training and have done no moral thinking. . . .
2. That in times of great decadence we are not to try to accommodate ourselves to decadent conditions by temporizing expedients, but by the highest moral remedies and by righteousness—*at whatever cost*. Practically I find that the people who came to me having used various mechanical means of preventing conception, have lost something in their married life which ought to have been more precious to them than life itself. All meddling with the sexual relation to secure facultative sterility degrades the wife to the level of a prostitute.

Therefore there is no right or decent way of controlling births but by total abstinence. . . .

Dr. John W. Williams

I make it a rule to refuse to discuss the question with perfectly healthy, normal persons. On the other hand, if I find that a wife is steadily losing ground as the result of rapidly recurring pregnancies, I send for the husband and say that in my opinion as a medical man it is highly advisable that his wife should not have another child for a specified length of time. In that event I advise him as to the most efficacious method of preventing conception; as I consider it more intelligent to prevent a breakdown than to treat it after it has occurred.

I give the same advice after certain serious obstetrical complications, and in women who are suffering from tuberculosis, certain forms of heart disease and other serious chronic disease, in which I know by experience that another pregnancy will subject the patient to serious danger. In such cases I consider it more conservative to give such advice than to be obliged to perform a therapeutic abortion after pregnancy has occurred.

Finally, in the presence of certain chronic diseases, which to my mind will always complicate the occurrence of pregnancy, and in which therapeutic abortion is necessary to relieve immediate danger to the patient's life, I hold that it is justifiable to render the patient sterile by operative means. . . .

In other words, I do not believe that the physician is justified in giving advice as to the prevention of conception solely for the convenience of his patients, but should limit it entirely to those cases which present a definite medical indication for the temporary or permanent avoidance of pregnancy. To my mind any other course practically places the physician in the same class as the professional abortionist.

Dr. R. C. Brannon

I beg to take issue with you, in regard to your propaganda for the control of births, as being subversive to religion, morals, and health of both men and women. This, when you come to sift the matter down to its final analysis, is what is shortening the lives of the human race, making weaklings in mind and body the children of strong men, and wrecking the nerves and bodies of women who ought to be the proud and happy mothers of a dozen healthy children.

The prevention of large families has caused an increase in insanity, tuberculosis, Bright's disease, diabetes and cancer, and I am willing to submit the proposition to the judgment of three of the greatest gynecologists in the United States. I have stepped in the breach and used my influence to curtail the bad practice of limiting the size of the family, as my experience as a physician of twenty years' practise has proven to my mind that it is the most hurtful, and wicked sin that was ever indulged in since the world was created. It is a swift and sure road to the grave.

Man was put here to multiply and replenish the earth. How terrible has been the punishment of many a rich man I have known—perhaps poor and struggling in early life, who decided he would escape the responsibility of rearing a large family, with the result when a little past life's prime his wife died of a cancer, and what enjoyment did either of them derive from his fortune of more than a half million dollars; filthy lucre begotten by miserly habits, that rightly should have been expended unselfishly in bringing up a large family that would have blessed the earth.

Introduction to Document 6

By the end of the decade, Sanger's arguments had fully taken on the Progressive Era style—fact-laden, scientific, and analytical. Her speech here comes from a 1920 forum on birth control held in New York City. Note that there is no apparent fear of arrest here; the debate over birth control had become part of open public discourse. She shared the stage with Winter Russell, a prominent New York City attorney.

DOCUMENT 6 *Debate Between Margaret Sanger and Winter Russell*

Winter Russell

. . . I am a member of the bar of the State of New York. I trust that I have due regard and respect for the statutes, the constitution, and the laws of this great city, state and nation. But I hold them as the veriest trash when they come up against the laws of Nature. The laws of Nature cannot be revised. They cannot be repealed. There is no power in this whole universe that can change these laws, and you have to deal with that.

That means you can't get pleasure without paying for it. Nature is inexorable in bringing about her retribution. It does not need any balance book. You can never embezzle. You can't cheat. You can't get away from it. . . .

You must pay at last for your own debt. Those are the laws. Now we recognize it in physics. Energy cannot be annihilated. Birth control says "yes." You shall pay the price. You can annihilate that energy and drink from the cup of pleasure, but you don't take the responsibility—the duty and the care. . . . It is along the lines of the people who are alchemists, who think they can turn the baser metals into gold. It is an age-long dream. It is a belief that has been held from the beginning of time. That thing cannot be done. That is the law of life—of God—that you have to pay. . . .

Margaret Sanger

. . . The only weapon that women have and the most uncivilized weapon that they have to use if they will not submit to having children every year or every year and a half, the weapon they use is abortion. We know how detrimental abortion is to the physical side as well as to the psychic side of the woman's life, and yet there are in this nation, because of these generalities and opinions that are here before us, that are stopping the tide of progress, we have more than one million women with abortions performed on them each year. . . . We speak of the rights of the unborn. I say that it is time to speak of those who are already born. . . .

We find in the South that where children come according to Nature, every year and one-half, that as soon as they are able, they are shuffled and hustled on in to take the place and compete with their father in the factories. That is the place that society has for the children of the poor. We find in other States, too, where it is only a question of a few years later that also the children, as soon as they are able to take their place in industry, are pushed out of the home, not because the mothers of these children are not just as anxious to see them in the universities and colleges, but because of the pitiless earnings that she must have to support those who are coming behind them.

Most of us know this. We know something about the actual conditions of life as it is among us. In some of the factories of Lowell and Fall River, Mass., it was found that of the children who work and toil there, under ten years of age, that 85% of them come from families of eight—their mothers have given birth to eight children—and we find in the South very much the same thing, excepting a higher percentage of 90 to 93% of the children there.

That is not the only thing. We have a condition not only as these that I have related, but we have a condition again that is more disastrous to the race than child labor or infant mortality, and that is the transmission of venereal disease to the race that is to come. . . . We know, too, that out of this terrible scourge of venereal disease that we have 90% of the insanity in this country, due to syphilis. Anyone who is dealing with fundamentals would know that these people should use means to protect themselves against having children. They should absolutely in due regard to themselves, to their children and to the race, not allow a child to be born while that disease is running riot in the system, and then we have that terrible consequence which is insanity. . . .

We have here 400,000 feeble-minded people in the United States, that any authority on this subject would say to you, "Not one of them should have been born." They never should have been born and sometimes these parents are perfectly normal, and yet this taint has gone through the blood and has left this perfectly normal, physical person, who arrives at the adult age with all its physical functions, and yet it has the mentality of a child eight years of age. The feeble-minded man or woman is of no use to itself or society, and it would be better if we were living in a real civilization that they should not have been born. Only 40,000 of this 400,000 are entered in institutions, and the others are living among us, producing and reproducing their progeny and providing abundant material and opportunity for the continuance of charities and other institutions for ages and generations more to come.

We found also in one institution—a so-called reformatory where they take the girls of the underworld—prostitutes—in Geneva, Ill., they find that 50% of these girls coming into the underworld—the prostitutes—was of this cause, that she belonged to the feeble-minded, and again we find that 89% of these came from large families. . . .

Also our child labor—we make laws in Washington against child labor, hoping we will wipe that out of existence. For fifty years they have been trying to wipe child labor off the books in the United States, but they have not succeeded and they will never succeed until they establish birth control clinics in those districts where these women are, where they put in birth control clinics, like they have in Holland—in every industrial section in the United States where women can come to trained nurses and physicians and get from them scientific information whereby they may control birth. . . .

Now, Mr. Russell has said some things that are very interesting to me, He tells us that we cannot have pleasure without pain. It is a man who is speaking. (*Laughter and applause.*) It is very peculiar that Nature only works on the one side of the human family when it comes to that law. She applies all the pain to the woman. It is absurd—a perfectly absurd argument in the face of rational intelligence (*applause*) to talk about marriage being for one purpose. . . .

Winter Russell

May I say at the outset that I did not say we could not have pleasure without pain. I said we could not have pleasure without paying for it and the man has to pay. (*Laughter.*) . . . Mrs. Sanger sees poverty, she sees misery and she sees unwanted children. To be sure, there are many thousands of these homes where, sad to say, the children are unwanted, but they have made this devout prayer to God, I believe, for children, and they have gotten them. They have gotten what I believe to be the greatest wealth and treasure of the Kingdom of Heaven that there is on the face of the earth, and when they get that, they have to pay for it. They have to pay and take the responsibility. . . .

I am going to give you a picture of the block on which I was born and brought up, that I have watched for 30 years. Thirty years ago I began to watch the block. There were 17 families, 34 people at the start; 34 people who were successful, they believe, in this little town of 3,500 people. It had a fine high school, a State Normal School—one of the foremost in the State. It had a Boys' School known nationally, if not internationally, and they were 34 people in 17 homes. . . .

Out of . . . 17 families, 9 are extinct. Nine are dead and gone. They have passed away. Is that race suicide? Out of the 8 who remain, out of the 34 people, out of these 8 families, there are 26 grandchildren. My father's family produced 12 of the 26. Out of 33 of the families, there are 14 grandchildren if you except mine. I think I am an exception. There is race suicide. Don't tell me that that is one exceptional block. I can duplicate that block on every street in that town except one blessed community, Little Canada. They were not Americans. They were vulgar. They were poor. They want big families, but from these poor families in Little Canada, there have come the French Canadians. From them come doctors, lawyers, and teachers, and they are inheriting the town. There is race suicide.

I can duplicate that block in practically every American city in this country. I can duplicate that block in every apartment house on the west side. . . . America is dying today—the America that we know.

Margaret Sanger

. . . I am speaking for the millions of women who are crushed with over child-bearing, whose lives are broken and who have become drudges in the family today. I am speaking for the mothers and the individual here and there does not concern me in the least. They may be an exception, but I know there are millions and millions of women who are married, who are just as self-controlled as anyone Mr. Russell can show us, who are living in a terror of pregnancy, and they have men who are just as good to them. Men are not all beasts. . . .

Birth control will free the mother from the trap of pregnancy. It will save the child from that procession of coffins, as well as from the toil of mill and factory.

Birth control will make parenthood a voluntary function instead of an accident as it is today. When motherhood and childhood is free, we then can go hand in hand with man, to remake the world, for the glorification as well as the emancipation of the human race. (*Applause.*) . . .

POSTSCRIPT

Margaret Sanger's drift toward intolerance grew more pronounced as the years passed. In 1922 she published *The Pivot of Civilization,* in which she argued that the "overfecundity" of the "degenerate classes" was responsible for poverty and crime. She used phrases like "human waste," "human weeds," the "unfit," and "dead weight" to describe the poor and the disabled; she argued that charity only encouraged overbreeding; she advocated that the state administer IQ tests to identify "degenerates" and prevent them from breeding uncontrollably. By 1932, she advocated in *The Birth Control Review* segregating or even sterilizing people deemed by the government to be genetically inferior.

Thus, birth control's gradual acceptance under the law was accompanied by a shift away from its radical beginnings. The legal barriers against transmitting contraceptive information and devices were gradually repealed, overturned, or ignored. Conservative women, even members of elite women's clubs, had generally opposed birth control because it seemed to assault motherhood, which had become both a hallowed role for women and a safeguard against male selfishness (men, after all, were still the prime breadwinners). Many women on the left also opposed birth control. They argued that the movement would not bring radical change, and some even claimed that contraceptives would only make women more vulnerable to sexual exploitation by men, who could now escape the consequences of their acts.

Still, a growing number of women insisted on having command over their own reproductive lives. In the 1920s and after, the birth control movement became thoroughly the creature of middle-class professionals: doctors, nurses, social workers, and public health administrators. Moreover, the movement grew quite bureaucratized, as activities were directed from central institutions, Margaret Sanger's American Birth Control League being prime among them. With bureaucratization and professionalization from the 1920s onward, the tone and goals of the movement changed profoundly. One result was a distinctly elitist shift in direction. When the early opponents of contraception spoke of "race suicide," they meant that "inferior" peoples—immigrants, the poor, and blacks—would outbreed and overwhelm oldstock, respectable white people. Sanger herself drifted toward that position, and by the 1920s, birth controllers often allied themselves with eugenicists.

Eugenics is the "science" of human engineering. While men like Theodore Roosevelt had argued that the "best" people—white, successful, and respectable—were breeding in numbers insufficient to keep up with more "virile" races, birth control advocates now claimed that legalization would help curb the masses' tendency to produce "retarded," "diseased" offspring. Contraceptives, in other words, might limit the "breeding" of "racially inferior" peoples. The eugenics movement had powerful supporters, and the elitist tendencies of professionalization gave birth controllers a common cause with those who wished to engineer human populations. Emblematic of the movement increasingly abandoning its working-class sympathies during the 1920s, the Sanger clinics began to keep records showing the nationality, religion, heredity, occupation, and union affiliation of patients. In her *Autobiography* (1938), Sanger even argued that the eugenics and birth control movements needed each other: "The eugenists wanted to shift the birth-control emphasis from less children for the poor to more children for the rich. We went back of that and sought first to stop the multiplication of the unfit." She no longer saw the poor as those who might be empowered to resist their oppression, but as the source of the unfit on the road to elimination.

QUESTIONS

Defining Terms

Identify in the context of the chapter each of the following:

Progressive style	Race suicide
Comstock Law of 1873	Packingtown
Jurgis Rudkis	Socialists
The Woman Rebel	Feminists
Meat Inspection Act	Antanas Kaztauskis
Louis Swift	

Probing the Sources

1. Do you think Upton Sinclair exaggerated the conditions in Packingtown? How does his account compare to the Reynolds-Neill Report? To Antanas Kaztauskis' story?
2. What religious reasons were given against the use of contraceptives? How did birth control advocates respond?
3. Why did Margaret Sanger and Upton Sinclair become involved in reform activities? Do their motives seem similar or different?
4. Outline the main arguments (both implicit and explicit) for birth control and against; for regulation of the meat packing industry and against.

Interpreting the Sources

1. What did Upton Sinclair mean when he said that he aimed at the public's heart but hit it in the stomach? How did Margaret Sanger's initial reasons for advocating birth control change over time?
2. What issues do these documents reveal about the role of government in protecting the health of citizens?
3. Do you find more similarities or differences in how Sanger and Sinclair thought about the poor? About immigrants?
4. How does the birth control debate resonate with contemporary discussions on abortion?

ADDITIONAL READING

The literature on the Progressive Era is extensive. Two classic works are Robert Wiebe, *The Search for Order* (1966), and Gabriel Kolko, *The Triumph of Conservatism* (1967). For a recent synthesis of historians' thinking, see Steven J. Diner, *A Very Different Age* (1998); for politics in the era, try Michael McGerr, *A Fierce Discontent* (2005). For background on Chicago's South Side, see Dominic Pacyga, *Polish Immigrants and Industrial Chicago* (2003). On the stockyards and Packingtown, see James R. Barrett, *Work and Community in the Jungle* (1988), and Louise Caroll Wade, *Chicago's Pride* (1988). *The Autobiography of Upton Sinclair* (1962) offers insight into the man, as do Kevin Mattson's *Upton Sinclair and the Other American Century* (2006) and Anthony Arthur's *Radical Innocent: Upton Sinclair* (2006). Related works include James Harvey Young, *Securing the Federal Food and Drug Act of 1906* (1989); Alan Dawley, *Struggles for Justice* (1991); and Elizabeth Sanders, *Roots of Reform* (1999). For the birth control movement, the best general history of sex and ideology is Estelle Friedman and John D'Emilio, *Intimate Matters* (1988). The literature on birth control is extensive; try Ellen Chesler, *Woman of Valor: Margaret Sanger and the Birth Control Movement in America* (1992); David M. Kennedy, *Birth Control in America* (1970); Andrea Tone, *Devices and Desires* (2001); and Linda Gordon, *The Moral Property of Women* (2007). Related works include Elaine Tyler May, *Great Expectations: Marriage and Divorce in Post Victorian America* (1980); Janet Farrell Brodie, *Contraception and Abortion in Nineteenth Century America* (1994); and Mary Odem, *Delinquent Daughters* (1996).

7

Selling the War

Recruitment Posters of World War I

Historical Context

If you have watched a televised sporting event—or any other program aimed at an 18 to 35 year-old age group—you have seen commercials designed to encourage young men and women to enlist in one or another of the armed services. The commercials are slick and professional; they feature attractive, well-conditioned young people and promise a better life replete with friends, adventure, and perhaps a touch of romance. They also appeal to values that Americans hold most dear. What are those values? And how do the commercials address them? These are the central questions that may be asked about such promotional campaigns, and though the values and forms of the commercials may change over the years, the ultimate object—the encouragement of enlistments—remains the same.

Take, for example, two popular marines commercials from the 1980s. The first begins with a scene from the court of King Arthur. Arthur, with his sword, Excalibur, in his hands, prepares to knight a young, handsome, physically ideal man. The knight-to-be dismounts from his powerful steed—the universal symbol in Western culture of nobility and masculine virility—and walks toward Arthur. The young man kneels, his head slightly bowed. Arthur lowers Excalibur to the man's shoulder, proclaiming him a knight. With a flash of lightning, the medieval knight is transformed into a modern marine. A voice and the on-screen message announce simply that the marines are "looking for a few good men." The second commercial centers on the process of forging and crafting a fine sword. It is filled with images of molten steel, a blacksmith forming a sword on his anvil, and an experienced craftsman finishing and polishing the sword. In the end, the sword finds its way into the hand of a marine, who demonstrates that he is trained fully in the handling of the weapon. Again a voice asserts that the marines are "looking for a few men with the mettle to be marines."

Together the two commercials drive home the point of yet another marine slogan: "The few, the proud, the Marines." But what are the values to which these commercials appeal? Patriotism? At no point is patriotism mentioned or scenes of defending the United States shown. Upward mobility? Again, not really. Although many armed-forces commercials promise technical training or the opportunity of future education, here the images of horses, swords, and knights have an anachronistic appeal. Few modern soldiers would care to go into battle mounted on a horse and armed only with a sword. Rather, these effective appeals are narcissistic. Not unlike the commercials for health spas or gymnasiums, they attempt to enlist those who believe (or would like to believe) that they are the physical elite who may join a highly selective club. The commercials traffic in self-image.

The army, the air force, and, most recently, the navy have chosen to appeal to other values. The air force officially counsels, "Aim high." The army suggests, "Be all you can be . . . and get an edge on life." The navy used to emphasize adventure with the slogan, "It's not just a job . . . it's an adventure." But beginning in 1988, its official slogan became, "You are tomorrow. . . . You are the Navy." All these slogans contain the same appeal—service in the armed forces is "a great place to start" a lucrative career. In one army commercial, a high school senior announces to his friends, while they engage in a late-night snack, that he has found a way to go to college; he will enlist in the army, and it will provide him with the opportunity to get a college education. Another army commercial shows a man and a woman meeting after a university class. To their mutual interest, they discover that the army provided them with a chance to attend college, and, of course, to meet. Here the promise of upward mobility is mixed with the promise of romance. It is important to note, however, that, once again, there are no overt appeals to patriotism or service to one's country, and, if military scenes are pictured at all, they are scenes of training, not combat.

Self-image and self-advancement—both values are important to modern American culture. A nation at war presents a different problem to armed forces recruiters. The army in a time of war might be "a great place to begin" one's career, but it may also be the place where one's life ends. Therefore, recruiters have to emphasize different values. World War I presented a series of difficult problems. Unlike World War II, there was no Pearl Harbor in World War I. The United States was not attacked, and millions of Americans—especially those with familial or emotional ties to Germany, Austria-Hungary, or Ireland—opposed the United States' entry into the war. For example, journalist H. L. Mencken openly defended Germany during the early years of the war. He ended letters to his German-American friends with "May all Englishmen roast forever in hell! A pox upon the English!" or "The Kaiser must and shall win!" And Mencken ended pro-German newspaper columns with "In Paris by Thanksgiving!" or "In Paris by Christmas!" Even people who did not cheer on the German war machine as Mencken did opposed President Woodrow Wilson's decision in April 1917 to involve the United States in the conflict. Intellectual Randolph Bourne clearly expressed his reasons for opposing America's decision to go to war. Far from being a noble struggle—"a war to end all wars," as Wilson phrased it—Bourne predicted that the war would become an imperialistic grab bag. In addition, at home it would foster the growth of governmental power, the suppression of civil liberties, and the curtailment of the free expression of ideas. War, Bourne wrote, "automatically sets in motion throughout society those irresistible forces of uniformity, for passionate cooperation with the Government in coercing into obedience the minority groups and individuals which lack the larger herd sense."

Bourne defined patriotism as "merely the emotion that fills the herd when it imagines itself engaged in mass defense or massed attack." And more than anything, he feared the mass herd instinct of people. Bourne's fear was fully justified.

Moved to a frenzied sense of anti-Germanicism, the "herd" was capable of tragic and great harm. It cried for "100 percent Americanism." It demanded that hamburger and sauerkraut be renamed liberty sandwich and liberty cabbage, that the German language and literature no longer be taught in public schools, that all things German be viewed with suspicion and disgust. Along with mindless hate came mindless violence. In Wyoming, a man who exclaimed "Hoch der Kaiser" on the day that Wilson delivered his war message was hanged, cut down while still alive, and forced to kneel and kiss the American flag. Near St. Louis, a mob attacked Robert Prager, a German-American who had actually tried to enlist in the United States Navy, bound him in an American flag, dragged him through the streets, and lynched him before a cheering crowd of five hundred "patriots." For this crime, the leaders of the mob were tried and found not guilty. After the trial, one jury member remarked, "Well, I guess nobody can say we aren't loyal now." Such episodes would lead social critic Walter Lippmann to write in his influential essay *Public Opinion* (1922) that most American citizens are "mentally children or barbarians . . . . The stream of public opinion is stopped by them in little eddies of misunderstanding, where it is discolored with prejudices and farfetched analogy."

Bourne particularly dreaded the role the government would play in creating this sense of mass conformity. "It will be coercion from above that will do the trick rather than patriotism from below," he cautioned. True to his prediction, soon after America's entry into the war, the government officially began to shape the public's attitude toward the war effort and Germany. During the first month of the war, Wilson and his military leaders organized the Committee on Public Information (CPI) and placed George Creel, a Progressive supporter of Wilson and a muckraker journalist, at the head of the agency. At first, the CPI was no crude propaganda mill. In the early months of the CPI, Creel saw his duty as providing information that enlightened Americans, not propaganda and censorship that altered or hid the truth. Like Wilson, Creel believed in the essential righteousness of the American cause, and he insisted that a mere recitation of "the facts" would be enough to convince anyone. As the war went on, however, the CPI engaged in an ever-increasing amount of propaganda. Its Four Minute Men, speakers who sang the praises of America's war effort, began to dwell more on German atrocities and less on American war aims; and upbeat films such as *Pershing's Crusaders* and *Old Colored Fighters* gave way to such hate productions as *Prussian Cur* and *The Kaiser, the Beast of Berlin.*

The American war message was spread in a number of ways. The CPI tirelessly pumped out propaganda—75 million pamphlets, 6,000 press releases, and 14,000 drawings. Some seventy-five thousand speakers stumped for their country. Certainly words—written or spoken—were important, but equally as important were the posters that supported America's war effort. Posters were employed, noted one authority on the subject, "to call for recruits . . . to request war loans, to make national policies acceptable, to spur industrial effort, to channel emotions such as courage or hate, to urge conservation of resources and inform the public of food and fuel substitutes." Often posters were used as part of some larger campaign and were augmented with personal appearances by celebrities, popular songs, press releases, flag ceremonies, and patriotic badges. Altogether, millions of posters were printed. For example, in the First Liberty Bond campaign, two million posters appeared; this number increased to five million for the Second Liberty Bond campaign and nine million for the Third Liberty Bond campaign.

To understand the impact of these posters, one has to try to imagine a time before television or even the mass use of radio. Although newspapers informed—or misinformed—the literate public, posters supplied a primary means of mass communication. Industries used posters to hawk their goods; newspapers and magazines used posters to entice readers; circuses and motion picture theaters used posters to attract spectators. Posters were everywhere—on the fences of baseball parks, on the sides of public and private buildings, and on the wooden sandwich boards that men and boys wore to advertise some product or event. When the British passenger liner the *Lusitania* was sunk by a German U-boat on May 7, 1915, the United States exploded with anger. Newspapers mourned the 128 Americans lost in the tragedy, and Wilson threatened war. But perhaps the horror and meaning of the event was most fully portrayed in a poster released by the Boston Committee of Public Safety in June of 1915. The crude but powerful image drawn by Fred Spear shows a drowning woman clothed in a gossamer gown sinking to the bottom of the sea. In her arms she maternally holds an infant. It is an almost surreal scene, both sensual and familial at the same time. "ENLIST" is the poster's simple message. The impact of the poster was felt across the nation.

Spear's poster—like the millions that would follow it—was "the weapon on the wall." Although it looked like art, in the fullest sense it was not art. Art seeks to extend the viewer's understanding of nature and life. War posters attempt to restrict the viewer's understanding. Peter Stanley, a historian of the subject, observed, "A successful poster was one capable of only one interpretation. Most of the posters . . . did not seek a dialogue: they imposed, imparted, and impelled, but did not inquire. They sought to persuade the viewer, and then to have him or her act in ways regarded as useful by the sponsors of the posters." To do this, they dealt with slogans and basic, easily comprehensible visual images. To strike the proper response, however, those images had to be part of the viewer's cultural baggage, and they had to speak to the viewer's deepest needs, desires, or fears.

A number of important illustrators and artists turned their talents to poster making during the war. In mid-April 1917, Charles Dana Gibson, creator of the Gibson Girl and the editor of the original *Life* magazine, called upon artists to enlist their creativity in the war effort. The result was the Division of Pictorial Publicity, which offered its services free of charge to the government. Such famous artists as James Montgomery Flagg, Howard Chandler Christy, and Joseph Pennell contributed to the output of the Division of Pictorial Publicity. Each artist brought to his work a distinctive style, and each labored to strike a particular chord in the viewer. James Montgomery Flagg appealed to simple, sentimental patriotism. In his most famous poster, a deadly serious Uncle Sam, modeled after himself, aims a pointed finger at the viewer and announces, "I WANT YOU for the U.S. ARMY." Another poster, which pictures a sleeping woman dressed in the Stars and Stripes, reads, "WAKE UP, AMERICA! CIVILIZATION CALLS EVERY MAN WOMAN AND CHILD!" Howard Chandler Christy employed sex to make his point. The Christy Girl exuded a wholesome sex appeal. In one navy recruitment poster, a Christy Girl exclaims, "GEE! I WISH I WERE A MAN . . . I'D JOIN THE NAVY." In another, a more sultry Christy Girl says, "I WANT YOU FOR THE NAVY." F. Strothman produced an effective Liberty Bond poster by portraying the Germans as Huns bent on destroying civilization. One of his posters shows a satan-eyed, spike-helmeted German, his bayonet and hands dripping blood, staring at the viewer over the smoldering rubble of a destroyed city. "Beat Back the HUN with LIBERTY BONDS," reads the poster.

THE DOCUMENTS:

Introduction to Document 1

George Creel began his working life as a journalist in Kansas City and Denver. But by the Progressive Era, he moved easily from crafting words as an investigative reporter to shaping sentences in the new field of advertising. He worked as a publicist for various causes, then as the United States entered World War I, he became the head of the government's efforts to sell the war. Just a few years later, in 1920, Creel wrote a memoir of his work. *How We Advertised America* was quite open in its praise of the arts of public relations. The book's subtitle gave away its author's theme: *The First Telling of the Amazing Story of the Committee on Public Information That Carried the Gospel of Americanism to Every Corner of the Globe.* Do you agree with Creel's claim that the war was as much a battle of ideas as of armies? Do you think that the Committee on Public Information was a news bureau or a propaganda agency? What does Creel say?

DOCUMENT 1 *From George Creel, How We Advertised America*

As Secretary Baker points out, the war was not fought in France alone. Back of the firing-line, back of armies and navies, back of the great supply-depots, another struggle waged with the same intensity and with almost equal significance attaching to its victories and defeats. It was the fight for the *minds* of men, for the "conquest of their convictions," and the battle-line ran through every home in every country.

It was in this recognition of Public Opinion as a major force that the Great War differed most essentially from all previous conflicts. The trial of strength was not only between massed bodies of armed men, but between opposed ideals, and moral verdicts took on all the value of military decisions. . . .

The Committee on Public Information was called into existence to make this fight for the "verdict of mankind," the voice created to plead the justice of America's cause before the jury of Public Opinion. . . . *In no degree was the Committee an agency of censorship, a machinery of concealment or repression. Its emphasis throughout was on the open and the positive. At no point did it seek or exercise authorities under those war laws that limited the freedom of speech and press.* In all things, from first to last, without halt or change, it was a plain publicity proposition, a vast enterprise in salesmanship, the world's greatest adventure in advertising.

Under the pressure of tremendous necessities an organization grew that not only reached deep into every American community, but that carried to every corner of the civilized globe the full message of America's idealism, unselfishness, and indomitable purpose. We fought prejudice, indifference, and disaffection at home and we fought ignorance and falsehood abroad. We strove for the maintenance of our own morale and the Allied morale by every process of stimulation; every possible expedient was employed to break through the barrage of lies that kept the people of the Central Powers in darkness and delusion; we sought the friendship and support of the neutral nations by continuous presentation of facts. We did not call it *propaganda,* for that word, in German hands, had come to be associated with deceit and corruption. Our effort was educational and informative throughout, for we had such confidence in our case as to feel that no other argument was needed than the simple, straightforward presentation of facts.

There was no part of the great war machinery that we did not touch, no medium of appeal that we did not employ. The printed word, the spoken word, the motion picture, the telegraph, the cable, the wireless, the poster, the sign-board—all these were used in our campaign to make our own people and all other peoples understand the causes that compelled America to take arms. All that was fine and ardent in the civilian population came at our call until more than one hundred and fifty thousand men and women were devoting highly specialized abilities to the work of the Committee, as faithful and devoted in their service as though they wore the khaki.

While America's summons was answered without question by the citizenship as a whole, it is to be remembered that during the three and a half years of our neutrality the land had been torn by a thousand divisive prejudices, stunned by the voices of anger and confusion, and muddled by the pull and haul of opposed interests. These were conditions that could not be permitted to endure. What we had to have was no mere surface unity, but a passionate belief in the justice of America's cause that should weld the people of the United States into one white-hot mass instinct with fraternity, devotion, courage, and deathless determination. The *war-will*, the will-to-win, of a democracy depends upon the degree to which each one of all the people of that democracy can concentrate and consecrate body and soul and spirit in the supreme effort of service and sacrifice. What had to be driven home was that all business was the nation's business, and every task a common task for a single purpose.

Starting with the initial conviction that the war was not the war of an administration, but the war of one hundred million people, and believing that public support was a matter of public understanding, we opened up the activities of government to the inspection of the citizenship. A voluntary censorship agreement safeguarded military information of obvious value to the enemy, but in all else the rights of the press were recognized and furthered. Trained men, at the center of effort in every one of the warmaking branches of government, reported on progress and achievement, and in no other belligerent nation was there such absolute frankness with respect to every detail of the national war endeavor.

As swiftly as might be, there were put into pamphlet form America's reasons for entering the war, the meaning of America, the nature of our free institutions, our war aims, likewise analyses of the Prussian system, the purposes of the imperial German government, and full exposure of the enemy's misrepresentations, aggressions, and barbarities. Written by the country's foremost publicists, scholars, and historians, and distinguished for their conciseness, accuracy, and simplicity, these pamphlets blew as a great wind against the clouds of confusion and misrepresentation. . . .

The Four Minute Men, an organization that will live in history by reason of its originality and effectiveness, commanded the volunteer services of 75,000 speakers, operating in 5,200 communities, and making a total of 755,190 speeches, every one having the carry of shrapnel.

With the aid of a volunteer staff of several hundred translators, the Committee kept in direct touch with the foreign-language press, supplying selected articles designed to combat ignorance and disaffection. It organized and directed twenty-three societies and leagues designed to appeal to certain classes and particular foreign-language groups, each body carrying a specific message of unity and enthusiasm to its section of America's adopted peoples.

It planned war exhibits for the state fairs of the United States, also a great series of interallied war expositions that brought home to our millions the exact nature of the struggle that was being waged in France. In Chicago alone two million people attended in two weeks, and in nineteen cities the receipts aggregated $1,432,261.36.

The Committee mobilized the advertising forces of the country—press, periodical, car, and outdoor—for the patriotic campaign that gave millions of dollars worth of free space to the national service.

It assembled the artists of America on a volunteer basis for the production of posters, window-cards, and similar material of pictorial publicity for the use of various government departments and patriotic societies. A total of 1,438 drawings was used.

It issued an official daily newspaper, serving every department of government, with a circulation of one hundred thousand copies a day. For official use only, its value was such that private citizens ignored the supposedly prohibitive subscription price, subscribing to the amount of $77,622.58.

It organized a bureau of information for all persons who sought direction in volunteer war-work, in acquiring knowledge of any administrative activities, or in approaching business dealings with the government. In the ten months of its existence it gave answers to eighty-six thousand requests for specific information.

It gathered together the leading novelists, essayists, and publicists of the land, and these men and women, without payment, worked faithfully in the production of brilliant, comprehensive articles that went to the press as syndicate features.

One division paid particular attention to the rural press and the plate-matter service. Others looked after the specialized needs of the labor press, the religious press, and the periodical press. The Division of Women's War Work prepared and issued the information of peculiar interest to the women of the United States, also aiding in the task of organizing and directing.

Through the medium of the motion picture, America's war progress, as well as the meanings and purposes of democracy, were carried to every community in the United States and to every corner of the world. "Pershing's Crusaders," "America's Answer," and "Under Four Flags" were types of feature films by which we drove home America's resources and determinations, while other pictures, showing our social and industrial life, made our free institutions vivid to foreign peoples. . . .

Turning away from the United States to the world beyond our borders, a triple task confronted us. First, there were the peoples of the Allied nations that had to be fired by the magnitude of the American effort and the certainty of speedy and effective aid, in order to relieve the war-weariness of the civilian population and also to fan the enthusiasm of the firing-line to new flame. Second, we had to carry the truth to the neutral nations, poisoned by German lies; and third, we had to get the ideals of America, the determination of America, and the invincibility of America into the Central Powers.

Unlike other countries, the United States had no subsidized press service with which to meet the emergency. As a matter of bitter fact, we had few direct news contacts of our own with the outside world, owing to a scheme of contracts that turned the foreign distribution of American news over to European agencies. The volume of information that went out from our shores was small, and, what was worse, it was concerned only with the violent and unusual in our national life. It was news of strikes and lynchings, riots, murder cases, graft prosecutions, sensational divorces, the bizarre extravagance of "sudden millionaires." Naturally enough, we were looked upon as a race of dollar-mad materialists, a land of cruel monopolists, our real rulers the corporations and our democracy a "fake."

Looking about for some way in which to remedy this evil situation, we saw the government wireless lying comparatively idle, and through the close and generous co-operation of the navy we worked out a news machinery that soon began to pour a steady stream of American information into international channels of communication. Opening an office in every capital of the world outside the Central Powers, a daily service went out from Tuckerton to the Eiffel Tower for use in France and then for relay to our representatives in Berne, Rome, Madrid, and Lisbon. From Tuckerton the service flashed to England, and from England there was relay to Holland, the Scandinavian countries, and

Russia. We went into Mexico by cable and land wires; from Darien we sent a service in Spanish to Central and South-American countries for distribution by our representatives; the Orient was served by telegraph from New York to San Diego, and by wireless leaps to Cavite and Shanghai. From Shanghai the news went to Tokio and Peking, and from Peking on to Vladivostok for Siberia. Australia, India, Egypt, and the Balkans were also reached, completing the world chain. . . .

Introduction to Document 2

The following posters proved effective during World War I. They managed to create a world without complexity, a world that was two-dimensional. By stereotyping Germans, women, and their fellow Americans, the artists were able to pique emotions and bend reality. What appeals did they make? What fears were aroused? What values are embedded in these images?

Remember, war poster art is political in that it attempts to arouse a civic response. The challenge of such visual documents is the act of interpretation. Each poster can be "read." For example, Germans in American World War I posters are often portrayed as faceless or apelike, giving rise to the visual impression that they represent a subhuman enemy. As another example, the eyes of the central figure in the posters can also be read. What do the eyes say to each viewer? Do they seek to elevate or denigrate, challenge or flirt with the viewer? Eyes that look up often increase the viewer's estimation of the subject, and ennoble the cause that is being advanced. Eyes that look directly at the viewer are often meant to challenge. To read the posters intelligently, you have to examine the small as well as the large details and constantly ask yourself, "What response is this meant to arouse?" Finally, since the posters are reprinted here in black and white, try to imagine what colors were used in the originals, for color is also meaningful. Some colors, like primary red and black, are threatening and foreboding; others, like green, light blue, and silver, are uplifting.

DOCUMENT 2 *The Posters*

Poster by James Montgomery Flagg. (National Archives)

Poster by Howard Chandler Christy. (National Archives)

Poster by Howard Chandler Christy. (National Archives)

Poster by F. Strothmann. (National Archives)

(National Archives)

Poster by James Montgomery Flagg. (National Archives)

Poster by James Montgomery Flagg. (National Archives)

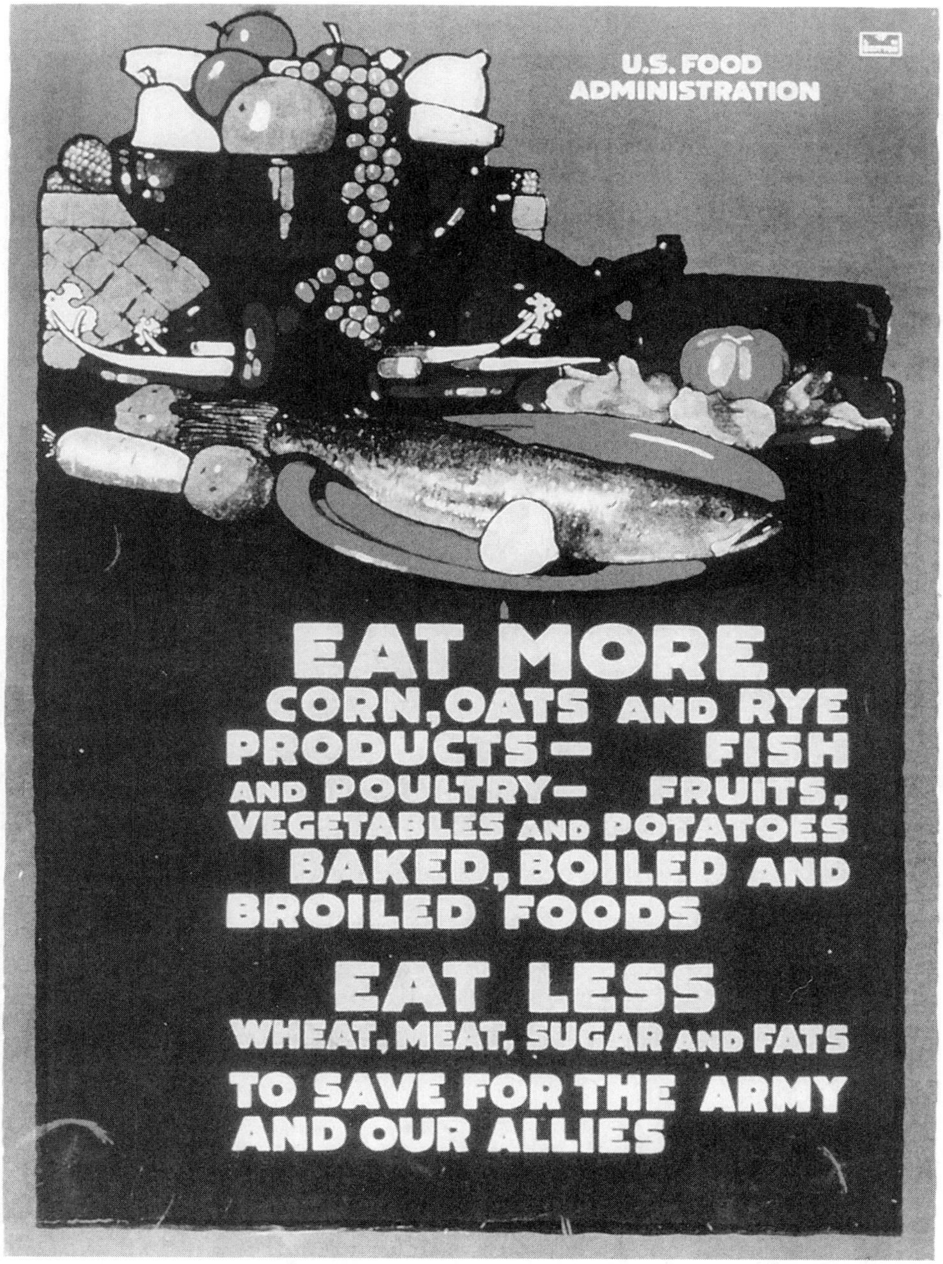

(National Archives)

(National Archives)

Poster by Sidney H. Riesenberg, Library of Congress, Prints and Photographs Division WWI Posters, [LC-USZC4-9856].

Poster by J. Paul Verrees. Library of Congress, Prints and Photographs Division, WWI Posters, [LC-USZ62-76848].

Poster by Haskell Coffin. (National Archives)

QUESTIONS

Defining Terms

Identify in the context of the chapter each of the following:

patriotism	"Be all you can be"
"100 percent Americanism"	George Creel
CPI	Fred Spear
the Gibson Girl	Liberty Bonds
Public Opinion	"GEE! I WISH I WERE A MAN"

Probing the Sources

1. What are the core values to which the posters speak? How do they compare to recruitment efforts that you have seen?
2. How are women portrayed in the posters? How are Germans portrayed in the posters?
3. What did the CPI do?
4. Why did America fight?

Interpreting the Sources

1. What advantages do visual appeals have over written appeals?
2. What similarities are there between the posters and such provocative writings as *The Jungle* and *How the Other Half Lives?*
3. How do you feel about the use of propaganda in a democracy?
4. Do you think advertising is a source of knowledge or deception? Give examples from your own experience.
5. How does World War I advertising differ from today's advertising for the military?

ADDITIONAL READING

See Joseph Darracott and Belinda Loftus, *First World War Posters* (1972); Philipp Fehl and Patricia Fenix, *World War I Propaganda Posters* (1969); Maurice Richards, *Posters of the First World War* (1969); and E. McNight Kauffer, *The Art of the Poster* (1924). On film, see Leslie DeBauche, *Reel Patriotism* (1997). David M. Kennedy, *Over Here: The First World War and American Society* (1980), explores the impact of the war on American society. Opposition to the war is discussed in H. C. Peterson and Gilbert C. Fite, *Opponents of War,* 1917–1918 (1957); William Preston, Jr., *Aliens and Dissenters: Federal Suppression of Radicals,* 1903–1933 (1953); and Frances R. Early, *A World Without War* (1997). Other works on the war include James Joll, *The Origins of the First World War* (1992); Thomas Knock, *To End All Wars: Woodrow Wilson and the Quest for a New World Order* (1992); and Ellis Hawley, *The Great War and the Search for Modern Order* (1992). On the history of advertising, see T. J. Jackson Lears, *Fables of Abundance* (1995); Roland Marchand, *Advertising the American Dream* (1986); and Stuart Ewen, *Captains of Consciousness* (1976).

8

Science on Trial

TENNESSEE VERSUS JOHN THOMAS SCOPES

HISTORICAL CONTEXT

During the 1920s, America was in many ways divided into two nations, one urban and one rural. Economic dynamism reigned in the cities. Business, particularly consumer industries, flourished. Urban Americans purchased cars and radios, vacuum cleaners, and other electrical appliances as never before. In rural America, however, there was no pronounced prosperity. Low prices for rural commodities stretched the financial resources of millions of farmers and took their toll on the small towns that depended on the business of farmers. Electrical lines had still not reached much of rural America, which remained as isolated as it had been in the nineteenth century. But more than economics divided urban and rural life. While many urban Americans reconciled their religious beliefs with scientific advancements in biology and geology, large numbers of rural Americans held to a strict Fundamentalist interpretation of the Bible. They insisted that the Rock of Ages was much younger than such scientists as Charles Darwin claimed. To be sure, Fundamentalism was not restricted just to rural America. But cultural and religious conservatism combined with economic stasis made the urban-rural division seem very wide.

Adherence to "that old-time religion" in small, rural Dayton, Tennessee, led to the decade's greatest showdown between the values of rural and urban America. Dayton lived in the shadow of urban prosperity. To its southwest, Chattanooga served as the hub of the region, attracting northern investment capital and surplus population. As for Dayton—the "other Dayton," people called it, referring to the bigger Dayton, Ohio—it enjoyed only modest, fitful growth and prosperity. To be sure, some citizens saw hopeful signs of a better future for Dayton. Most of its major streets were paved; a few automobiles navigated those streets; trains and buses made regular stops; and the tax rate was one of the lowest in the state. And Dayton was the county seat for a large farming community. But with all this, the town's business section was small and the town's prospects for the future were not great. To most outsiders, Dayton seemed—and largely was—a quiet, sleepy southern town where little changed but the seasons. Commenting on the lack of social experimentation in the town, historian Ray Ginger noted:

> Whiskey had been banned by local option since 1903. Dayton had no gamblers and no abandoned women—unless one chooses to think that all of its women had been

> abandoned. They did not smoke cigarettes, wear cosmetics, or bob their hair. They never attended trials. No woman had ever served on a jury in the county. The women's clubs stayed out of civic affairs. That was men's business. White men. The town's two hundred Negroes observed the law and stayed in their prescribed place.

In 1925, it was not just Dayton that seemed backward; the entire state of Tennessee appeared behind the times to liberal-thinking, religiously progressive Americans. In that year, John Washington Butler, a decent, respected forty-nine-year-old farmer who had been elected to the Tennessee legislature the previous year, introduced a bill to make it illegal to teach the theory of evolution in the state's public schools. Butler's crusade was fired by passionate intensity, and those who opposed the bill were paralyzed by a lack of conviction. The faculty of the University of Tennessee maintained a deafening public silence, although in private many opposed the bill. The officials of the state's department of education were similarly mute, and the leaders of the Tennessee Academy of Science joined the silent chorus. As for the legislators themselves, they sat back and hoped that the entire embarrassment would go away. Describing the curious legislative process, William Manchester wrote:

> The House of Representatives—believing, its leaders claimed, that the Senate would kill it—passed the bill overwhelmingly. The Senate, thinking the governor would veto it, did likewise, and the governor, to the astonishment of that body, signed it on March 21, 1925. Butler's theology . . . had been translated into law by the irresponsible canons of political chance.

The passage of the antievolution law did not end the public debate over the issue. In fact, it did just the opposite. In Dayton, George Rappelyea, a native of New York who was the manager of the Cumberland Coal and Iron Company of Dayton, expressed the opinion that the law was bunk. Down at Robinson's Drug Store, several natives of Dayton disagreed. Both sides discussed the merits of their case, but getting nowhere, they called in an outside opinion. Rappelyea summoned John Scopes, the local biology teacher, from the tennis courts and asked his opinion of the law. Scopes remarked that it would be impossible to teach biology without breaking the new law and that he had already broken the antievolution law in the classroom. The discussion—the heat it generated and the passions it inflamed—gave Rappelyea an idea. Why not have a test case for the law in Dayton? Scopes could teach a class on evolution, the police could arrest him for breaking the Butler law, and a trial could be staged in Dayton. It would put Dayton on the map and be good for local business at the same time. The trial will be "a big sensation," Rappelyea said. "Why not bring a lot of doctors and preachers here? Let's get H. G. Wells and a lot of big fellows." At first Scopes declined the offer. The thought of having an arrest and conviction on his record did not sit well with him. But eventually, he relented. "It was just a drugstore discussion that got past control," he later remarked.

H. G. Wells did not travel to Dayton, but a lot of other "big fellows" did. William Jennings Bryan quickly offered his services to the Christian defenders of the Butler law. Bryan was nearing the end of a long, industrious, and distinguished, if a bit disappointing, career. In 1896, he had exploded on the national scene with his "Cross of Gold" speech at the Democratic Presidential Convention in Chicago.

Claiming to represent the toiling masses—the American producers—Bryan had generated support for the free silver cause and won the Democratic nomination for the presidency. A great orator and a passionate believer, Bryan threw his heart and soul into the campaign, but he lost the election. Only thirty-six years of age in 1896, he was young enough to try again. In 1900, he was nominated by the Democratic party to run once more for the presidency; again he lost. In 1908, the Democrats again chose Bryan to carry their standard, and for the third time he lost. After the 1908 election, he became increasingly involved in social crusades. In 1909, he announced his conversion to the prohibitionist cause and joined the fight for a national prohibition amendment. For a brief time before World War I, he served as Woodrow Wilson's secretary of state. After the Great War ended, Bryan became an antievolutionist. With the same passion with which he had once embraced free silver, he latched onto the idea that Darwinism was the root of the world's troubles. People had to shun liberal modernism and return to the teachings of the Bible. "You believe in the ages of rocks: I believe in the Rock of Ages," he told his opponents. For Bryan it was a simple issue of good and evil. He did not see—or refused to acknowledge—the complexity of the issue. As Ray Ginger observed, "His perception changed every shade of gray into a dismal black or a dazzling white. He saw no object as it really was. The people were an Absolute Good, the gold power was an Absolute Evil, as was Darwinism." Consistent with this view, in 1924 Bryan drafted the text of an antievolution resolution passed by the Florida legislature, which made it illegal "to teach as true Darwinism or any other hypothesis that links man in blood relationship to any other form of life." Thus, when the call came from Dayton to stand witness for his beliefs, Bryan hurried to Tennessee to defend the Butler law.

Clarence Seward Darrow ventured to Dayton to defend Scopes and the Darwinian view of evolution. Like Bryan, Darrow was a product of rural America. He had been born and reared in Kinsman, Ohio, the son of a man who had attended Meadville Theological Seminary, preached for a short time, and then undergone a crisis in faith from which he emerged an agnostic. Clarence Darrow was clearly his father's son. He was skeptical of philosophical and religious absolutes, and he placed more faith in scientific rationalism than the untested teachings of the would-be guardians of public and private morality. Although he loved rural America—and held dear the independent rural ideal—he had made his reputation in Chicago and is most closely identified with urban society. And like the urban society of his day, Darrow presented a mass of contradictions: He started his career as a railroad lawyer but became the country's leading defense attorney; he passionately defended the rights of blacks but scoffed at equal rights for women; and he lived well and spent lavishly but harbored a belief in socialism. Yet of one thing he was certain: The state should defend, not restrict, a person's right of self-expression, and free speech was the foremost example of self-expression. It was this principle that drew Darrow from Chicago to Dayton. Scopes had the right to teach the theory of evolution even if the Tennessee legislature said he could not.

Joining Darrow and Bryan in Dayton were journalists, preachers, and an odd assortment of curious spectators. There was the white-haired, wild-eyed T. T. Martin, field secretary for the Anti-Evolution League, who urged all who would listen to "Drive Hell out of the high Schools." There was a party of Seventh Day Adventists who drove around Dayton in an automobile that proudly displayed a sign

Clarence Darrow and William Jennings Bryan at the Scopes trial. (AP Images)

proclaiming, "Get Right with God." There were the many mountaineers who came into Dayton to see what all the commotion was about. One of the mountain people explained his position and that of many of Butler's defenders: "Well, brother, my way's the safest; just believe what the Bible says and quit trying to figure out something different."

Of all the reporters who traveled to Dayton, H. L. Mencken was the most notorious. He was the consummate cynic. A newspaperman from Baltimore, he was opposed to all that was smug and confident in the American character. He attacked American puritanism, decried the country's worship of business, and lambasted conventional morality and religion. For Mencken, Bryan represented the worst side of the American character. Bryan's confident refusal to subject any of his beliefs to questioning and his willingness to use the power of the federal government to make other people live by his rules repelled Mencken. And in the *Scopes* trial, Mencken saw repressive Bryanism writ large. On the day the trial began, Mencken wrote:

> The trial of the infidel Scopes . . . will greatly resemble, I suspect, the trial of a prohibition agent accused of mayhem in Union Hill, New Jersey. That is to say, it will be conducted with the most austere regard for the highest principles of jurisprudence. Judge and jury will go to extreme lengths to assure the prisoner the last and least of his rights. He will be protected in his person and feelings by the full military and naval power of the State of Tennessee. No one will be permitted to pull his nose, to pray publicly for his condemnation or even to make a face at him. But all the same he will

be bumped off inevitably when the time comes, and to the applause of all right-thinking men.

The *Scopes* trial dominated the public's interests. Indeed, in the still, intense summer heat of Dayton, Bryan and Darrow defended two different worldviews, one rooted in America's rural past and the other based on the tenets of scientific modernism. For Americans in 1925, the *Scopes* trial symbolized their country in transition. When Darrow and Bryan engaged in their famous confrontation, two worlds collided.

THE DOCUMENTS

Introduction to Documents 1 through 3

Document 1 is an excerpt from George William Hunter's *Civic Biology,* the textbook, published in 1914, that John Scopes used to teach evolution. Note the racial and class attitudes in this "scientific" text.

Document 2, Clarence Darrow's examination of William Jennings Bryan in the case of *Tennessee v. John Thomas Scopes,* has been edited to highlight the conflict between the two men. Most of the normal legal objections and rulings have been removed. Because of the extreme heat of the day, the examination was moved outdoors, and it lasted all day.

Five days after the end of the Scopes trial, Bryan suffered a cerebral hemorrhage and died. Document 3, H. L. Mencken's "In Memoriam: W. J. B.," was published in the Baltimore *Evening Sun* on July 27, 1925, the day after Bryan's death. Mencken rewrote the piece for the October 1925 issue of the *American Mercury.* Document 3 is selected from the second version. It, more than any other document, suggests the level of hostility between urban and rural America.

DOCUMENT 1 *From Civic Biology*

George William Hunter

The Doctrine of Evolution.—We have now learned that animal forms may be arranged so as to begin with very simple one-celled forms and culminate with a group which contains man himself. This arrangement is called the *evolutionary series*. Evolution means change, and these groups are believed by scientists to represent stages in complexity of development of life on the earth. Geology teaches that millions of years ago, life upon the earth was very simple, and that gradually more and more complex forms of life appeared, as the rocks formed latest in time show the most highly developed forms of animal life. The great English scientist, Charles Darwin, from this and other evidence, explained the theory of evolution. This is the belief that simple forms of life on the earth slowly and gradually gave rise to those more complex and that thus ultimately the most complex forms came into existence. . . .

Evolution of Man.—Undoubtedly there once lived upon the earth races of men who were much lower in their mental organization than the present inhabitants. If we follow the early history of man upon the earth, we find that at first he must have been little better than one of the lower animals. He was a nomad, wandering from place to place, feeding upon whatever living things he could kill with his hands. Gradually he must have learned to use weapons, and thus kill his prey, first using rough stone implements for this purpose. As man became more civilized, implements of bronze and of iron were used. About this time the subjugation and domestication of animals began to take place. Man then began to cultivate the fields, and to have a fixed place of abode other than a cave. The beginnings of civilization were long ago, but even to-day the earth is not entirely civilized.

The Races of Man.—At the present time there exist upon the earth five races or varieties of man, each very different from the other in instincts, social customs, and, to an extent, in structure. These are the Ethiopian or negro type, originating in Africa; the Malay or brown race, from the islands of the Pacific; the American Indian; the Mongolian or yellow race, including the natives of China, Japan, and the Eskimos; and finally, the highest type of all, the Caucasians, represented by the civilized white inhabitants of Europe and America. . . .

Improvement of Man.—If the stock of domesticated animals can be improved, it is not unfair to ask if the health and vigor of the future generations of men and women on the earth might not be improved by applying to them the laws of selection. This improvement of the future race has a number of factors in which we as individuals may play a part. . . .

Eugenics.—When people marry there are certain things that the individual as well as the race should demand. The most important of these is freedom from germ diseases which might be handed down to the offspring. Tuberculosis, syphilis, that dread disease which cripples and kills hundreds of thousands of innocent children, epilepsy, and feeble-mindedness are handicaps which it is not only unfair but criminal to hand down to posterity. The science of being well born is called *eugenics*.

The Jukes.—Studies have been made on a number of different families in this country, in which mental and moral defects were present in one or both of the original parents. The "Jukes" family is a notorious example. The first mother is known as "Margaret, the mother of criminals." In seventy-five years the progeny of the original generation has cost the state of New York over a million and a quarter of dollars, besides giving over to the care of prisons and asylums considerably over a hundred feeble-minded, alcoholic, immoral, or criminal persons. Another case recently studied is the "Kallikak" family. This family has been traced back to the War of the Revolution, when a young soldier named Martin Kallikak seduced a feeble-minded girl. She had a feeble-minded son from whom there have been to the present time 480 descendants. Of these 33 were sexually immoral, 24 confirmed drunkards, 3 epileptics, and 143 *feeble-minded.* The man who started this terrible line of immorality and feeble-mindedness later married a normal Quaker girl. From this couple a line of 496 descendants have come, with *no* cases of feeble-mindedness. The evidence and the moral speak for themselves!

Parasitism and Its Cost of Society.—Hundreds of families such as those described above exist to-day, spreading disease, immorality, and crime to all parts of this country. The cost to society of such families is very severe. Just as certain animals or plants become parasitic on other plants or animals, these families have become parasitic on society. They not only do harm to others by corrupting, stealing, or spreading disease, but they are actually protected and cared for by the state out of public money. Largely for them the poorhouse and the asylum exist. They take from society, but they give nothing in return. They are true parasites.

The Remedy.—If such people were lower animals, we would probably kill them off to prevent them from spreading. Humanity will not allow this, but we do have the remedy of separating the sexes in asylums or other places and in various ways preventing intermarriage and the possibilities of perpetuating such a low and degenerate race. Remedies of this sort have been tried successfully in Europe and are now meeting with success in this country.

Blood Tells.—Eugenics show us, on the other hand, in a study of the families in which are brilliant men and women, the fact that the descendants have received the *good* inheritance from their ancestors. The following, taken from Davenport's *Heredity in Relation to Eugenics*, illustrates how one family has been famous in American History.

In 1667 Elizabeth Tuttle, "of strong will, and of extreme intellectual vigor, married Richard Edwards of Hartford, Conn., a man of high repute and great erudition. From their one son descended another son, Jonathan Edwards, a noted divine, and president of Princeton College. Of the descendants of Jonathan Edwards much has been written; a brief catalogue must suffice: Jonathan Edwards, Jr., president of Union College; Timothy Dwight, president of Yale; Sereno Edwards Dwight, president of Hamilton College; Theodore Dwight Woolsey, for twenty-five years president of Yale College; Sarah, wife of Tapping Reeve, founder of Litchfield Law School, herself no mean lawyer; Daniel Tyler, a general in the Civil War and founder of the iron industries of North Alabama; Timothy Dwight, second, president of Yale University from 1886 to 1898; Theodore William Dwight, founder and for thirty-three years warden of Columbia Law School; Henrietta Frances, wife of Eli Whitney, inventor of the cotton gin, who, burning the midnight oil by the side of her ingenious husband, helped him to his enduring fame; Merrill Edwards Gates, president of Amherst College; Catherine Maria Sedgwick of graceful pen; Charles Sedgwick Minot, authority on biology and embryology in the Harvard Medical School; Edith Kermit Carow, wife of Theodore Roosevelt; and Winston Churchill, the author of *Coniston* and other well-known novels."

Of the daughters of Elizabeth Tuttle distinguished descendants also came: Robert Treat Paine, signer of the Declaration of Independence; Chief Justice of the United States Morrison R. Waite; Ulysses S. Grant and Grover Cleveland, presidents of the United States. These and many other prominent men and women can trace the characters which enabled them to occupy the positions of culture and learning they held back to Elizabeth Tuttle.

Euthenics.—Euthenics, the betterment of the environment, is another important factor in the production of a stronger race. The strongest physical characteristics may be ruined if the surroundings are unwholesome and unsanitary. The slums of a city are "at once symptom, effect, and cause of evil." A city which allows foul tenements, narrow streets, and crowded slums to exist will spend too much for police protection, for charity, and for hospitals.

Every improvement in surroundings means improvement of the chances of survival of the race. In the spring of 1913 the health department and street-cleaning department of the city of New York cooperated to bring about a "clean up" of all filth, dirt, and rubbish from the houses, streets, and vacant lots in that city. During the summer of 1913 the health department reported a smaller percentage of deaths of babies than ever before. We must draw our own conclusions. Clean streets and houses, clean milk and pure water, sanitary housing, and careful medical inspection all do their part in maintaining a low rate of illness and death, thus reacting upon the health of the citizens of the future. . . .

DOCUMENT 2 ***Darrow versus Bryan***

Mr. Hays [defense attorney]: The defense desires to call Mr. Bryan as a witness. . . .

Darrow: You have given considerable study to the Bible, haven't you, Mr. Bryan?

Bryan: Yes, sir, I have.

D: Well, we all know you have; we are not going to dispute that at all. But you have written and published articles almost weekly, and sometimes have made interpretations of various things?

B: I would not say interpretations, Mr. Darrow, but comments on the lesson.
D: If you comment to any extent, these comments have been interpretations.
B: I presume that my discussion might be to some extent interpretations, but they have not been primarily intended as interpretations. . . .
D: Do you claim that everything in the Bible should be literally interpreted?
B: I believe everything in the Bible should be accepted as it is given there; some of the Bible is given illustratively. For instance: "Ye are the salt of the earth." I would not insist that man was actually salt, or that he had flesh of salt, but it is used in the sense of salt as saving God's people.
D: But when you read that Jonah swallowed the whale—or that the whale swallowed Jonah—excuse me, please—how do you literally interpret that?
B: When I read that a big fish swallowed Jonah—it does not say whale.
D: Doesn't it? Are you sure?
B: That is my recollection of it. A big fish, and I believe it, and I believe in a God who can make a whale and can make a man and make both do what He pleases . . .
B: Yes, sir. Let me add: one miracle is just as easy to believe as another.
D: It is for you.
B: It is for me.
D: Just as hard?
B: It is hard to believe for you, but easy for me. A miracle is a thing performed beyond what man can perform. When you get beyond what man can do, you get within the realm of miracles; and it is just as easy to believe in the miracle of Jonah as any other miracle in the Bible.
D: Perfectly easy to believe that Jonah swallowed the whale?
B: If the Bible said so; the Bible doesn't make as extreme statements as evolutionists do. . . .
D: Do you believe Joshua made the sun stand still?
B: I believe what the Bible says. I suppose you mean that the earth stood still?
D: I don't know. I am talking about the Bible now.
B: I accept the Bible absolutely.
D: The Bible says Joshua commanded the sun to stand still for the purpose of lengthening the day, doesn't it; and you believe it?
B: I do.
D: Do you believe at that time the sun went around the earth?
B: No, I believe that the earth goes around the sun.
D: Do you believe that the men who wrote it thought that the day could be lengthened or that the sun could be stopped?
B: I don't know what they thought.
D: You don't know?
B: I think they wrote the fact without expressing their own thoughts. . . .
D: Have you an opinion as to whether—whoever wrote the book, I believe Joshua, the Book of Joshua, thought the sun went around the earth or not? . . .
B: I believe that the Bible is inspired, with an inspired author. Whether one who wrote as he was directed to write understood the things he was writing about, I don't know.
D: Whoever inspired it? Do you think whoever inspired it believed that the sun went around the earth?
B: I believe it was inspired by the Almighty, and He may have used language that could be understood at that time.

D: Was—
B: Instead of using language that could not be understood until Darrow was born. (*Laughter and applause*)
D: So, it might have been subject to construction, might it not? . . .
B: He was using language at that time the people understood. . . .
D: You believe the story of the flood to be a literal interpretation?
B: Yes, sir.
D: When was that flood?
B: I would not attempt to fix the date. The date is fixed, as suggested this morning.
D: About 4004 B.C.?
B: That has been the estimate of a man that is accepted today. I would not say it is accurate.
D: That estimate is printed in the Bible?
B: Everybody knows, at least, I think most of the people know, that was the estimate given.
D: But what do you think the Bible itself says? Don't you know how it was arrived at?
B: I never made a calculation.
D: A calculation from what?
B: I could not say.
D: From the generations of man?
B: I would not want to say that.
D: What do you think?
B: I do not think about things I don't think about.
D: Do you think about things you do think about?
B: Well, sometimes. (*Laughter*)
Policeman: Let us have order. . . .
B: These gentlemen have not had much chance—they did not come here to try this case. They came here to try revealed religion. I am here to defend it, and they can ask me any question they please.
The Court: All right. (*Applause*)
D: Great applause from the bleachers.
B: From those whom you call "yokels."
D: I have never called them yokels.
B: That is the ignorance of Tennessee, the bigotry.
D: You mean who are applauding you? (*Applause*)
B: Those are the people whom you insult.
D: You insult every man of science and learning in the world because he does not believe in your fool religion.
The Court: I will not stand for that. . . .
D: How long ago was the flood, Mr. Bryan?
B: Let me see Usher's calculation about it?
D: Surely. (*He hands a Bible to the witness*)
B: It is given here as 2348 years B.C.
D: Well, 2348 years B.C. You believe that all the living things that were not contained in the ark were destroyed?
B: I think the fish may have lived.
D: Outside of the fish?
B: I cannot say.
D: You cannot say?
B: No, except that just as it is, I have no proof to the contrary.

D: I am asking you whether you believe?

B: I do.

D: That all living things outside of the fish were destroyed?

B: What I say about the fish is merely a matter of humor.

D: I understand. . . .

B: I accept that, as the Bible gives it, and I have never found any reason for denying, disputing, or rejecting it. . . .

D: Don't you know there are any number of civilizations that are traced back to more than 5000 years?

B: I know we have people who trace things back according to the number of ciphers they have. But I am not satisfied they are accurate.

D: You are not satisfied there is any civilization that can be traced back 5000 years?

B: I would not want to say there is because I have no evidence of it that is satisfactory.

D: Would you say there is not?

B: Well, so far as I know, but when the scientists differ, from 24,000,000 to 306,000,000 in their opinion, as to how long ago life came here, I want them nearer, to come nearer together before they demand of me to give up my belief in the Bible. . . .

D: Let me make this definite. You believe that every civilization on the earth and every living thing, except possibly fishes, that came out of the ark were wiped out by the flood?

B: At that time.

D: At that time. And then, whatever human beings, including all the tribes, that inhabited the world, and have inhabited the world, and who run their pedigree straight back, and all the animals, have come onto the earth since the flood?

B: Yes.

D: Within 4200 years. Do you know a scientific man on the face of the earth that believes any such thing?

B: I cannot say, but I know some scientific men who dispute entirely the antiquity of man as testified to by other scientific men.

D: Oh, that does not answer the question. Do you know of a single scientific man on the face of the earth that believes any such thing as you stated, about the antiquity of man?

B: I don't think I have ever asked one the direct question.

D: Quite important, isn't it?

B: Well, I don't know as it is.

D: It might not be?

B: If I had nothing else to do except speculate on what our remote ancestors were and what our remote descendants may be—but I have been more interested in Christians living right now, to make it much more important than speculation on either the past or the future.

D: You have never had any interest in the age of the various races and people and civilization and animals that exist upon the earth today? Is that right?

B: I have never felt a great deal of interest in the effort that has been made to dispute the Bible by the speculations of men, or the investigations of men. . . .

D: . . . Now, I ask you if you know if it was interesting enough, or important enough for you to try to find out about how old these ancient civilizations were?

B: No; I have not made a study of it.

D: Don't you know that the ancient civilizations of China are 6000 or 7000 years old, at the very least?

B: No; they would not run back beyond the creation, according to the Bible, 6000 years.

D: You don't know how old they are, is that right?

B: I don't know how old they are, but probably you do. I think you would give the preference to anybody who opposed the Bible, and I give the preference to the Bible.

D: I see. Well, you are welcome to your opinion. Have you any idea how old the Egyptian civilization is?

B: No.

D: Do you know of any record in the world, outside of the story of the Bible, which conforms to any statement that it is 4200 years ago or thereabouts that all life was wiped off the face of the earth?

B: I think they have found records. . . .

D: Mr. Bryan, don't you know that there are many old religions that describe the flood?

B: No, I don't know.

D: You know there are others besides the Jewish?

B: I don't know whether there are records of any other religion which refer to this flood.

D: Don't you ever examine religion so far as to know that?

B: Outside of the Bible?

D: Yes.

B: No; I have not examined to know that, generally.

D: You have never examined any other religions?

B: Yes, sir.

D: Have you ever read anything about the origins of religions?

B: Not a great deal.

D: You have never examined any other religion?

B: Yes, sir.

D: And you don't know whether any other religion ever gave a similar account of the destruction of the earth by the flood?

B: The Christian religion has satisfied me, and I have never felt it necessary to look up some competing religions. . . .

D: Mr. Bryan, am I the first man you ever heard of who has been interested in the age of human societies and primitive man?

B: You are the first man I ever heard speak of the number of people at those different periods.

D: Where have you lived all your life?

B: Not near you. (*Laughter and applause*)

D: Nor near anybody of learning?

B: Oh, don't assume you know it all.

D: Do you know there are thousands of books in our libraries on all those subjects I have been asking you about?

B: I couldn't say, but I will take your word for it.

D: Did you ever read a book on primitive man? Like Tyler's *Primitive Culture*, or Boas, or any of the great authorities?

B: I don't think I ever read the ones you have mentioned.

D: Have you read any?

B: Well, I have read a little from time to time. But I didn't pursue it, because I didn't know I was to be called as a witness.

D: You have never in all your life made any attempt to find out about the other peoples of the earth—how old their civilizations are—how long they had existed on earth, have you?

B: No, sir; I have been so well satisfied with the Christian religion that I have spent no time trying to find arguments against it. . . .

Stewart: I want to interpose another object. What is the purpose of this examination?

B: The purpose is to cast ridicule on everybody who believes in the Bible, and I am perfectly willing that the world shall know that these gentlemen have no other purpose than ridiculing every Christian who believes in the Bible.

D: We have the purpose of preventing bigots and ignoramuses from controlling the education of the United States and you know it, and that is all.

B: I am glad to bring out that statement. I want the world to know that this evidence is not for the view Mr. Darrow and his associates have filed affidavits here stating, the purpose of which, I understand, is to show that the Bible story is not true.

Malone: Mr. Bryan seems anxious to get some evidence in the record that would tend to show that those affidavits are not true.

B: I am not trying to get anything into the record. I am simply trying to protect the Word of God against the greatest atheist or agnostic in the United States. (*Prolonged applause*) I want the papers to know I am not afraid to get on the stand in front of him and let him do his worst. I want the world to know. (*Prolonged applause*)

D: I wish I could get a picture of these clackers. . . .

D: Mr. Bryan, do you believe that the first woman was Eve?

B: Yes.

D: Do you believe she was literally made out of Adam's rib?

B: I do.

D: Did you ever discover where Cain got his wife?

B: No, sir; I leave the agnostics to hunt for her.

D: You have never found out?

B: I have never tried to find out.

D: You have never tried to find out?

B: No.

D: The Bible says he got one, doesn't it? Were there other people on the earth at that time?

B: I cannot say.

D: You cannot say. Did that ever enter your consideration?

B: Never bothered me.

D: There were no others recorded, but Cain got a wife.

B: That is what the Bible says.

D: Where she came from you do not know. All right. Does the statement, "The morning and the evening were the first day," and "The morning and the evening were the second day," mean anything to you?

B: I do not think it necessarily means a twenty-four-hour day.

D: You do not?

B: No.

D: What do you consider it to be?

B: I have not attempted to explain it. If you will take the second chapter—let me have the book. (*Examines the Bible*) The fourth verse of the second chapter says: "These are the generations of the heavens and of the earth, when they were created in the day that the Lord God made the earth and the heavens." The word "day" there in the very next chapter is used to describe a period. I do not see that there is any necessity for construing the words, "the evening and the morning," as meaning necessarily a twenty-four-hour day, "in the day when the Lord made the heaven and the earth."

D: Then, when the Bible said, for instance, "and God called the firmament heaven. And the evening and the morning were the second day," that does not necessarily mean twenty-four hours?

B: I do not think it necessarily does.

D: Do you think it does or does not?

B: I know a great many think so.

D: What do you think?

B: I do not think it does.

D: You think those were not literal days?

B: I do not think they were twenty-four-hour days.

D: What do you think about it?

B: That is my opinion—I do not know that my opinion is better on that subject than those who think it does.

D: You do not think that?

B: No. But I think it would be just as easy for the kind of God we believe in to make the earth in six days as in six years or in 6,000,000 years or in 600,000,000 years. I do not think it important whether we believe one or the other.

D: Do you think those were literal days?

B: My impression is they were periods, but I would not attempt to argue as against anybody who wanted to believe in literal days.

D: Have you any idea of the length of the periods?

B: No; I don't.

D: Do you think the sun was made on the fourth day?

B: Yes.

D: And they had evening and morning without the sun?

B: I am simply saying it is a period.

D: They had evening and morning for four periods without the sun, do you think?

B: I believe in creation as there told, and if I am not able to explain it I will accept it. Then you can explain it to suit yourself.

D: Mr. Bryan, what I want to know is, do you believe the sun was made on the fourth day?

B: I believe just as it says there.

D: Do you believe the sun was made on the fourth day?

B: Read it.

D: I am very sorry; you have read it so many times you would know, but I will read it again:

"And God said, let there be lights in the firmament of the heaven, to divide the day from the night; and let them be for signs, and for seasons, and for days, and years. And let them be for lights in the firmament of the heaven, to give light upon the earth; and it was so. And God made two great lights; the greater light to rule the day, and the lesser light to rule the night; He made the stars also. And God set them in the firmament of the heaven, to give light upon the earth, and to rule over the day and over the night, and to divide the light from the darkness; and God saw that it was good. And the evening and the morning were the fourth day."

Do you believe, whether it was a literal day or a period, the sun and the moon were not made until the fourth day?

B: I believe they were made in the order in which they were given there. . . .

D: Cannot you answer my question?

B: I have answered it. I believe that it was made on the fourth day, in the fourth day.

D: And they had the evening and the morning before that time for three days or three periods. All right, that settles it. Now, if you call those periods, they may have been a very long time. . . .

B: Your Honor, I think I can shorten this testimony. The only purpose Mr. Darrow has is to slur at the Bible, but I will answer his question. I will answer it all at once, and I have no objection in the world, I want the world to know that this man, who does not believe in a God, is trying to use a court in Tennessee—

D: I object to that.

B: (*Continuing*)—to slur at it, and while it will require time. I am willing to take it.

D: I object to your statement. I am examining you on your fool ideas that no intelligent Christian on earth believes.

The Court: Court is adjourned until tomorrow morning.

DOCUMENT 3 ***"In Memoriam: W. J. B."***

H. L. Mencken

Has it been duly marked by historians that William Jennings Bryan's last secular act on this globe of sin was to catch flies? A curious detail, and not without its sardonic overtones. He was the most sedulous fly-catcher in American history, and in many ways the most successful. His quarry, of course, was not *Musca domestica* but *Homo neandertalensis*. For forty years he tracked it with coo and bellow, up and down the rustic backways of the Republic. Wherever the flambeaux of Chautauqua smoked and guttered, and the bilge of idealism ran in the veins, and Baptist pastors dammed the brooks with the sanctified, and men gathered who were weary and heavy laden, and their wives who were full of Peruna and as fecund as the shad (*Alosa sapidissima*), there the indefatigable Jennings set up his traps and spread his bait. He knew every country town in the South and West, and he could crowd the most remote of them to suffocation by simply winding his horn. The city proletariat, transiently flustered by him in 1896, quickly penetrated his buncombe and would have no more of him; the cockney gallery jeered him at every Democratic national convention for twenty-five years. But out where the grass grows high, and the horned cattle dream away the lazy afternoons, and men still fear the powers and principalities of the air—out there between the corn-rows he held his old puissance to the end. There was no need of beaters to drive in his game. The news that he was coming was enough. For miles the flivver dust would choke the roads. And when he rose at the end of the day to discharge his Message there would be such breathless attention, such a rapt and enchanted ecstasy, such a sweet rustle of amens as the world had not known since Johann fell to Herod's ax.

There was something peculiarly fitting in the fact that his last days were spent in a one-horse Tennessee village, beating off the flies and gnats, and that death found him there. The man felt at home in such simple and Christian scenes. He liked people who sweated freely, and were not debauched by the refinements of the toilet. Making his progress up and down the Main street of little Dayton, surrounded by gaping primates from the upland valleys of the Cumberland Range, his coat laid aside, his bare arms and hairy chest shining damply, his bald head sprinkled with dust—so accoutred and on display, he was obviously happy. He liked getting up early in the morning, to the tune of cocks crowing on the dunghill. He liked the heavy, greasy victuals of the farmhouse kitchen. He liked country lawyers, country pastors, all country people. He liked country sounds and country smells.

I believe that this liking was sincere—perhaps the only sincere thing in the man. His nose showed no uneasiness when a hillman in faded overalls and hickory shirt accosted him on the street, and besought him for light upon some mystery of Holy Writ. The simian gabble of the cross-roads was not gabble to him, but wisdom of an occult and superior sort. In the presence of city folks he was palpably uneasy. Their clothes, I suspect, annoyed him, and he was suspicious of their too delicate manners. He knew all the while that they were laughing at him—if not at his baroque theology, then at least at his alpaca pantaloons. But the yokels never laughed at him. To them he was not the huntsman but the prophet, and toward the end, as he gradually forsook mundane politics for more ghostly concerns, they began to elevate him in their hierarchy. When he died he was the peer of Abraham. His old enemy, Wilson, aspiring to the same white and shining robe, came down with a thump. But Bryan made the grade. His place in Tennessee hagiography is secure. If the village barber saved any of his hair, then it is curing gall-stones down there today.

But what label will he bear in more urbane regions? One, I fear, of a far less flattering kind. Bryan lived too long, and descended too deeply into the mud, to be taken seriously hereafter by fully literate men, even of the kind who write schoolbooks. There was a scattering of sweet words in his funeral notices, but it was no more than a response to conventional sentimentality. The best verdict the most romantic editorial writer could dredge up, save in the humorless South, was to the general effect that his imbecilities were excused by his earnestness—that under his clowning, as under that of the juggler of Notre Dame, there was the zeal of a steadfast soul. But this was apology, not praise; precisely the same thing might be said of Mary Baker G. Eddy. The truth is that even Bryan's sincerity will probably yield to what is called, in other fields, definitive criticism. . . .

This talk of sincerity, I confess, fatigues me. If the fellow was sincere, then so was P. T. Barnum. The word is disgraced and degraded by such uses. He was, in fact, a charlatan, a mountebank, a zany without sense or dignity. His career brought him into contact with the first men of his time; he preferred the company of rustic ignoramuses. It was hard to believe, watching him at Dayton, that he had traveled, that he had been received in civilized societies, that he had been a high officer of state. He seemed only a poor clod like those around him, deluded by a childish theology, full of an almost pathological hatred of all learning, all human dignity, all beauty, all fine and noble things. He was a peasant come home to the barnyard. Imagine a gentleman, and you have imagined everything that he was not. What animated him from end to end of his grotesque career was simply ambition—the ambition of a common man to get his hand upon the collar of his superiors, or, failing that, to get his thumb into their eyes. He was born with a roaring voice, and it had the trick of inflaming half-wits. His whole career was devoted to raising those half-wits against their betters, that he himself might shine.

His last battle will be grossly misunderstood if it is thought of as a mere exercise in fanaticism—that is, if Bryan the Fundamentalist Pope is mistaken for one of the bucolic Fundamentalists. There was much more in it than that, as everyone knows who saw him on the field. What moved him, at bottom, was simply hatred of the city men who had laughed at him so long, and brought him at last to so tatterdemalion an estate. He lusted for revenge upon them. He yearned to lead the anthropoid rabble against them, to punish them for their execution upon him by attacking the very vitals of their civilization. He went far beyond the bounds of any merely religious frenzy, however inordinate. When he began denouncing the notion that man is a mammal even some of the hinds at Dayton were agape. And when, brought upon Clarence Darrow's cruel hook, he writhed and tossed in a very fury of malignancy, bawling against the veriest elements of sense and decency like a man frantic—when he came to that tragic climax of his striving there were snickers among the hinds as well as hosannas.

Upon that hook, in truth, Bryan committed suicide, as a legend as well as in the body. He staggered from the rustic court ready to die, and he staggered from it ready to be forgotten, save as a character in a third-rate farce, witless and in poor taste. It was plain to everyone who knew him, when he came to Dayton, that his great days were behind him—that, for all the fury of his hatred, he was now definitely an old man, and headed at last for silence. There was a vague, unpleasant manginess about his appearence; he somehow seemed dirty, though a close glance showed him as carefully shaven as an actor, and clad in immaculate linen. All the hair was gone from the dome of his head, and it had begun to fall out, too, behind his ears, in the obscene manner of Samuel Gompers. The resonance had departed from his voice; what was once a bugle blast had become reedy and quavering. Who knows that, like Demosthenes, he had a lisp? In the old days, under the magic of his eloquence, no one noticed it. But when he spoke at Dayton it was always audible.

When I first encountered him, on the sidewalk in front of the office of the rustic lawyers who were his associates in the Scopes case, the trial was yet to begin, and so he was still expansive and amiable. I had printed in the *Nation*, a week or so before, an article arguing that the Tennessee anti-evolution law, whatever its wisdom, was at least constitutional—that the yahoos of the State had a clear right to have their progeny taught whatever they chose, and kept secure from whatever knowledge violated their superstitions. The old boy professed to be delighted with the argument, and gave the gaping bystanders to understand that I was a publicist of parts. Not to be outdone, I admired the preposterous country shirt that he wore—sleeveless and with the neck cut very low. We parted in the manner of two ambassadors.

But that was the last touch of amiability that I was destined to see in Bryan. The next day the battle joined and his face became hard. By the end of the week he was simply a walking fever. Hour by hour he grew more bitter. What the Christian Scientists call malicious animal magnetism seemed to radiate from him like heat from a stove. From my place in the courtroom, standing upon a table, I looked directly down upon him, sweating horribly and pumping his palm-leaf fan. His eyes fascinated me; I watched them all day long. They were blazing points of hatred. They glittered like occult and sinister gems. Now and then they wandered to me, and I got my share, for my reports of the trial had come back to Dayton, and he had read them. It was like coming under fire.

Thus he fought his last fight, thirsting savagely for blood. All sense departed from him. He bit right and left, like a dog with rabies. He descended to demagogy so dreadful that his very associates at the trial table blushed. His one yearning was to keep his yokels heated up—to lead his forlorn mob of imbeciles against the foe. That foe, alas, refused to be alarmed. It insisted upon seeing the whole battle as a comedy. Even Darrow, who knew better, occasionally yielded to the prevailing spirit. One day he lured poor Bryan into the folly I have mentioned: his astounding argument against the notion that man is a mammal. I am glad I heard it, for otherwise I'd never believe it. There stood the man who had been thrice a candidate for the Presidency of the Republic—there he stood in the glare of the world, uttering stuff that a boy of eight would laugh at. The artful Darrow led him on: he repeated it, ranted for it, bellowed it in his cracked voice. So he was prepared for the final slaughter. He came into life a hero, a Galahad, in bright and shining armor. He was passing out a poor mountebank.

POSTSCRIPT

After nine minutes of deliberation, the jury found Scopes guilty of violating the Butler law, and the court fined him $100. The verdict was later reversed on a technical defect in the trial.

QUESTIONS

Defining Terms

Identify in the context of the chapter each of the following:

Fundamentalism	Darwinism
John Butler	George Rappelyea
John Scope	William J. Bryan
Clarence Darrow	H. L. Mencken
Civic Biology	eugenics

Probing the Sources

1. What was the purpose of Darrow's examination of Bryan? How did Darrow characterize Bryan? How did Bryan characterize Darrow?
2. Bryan was the self-proclaimed defender of rural values and Fundamentalist beliefs. H. L. Mencken opposed Bryan and those who blindly followed him. What social and class tensions boil beneath Mencken's bilious obituary of Bryan?
3. Darrow placed his faith in science, but science had its own prejudices. What class and racial prejudices were being taught under the guise of science?
4. As a representative of urban America, how did Mencken regard rural America?

Interpreting the Sources

1. What issues and tensions were highlighted by the *Scopes* trial?
2. Are any of the larger issues that were debated in the *Scopes* trial still important today? Which ones? Why? How?
3. During which periods in American history has religious Fundamentalism been particularly strong? In what ways does Fundamentalism represent a social as well as a religious movement?
4. What was at stake for men like Darrow and Bryan in the trial?

ADDITIONAL READING

Ray Ginger, *Six Days or Forever* (1958), tells the story of the *Scopes* trial in all its detail and with all its color. Also see Edward J. Larson, *Summer for the Gods: The Scopes Trial and America's Continuing Debate over Science and Religion* (1997); and Ronald L. Numbers, *Darwinism Comes to America* (1998). For the religious issues involved, see

Norman F. Furniss, *The Fundamentalist Controversy, 1918–1933* (1958). Bryan's last years are covered in Lawrence Levine, *Defender of the Faith* (1965). For an excellent biography of Bryan, see Michael Kazin, *A Godly Hero,* (2006). Clarence Darrow told his own story in *The Story of My Life* (1932). For Mencken, see William Manchester, *Disturber of the Peace* (1952), and Fred Hobson, *Mencken: A Life* (1995). Other important works on the 1920s and their legacy include, Lynn Dumenil, *The Modern Temper* (1995); Susan Smulyan, *Selling Radio* (1994); Roland Marchand, *Advertising the American Dream* (1985); Desmond King, *Making Americans* (2000); and David Goldberg, *Discontented America* (1999). For a long view of evolution, see Edward J. Lanson, *Evolution: The Remarkable History of a Scientific Theory* (2004).

9

Writing the Great Depression

Historical Context

Great literature, we like to believe, is timeless, so Shakespeare's works will endure forever. No doubt he gave voice to emotional truths that touch very diverse people. But interpretations of the meanings of Shakespeare's plays have varied widely over the years, and these interpretations have been shaped by events taking place in the interpreters' own times. Shakespeare himself was enmeshed in the social, religious, and political issues of Elizabethan England, and his plays are full of direct and indirect references to those issues. To give an example from American literary history, Herman Melville's *Moby Dick* (1851) was mostly ignored during the nineteenth century; it became acknowledged as great literature only in the 1920s, long after the author's death. Melville's work tended to be very skeptical of human perfectibility and social progress, and such skepticism resonated more for the intellectuals of the early twentieth century than for those in the nineteenth century.

Artists and writers always are influenced by the context of their times, and how their works are received depends on the historically shaped beliefs of those who behold them. This was especially true during the 1930s. Of course, the descent into economic depression that began with the stock market crash of October 1929 was felt most directly in material life. The previous decade had brought prosperity for middle- and upper-class Americans. True, the twenties were hard times for farmers and the urban poor, but a larger number of Americans than ever before had more income and could afford more consumer goods than at any time in U.S. history. With the Great Depression, however, came massive cuts in wages and employment. Per capita disposable income dropped about one-third, while the unemployment rate reached 25 percent in the early thirties. Working-class people were hit hardest, for they had few resources to fall back on, but the downward spiral of the economy tugged at almost everyone. To put it simply, most families still had the necessities of life, and even some luxuries, but most families also had less than before. More important, the number of families slipping into impoverishment grew dramatically.

Beyond the shrinkage of material resources, Americans' confidence was shaken. No one seemed to know when, how, or if the crisis would end; Franklin Roosevelt's New Deal helped some, but politicians and economists had no permanent solutions. The depression made people question the most fundamental tenets of the

American creed: that our economy and society ensured a brighter future for all, that equality of opportunity was the American way, that hard work would be rewarded, and that the American dream of prosperity still worked. How could they believe such things when the leaders and heroes of the twenties—businessmen, financiers, and great captains of wealth—seemed as confused as everyone else, when breadlines grew ever longer, and when unemployment and poverty wore the familiar faces of family members and friends?

Much of the art and literature of the era reflected these changed perceptions. It was not as if the writers and artists of the twenties had been celebrants of American culture. On the contrary, the carnage of World War I, the meanness of the Versailles treaty, the postwar era's gaudy materialism—these all alienated many talented people, making them a "lost generation" of American writers. Several exiled themselves to Paris (Ernest Hemingway and F. Scott Fitzgerald among them), but even those who stayed in the United States wrote with a bitterness born of betrayal. John Dos Passos captured his generation's loathing of the money grubbing, the spiritual emptiness, and the unseemly hedonism just behind the espousal of democratic ideals. Most writers would have agreed with H. L. Mencken that the more a man declared his own honesty, patriotism, or piety, the more likely he was to be a scoundrel or a thief. Above all, the literature of the twenties stressed the individual's need to make a separate peace with the world; each person must suffer his or her pain alone and must find his or her own joy or community, but all must know that God, human society, and money could not save them.

Ironically, the literature during the Great Depression contained less of this cynicism. In the midst of the crisis, writers and artists no longer felt so peripheral to their culture. The worship of money that characterized most of the twenties culture marginalized all who felt that the life of the mind—scholarship, artistic creation, the humanities—counted for more than mere dollars. As the Great Depression ground on, Americans' belief that millionaires were heroes worthy of emulation grew shaky. For some intellectuals, there was a strange exhilaration in others' loss of faith in the American dream. If the competitive economy had atomized people, the depression could bring them together as each others' keepers, and there is no doubt that the rediscovery of communities—of workers, regions, and racial or ethnic groups—was an important theme of the writing of the decade.

Moreover, the crisis called for new *ideas,* intellectuals' specialty. On the most functional level, this meant the channeling of university people like economists and sociologists into the government. But even novelists and painters became tied to the Roosevelt administration. The New Deal appropriated funds for agencies like the Federal Writers Project (in which the government underwrote the creation of plays, oral histories, and travel guides), the Works Progress Administration (which hired unemployed artists to paint murals on new federal buildings), and the Farm Security Administration (in which unemployed photographers—including such respected camera artists as Dorothea Lange, Walker Evans, and Ansel Adams—documented the lives of homeless families, unemployed workers, and southern tenant farmers). So a small amount of government aid and, more important, a sense of being socially useful made the Great Depression a period of great energy and excitement in the arts.

This notion of being socially useful took highly political forms. For some, the crisis intensified a hatred of modernity, including cities, factories, and all that was progressive. This tendency was exemplified by the southern agrarians, a group of fiction writers, poets, and historians who self-consciously rejected the booming growth and power of the twentieth century to extol the virtues of small-scale life on the land, more particularly in the rural South. The agrarians were fundamentally conservative and nostalgic, and certainly they were blind to the poverty and racism of the southern past. Still, theirs was a powerful critique of the aggrandizing, money-worshiping, progress-loving elements of American culture.

More commonly, artists and writers turned to the left. Many believed that capitalism, with its enormous concentrations of private wealth and power, made a few rich while it impoverished the masses, and the Great Depression certainly seemed to offer evidence. Their political and economic solutions varied widely, from New Deal reforms through socialism, communism, and anarchism. What united them, however, was their commitment to depicting common folk struggling against the system that exploited them. Much of the cynicism of the twenties was gone, for the new literature sought to be a tool of empowerment. Rather than maintaining a detached and critical distance from America, intellectuals now strove to make the arts and humanities instruments of change by depicting ordinary people in their daily struggles, sometimes being overwhelmed, and sometimes winning symbolic or real triumphs.

Poverty, exploitation, disease—the arts revealed life in all of its grimness. Indeed, the primary task of creative expression, many would have argued, was to expose human misery and to unmask the evil system that caused it. However, it was at this historical moment of crisis that glimmers of hope also appeared in literature, hope arising from a renewed faith that masses of men and women could be makers of their own destinies, that they might seize as their birthright America's unfulfilled democratic promise.

Such an environment was not congenial to "art for art's sake," the belief that creativity was pure mental work that soared above the "real world." The view was that artists and intellectuals must never again become mere aesthetes, escaping from daily life to challenge themselves only by creating beautiful, if empty, works. They had an obligation to engage the issues confronting people. One can even see this shift in the styles of artistic expression: a renewed emphasis on realism and naturalism in fiction, less stress on abstraction in painting, and, above all, a shift to the documentary style, a mode of expression that seemed to deny the presence of the artist altogether. Documentary style pretends to be artless: the camera just records what is going on; the writer merely reports what she sees. The documentary style—seemingly objective, dispassionate, and factually accurate—became very common in fiction and nonfiction and in film and photography, for it appeared to reveal human suffering in the most clear and unmediated way and by so doing, sounded an unmistakable call for reform.

"Migrant Mother," by Dorothea Lange, 1936. (Library of Congress)

Homeless family on the Road by Dorothea Lange.1938 © The Dorothea Lange Collection, Oakland Museum of California, City of Oakland. Gift of Paul S. Taylor.

Photographers working for New Deal agencies, most notably the Farm Security Administration, produced powerful images of the victims of the Great Depression. While the program provided employment for the artists, their photographs helped engender support for New Deal relief agencies.

Rural family during the depression, by Ben Shahn. (Library of Congress)

THE DOCUMENTS

Introduction to Document 1

During the Great Depression, Franklin and Eleanor Roosevelt and other members of the government received thousands of letters, some asking for assistance, others applauding the New Deal, still others condemning it. Document 1 gives a sense of the range of opinions expressed by citizens, including racist and nativist attacks on the poor, warnings that the New Deal smacked of communism, and declarations that, if something more was not done soon, revolution was inevitable. But above all, there were pleas for help from the poor.

DOCUMENT 1 **Americans Write to Their Leaders**

ElKader Iowa Sep the 11 1934

Mr. FranKlin Roosevelt
Dear President Roosevelt

I am in a terrible perdicament So I thought of you to send my plea of trouble to you because I drempt the other night that I Should write to you thinking that may = be I could get Some help from you as long as no one els will help me out I am an old woman Seventy two years old and an invalid that is the worst of it I can't get around at all. I bin Sitting in a chair for years already if I am not in bed I can't walk alone atall So that makes it pretty hard fore me to be put out of my home the one I worked so hard for over forty-Six years, So please help me Some way or I will half to Sine my last bit away if I could only raise thirteen Hundred Dollars than I could Stay in my home Oh. So please help me Mr. Roosevelt and answer right away or els it will be to late if I ever get onto my feet I Sure will try and pay you back. I helped So many out but it Seems now that I am in the grattes trouble no = body will help me So please Mr. Roosevelt help me Sincerly Mrs. A. M. U.

February 1936

Mr. and Mrs. Roosevelt
Wash. D.C.
Dear Mr. President:

I'm a boy of 12 years. I want to tell you about my family My father hasn't worked for 5 months He went plenty times to relief, he filled out application. They won't give us anything. I don't know why. Please you do something. We haven't paid 4 months rent, Everyday the landlord rings the door bell, we don't open the door for him. We are afraid that will be put out, been put out before, and don't want to happen again. We haven't paid the gas bill, and the electric bill, haven't paid grocery bill for 3 months. My brother goes to Lane Tech. High School. he's eighteen years old, hasn't gone to school for 2 weeks because he got no carfare. I have a sister she's twenty years, she can't find work. My father he staying home. All the time he's crying because he can't find work. I told him why are you crying daddy, and daddy said why shouldn't I cry when there is nothing in the house. I feel sorry for him. That night I couldn't sleep. The next morning I wrote this letter to you, in my room. Were American citizens and were born in Chicago, Ill. and I don't know why they don't help us Please answer right away because we need it. will starve Thank you.

God bless you.

Anonymous
Chicago, Ill.

Fayetteville, W.Va.
Nov. 4, 1936

[Dear Mrs. Roosevelt,]

. . . Personally I have found that the more you give the lower classes the more they want. Never satisfied. In my charitable work I become discouraged and it makes me know what your husband is up against. The people (some) are so simple-minded. They think the President is going to keep on giving. My gardener (White) and my maid (col.) voted democratic this election, not from coercion on my part but because "Roosevelt will take care of us." . . .

I am very sincerely yours,
Mrs. N. J. S.

New York, N.Y.
October 1939

Mr. Harry Hopkins
Washington, D.C.
Dear Mr. Hopkins:

Will you please investigate the various relief agencies in many cities of the United States. The cities where there are a large foreign and jewish population. No wonder the cities are now on the verge of bankruptcy because we are feeding a lot of ignorant foreigners by giving them relief. And, they are turning against us every day. I would suggest to deport all foreigners and jews who are not citizens over the United States back to any land where they choose to go and who will admit them. As America is now over crowded with too much immigration and it can not feed even its own citizens without feeding the citizens of other foreign nations. I have found out after careful investigation that we are feeding many foreigners who send out their wives to work and who have money in the bank. While the men drink wine and play cards in saloons and cafes. I have spoken to one Italian whom I met. And I ask him what he was doing for a living. He said me drinka da dago red wine and play cards and send the wife out to work. Isn't a very good thing for us to support them. No wonder the taxpayers are grumbling about taxes. Most of them are a race of black hands murders boot leggers bomb throwers. While most of the sheeney jews as they are called are a race of dishonest people who get rich by swindling, faking and cheating the poor people. Besides the jews are responsible by ruining others in business by the great amount of chisling done. And selling even below the cost prices, in order to get all the others business. The foreigners and jews spend as little as they can to help this country. And, they live as cheap as they can. And, work as cheap as they can, and save all the money they can. And when they have enough they go back to their country. Why don't we deport them under the section of the United States Immigration Laws which relates to paupers and those who become a public charge. The Communist Party is composed mostly by foreigners and jews. The jews are the leaders of the movement and urge the downfall of this government. . . .

A Taxpayer

Hornell, New York
March 7, 1934

U.S. Senator Robert F. Wagner
Senate Building,
Washington, D.C.

My *Dear Senator:*

It seems very apparent to me that the Administration at Washington is accelerating its pace towards socialism and communism. Nearly every public statement from Washington is against stimulation of business which would in the end create employment.

Everyone is sympathetic to the cause of creating more jobs and better wages for labor; but, a program continually promoting labor troubles, higher wages, shorter hours, and less profits for business, would seem to me to be leading us fast to a condition where the Government must more and more expand it's relief activities, and will lead in the end to disaster to all classes. . . .

I am not addicted to annoying public office holders with correspondence but if there are any private rights left in this country, then I would appreciate an early reply to this letter, so that I may take such action as is still possible to protect myself and family.

With kindest personal regards,
Yours truly,
W. L. C. [male]

Nashville, Tenn.
8/15/36

Mrs. Franklin D. Roosevelt,
Dear Lady

Will you please warn the people of whats going to happen in America if these property owners dont quit making industrial slaves out of their laborers and working them on starvation wages, paying them a wage whereby they cannot obtain the desires of life, or else installing machinery and laying the common laborer off of his job to starve to death.

We dont want a revolution in this country where innocent men, women, and children will be shot down without mercy like they are doing in spain and also like they did in Russia. We want peace on earth good will toward men. You know mrs. Roosevelt with the majority of us poor people we desire good things as well as the higher classes of society. For instance we desire a nice home to live in with sanitary surroundings. we desire a nice refrigadaire, electric stove, fan, nice furniture, radio, a nice car with money to take a vacation, but one cannot have these desires of life at a wage of 8.00 10.00 or $12.00 per week, and if we could, we could not accumalate no money and would have to go on being industrial slaves and our children would fall under the same yoke of bondage that we and our fore parents were under. And never be considered no more than an ordinary slaves. . . .

Mrs. Roosevelt this nation is hanging over a giant powder keg just waiting for someone to light a match. You see I am forced to mingle with the poorer classes and I hear what they have to say. As far as I am concerned I dont believe in taking the carnal weapon against my fellow man. Therefore all I can do is stand still and see the salvation of the lord. I am thirty four years old married and have one daughter. I have a eighth grade education. I got a job last week as labourer on the new courthouse here, although I am a painter by trade, and just because I am a little crippled on my right side the contractor would not work me, he said the insurance company would not allow him to.

And so I cannot see a very bright prospect in life. Although my wife slaves in a cotton mill but I want a job so as I can get her out of it, for I am afraid she has contracted tuburcolosis, hoping an answer I remain

Yours,
Sincerely,
D. B. P. [male]

Introduction to Document 2

Tom Kromer grew up in West Virginia, where his father had been a coal miner and then a glassblower. Tom was a talented student, and he enrolled at Marshall College, but the death of his father and his own lack of funds caused him to drop out before finishing a degree. The Great Depression soon followed, and Kromer was left a vagrant. For a few years, he rode freight trains across the country. Finally, he was able to join the Civilian Conservation Corps, which afforded him the time and money to write his autobiographical *Waiting for Nothing* (1935). The author Lincoln Steffens assisted Kromer in having the manuscript published by Alfred A. Knopf. Perhaps more than any other depression-era book, this one gave a sense, not only of hopeless wandering, but also of the terror of being homeless. Kromer left nothing out: the alcoholism, the cruelty of the police and the middle class, the violence of "stiffs" against each other, and the ever-pressing need for "three hots and a flop"—food and shelter.

DOCUMENT 2 **From Waiting for Nothing**

Tom Kromer

I crouch here in this doorway of the blind baggage. For five hours I have huddled here in the freezing cold. My feet dangle down beneath the car. The wind whistles underneath and swings them back and forth. The wheels sing over the rails. Up in front of me the engine roars through the blackness, that is blacker than the night. The smoke and the fire belch into the sky and scatter into scorching sparks that burn my back and neck. I do not feel the wind that swings my legs. They are frozen. I have no feeling in them. I slink far back in this door and put my hands over my face. Great God, but I am miserable. I cannot stand this much longer. I was a fool for nailing the blind baggage of this passenger. I was a fool, and now I am freezing to death.

I think. How am I ever going to get off this drag if it ever does stop? I can't walk. My feet, that are frozen, will not hold me up. I sit here and think, and I doze. I awake with a jerk.

"You damn fool," I say, "you can't go to sleep here. You will fall under those wheels that sing beneath you. Those wheels would make quick work of you, all right. Those wheels would make mincemeat of you. You would not be cold any more."

I begin to sing. I sing loud. I yell at the top of my voice, because of the roar of the wheels and the sound of the wind underneath me. I don't want to fall under those wheels. I am only a stiff, and I know that a stiff is better off dead, but I don't want to fall under those wheels. I can feel myself getting dopey. I try to sing louder. I try to hear my voice over the sound of the wind and the cars, but I cannot. I cannot keep awake. I can see that I cannot keep awake. I am falling asleep. I wonder if this is the way a guy freezes to death. I am not so cold now. I am almost warm. The wind roars just as loud as before. It must be just as cold as it was before. But I am not cold. I am warm. Great Christ, I must not let myself freeze to death. I swing my arms. I reach my head far out over the side of the car. The wind tears at my face, but I keep it there until the tears run down my cheeks. Oh, Christ, won't this drag never stop?

I feel the buckle of this drag beneath me. I feel it jerk and throw me forward. I hear the whine of air for brakes. I grab the sides of this car with all my might. My frozen fingers slip, then hold. I am not scared. I am not afraid. I just grab the sides of the car and hold. I feel this train slacken speed. I see the scattered lights of a town. Only a few lights, but I see that this drag is going to stop. I begin to laugh. I laugh like a crazy man when I see that this drag is going to stop.

I hang on with all my might. There will be a jerk when this drag stops. I do not want to go under those wheels. We pull to a stop in front of this jerk-water station. There will be no bulls [police] in this place. The thing to do is to get off this drag before it starts again. It will not stay here long. How am I going to reach the ground? My legs are numb. They are frozen. They will not hold me up. I rub them fast and hard. I feel them sting and burn as the blood begins to run. I try to move them. I can move them. I can see them move. But I feel nothing when they move. I pull myself to my feet. I am standing. I can see that I am standing, but I cannot feel the car beneath my feet. I reach out over the side of the car and grab the ladder. I climb down. I hold with one hand and guide my legs with the other, but I climb down. I stop at this last step. It is a long way to the ground for my frozen feet. I jump. I fall face-down in the cinders at the side of the track. This drag whistles the high ball. She pulls out. I lie here in the cinders with my bleeding face and watch the coaches go by. I lie here in the cinders with my frozen legs that have no feeling in them. I shiver as I think of that blind baggage with the roar of the wheels and the sound of the wind underneath. I push my fists into the ground and get to my feet. I grimace at the pain that shoots through my legs, but I grit my teeth and walk.

What I want right now is a cup of coffee. A cup of good hot coffee will always warm a guy up. I am too cold to want to eat. I make it to the main stem of this town. There are lights in the few stores that are still open. I pass a restaurant. There is a sign in the window. It says: "Try our ten-cent hamburgers." I wonder if they would let a frozen stiff try their ten-cent hamburgers. I walk in. There are two customers eating. I walk up to this bird behind the counter. He backs away. He glances at his cash register. He has a scared look on his face. I look in the mirror that lines the wall. I do not blame this guy for being scared. What I see scares me, too. My face is as black as the ace of spades. It is smeared with blood from the cuts of the cinders as they scraped my face. I hit those cinders hard.

"Buddy," I say, "I am broke. Could you spare me a cup of coffee?"

"I can't spare you nothin'," he says. "Beat it before I throw you out."

Imagine this bastard. I am half starved and half froze, and he turns me down for a lousy cup of coffee. I am too cold to even cuss him out. I want to cuss him out, but I am too cold. I walk down the street and hit these other two restaurants. They turn me down flat. I can't get me anything to warm me up. But there is one thing I will have to get, and that is a flop. In weather like this a stiff has got to have a flop.

"Where is the town bull?" I say to this guy on the corner.

"You will find him in the garage," he says. "He will be shootin' the bull by the stove in the garage."

I walk over to this garage and find this hick cop by the stove in the office.

"Chief," I say, "I want to get locked up in the can. I am on the fritz with no place to flop."

"The jail ain't no hotel," he says. "I can't lock you up. I can't louse the jail up by locking you up."

Well, if this is not a hell of a note! A stiff can't even break into a lousy can. They call this a free country, and a stiff can't even break into jail to get away from the cold and the wind.

"Can I warm up a little by your fire?" I say. "I am froze."

"Get this straight," this bull says; "we have no use for lousy stiffs in this town. The best thing you can do is to hit the highway away from here."

"What is a stiff supposed to do, shoot himself?" I say.

"If I catch you in this town tomorrow, it will be a good thing if you do shoot yourself," he says.

I go out to the street and walk. I walk fast. I do not feel like walking fast, but I have to to keep from freezing to death. That's how cold I am. I pass a pecan grove. Over away from the road I can see a shack with a light in it. I knock on the door. An old man comes to the door with a lantern in his hand.

"Hello," I say. "Have you got somewhere a guy could flop for the night around here? I am freezing to death, with no place to flop."

He puts his hand on the top of my head.

"Son, do you believe in Christ?" he says.

"Sure," I say, "I believe in Christ. Have you got some place I could flop around here?"

"The last days are upon us," he says. "The sound of the trumpet is soon upon us. Repent or you burn in everlasting flame."

This guy is as batty as a loon. I can see that.

"Have you got some place I could flop outside?" I say. "An old shed or something?"

Outside will not be too far away from this guy. He is ready for the booby-hatch.

"The lamb that is lost is the care of the Lord," he says.

He leads the way to this building where they store the pecans. It is a big place. The floor is covered with piles of these pecans. He takes a shovel and digs a hole down in one of these piles, he puts two burlap sacks in the bottom of it.

"Son," he says, "lay down in this hole and rest."

I get in.

He covers me up with pecans, and piles sacks on top of me. My face is all that is sticking out of the hole. He puts a sack over my face.

"Rest that you may better fight the battles of the Lord," he says.

He takes his lantern and goes back to his shack.

It is pitch-dark in here now. I lie under these pecans and think. Here I am lying down in a hole. Here I am covered up with pecans. Before I went on the fritz, I was lying nights in a feather bed. I thought I was hard up then. I had a decent front. I had my three hots and a flop. Can you imagine a guy thinking he is hard up when he has his three hots and a flop? That was two years ago, but two years are ten years when you are on the fritz. I look ten years older now. I looked like a young punk then. I was a young punk. I had some color in my cheeks. I have hit the skids since then. This is as low down as a guy can get, being down in a hole with pecans on top of him for covers. If a guy had any guts, he wouldn't put up with this. I think. Why should one guy have a million dollars, and I am down in a hole with pecans on top of me for covers? Maybe that guy has brains. Maybe he works hard. I don't know. What is that to me if he is there and I am here? Religion, they say in the missions. Religion and morals. What are religion and morals to me, if I am down in a hole with pecans on top of me? Who is there to say that this world belongs to certain guys? What right has one guy to say: This much of the world is mine; you can't sleep here?

I lie here in the darkness and think. It is too cold to sleep. On the blind baggage of the drag I could not keep my eyes open. Now I cannot close them. I listen to these rats that rustle across the floor. I pull this sack off my face and strain my eyes through the blackness. I am afraid of rats. Once in a jungle [hobo camp] I awoke with two on my face. Since then I dream of rats that are as big as cats, who sit on my face and gnaw at my nose and eyes. I cannot see them. It is too dark. I cannot lie here and wait with my heart thumping against my ribs like this. I cannot lie here and listen to them patter across the floor, and me not able to see them. I pull myself out of these pecans and get to my feet. I tiptoe out to the road. I do not want to wake this crazy old codger who dug the hole for me. I do not want to hurt his feelings, and besides, he might go off his nut.

I walk. I lower my head far down to keep the whistling wind from cutting my face like a knife. I listen to the creak of the trees as the wind tears through them. I keep to the left of the road. I cannot hear the sounds of the cars as they come up behind me. You can hear nothing for the roar of the wind. From time to time I turn my head to stare through the night for signs of a headlight. When I see one, I stop in my tracks and hold out my hand for a ride. They do not stop when they see me raise my hand. They step on the gas and go faster. They do not care to pick up a worn-out stiff with blisters on his feet. It is night. They are afraid. They are afraid of being knocked in the head. I do not blame them for being afraid. You cannot tell what a stiff might do when he is as cold and fagged as I am. A stiff is not himself when he is as cold as I am.

I reach the town and skirt it. I am afraid of rats, and this town bull has a face like a rat. I reach the yards and crawl into one of these cars that line the tracks. I shove the doors almost shut. I do not shut it tight. If they start moving these cars during the night, I want to be ready for a quick get-away. I take this newspaper out of my pocket and spread it on the floor. I take off my shoes and use them for a pillow. I lie down, I am all in. I am asleep in a minute.

I do not know how long I am asleep. I awake with a jerk. Something has awakened me. All at once I am wide-eyed and staring. There is a feeling of queerness in the top of my head. I know that feeling. I get that feeling when there is something wrong. I had that feeling once when a drag I was on went over the ditch. That feeling was in the top of my head just before a guy I was talking to on the street dropped dead. My breath comes in short gasps. There is a crawling feeling all over me. A tingle starts at my feet and runs to my hair. I feel a chill in the roots of my hair. I know what that is. My hair is standing up.

I raise up on my elbow. The rustle I make as I move on the paper sounds like thunder in the quietness of the car. A ray of light comes through the opening in the door. It is not strong enough to reach to the other end of the car, but I know that there is nothing there. It is in back of me. Whatever it is that is in this car is in back of me. . . .

Then, through the dark, comes this squeal. It is a wild squeal. A squeal like something is mad and crazy. It is like something that has lost its mind. I feel it bound through the air and land on my back. It knocks me down to the floor. These sharp claws bite into the nape of my neck. The long fingers grip my throat so that my breath comes in sobs. I am strangling. I grab at these claws. I feel a man's wrist. A strong wrist. A wrist that is all covered with hair like an animal's. I am down on my belly on the floor of the car. These fingers like hot iron press tighter and tighter. I feel these knees that bore into the small of my back. My neck wrenches backward. So far back I wait to hear it snap. Dizzier I get, and dizzier. Like in a dream I know that these claws that bite into my neck are trying to kill me, to choke me to death. I struggle blindly in the darkness.

I throw myself to my back. I feel the claws loosen their grip. I feel them slide off my neck and tear the flesh off in strips. I feel the burn on my throat and the moistness that I know is blood. I stumble to my feet as he sprawls on the floor. I am facing him now in the dark. He scrambles to his feet. He is only a shapeless mass in front of me. It is a shapeless mass that wants to kill me, to choke me till there is no life in me. I see it hurl itself through the air. I brace myself against the side of the car and kick out with my foot with all my might. I feel it hit, hard. I hear a grunt, a squeally grunt that a pig might give. My foot is buried in his belly. He thuds to the floor. He rolls over and over, but he is up again in a second. There is a flash in his hand. Through the ray of light that comes through the door I see this flash. My spine creeps. I know what that flash is. It is a knife. I cannot let him get at me with the knife. I cannot let him rip me open with the knife. He is going to murder me with the knife. I have to get out of here. Great Christ, I have to get out of here. I leap towards the door and reach it. I claw at it and try to pry it open. It is caught. The splinters bury themselves in my finger-nails. I do not notice the pain. I am too afraid to notice the pain of a splinter in my nails. Again behind me I hear that scream.

I swing around. The knife flashes through the air above my head. I grab at the hairy wrist that holds the knife. The razor-sharp edge slashes my arms. I know it slashes my arms because of the scorched feeling and the wet that spurts against my face. I struggle with the wrist that holds the knife and the arm that clubs at my head. I am getting weak. The loss of blood has made me weak. I cannot hold the arm that clutches the knife. I glue my eyes to this flash that quivers and shakes over my head as we strain in the ray that comes through the door from the moonlight. Nearer it comes and nearer. I twist the wrist with all my strength. I twist till I hear the snap of it through our panting and scuffling. I hear this scream again as the arm goes limp and the knife clatters to the box-car floor. I start to dive for the knife on the floor and feel this fist that smashes to my face. I sprawl to the other end of the car. I grope in the dark and try to get up. I cannot. I am too weak to get to my feet. I lie here and tremble on the floor.

Through the ray of light that comes from the door I see this guy stand and stare at the floor. The gleam of the knife is there. He does not pick it up. He is not looking at the knife. It is this pool of blood from my slashed-up arm he is staring at. He stares like a guy in a trance at this blood. He flops to his knees and splashes his hands in the blood and screams. He splashes his hands in the pool of blood and smears it all over his face. I can see him quiver and shake and hear his jabber as he smears the blood. I lie here and wait for the flash of the knife, but it does not come. He leaps to his feet and jumps towards the door of the car. He jabbers and babbles as he shoves against it. He slides it open and leaps to the tracks. I can hear his screams as he crashes through the thickets.

I lie in the darkness with my bloody arm and shiver and sob in my breath.

Introduction to Documents 3 and 4

In the following two pieces, Meridel Le Sueur offers us chilling visions of how women were affected by the depression. "Women on the Breadlines" (1932), from which Document 3 is excerpted, captures some of the same wandering, hopeless quality of Kromer's novel. As Le Sueur points out, however, many vagrant women would rather have starved alone than face the shame of asking for help. "Women on the Breadlines" appeared in *New Masses,* the cultural organ of the Communist Party of America. The editors appended a note criticizing the article for its despairing tone. In Document 4, "I Was Marching," which appeared in *New Masses* two years later, Le Sueur took a much more affirmative position. The immediate subject was the 1934 Minneapolis Teamsters strike. Here Le Sueur captured the terrors of the strike; this time, however, collective resistance triumphed over individual hopelessness.

DOCUMENT 3 ***"Women on the Breadlines"***

Meridel Le Sueur

I am sitting in the city free employment bureau. It's the woman's section. We have been sitting here now for four hours. We sit here every day, waiting for a job. There are no jobs. Most of us have had no breakfast. Some have had scant rations for over a year. Hunger makes a human being lapse into a state of lethargy, especially city hunger. Is there any place else in the world where a human being is supposed to go hungry amidst plenty without an outcry, without protest, where only the boldest steal or kill for bread, and the timid crawl the streets, hunger like the beak of a terrible bird at the vitals?

We sit looking at the floor. No one dares think of the coming winter. There are only a few more days of summer. Everyone is anxious to get work to lay up something for that long siege of bitter cold. But there is no work. Sitting in the room we all know it. That is why we don't talk much. We look at the floor dreading to see that knowledge in each other's eyes. There is a kind of humiliation in it. We look away from each other. We look at the floor. It's too terrible to see this animal terror in each other's eyes.

So we sit hour after hour, day after day, waiting for a job to come in. There are many women for a single job. A thin sharp woman sits inside the wire cage looking at the book. For four hours we have watched her looking at the book. She has a hard little eye. In the small bare room there are half a dozen women sitting on the benches waiting. Many come and go. Our faces are all familiar to each other, for we wait here every day.

This is a domestic employment bureau. Most of the women who come here are middle aged, some have families, some raised their families and are now alone, some have men who are out of work. Hard times and the man leaves to hunt for work. He doesn't find it. He drifts on. The woman probably doesn't hear from him for a long time. She expects it. She isn't surprised. She struggles alone to feed the many mouths. Sometimes she gets help from the charities. If she's clever she can get herself a good living from the charities, if she's naturally a lick spittle, naturally a little docile and cunning. If she's proud then she starves silently, leaving her children to find work, coming home after a day's searching to wrestle with her house, her children.

Some such story is written on the faces of all these women. There are young girls too, fresh from the country. Some are made brazen too soon by the city. There is a great exodus of girls from the farms into the city now. Thousands of farms have been vacated completely in Minnesota. The girls are trying to get work. The prettier ones can get jobs in the stores when there are any, or waiting on table but these jobs are only for the attractive and the adroit, the others, the real peasants, have a more difficult time. . . .

It's one of the great mysteries of the city where women go when they are out of work and hungry. There are not many women in the bread line. There are no flop houses for women as there are for men, where a bed can be had for a quarter or less. You don't see women lying on the floor at the mission in the free flops. They obviously don't sleep in the jungle or under newspapers in the park. There is no law I suppose against their being in these places but the fact is they rarely are.

Yet there must be as many women out of jobs in cities and suffering extreme poverty as there are men. What happens to them? Where do they go? Try to get into the Y.W.C.A. without any money or looking down at heel. Charities take care of very few and only those that are called "deserving." The lone girl is under suspicion by the virgin women who dispense charity.

I've lived in cities for many months broke, without help, too timid to get in bread lines. I've known many women to live like this until they simply faint on the street from privations, without saying a word to anyone. A woman will shut herself up in a room until it is taken away from her, and eat a cracker a day and be as quiet as a mouse so there are no social statistics concerning her.

I don't know why it is, but a woman will do this unless she has dependents, will go for weeks, verging on starvation, crawling in some hole, going through the streets ashamed, sitting in libraries, parks, going for days without speaking to a living soul like some exiled beast, keeping the runs mended in her stockings, shut up in terror in her own misery, until she becomes too super sensitive and timid to even ask for a job.

Bernice says even strange men she has met in the park have sometimes, that is in better days, given her a loan to pay her room rent. She has always paid them back.

In the afternoon the young girls, to forget the hunger and the deathly torture and fear of being jobless, try and pick up a man to take them to a ten cent show. They never go to more expensive ones, but they can always find a man willing to spend a dime to have the company of a girl for the afternoon.

Sometimes a girl facing the night without shelter will approach a man for lodging. A woman always asks a man for help. Rarely another woman. I have known girls to sleep in men's rooms for the night, on a pallet without molestation, and given breakfast in the morning.

It's no wonder these young girls refuse to marry, refuse to rear children. They are like certain savage tribes, who, when they have been conquered refuse to breed.

Not one of them but looks forward to starvation, for the coming winter. We are in a jungle and know it. We are beaten, entrapped. There is no way out. Even if there were a job, even if that thin acrid woman came and gave everyone in the room a job for a few days, a few hours, at thirty cents an hour, this would all be repeated tomorrow, the next day and the next.

Not one of these women but knows, that despite years of labour there is only starvation, humiliation in front of them. . . .

So we sit in this room like cattle, waiting for a non existent job, willing to work to the farthest atom of energy, unable to work, unable to get food and lodging, unable to bear children; here we must sit in this shame looking at the floor, worse than beasts at a slaughter.

It is appalling to think that these women sitting so listless in the room may work as hard as it is possible for a human being to work, may labour night and day, like Mrs. Gray wash street cars from midnight to dawn and offices in the early evening, scrubbing for fourteen and fifteen hours a day, sleeping only five hours or so, doing this their whole lives, and never earn one day of security, having always before them the pit of the future.

The endless labour, the bending back, the water soaked hands, earning never more than a week's wages, never having in their hands more life than that.

It's not the suffering, not birth, death, love that the young reject, but the suffering of endless labour without dream, eating the spare bread in bitterness, a slave without the security of a slave.

Editorial Note: This presentation of the plight of the unemployed woman, able as it is, and informative, is defeatist in attitude, lacking in revolutionary spirit and direction which characterize the usual contribution to *New Masses*. We feel it our duty to add, that there is a place for the unemployed woman, as well as man, in the ranks of the unemployed councils and in all branches of the organized revolutionary movement. Fight for your class, read *The Working Woman*, join the Communist Party.

DOCUMENT 4 *"I Was Marching"*

Meridel Le Sueur

I have never been in a strike before. It is like looking at something that is happening for the first time and there are no thoughts and no words yet accrued to it. If you come from the middle class, words are likely to mean more than an event. You are likely to think about a thing, and the happening will be the size of a pin point and the words around the happening very large, distorting it queerly. It's a case of "Remembrance of things past." When you are in the event, you are likely to have a distinctly individualistic attitude, to be only partly there, and to care more for the happening afterwards than when it is happening. That is why it is hard for a person like myself and others to be in a strike.

Besides, in American life, you hear things happening in a far and muffled way. One thing is said and another happens. Our merchant society has been built upon a huge hypocrisy, a cut-throat competition which sets one man against another and at the same time an ideology mouthing such words as "Humanity," "Truth," the "Golden Rule," and such. Now in a crisis the word falls away and the skeleton of that action shows in terrific movement.

For two days I heard of the strike. I went by their headquarters, I walked by on the opposite side of the street and saw the dark old building that had been a garage and lean, dark young faces leaning from the upstairs windows. I had to go down there often. I looked in. I saw the huge black interior and live coals of living men moving restlessly and orderly, their eyes gleaming from their sweaty faces.

I saw cars leaving filled with grimy men, pickets going to the line, engines roaring out. I stayed close to the door, watching. I didn't go in. I was afraid they would put me out. After all, I could remain a spectator. A man wearing a polo hat kept going around with a large camera taking pictures.

I am putting down exactly how I felt, because I believe others of my class feel the same as I did. I believe it stands for an important psychic change that must take place in all. I saw many artists, writers, professionals, even business men and women standing across the street, too, and I saw in their faces the same longings, the same fears.

The truth is I was afraid. Not of the physical danger at all, but an awful fright of mixing, of losing myself, of being unknown and lost. I felt inferior. I felt no one would know me there, that all I had been trained to excel in would go unnoticed. I can't describe what I felt, but perhaps it will come near it to say that I felt I excelled in competing with others and I knew instantly that these people were *NOT* competing at all, that they were acting in a strange, powerful trance of movement *together*. And I was filled with longing to act with them and with fear that I could not. I felt I was born out of every kind of life, thrown up alone, looking at other lonely people, a condition I had been in the habit of defending with various attitudes of cynicism, preciosity, defiance and hatred.

Looking at that dark and lively building, massed with men, I knew my feelings to be those belonging to disruption, chaos and disintegration and I felt their direct and awful movement, mute and powerful, drawing them into a close and glowing cohesion like a powerful conflagration in the midst of the city. And it filled me with fear and awe and at the same time hope. I knew this action to be prophetic and indicative of future actions and I wanted to be part of it.

Our life seems to be marked with a curious and muffled violence over America, but this action has always been in the dark, men and women dying obscurely, poor and poverty marked lives, but now from city to city runs this violence, into the open, and colossal happenings stand bare before our eyes, the street churning suddenly upon the pivot of mad violence, whole men suddenly spouting blood and running like living sieves, another holding a dangling arm shot squarely off, a tall youngster, running, tripping over his intestines, and one block away, in the burning sun, gay women shopping and a window dresser trying to decide whether to put green or red voile on a mannikin.

In these terrible happenings you cannot be neutral now. No one can be neutral in the face of bullets.

The next day, with sweat breaking out on my body, I walked past the three guards at the door. They said, "Let the women in. We need women." And I knew it was no joke. . . .

I found the kitchen organized like a factory. Nobody asks my name. I am given a large butcher's apron. I realize I have never before worked anonymously. At first I feel strange and then I feel good. The forewoman sets me to washing tin cups. There are not enough cups. We have to wash fast and rinse them and set them up quickly for buttermilk and coffee as the line thickens and the men wait. . . .

Then I am changed and put to pouring coffee. At first I look at the men's faces and then I don't look any more. It seems I am pouring coffee for the same tense, dirty sweating face, the same body, the same blue shirt and overalls. Hours go by, the heat is terrific. I am not tired. I am not hot. I am pouring coffee. I am swung into the most intense and natural organization I have ever felt. I know everything that is going on. These things become of great matter to me.

Eyes looking, hands raising a thousand cups, throats burning, eyes bloodshot from lack of sleep, the body dilated to catch every sound over the whole city. Buttermilk? Coffee?

"Is your man here?" the woman cutting sandwiches asks me.

"No," I say, then I lie for some reason, peering around as if looking eagerly for someone, "I don't see him now."

But I was pouring coffee for living men. . . .

That night at eight o'clock a mass-meeting was called of all labor. It was to be in a parking lot two blocks from headquarters. All the women gather at the front of the building with collection cans, ready to march to the meeting. I have not been home. It never occurs to me to leave. The twilight is eerie and the men are saying that the chief of police is going to attack the meeting and raid headquarters. The smell of blood hangs in the hot, still air. Rumors strike at the taut nerves. The dusk looks ghastly with what might be in the next half hour.

"If you have any children," a woman said to me, "you better not go." I looked at the desperate women's faces, the broken feet, the torn and hanging pelvis, the worn and lovely bodies of women who persist under such desperate labors. I shivered, though it was 96 and the sun had been down a good hour.

The parking lot was already full of people when we got there and men swarmed the adjoining roofs. An elegant café stood across the street with water sprinkling from its roof and splendidly dressed men and women stood on the steps as if looking at a show.

The platform was the bullet riddled truck of the afternoon's fray. We had been told to stand close to this platform so we did, making the center of a wide massed circle that stretched as far as we could see. We seemed buried like minerals in a mass, packed body to body. I felt again that peculiar heavy silence in which there is the real form of the happening. My eyes burn. I can hardly see. I seem to be standing like an animal in ambush. I have the brightest, most physical feeling with every sense sharpened peculiarly. The movements, the masses that I see and feel I have never known before. I only partly know what I am seeing, feeling, but I feel it is the real body and gesture of a future vitality. I see that there is a bright clot of women drawn close to a bullet riddled truck. I am one of them, yet I don't feel myself at all. It is curious. I feel most alive and yet for the first time in my life I do not feel myself as separate. I realize then that all my previous feelings have been based on feeling myself separate and distinct from others and now I sense sharply faces, bodies, closeness and my own fear is not my own alone, nor my hope. . . .

[THE NEXT DAY.]

The strikers keep moving up cars. We keep moving back together to let cars pass and form between us and a brick building that flanks the parking lot. . . . We all watched carefully the placing of the cars. Sometimes we looked at each other. I didn't understand that look. I felt uneasy. It was as if something escaped me. And then suddenly, on my very body, I knew what they were doing, as if it had been communicated to me from a thousand eyes, a thousand silent throats, as if it had been shouted in the loudest voice.

THEY WERE BUILDING A BARRICADE.

Two men died from that day's shooting. Men lined up to give one of them a blood transfusion, but he died. Black Friday men called the murderous day. Night and day workers held their children up to see the body of Ness who died. Tuesday, the day of the funeral, one thousand more militia were massed downtown.

It was still over ninety in the shade. I went to the funeral parlors and thousands of men and women were massed there waiting in the terrific sun. One block of women and children were standing two hours waiting. I went over and stood near them. I didn't know whether I could march. I didn't like marching in parades. Besides, I felt they might not want me.

I stood aside not knowing if I would march. I couldn't see how they would ever organize it anyway. No one seemed to be doing much.

At three-forty some command went down the ranks. I said foolishly at the last minute, "I don't belong to the auxiliary—could I march?" Three women drew me in. "We want all to march," they said gently. "Come with us."

The giant mass uncoiled like a serpent and straightened out ahead and to my amazement on a lift of road I could see six blocks of massed men, four abreast, with bare heads, moving straight on and as they moved, uncoiled the mass behind and pulled it after them, I felt myself walking, accelerating my speed with the others as the line stretched, pulled taut, then held its rhythm.

Not a cop was in sight. The cortege moved through the stop-and-go signs, it seemed to lift of its own dramatic rhythm, coming from the intention of every person there. We were moving spontaneously in a movement, natural, hardy and miraculous.

We passed through six blocks of tenements, through a sea of grim faces and there was not a sound. There was the curious shuffle of thousands of feet, without drum or bugle, in ominous silence, a march not heavy as the military, but very light, exactly with the heart beat.

I was marching with a million hands, movements, faces and my own movement was repeating again and again, making a new movement from the many gestures, the walking, falling back, the open mouth crying, the nostrils stretched apart, the raised hand, the blow falling, and the outstretched hand drawing me in.

I felt my legs straighten. I felt my feet join in that strange shuffle of thousands of bodies moving with direction, of thousands of feet and my own breath with the gigantic breath. As if an electric charge had passed through me, my hair stood on end. I was marching.

Introduction to Document 5

Like Kromer's *Waiting for Nothing,* Michael Gold's *Jews Without Money* (1930) might best be called documentary fiction. Gold reveals how many Jews of his own American-born generation remained victims of poverty and discrimination. Gold was a member of the Communist party, indeed a leader in the move to radicalize art and literature during the depression. *Jews Without Money* did not romanticize poverty, nor did it dwell on a particular political agenda; Gold was content to dramatize people's sense of being locked into a system that promised prosperity, but delivered despair. Although Gold grew up before the Great Depression, his book came out during the crisis. His description of his own youth spoke with passion to readers about the devastation wrought on families during the 1930s.

DOCUMENT 5 From *Jews Without Money*

Michael Gold

The neighbors were talking about us. They were worrying. In the tenement each woman knew what was cooking for supper in her neighbor's pot. Each knew the cares, too, that darkened a neighbor's heart.

One night a neighbor called. He kissed the *mezzuzah* over the door, and wiped his feet on the burlap rags. Then he timidly entered our kitchen like an intruder.

"Good evening, Mr. Lipzin," said my mother. "Please sit down."

"Good evening," he stammered, seating himself. "It was raining to-day, and I did not sell many bananas, so I brought you some. Maybe your children like bananas."

He handed my mother a bunch of bananas, and she took them, saying, "Thanks, Mr. Lipzin."

The pot-bellied little peddler shyly fingered his beard. He had come for a purpose, but was too embarrassed to speak. . . .

My father fidgeted uneasily. He was about to say something to break the spell cast by the tongue-tied peddler, when Mr. Lipzin became articulate. "Excuse me, but my wife nagged me into coming here," he stammered. "She is worrying about you. Excuse me, but they say you have been out of work a long time and can find nothing to do, Mr. Gold."

"Yes, Mr. Lipzin, why should one conceal it?" said my father. "Life is dark for us now."

"*Nu,*" said the little peddler, as he wiped his forehead, "so that is why my wife nagged me to see you. If there is nothing else, one can at least make a kind of living with bananas. I have peddled them, with God's help, for many years. It is a hard life, but one manages to live. . . ."

My father stood up and folded his arms haughtily.

"And you are suggesting, Mr. Lipzin, that I, too, should go out peddling bananas?" he asked.

The peddler sweated like a runner with embarrassment. He stood up and edged toward the door to make his escape.

"No, no, God forbid," he stammered. "Excuse me, it was my wife who nagged me to come here. No, no, Mr. Gold! Good evening to you all; may God be with you!"

He went out, mopping his fiery face with a bandanna. My father stared after him, his arms still folded in that fierce, defiant attitude.

"What a gall! What meddling neighbors we have! To come and tell me that I ought to peddle these accursed bananas! After my fifteen years in America, as if I were a greenhorn! I, who once owned a suspender shop, and was a foreman of house painters! . . ."

Two weeks after Mr. Lipzin's visit [my father] was in the street with a pushcart, peddling the accursed bananas.

He came back the first night, and gave my mother a dollar bill and some silver. His face was gray; he looked older by ten years; a man who had touched bottom. My mother tried to comfort him, but for days he was silent as one who has been crushed by a calamity. Hope died in him; months passed, a year passed; he was still peddling bananas.

I remember meeting him one evening with his pushcart. . . . I recognized him, a hunched, frozen figure in an old overcoat standing by a banana cart. He looked so lonely, the tears came to my eyes. Then he saw me, and his face lit with his sad, beautiful smile—Charlie Chaplin's smile.

"Ach, it's Mikey," he said. "So you have sold your papers! Come and eat a banana."

He offered me one. I refused it. I was eleven years old, but poisoned with a morbid proletarian sense of responsibility. I felt it crucial that my father *sell* his bananas, not give them away. He thought I was shy, and coaxed and joked with me, and made me eat the banana. It smelled of wet straw and snow.

"You haven't sold many bananas to-day, pop," I said anxiously.

He shrugged his shoulders.

"What can I do? No one seems to want them."

It was true. The work crowds pushed home morosely over the pavements. The rusty sky darkened over New York buildings, the tall street lamps were lit, innumerable trucks, street cars and elevated trains clattered by. Nobody and nothing in the great city stopped for my father's bananas. . . .

"Look at me," he said. "Twenty years in America, and poorer than when I came. A suspender shop I had, and it was stolen from me by a villain. A house painter foreman I became, and fell off a scaffold. Now bananas I sell, and even at that I am a failure. It is all luck." He sighed and puffed at his pipe.

"Ach, Gott, what a rich country America is! What an easy place to make one's fortune! Look at all the rich Jews! Why has it been so easy for them, so hard for me? I am just a poor little Jew without money."

"Poppa, lots of Jews have no money," I said to comfort him.

"I know it, my son," he said, "but don't be one of them. It's better to be dead in this country than not to have money. Promise me you'll be rich when you grow up, Mikey!"

"Yes, poppa."

"Ach," he said fondly, "this is my one hope now! This is all that makes me happy! I am a greenhorn, but you are an American! You will have it easier than I; you will have luck in America!"

"Yes, poppa," I said, trying to smile with him. But I felt older than he; I could not share his naïve optimism; my heart sank as I remembered the past and thought of the future. . . .

At the age of twelve I carried in my mind a morbid load of responsibility.

I had been a precocious pupil in the public school, winning honors not by study, but by a kind of intuition. I graduated a year sooner than most boys. At the exercises I was valedictory orator.

My parents were proud, of course. They wanted me to go on to high school, like other "smart" boys. They still believed I would be a doctor.

But I was morbid enough to be wiser than my parents. Even then I could sense that education is a luxury reserved for the well-to-do. I refused to go to high school. More than half the boys in my graduating class were going to work; I chose to be one of them.

It was where I belonged. I figured it out on paper for my parents. Four years of high school, then six years of college before one could be a doctor. Ten years of study in all, with thousands of dollars needed for books, tuition, and the rest.

There were four of us in my family. My mother seemed unable to work. Would my father's banana peddling keep us alive during those ten years while I was studying?

Of course not. I was obstinate and bitter; my parents wept, and tried to persuade me, but I refused to go to high school.

Miss Barry, the English teacher, tried to persuade me, too. She was fond of me. She stared at me out of wistful blue eyes, with her old maid's earnestness, and said:

"It would be a pity for you to go into a factory. I have never seen better English compositions than yours, Michael."

"I must work, Miss Barry," I said. I started to leave. She took my hand. I could smell the fresh spring lilacs in the brass bowl on her desk.

"Wait," she said earnestly, "I want you to promise me to study at night. I will give you a list of the required high school reading; you can make up your Regents' counts that way. Will you do it?"

"Yes, Miss Barry," I lied to her sullenly.

I was trying to be hard. For years my ego had been fed by every one's praise of my precocity. I had always loved books; I was mad about books; I wanted passionately to go to high school and college. Since I couldn't, I meant to despise all that nonsense.

"It will be difficult to study at night," said Miss Barry in her trembly voice, "but Abraham Lincoln did it, and other great Americans."

"Yes, Miss Barry," I muttered.

She presented me with a parting gift. It was a volume of Emerson's Essays, with her name and my name and the date written on the flyleaf.

I thanked her for the book, and threw it under the bed when I got home. I never read a page in it, or in any book for the next five years. I hated books; they were lies, they had nothing to do with life and work.

It was not easy to find my first job. I hunted for months, in a New York summer of furnace skies and fogs of humidity. I bought the *World* each morning, and ran through the want ads:

Agents Wanted—Addressers Wanted—Barbers Wanted—Bushelmen Wanted—Butchers Wanted—Boys Wanted—

That fateful ad page brings news of life and death each morning to hundreds of thousands. How often have I read it with gloomy heart. Even to-day the sight of it brings back the ache and hopelessness of my youth.

There was a swarm of boys pushing and yapping like homeless curs at the door of each job. I competed with them. We scrambled, flunkeyed and stood at servile attention under the boss's eye, little slaves on the block.

No one can go through the shame and humiliation of the job-hunt without being marked for life. I hated my first experience at it, and have hated every other since. There can be no freedom in the world while men must beg for jobs.

I rose at six-thirty each morning, and was out tramping the streets at seven. There were always hundreds of jobs, but thousands of boys clutching after them. The city was swarming with these boys, aimless, bewildered and as hungry for work as I was.

I found a job as errand boy in a silk house. But it was temporary. The very first morning the shipping clerk, a refined Nordic, suddenly realized I was a Jew. He politely fired me. They wanted no Jews. In this city of a million Jews, there was much anti-Semitism among business firms. Many of the ads would read: Gentile Only. Even Jewish business houses discriminated against Jews. How often did I slink out of factory or office where a foreman said Jews were not wanted. How often was I made to remember I belonged to the accursed race, the race whose chief misfortune it is to have produced a Christ.

At last I found a job. It was in a factory where incandescent gas mantles were made, a dark loft under the elevated trains on the Bowery near Chatham Square.

This was a spectral place, a chamber of hell, hot and poisoned by hundreds of gas flames. It was suffocating with the stink of chemicals.

I began to sweat immediately. What was worse, I could not breathe. The place terrified me. The boss came up and told me to take off my coat. He was a grim little man, thick as a cask about the middle, and dressed in a gaudy pink silk shirt. He chewed a cigar.

His face was morbid and hard like a Jewish gangster's.

"Monkey Face," he called, "show this new kid what to do."

An overgrown Italian boy approached, in pants and undershirt streaked with sweat. His slit nose, ape muzzle, and tiny malicious eyes had earned him his appropriate nickname.

"Come here, kid," he said. I followed him down the loft. There were thirty unfortunate human beings at work. Men sat at a long table testing mantles. Their faces were death masks, fixed and white. Great blue spectacles shielded their eyes.

Little Jewish and Italian girls dipped racks of mantles in chemical tanks. Boys stood before a series of ovens in which sixty gas jets blazed. They passed in the racks for the chemicals to burn off. Every one dripped with sweat; every one was haggard, as though in pain.

"Where did yuh work last?" growled Monkey Face.

"It's my first job. I'm just out of school."

"Yeh?" he snickered. "Just out of school, huh? Well, yuh struck a good job, kid; it'll put hair on your chest. Here, take dis."

I took the iron rack he gave me, and dropped it at once. It scorched my hand. Monkey Face laughed at the joke.

"You son-of-a-bitch!" I said, "it's hot."

He pushed his apish face close to mine.

"Yuh little kike, I'll bite your nose off if yuh get fresh wit' me! I'm your boss around here."

He went away. I worked. Racks of mantles were brought me, and I burned them off. Hell flamed and stank around me. At noon the boss blew a whistle. We sat on benches for our half-hour lunch. I could not eat for nausea. I wanted air, air, but there was no time for air.

There was no time for anything but work in that evil hell-hole. I sweated there for six months. Monkey Face tortured me. I lost fifteen pounds in weight. I raged in nightmares in my sleep. I forgot my college dreams; I forgot everything, but the gas mantles.

My mother saw how thin I was becoming. She forced me to quit that job. I was too stupefied to have done this myself. Then I read the Want Ads for another month. I found a job in a dark Second Avenue rat-hole, a little printing shop. Here I worked for another five months until I injured my hand in a press.

Another spell of job-hunting. Then a brief interval in a matzoth bakery. Job in an express company. Job in a mail order house. Job in a dry goods store.

Jobs, jobs. I drifted from one to the other, without plan, without hope. I was one of the many. I was caught like my father in poverty's trap. I was nothing, bound for nowhere. . . .

And I worked. And my father and mother grew sadder and older. It went on for years. I don't want to remember it all; the years of my adolescence. Yet I was only one among a million others.

QUESTIONS

Defining Terms

Identify in the context of the chapter each of the following:

New Deal	the American Dream
socialism	southern agrarians
Tom Kromer	Communist Party
Meridel Le Sueur	1934 Minneapolis Teamsters Strike
New Masses	Mike Gold

Probing the Sources

1. Why did people write to President and Mrs. Roosevelt? What did they ask for, and what opinions did they express about the origins and solution of the economic crisis?
2. In what sense were these pieces hopeful or despairing? Did any of them offer a vision of collective over individual action?
3. According to these accounts, in what specific ways did the Great Depression affect people in their daily lives?
4. How did the letters to the president compare to the fiction you read?
5. What impact did the depression have on women?

Interpreting the Sources

1. Why did Kromer and Gold blur the line between fiction and autobiography?
2. Why are images of strikes and unions so powerful in Le Sueur's writings? Do you think she responded to the editor's criticism at the end of "Women on the Breadlines"?
3. What did Mike Gold mean by "Jews without money"?
4. While they certainly hated human misery, in what sense did these writers welcome the crisis?
5. What are the advantages and disadvantages of using fiction to study history?

ADDITIONAL READING

On the economic aspects of the crisis, see Lester V. Chandler, *America's Greatest Depression* (1970). For an account of the Roosevelt administration, try William E. Leuchtenburg's *The FDR Years: On Roosevelt and His Legacy* (1995). The flavor of the times is captured in Studs Terkel's oral history *Hard Times* (1970) and Ann Banks's *First Person America* (1981). In *Voices of Protest* (1982), Alan Brinkley discusses the popular appeal of two depression-era demagogues, Huey Long and Father Coughlin. Important recent works include, Robert McElvaine, *The Great Depression* (1984); David Kennedy, *Freedom from Fear* (1999); Alan Brinkley, *The End of Reform* (1995); Ronald Edsforth, *The New Deal* (2000); Anthony Lee, *Painting on the Left* (1999); and Lewis Erenberg, *Swingin' the Dream* (1998). For Oklahoma and Arkansas migrants, see James Gregory, *American Exodus: The Dust Bowl Migration and California Okie Subculture* (1989). On workers' response to the crisis, see Lizabeth Cohen, *Making a New Deal* (1991). On the depression and race, see Patricia Sullivan, *Days of Hope: Race and Democracy in the New Deal Era* (1996). And see Michael Denning's *The Cultural Front* (1996), and Lawrence and Cornelia Levine, *The People and the President* (2002).

10

The Good War

Historical Context

The sheer size of American efforts in World War II was staggering. More than 16 million men and women served in the armed forces; some 320,000 were killed and another 800,000 wounded. Women and minorities served in unprecedented numbers. The war also demanded the total mobilization of economic resources. From an unemployment high of around 25 percent in 1933, the war virtually eliminated joblessness a decade later, as rural people, African Americans, and Mexicans poured into the cities to work in the war-related industries. The media, especially radio and the movies, brought current events home as never before, and the government's Office of War Information saw to it that the nation's fighting spirit remained high.

At the beginning of 1941, almost a year before we entered the conflict, the United States was a nervous island of peace in a world torn by war. In Europe the Nazi's were on the march. During the previous year Adolf Hitler's German armies' blitzkrieg assaults had overrun Denmark, Norway, Belgium, Holland, and France. Nazi planes had rained death and destruction over large sections of southern England, bombing London repeatedly in the great Blitz. In Eastern Europe Joseph Stalin's Soviet forces had defeated tiny Finland, and in the Mediterranean Benito Mussolini's Italian forces had attacked Greece. Finally, Japan—which had already invaded Manchuria and China—signed an ominous alliance with Germany and Italy, proclaimed "a new order in Eastern Asia," and promptly invaded French Indochina.

Through all this fighting the United States had kept its distance, maintaining fragile neutrality. But for President Franklin D. Roosevelt neutrality in action did not imply neutrality in thought. He wanted peace, but not peace at any price. After winning reelection in November for an unprecedented third term, he began to move more boldly in foreign affairs, expressing opinions and requesting legislation that placed the United States in harm's way. On the night of January 6, 1941, in his annual message to Congress, he spelled out the dangers. He began by telling the crowded galleries what they already knew: "[A]t no previous time has American security been as seriously threatened from without as it is today. . . . " He emphasized that some ideas were worth dying for.

Toward the end of his address, Roosevelt outlined the four core values he hoped the world would embrace: "The first is freedom of speech and expression—everywhere in the world. The second is freedom of every person to worship God in his own way—everywhere in the world. The third is freedom from want—which, translated into world terms, means economic understanding that secures to every nation a healthy peacetime life for its inhabitants—everywhere in the world. The fourth is freedom from fear—which, translated into world terms, means a world-wide reduction of armaments to such a point and in such a fashion that no nation will be in a position to commit an act of physical aggression against any neighbor—anywhere in the world."

In straightforward language Roosevelt's "Four Freedoms" proposed a "moral order." His were not fighting words as much as they were fighting ideas. But after the United States entered the war in December 1941, Roosevelt's advisers knew that they needed more than words and ideas to spread the President's message. They needed images—powerful, emotional visual symbols—to give a face to the American war effort. To do this, his administration turned to Norman Rockwell, the country's pre-eminent illustrator and best-loved artist. Since the second decade of the century, Rockwell's *Saturday Evening Post* covers had brilliantly captured the mythical small-town, middle-class, white, Protestant America. A boy in a baseball cap, a red-headed girl in pigtails, Santa Claus getting ready for Christmas, a barbershop quartet singing in harmony—these were some of Rockwell's favorite subjects.

Rockwell's assignment was to turn Roosevelt's words into images. He did so brilliantly. The four paintings—*Freedom of Speech, Freedom of Worship, Freedom from Want,* and *Freedom from Fear*—ran as covers for *The Saturday Evening Post* from February 20, 1943, to March 13, 1943. They were then reproduced and distributed across the nation as pictures and posters, reminders to millions of Americans of the cause for which their soldiers were fighting and dying.

The images Rockwell created were dramatic and compelling, each of them instantly familiar. In *Freedom of Speech* a humbly dressed young man stands alone in a town meeting to express his views while other, older men lift their eyes in admiration, if not agreement. *Freedom of Worship* portrays the diversity of America, presenting men and women; blacks and whites; Catholics, Protestants, and Jews worshipping together. Across the bottom of the picture in gold letters are the words; "Each according to the dictates of his own conscience." *Freedom from Want* presents a warm Thanksgiving meal as a big, loving family gathers round the table. *Freedom from Fear* shows a mother and father tucking in their two young children safely into bed for the night. The tension in the painting is provided by the folded newspaper held by father; the half visible headline reads "BOMBINGS KI . . . HORROR HIT. . . . "

In essence, Rockwell's painting presented America exactly how most Americans wanted to see themselves. It was an America that provided food for the hungry, safety for the defenseless, freedom for the persecuted, and respect for each person's opinions. All this, of course, silently contrasted with America's wartime enemies. The freedoms Roosevelt and Rockwell exulted were absent in Germany, Italy, and Japan, and were threatened around the world.

The contrasts between "us" and "them," the defenders and the aggressors, freedom extenders and freedom deniers, gave rise to the notion of World War II as the "Good War." It is difficult to describe any war as "good," but certainly World War II was a just war. It was, after all, a war fought against tyrants who ruthlessly compiled a long list of war crimes ranging from cruel treatment of prisoners to the Holocaust. For more than sixty years, histories, novels, comic books, movies, and television shows have presented the "Good War" of Roosevelt and Rockwell. More recently, the film *Saving Private Ryan,* the television series *The Band of Brothers,* and the book *The Greatest Generation* have reinvigorated the "Good War" ideal, while turning it into a media cash cow.

Are the books and films and television shows wrong? Were Roosevelt's words and Rockwell's images false? No, not really. The Americans and their Allies that fought against Nazi Germany and Imperial Japan confronted governments capable of great evil, governments without respect for human lives or civil liberties, governments determined to extend their influence and racial ideology at the expense of other countries. The troubling aspect of the Four Freedoms is that it was a light pointed outward toward a dark and troubled world. It exposed the evils of Germany and Japan but said very little about the problems inside of the United States. For some American minorities—African Americans, Mexican Americans, and Japanese Americans—images of the "Good War" were complicated by problems at home.

Blacks were particularly aware that racist ideology was not unusual in the United States. Throughout the late 1930s and early 1940s, as Germany marched to battle in Europe and ultimately declared war on the United States, African American journalists and political leaders pointed out that Klansman and anti-Semites in America supported "Hitlerism" at home. NAACP leader Roy Wilkins urged Americans to resist the oppression of "citizens who happen not to be white." One African American journalist commented, "The only difference between the Japanese murdering defenseless Chinese and the lynching of Negroes by their fellow Americans is one of degree." The journalist hoped that the racist barbarities of the Germans and the Japanese would make Americans "stop and think" about racial injustices committed in the United States.

Even after the Japanese bombed Pearl Harbor and the U.S. entered the fray, African Americans stressed that the war against racist ideology had a home front. Southern bases where Jim Crow customs were rigidly practiced, discrimination in defense plants, segregation inside the United States Army and Navy—all pointed to the fact that racism was a world problem. African American journalists called for a "double victory" (VV) campaign that would defeat fascism abroad and racism at home. Why, they asked, could black and white soldiers die together fighting in Europe and Asia but not eat together in a restaurant in Washington, D.C.? As African American poet Langston Hughes wrote during the war: "You tell me that hitler/ Is a mighty bad man/ I guess he took lessons/ From the ku klux klan."

Japanese Americans contended with other difficulties. Although German Americans and Italian Americans were generally treated leniently during the war, the government sent more than one hundred thousand Japanese Americans to ten internment camps located in six western states. The camps were little more than prisons, but the detainees had committed no crimes. Overcrowded wooden barracks, barbed wire, armed guards, dusty wind-swept conditions, bad food, and substandard medical conditions greeted the innocent victims of prejudice. Although many Japanese Americans questioned the legality of internment, the Supreme Court in *Korematsu v. United States* (1944) upheld the government's action.

Other American minorities also suffered during the Good War. Mexican Americans in western states faced hostility and discrimination. During the Great Depression the government deported tens of thousands of Mexicans and Mexican Americans—U.S. citizens—back to Mexico in a program of "repatriation." Less than a decade later, confronted by war-time labor shortages, the government's Bracero (work hands) Program welcomed immigrants from Mexico. This led to ethnic and cultural clashes in the Southwest. Anglos viewed Latino youths as low-level war profiteers, stereotyping them as long-haired, zoot-suited, knife-carrying criminals. The ethnic tensions simmered in Los Angeles, boiling over into violence in the June 1943 Zoot Suit riots. Although American servicemen provoked most of the violence, the riots were blamed on Latino men.

Despite the discrimination they faced at home, African Americans, Mexican Americans, and Japanese Americans fought for their country. They reinterpreted the struggle as an opportunity to prove their devotion to American freedom. The World War II era might not have been as unblemished as the movies depicted, but Americans overwhelmingly supported the *ideal* of the four freedoms. They recognized the threat posed by Japan and Germany, and in the long run, fighting racism overseas sometimes spilled over to fighting it at home.

The following documents examine the idea of "The Good War." They address how the government presented American values and how those very values failed to embrace all Americans. More than any other issue, the war against Germany and Japan challenged racist assumptions. Adolf Hitler's theories of a "master race," and his persecution of minorities helped establish America's wartime agenda. In fighting against fascism and racism, America was fighting for political freedom and racial tolerance—at least that is what wartime publicity said. If the realities of American society often fell short of our ideals, that tension helped shape postwar American politics.

THE DOCUMENTS

Introduction to Documents 1 and 2

The first two documents articulate the values that the Roosevelt administration believed were essential to any civilized society. Delivered on January 6, 1941, almost a full year before the United States entered the war, FDR's "Four Freedoms" speech attempted both to prepare Americans for the looming conflict and express the country's core beliefs. Norman Rockwell gave visual form to Roosevelt's "Four Freedoms," and his paintings were seen all over America when the *Saturday Evening Post* published them as cover art early in 1943. Reading Roosevelt's words and examining Rockwell's paintings in the context of World War II leads to a series of questions. For example, were FDR's "Four Freedoms" simply a ruse to prepare Americans for war? In Rockwell's paintings, where does art end and propaganda begin? Can propaganda be art? What is the emotional appeal of "the four freedoms"?

DOCUMENT 1 ***Franklin D. Roosevelt Presidential Library and Museum***

Annual Message to Congress
January 6, 1941

Mr. President, Mr. Speaker, Members of the Seventy-seventh Congress:

I address you, the Members of the Seventy-seventh Congress, at a moment unprecedented in the history of the Union. I use the word "unprecedented," because at no previous time has American security been as seriously threatened from without as it is today. . . .

Every realist knows that the democratic way of life is at this moment being directly assailed in every part of the world—assailed either by arms, or by secret spreading of poisonous propaganda by those who seek to destroy unity and promote discord in nations that are still at peace.

During sixteen long months this assault has blotted out the whole pattern of democratic life in an appalling number of independent nations, great and small. The assailants are still on the march, threatening other nations, great and small.

Therefore, as your President, performing my constitutional duty to "give to the Congress information of the state of the Union," I find it, unhappily, necessary to report that the future and the safety of our country and of our democracy are overwhelmingly involved in events far beyond our borders. . . .

The need of the moment is that our actions and our policy should be devoted primarily—almost exclusively—to meeting this foreign peril. For all our domestic problems are now a part of the great emergency.

Just as our national policy in internal affairs has been based upon a decent respect for the rights and the dignity of all our fellow men within our gates, so our national policy in foreign affairs has been based on a decent respect for the rights and dignity of all nations, large and small. And the justice of morality must and will win in the end.

Our national policy is this:

First, by an impressive expression of the public will and without regard to partisanship, we are committed to all-inclusive national defense.

Second, by an impressive expression of the public will and without regard to partisanship, we are committed to full support of all those resolute peoples, everywhere, who are resisting aggression and are thereby keeping war away from our Hemisphere. By this support, we express our determination that the democratic cause shall prevail; and we strengthen the defense and the security of our own nation.

Third, by an impressive expression of the public will and without regard to partisanship, we are committed to the proposition that principles of morality and considerations for our own security will never permit us to acquiesce in a peace dictated by aggressors and sponsored by appeasers. We know that enduring peace cannot be bought at the cost of other people's freedom.

In the recent national election there was no substantial difference between the two great parties in respect to that national policy. No issue was fought out on this line before the American electorate. Today it is abundantly evident that American citizens everywhere are demanding and supporting speedy and complete action in recognition of obvious danger.

Therefore, the immediate need is a swift and driving increase in our armament production. . . .

Let us say to the democracies: "We Americans are vitally concerned in your defense of freedom. We are putting forth our energies, our resources and our organizing powers to give you the strength to regain and maintain a free world. We shall send you, in ever-increasing numbers, ships, planes, tanks, guns. This is our purpose and our pledge."

In fulfillment of this purpose we will not be intimidated by the threats of dictators that they will regard as a breach of international law or as an act of war our aid to the democracies which dare to resist their aggression. Such aid is not an act of war, even if a dictator should unilaterally proclaim it so to be.

When the dictators, if the dictators, are ready to make war upon us, they will not wait for an act of war on our part. They did not wait for Norway or Belgium or the Netherlands to commit an act of war.

Their only interest is in a new one-way international law, which lacks mutuality in its observance, and, therefore, becomes an instrument of oppression.

The happiness of future generations of Americans may well depend upon how effective and how immediate we can make our aid felt. No one can tell the exact character of the emergency situations that we may be called upon to meet. The Nation's hands must not be tied when the Nation's life is in danger.

We must all prepare to make the sacrifices that the emergency—almost as serious as war itself—demands. Whatever stands in the way of speed and efficiency in defense preparations must give way to the national need.

A free nation has the right to expect full cooperation from all groups. A free nation has the right to look to the leaders of business, of labor, and of agriculture to take the lead in stimulating effort, not among other groups but within their own groups.

The best way of dealing with the few slackers or trouble makers in our midst is, first, to shame them by patriotic example, and, if that fails, to use the sovereignty of Government to save Government.

As men do not live by bread alone, they do not fight by armaments alone. Those who man our defenses, and those behind them who build our defenses, must have the stamina and the courage which come from unshakable belief in the manner of life which they are defending. The mighty action that we are calling for cannot be based on a disregard of all things worth fighting for.

The Nation takes great satisfaction and much strength from the things which have been done to make its people conscious of their individual stake in the preservation of democratic life in America. Those things have toughened the fibre of our people, have renewed their faith and strengthened their devotion to the institutions we make ready to protect.

Certainly this is no time for any of us to stop thinking about the social and economic problems which are the root cause of the social revolution which is today a supreme factor in the world.

For there is nothing mysterious about the foundations of a healthy and strong democracy. The basic things expected by our people of their political and economic systems are simple. They are:

Equality of opportunity for youth and for others.
Jobs for those who can work.
Security for those who need it.
The ending of special privilege for the few.
The preservation of civil liberties for all.
The enjoyment of the fruits of scientific progress in a wider and constantly rising standard of living.

These are the simple, basic things that must never be lost sight of in the turmoil and unbelievable complexity of our modern world. The inner and abiding strength of our economic and political systems is dependent upon the degree to which they fulfill these expectations.

Many subjects connected with our social economy call for immediate improvement. As examples:

<u>We should bring more citizens under the coverage of old-age pensions and unemployment insurance.</u>

We should widen the opportunities for adequate medical care.

We should plan a better system by which persons deserving or needing gainful employment may obtain it.

I have called for personal sacrifice. I am assured of the willingness of almost all Americans to respond to that call. . . .

In the future days, which we seek to make secure, we look forward to a world founded upon four essential human freedoms.

The first is freedom of speech and expression—everywhere in the world.

The second is freedom of every person to worship God in his own way—everywhere in the world.

The third is freedom from want—which, translated into world terms, means economic understandings which will secure to every nation a healthy peacetime life for its inhabitants—everywhere in the world.

The fourth is freedom from fear—which, translated into world terms, means a worldwide reduction of armaments to such a point and in such a thorough fashion that no nation will be in a position to commit an act of physical aggression against any neighbor—anywhere in the world.

That is no vision of a distant millennium. It is a definite basis for a kind of world attainable in our own time and generation. That kind of world is the very antithesis of the so-called new order of tyranny which the dictators seek to create with the crash of a bomb.

To that new order we oppose the greater conception—the moral order. A good society is able to face schemes of world domination and foreign revolutions alike without fear.

Since the beginning of our American history, we have been engaged in change—in a perpetual peaceful revolution—a revolution which goes on steadily, quietly adjusting itself to changing conditions—without the concentration camp or the quick-lime in the ditch. The world order which we seek is the cooperation of free countries, working together in a friendly, civilized society.

This nation has placed its destiny in the hands and heads and hearts of its millions of free men and women; and its faith in freedom under the guidance of God. Freedom means the supremacy of human rights everywhere. Our support goes to those who struggle to gain those rights or keep them. Our strength is our unity of purpose. To that high concept there can be no end save victory.

DOCUMENT 2

Norman Rockwell, whose illustrations were widely known and beloved byAmericans, painted his version of Roosevelt's four freedoms--freedom of speech, of worship, from want, from fear--as cover-art for the Saturday Evening Post early in 1943, when the United States was embroiled in World War II and the outcome of that conflict was far from certain.What messages, emotional and intellectual, were conveyed by these images? (Printed by permission of the Norman Rockwell Family Agency. Copyright © 2007 the Norman Rockwell Family Entities. The Library of Congress.)

Introduction to Documents 3 and 4

The racist ideology of the Nazi and Japanese regimes brought into sharp focus the racism that plagued American society. Throughout the war African American journalists and soldiers criticized the existence of segregated armed forces and Jim Crow facilities in Southern training camps. Although Executive Order #8802 outlawed discrimination in defense work or government service because of "race, creed, color, or national origin," the 1941 order was often ignored or evaded. The following editorials point out the irony of a segregated, racially divided nation claiming to fight for freedom and toleration. Both appeared in *The Crisis,* the journal of the National Association for the Advancement of Colored People. Founded in 1909 on the one hundredth anniversary of Abraham Lincoln's birth, the NAACP was America's oldest civil rights organization. The first editorial appeared just before the Japanese attack on Pearl Harbor, and discussed the problem of discrimination in the military. The second editorial, published a year later and addressed as an open letter to President Roosevelt, made much broader claims for equality at home based on America's professed ideals.

DOCUMENT 3 *The Army Must Act*

If the government expects any support from Negro public opinion in the future it must insist that the War Department take positive action to bring to trial all the persons responsible for the incident at Fort Bragg, N.C., on August 6 in which a Negro private and a white military policeman were killed in a fight on a bus.

In a sense, this Fort Bragg incident is the acid test of the Army and Negroes. The first test came last spring in the lynching of Private Felix Hall who was found hanging from a tree within the borders of Fort Benning, Ga. In that matter—one of intense interest to all Negro Americans—the Army so far has announced merely that it is conducting an investigation.

But at Fort Bragg, the situation is different. The killings were the direct result of the Army policy of segregating and humiliating Negro soldiers and then placing military police duty over them largely in the hands of ignorant, prejudiced, white southern soldiers. . . .

Information gathered by white and Negro newspaper reporters at Fort Bragg shows that Negro soldiers, including one commissioned officer and several non-commissioned officers, were rounded up, humiliated, cursed, beaten, and threatened with cocked pistols and shotguns by white military police. The soldiers they arrested and beat up were not involved in any way in the shooting, were not on the bus in question, were not even in the vicinity of the shooting, and knew nothing whatever about it.

The whole incident resembles exactly the aftermath of an alleged crime by a Negro in any southern community. A reign of terror is instituted in which any colored person, man, woman, or child, is subject to raiding and punishment by any white person.

At Fort Bragg all Army discipline was thrown to the winds. In a minute the Negro soldiers became "just Negroes" subject to the whims of any white man. It will be useless for the Army to try to dodge responsibility for this affair. *The white military police would not have beaten up scores of Negro soldiers, would not have interfered with Negro civilians in towns away from Army posts, and would not have staged a "lynching roundup" after the Fort Bragg double killing if their commanding officers had not approved such action.*

The chief villain in this piece is the officer in charge of military police. The next is the commander of the colored troops at Ft. Bragg, and the next is the commandant of the whole post. The poor white boys who do the beating and shooting are merely instruments of a policy maintained by these men and the War Department.

We shall see what we shall see. Negro Americans might as well discover at the beginning whether they are to fight and die for democracy for the Lithuanians, the Greeks, and the Brazilians, or whether they had better fight and die for a little democracy for themselves. . . .

DOCUMENT 4 *An Open Letter to President Roosevelt—An Editorial*

Dear Mr. President:

Early in 1943, a year and a month after Pearl Harbor, you will stand before the Congress and give your message on the State of the Nation. On this occasion, Mr. President, we venture to inject our observations upon the feelings of one-tenth of the population of our nation, a tenth which has been loyal to America since that day on Boston Common when a black man was the first to die before the guns of the Redcoats in the war for Independence.

We venture this injection not because we feel our reactions are of paramount importance, but because you, yourself, and, indeed all the great statesmen of the United Nations cause, have said that without unity, without marching along together and fighting shoulder to shoulder, we will lose this war and fall victim to the dictators.

We believe, therefore, that any practice which threatens that unity, which alienates a tenth of our people at a time when our life as a nation may depend upon mustering ten tenths, is worthy of your attention as we proceed upon the second year of war.

WHAT YOU HAVE DONE

We are not unaware of what you have done thus far on this problem. In the fall of 1940 you promised that Negroes would be placed in every major branch of the Army, that they would be trained as commissioned officers on a non-segregated basis. You even broke with Army tradition and announced that Negroes would be trained as combat aviators. You appointed a Negro as civilian aide to the Secretary of War and elevated a Negro colonel, a veteran of Regular Army service, to the rank of brigadier general, the first such rank ever held by a Negro in an American army. Our women were accepted in the WAACS.

On the production front you issued Executive Order 8802, directing the abolishing of discrimination in employment in war industries and government agencies. You set up the President's Committee on Fair Employment Practice to examine into violations of this order.

In your speeches, and particularly in the one of January 6, 1942, you decried racial discrimination "in any of its ugly forms" and called upon our people to unite against the Axis.

Your administrative officers have taken Negroes into government offices to aid in the further integration of Negro citizens into the war effort and into the life of the country. Your good wife has gone the length and breadth of this land, and over the seas, never neglecting our segment of the population in her travels and comments.

For these actions you and she have suffered vile and un-American condemnation and calumny from some quarters which see not the whole nation and its welfare, not the human family and its multi-colored members, but only their narrow section through their prejudiced eyes and little selves. We are grateful for these things, Mr. President, and for the broad measures which have operated, in some degree, to extend to every American, regardless of race, creed, or color, that equality of opportunity to which Americans are entitled.

BUT . . .

However, despite your exhortations to unity, and your acts clearly indicating unity as a national policy, the thirteen millions of Negro American citizens have not been made an integral part of the nation's war effort; they are not geared as they should be—or as they passionately desire to be—to an all-out drive for victory.

Their fighting men are, as you promised, in every major branch of the army. Many of them are serving on battlefronts far from our shores. But in their own army they find themselves set apart from their fellow fighters for freedom, in their army theatres, canteens, living quarters and transportation. The manifold methods by which this separation is emphasized have sapped morale sadly and embittered our men—some almost to the point of mutiny.

There are Negro officers, as you promised, but the line officers are confined to the lowest ranks, and promotions are slow in coming. In the 93rd division at Fort Huachuca, Ariz., that complete small army of which Negroes are so proud, we understand there is only *one* Negro captain in the line. We know that we did not have many veteran officers at the start, but we have watched newly-trained white officers rise steadily above our men—in our own division.

Off the military reservations our fighting men have been treated so viciously by their own fellow Americans that many of them have wondered whether the enemy is really across the seas, or here at home. Notorious in this studied cruelty to Negro soldiers has been Alexandria, La.

We are proud, too, of our few fighting pursuit pilots in the Army Air Forces, but none of our lads is a bomber pilot, a bombardier, a navigator, an aerial gunner.

The Navy remains adamant against commissions for our men and has excluded us from the V-1 program. It also bars our women from the WAVES.

On the production front the pressure of sheer necessity has forced the employment of our people in most places, but in too many communities your Executive Order 8802 is being defied and sabotaged by management and labor alike. In too many instances menial tasks and unskilled labor are all that we may secure. In some few instances we are still rigidly excluded from any type of employment.

On what we may call the civilian front we are still lynched. Six persons—two of them boys in their teens—fell victim to mobs during 1942. Millions of us are still disfranchised by one method or another. Six million white Americans and four million of us are barred from the ballot box by the poll tax alone. We still suffer humiliations and discriminations in public places, in travel and in housing.

We, who are willing and anxious to fight for the Four Freedoms, are not free.

OUR NATION IS HURT

Less than a month ago Governor Frank Dixon of Alabama defied the Federal government, the whole war effort, to include the Negro in the fight against oppression, bigotry, and hatred. In this philosophy, Mr. President, we are supposed to fight and die for the freedom of the remotest corners of the world, for every other people, but to be content to remain in, or return to, a "place" in Governor Dixon's world.

We are concerned not alone because of what these things have done to our part of the population, but because of what they are doing to our war effort. We do not live in this world alone. Alabama cannot draw a ring around itself and stand or fall by its vision, its philosophy. There are billions of eyes upon America. Victory itself, and any success we may have in the post-war world may well depend upon the justice we demonstrate now in our treatment of the largest black citizen-minority in a democracy anywhere on earth.

It is needless to protest once again our loyalty to our country. That has been proved generation after generation. But we are loyal to the ideals of this nation, not to the practices which meet us on every hand. Our boys, to the last one, are not fighting—and are not offering to die—to perpetuate those practices. . . .

They and we would be heartened and strengthened anew if you, Mr. President, would speak out, notifying the foes of liberty *everywhere* exactly what America expects to buy with the blood and billions she is expending.

Introduction to Documents 5 and 6

On February 19, 1942, President Roosevelt authorized the war department to ship almost 112,000 West Coast Japanese, most of them American citizens, to "relocation" centers. The order was based upon the notion that persons of Japanese ancestry presented a clear and present threat to American security, that loyalty to Japan might lead some of them to sabotage the American war effort. Although the order was later upheld in *Korematsu v. United States* (1944), not all of Supreme Court justices concurred with the majority opinion. In fact, Justice Frank Murphy in his dissenting opinion charged that the order "goes over 'the brink of constitutional power' and falls into the ugly abyss of racism." Document 5 presents the majority opinion in *Hirabayashi v. United States* (1943), the first case that tested the constitutionality of the order. In this case, an American citizen of Japanese ancestry refused to register for evacuation. More, he deliberately violated a curfew that ordered people of Japanese ancestry to stay within their homes after 8:00 p.m. every night. The legal question, then, centered on the President's Executive Order #9066 and Congress's ratification of that order mandating the internment camps. How did the court rule and why? The next document gives us the voice of an American citizen incarcerated in one of the camps. How would Ted Nakashima argue with the Supreme Court? Why does he spend so much time describing his family? What does he mean that being called a "Jap" hurt most of all? How were the experiences of African Americans and Japanese Americans similar during the war? Different?

DOCUMENT 5 *Hirabayashi v. United States*

Opinion of the Court

. . . The war power of the national government is "the power to wage war successfully." . . . It extends to every matter and activity so related to war as substantially to affect its conduct and progress. The power is not restricted to the winning of victories in the field and the repulse of enemy forces. It embraces every phase of the national defense, including the protection of war materials and the members of the armed forces from injury and from the dangers which attend the rise, prosecution and progress of war. . . . Since the Constitution commits to the Executive and to Congress the exercise of the war power in all the vicissitudes and conditions of warfare, it has necessarily given them wide scope for the exercise of judgment and discretion in determining the nature and extent of the threatened injury or danger and in the selection of the means for resisting it. . . . Where, as they did here, the conditions call for the exercise of judgment and discretion and for the choice of means by those branches of the Government on which the Constitution has placed the responsibility of war-making, it is not for any court to sit in review of the wisdom of their action or substitute its judgment for theirs.

The actions taken must be appraised in the light of the conditions with which the President and Congress were confronted in the early months of 1942, many of which, since disclosed, were then peculiarly within the knowledge of the military authorities. On December 7, 1941, the Japanese air forces had attacked the United States Naval Base at

Pearl Harbor without warning, at the very hour when Japanese diplomatic representatives were conducting negotiations with our State Department ostensibly for the peaceful settlement of differences between the two countries. Simultaneously or nearly so, the Japanese attacked Malaysia, Hong Kong, the Philippines, and Wake and Midway Islands. On the following day their army invaded Thailand. Shortly afterwards they sank two British battleships. On December 13th, Guam was taken. On December 24th and 25th they captured Wake Island and occupied Hong Kong. On January 2, 1942, Manila fell, and on February 10th Singapore, Britain's great naval base in the East, was taken. On February 27th the battle of the Java Sea resulted in a disastrous naval defeat to the United Nations. By the 9th of March Japanese forces had established control over the Netherlands East Indies; Rangoon and Burma were occupied; Bataan and Corregidor were under attack.

Although the results of the attack on Pearl Harbor were not fully disclosed until much later, it was known that the damage was extensive, and that the Japanese by their successes had gained a naval superiority over our forces in the Pacific which might enable them to seize Pearl Harbor, our largest naval base and the last stronghold of defense lying between Japan and the west coast. That reasonably prudent men charged with the responsibility of our national defense had ample ground for concluding that they must face the danger of invasion, take measures against it, and in making the choice of measures consider our internal situation, cannot be doubted.

The challenged orders were defense measures for the avowed purpose of safeguarding the military area in question, at a time of threatened air raids and invasion by the Japanese forces, from the danger of sabotage and espionage. As the curfew was made applicable to citizens residing in the area only if they were of Japanese ancestry, our inquiry must be whether in the light of all the facts and circumstances there was any substantial basis for the conclusion, in which Congress and the military commander united, that the curfew as applied was a protective measure necessary to meet the threat of sabotage and espionage which would substantially affect the war effort and which might reasonably be expected to aid a threatened enemy invasion. The alternative which appellant insists must be accepted is for the military authorities to impose the curfew on all citizens within the military area, or on none. In a case of threatened danger requiring prompt action, it is a choice between inflicting obviously needless hardship on the many, or sitting passive and unresisting in the presence of the threat. We think that constitutional government, in time of war, is not so powerless and does not compel so hard a choice if those charged with the responsibility of our national defense have reasonable ground for believing that the threat is real. . . .

In the critical days of March 1942, the danger to our war production by sabotage and espionage in this area seems obvious. . . . At a time of threatened Japanese attack upon this country, the nature of our inhabitants' attachments to the Japanese enemy was consequently a matter of grave concern. Of the 126,000 persons of Japanese descent in the United States, citizens and non-citizens, approximately 112,000 resided in California, Oregon and Washington at the time of the adoption of the military regulations. Of these approximately two-thirds are citizens because born in the United States. Not only did the great majority of such persons reside within the Pacific Coast states but they were concentrated in or near three of the large cities, Seattle, Portland and Los Angeles, all in Military Area No. 1.

There is support for the view that social, economic and political conditions which have prevailed since the close of the last century, when the Japanese began to come to this country in substantial numbers, have intensified their solidarity and have in large measure prevented their assimilation as an integral part of the white population. In addition, large numbers of children of Japanese parentage are sent to Japanese language schools outside the regular hours of public schools in the locality. Some of these schools are generally believed to be sources of Japanese nationalistic propaganda, cultivating allegiance to Japan.

Considerable numbers, estimated to be approximately 10,000, of American-born children of Japanese parentage have been sent to Japan for all or a part of their education.

Congress and the Executive, including the military commander, could have attributed special significance, in its bearing on the loyalties of persons of Japanese descent, to the maintenance by Japan of its system of dual citizenship. Children born in the United States of Japanese alien parents, and especially those children born before December 1, 1924, are under many circumstances deemed, by Japanese law, to be citizens of Japan. No official census of those whom Japan regards as having thus retained Japanese citizenship is available, but there is ground for the belief that the number is large. . . .

As a result of all these conditions affecting the life of the Japanese, both aliens and citizens, in the Pacific Coast areas, there has been relatively little social intercourse between them and the white population. The restrictions, both practical and legal, affecting the privileges and opportunities afforded to persons of Japanese extraction residing in the United States, have been sources of irritation and may well have tended to increase their isolation, and in many instances their attachments to Japan and its institutions.

Viewing these data in all their aspects, Congress and the Executive could reasonably have concluded that these conditions have encouraged the continued attachment of members of this group to Japan and Japanese institutions. These are only some of the many considerations which those charged with the responsibility for the national defense could take into account in determining the nature and extent of the danger of espionage and sabotage, in the event of invasion or air raid attack. The extent of that danger could be definitely known only after the event and after it was too late to meet it. Whatever views we may entertain regarding the loyalty to this country of the citizens of Japanese ancestry, we cannot reject as unfounded the judgment of the military authorities and of Congress that there were disloyal members of that population, whose number and strength could not be precisely and quickly ascertained. We cannot say that the war-making branches of the Government did not have ground for believing that in a critical hour such persons could not readily be isolated and separately dealt with, and constituted a menace to the national defense and safety, which demanded that prompt and adequate measures be taken to guard against it.

Appellant does not deny that, given the danger, a curfew was an appropriate measure against sabotage. It is an obvious protection against the perpetration of sabotage most readily committed during the hours of darkness. If it was an appropriate exercise of the war power its validity is not impaired because it has restricted the citizen's liberty. Like every military control of the population of a dangerous zone in war time, it necessarily involves some infringement of individual liberty, just as does the police establishment of fire lines during a fire, or the confinement of people to their houses during an air raid alarm—neither of which could be thought to be an infringement of constitutional right. Like them, the validity of the restraints of the curfew order depends on all the conditions which obtain at the time the curfew is imposed and which support the order imposing it.

But appellant insists that the exercise of the power is inappropriate and unconstitutional because it discriminates against citizens of Japanese ancestry, in violation of the Fifth Amendment. The Fifth Amendment contains no equal protection clause and it restrains only such discriminatory legislation by Congress as amounts to a denial of due process. . . .

Distinctions between citizens solely because of their ancestry are by their very nature odious to a free people whose institutions are founded upon the doctrine of equality. For that reason, legislative classification or discrimination based on race alone has often been held to be a denial of equal protection. . . . We may assume that these considerations would be controlling here were it not for the fact that the danger of espionage and sabotage, in time of war and of threatened invasion, calls upon the military authorities to scrutinize every relevant fact bearing on the loyalty of populations in the danger areas. Because racial discriminations are in most circumstances irrelevant and therefore prohibited, it by no means follows that, in dealing with the perils of war, Congress and the Executive are wholly precluded from taking into account those facts and circumstances which are relevant to measures for our national defense and for the successful prosecution of the war, and which may in fact place citizens of one ancestry in a different category from others. "We must never forget, that it is *a constitution* we are expounding," "a constitution intended to endure for ages to come, and, consequently, to be adapted to the various *crises* of human affairs." The adoption by Government, in the crisis of war and of threatened invasion, of measures for the public safety, based upon the recognition of facts and circumstances which indicate that a group of one national extraction may menace that safety more than others, is not wholly beyond the limits of the Constitution and is not to be condemned merely because in other and in most circumstances racial distinctions are irrelevant.

Here the aim of Congress and the Executive was the protection against sabotage of war materials and utilities in areas thought to be in danger of Japanese invasion and air attack. We have stated in detail facts and circumstances with respect to the American citizens of Japanese ancestry residing on the Pacific Coast which support the judgment of the war-waging branches of the Government that some restrictive measure was urgent. We cannot say that these facts and circumstances, considered in the particular war setting, could afford no ground for differentiating citizens of Japanese ancestry from other groups in the United States. The fact alone that attack on our shores was threatened by Japan rather than another enemy power set these citizens apart from others who have no particular associations with Japan. . . .

DOCUMENT 6 *Concentration Camp: U.S. Style*

by Ted Nakashima

Unfortunately in this land of liberty, I was born of Japanese parents; born in Seattle of a mother and father who have been in this country since 1901. Fine parents, who brought up their children in the best American way of life. My mother served with the Volunteer Red Cross Service in the last war—my father, an editor, has spoken and written Americanism for forty years.

Our family is almost typical of the other unfortunates here at the camp. The oldest son, a licensed architect, was educated at the University of Washington, has a master's degree from the Massachusetts Institute of Technology and is a scholarship graduate of the American School of Fine Arts in Fontainebleau, France. He is now in camp in Oregon with his wife and three-months-old child. He had just completed designing a much needed defense housing project at Vancouver, Washington.

The second son is an M.D. He served his internship in a New York hospital, is married and has two fine sons. The folks banked on him, because he was the smartest of us three boys. The army took him a month after he opened his office. He is now a lieutenant in the Medical Corps, somewhere in the South.

I am the third son, the dumbest of the lot, but still smart enough to hold down a job as an architectural draftsman. I have just finished building a new home and had lived in it three weeks. My desk was just cleared of work done for the Army Engineers, another stack of 391 defense houses was waiting (a rush job), when the order came to pack up and leave for this resettlement center called "Camp Harmony."

Mary, the only girl in the family, and her year-old son, "Butch," are with our parents—interned in the stables of the Livestock Exposition Buildings in Portland.

Now that you can picture our thoroughly American background, let me describe our new home.

The resettlement center is actually a penitentiary—armed guards in towers with spotlights and deadly tommy guns, fifteen feet of barbed-wire fences, everyone confined to quarters at nine, lights out at ten o'clock. The guards are ordered to shoot anyone who approaches within twenty feet of the fences. No one is allowed to take the two-block-long hike to the latrines after nine, under any circumstances.

The apartments, as the army calls them, are two-block-long stables, with windows on one side. Floors are shiplaps on two-by-fours laid directly on the mud, which is everywhere. The stalls are about eighteen by twenty-one feet; some contain families of six or seven persons. Partitions are seven feet high, leaving a four-foot opening above. The rooms aren't too bad, almost fit to live in for a short while.

The food and sanitation problems are the worst. We have had absolutely no fresh meat, vegetables or butter since we came here. Mealtime queues extend for blocks; standing in a rainswept line, feet in the mud, waiting for the scant portions of canned wieners and boiled potatoes, hash for breakfast or canned wieners and beans for dinner. Milk only for the kids. Coffee or tea dosed with saltpeter and stale bread are the adults' staples. Dirty, unwiped dishes, greasy silver, a starchy diet, no butter, no milk, bawling kids, mud, wet mud that stinks when it dries, no vegetables—a sad thing for the people who raised them in such abundance. Memories of a crisp head of lettuce with our special olive oil, vinegar, garlic and cheese dressing.

Today one of the surface sewage-disposal pipes broke and the sewage flowed down the streets. Kids play in the water. Shower baths without hot water. Stinking mud and slops everywhere.

Can this be the same America we left a few weeks ago?

As I write, I can remember our little bathroom—light coral walls. My wife painting them, and the spilled paint in her hair. The open towel shelving and the pretty shower curtains which we put up the day before we left. How sanitary and clean we left it for the airlines pilot and his young wife who are now enjoying the fruits of our labor.

It all seems so futile, struggling, trying to live our old lives under this useless, regimented life. The senselessness of all the inactive manpower. Electricians, plumbers, draftsmen, mechanics, carpenters, painters, farmers—every trade—men who are able and willing to do all they can to lick the Axis. Thousands of men and women in these camps, energetic, quick, alert, eager for hard, constructive work, waiting for the army to do something for us, an army that won't give us butter.

I can't take it! I have 391 defense houses to be drawn. I left a fine American home which we built with our own hands. I left a life, highballs with our American friends on week-ends, a carpenter, laundry-truck driver, architect, airlines pilot—good friends, friends who would swear by us. I don't have enough of that Japanese heritage "*ga-man*"—a code of silent suffering and ability to stand pain.

Oddly enough I still have a bit of faith in army promises of good treatment and Mrs. Roosevelt's pledge of a future worthy of good American citizens. I'm banking another $67 of income tax on the future. Sometimes I want to spend the money I have set aside for income tax on a bit of butter or ice cream or something good that I might have smuggled through the gates, but I can't do it when I think that every dollar I can put into "the fight to lick the Japs," the sooner I will be home again. I must forget my stomach.

What really hurts most is the constant reference to us evacués as "Japs." "Japs" are the guys we are fighting. We're on this side and we want to help.

Why won't America let us?

The New Republic, *June 15, 1942*

Introduction to Document 7

Relations between whites and Latinos were never easy, but the years leading up to World War II had been particularly difficult. During the Great Depression, 400,000 Mexicans and American citizens of Mexican descent were shipped south. These people, it was said, took jobs away from white Americans, and the government began a massive—and illegal—campaign of "repatriation." But with a war-induced labor shortage, new immigrants were again allowed into California under the Bracero Program of 1942, which caused very uneasy labor relations.

By 1943, reports of alleged gang violence reached their peak in the local press. The stereotyped image of Mexican youths—each sporting long hair, a zoot suit, and a blade in his pocket—filled the newspapers. Headlines referred to "Zoot-Suited Gangsters," "Hoodlums," "Boy Gang Rioters," "Mexican Good Squads," and "Pachuco Killers." Edward Duran Ayers, a spokesman for the L.A. County Sheriff's Department, declared that Mexicans were descendants of blood-thirsty Aztecs, and he added, "the Caucasian, especially the Anglo-Saxon, when engaged in fighting, particularly among youths, resorts to fisticuffs, and may at times kick each other, which is considered unsportive, but this Mexican element considers all that to be a sign of weakness, and all he knows and feels is a desire to use a knife or some lethal weapon." Ayers went on to say that the tendency toward violence was a biological trait of Mexicans, blacks, and Native Americans.

Ayers' words did not fit well with the wartime ideal of a Grand Alliance that included Mexico and other Latin American nations standing shoulder-to-shoulder with the United States. But by the spring of 1943, some of the strains of war were beginning to show. The news from Europe and Asia was not good. On the home front, rumors of Japanese spy rings subverting the American war effort grabbed newspaper headlines, even though almost all Japanese Americans had been forced into internment camps a year earlier. Coal miners went out on strike in May 1943 amid accusations of treason and disloyalty. Reports also circulated the news that juvenile delinquency was rampant, while the Federal Bureau of Investigation reported a growing problem with draft dodging.

In June 1943, civil disturbances broke out in New York City, Los Angeles, Detroit, Philadelphia, and smaller cities. All of these events began when police, soldiers, or white citizens confronted members of minority groups. Rioting in Detroit left thirty-four people dead (twenty-seven blacks and seven whites) and hundreds wounded. The battles that broke out in L.A. two weeks earlier were not so deadly, but the following newspaper stories and memoranda offer a window on civil strife in the midst of war.

DOCUMENT 7

28 Zoot Suiters Seized on Coast After Clashes with Service Men

Los Angeles, June 6—Subdued and no longer ready to do battle, twenty-eight zoot-suiters, stripped of their garish clothing and with county jail barbers hopefully eyeing their flowing duck-tail haircuts, languished behind bars today after a second night of battle with officers and service men.

The arrests came after a "war" declared by service men, mostly sailors, on zoot-suit gangs which have been preying on the East Side as well as molesting civilians. Impetus was given to the clean-up campaign when the wives of two sailors were criminally attacked by the youths.

Cruising in taxicabs and cars, and occasionally spearing into enemy territory on foot in precise platoon drill, the service men routed the gangs, depriving them of crude weapons.

Favored for fighting by the youths were lengths of rope weighted with wire and lead, tire chains and wrenches, hammers and heavy bottles, some with the tops broken off.

Deputy sheriffs and police riot squads patrolled the "No Man's Land," breaking up fights where possible.

Sixteen Mexican youths, all armed with some sort of bludgeon, were arrested. They were said to have tried to keep Deputy Sheriffs Foster Kellogg and E. N. Smith from arresting one of their number.

The entire lot was booked in the county jail on riot charges after flying squadrons of officers arrived on the scene.

The suspects, who were in a truck, said they were on their way to "have it out" with a bunch of sailors who had sent word they would be at California and Temple Streets to accommodate any of the zoot-suiters who thought Uncle Sam's fighting men were not just that.

New York Times, *June 7, 1943*

City, Navy Clamp Lid on Zoot-Suit Warfare

. . . Throughout tense hours last night the zoot-suit war was held to sporadic clashes by a combination of strong police patrols and a Navy order listing Los Angeles as a restricted area for men of the Navy, Marine Corps and Coast Guard.

Nearly 1000 uniformed and special officers took up assigned positions throughout the downtown and East Side sections of the city at dusk. Others patrolled the streets in cruising cars, keeping a throng of sight-seers moving.

Crowds were dispersed almost as soon as they gathered and few youths in zoot suits were seen as groups of soldiers moved through the district with the watchful eyes of men looking for trouble. . . .

Los Angeles Times, *June 9, 1943*

Memo from Marine Commander Clarence Fogg to the District Patrol Officer, June 8, 1943

Continued disorder.

Hundreds of service men prowling downtown Los Angeles mostly on foot—disorderly—apparently on prowl for Mexicans.

Have by joint agreement with Army Provost Marshall declared following Los Angeles city territory out of bounds to all Navy, Marines, Coast Guard, and Army personnel: Main Street east to Los Angeles city limits.

All shore patrol are concentrated in the downtown area. Disorderly personnel are being arrested by shore patrol. Expect adverse publicity in morning newspaper.

Los Angeles Police have called in all off-duty men and auxiliary police to handle situation.

Naval Reserve Armory did not grant liberty. Men involved are from Marine activities, San Diego and El Toro, Navy activity composed of Roosevelt Base, Port Hueneme, and Destroyer Base, San Diego.

Situation under control at present except for widely separated incidents.

Groups vary in size from 10 to 150 men and scatter immediately when shore patrol approach. Men found carrying hammock clues, belts, knives, and tire irons when searched by patrol after arrest. . . .

Senior Patrol Office will call District Patrol Officer at about 1000 today, June 8, 1943, if there is anything additional to report.

Military police patrols roamed the streets on foot and in jeeps, augmenting the work of city police. Many women and girls strolled the sidewalks with soldier escorts and the bars were crowded with servicemen awaiting the sound of a police whistle or a scuffle.

Only a sprinkling of sailors was seen, however, as the ban ordered by Rear Admiral D. W. Bagley, commandant of the 11th Naval District, went into effect.

Admiral Bagley issued the "precautionary measure" as a result of clashes between Navy men and the youths.

The official Navy announcement described the sailors as acting in "self-defense against the rowdy element" and defined the order as applying to all Navy personnel except those granted special authorization by commanders of naval stations in the area. . . .

Yesterday's incidents in the zoot war included insults hurled at Navy men in the Chavez Ravine area. . . . After shouting taunts and abuse mixed with dire threats, the youths sped away.

Earlier in the day police reported that Donald J. Jackson, 20-year-old sailor, had been knifed by a gang of youths at First St. and Evergreen Ave. shortly after noon, while his companion, James R. Phelps, 19, another sailor, escaped injury by fleeing.

The attack was reported to the Hollenbeck Heights police, who began a roundup of suspects in the vicinity. Jackson received a five-inch cut in the stomach and a slight cut on the head and was treated at the Georgia Street Receiving Hospital, where his condition was said to be serious.

Shortly after, D. A. Mainhurst, 23, a sailor who had just reached the city from San Diego, reported to Newton St. police that he was beaten and kicked by a gang of zoot suiters at Central Ave. and Olympic Blvd. as he was waiting for a bus. . . .

He told police that about eight men attacked him from behind, knocked him down and kicked him. He escaped and took refuge in a service station, from which the gangsters dragged him and began beating him when nearby residents came to his rescue and the gang fled.

Phelps and Jackson said they were walking peaceably along the street at First St. and Evergreen Ave. when at least 15 zoot suiters jumped from automobiles and attacked them, slashing Jackson.

All this occurred shortly before Army and Navy officers conferred with Mayor Bowron and Chief of Police Horrall in the Mayor's office regarding plans for halting the disturbances. Full cooperation was pledged by the military officials, who were not aware at the time that Admiral Bagley had made Los Angeles a restricted area for his personnel. . . .

In the Monday night rioting which blocked traffic on S. Main St. and Broadway for a time, at least 50 zoot-suit youths were beaten and, in many cases, stripped of their outer clothing.

Thousands of civilians assembled in the area and, according to Chief Horrall, "egged on" the servicemen, who banded together and took on all persons they found clad in zoot suits.

In the police roundup which followed, more than 200 youths, only a few of them in zoot suits, were arrested and booked in the Georgia Street Juvenile Bureau on suspicion of inciting to riot. Nearly 500 servicemen were taken in custody by military authorities and police but these were sent back to their stations early yesterday.

The Battle Between Marines and "Pachucos"

. . . The Coordinator of Latin-American Youths . . . informed us . . . that during a meeting in which the situation created by the riots between the "pachucos" and the marines was discussed, a decision was reached to send the following telegram to Mr. Elmer Davis, Head of the Office of War Information in Washington; to Mr. Alan Cranston, Head of the Division of Foreign Languages, of the same office, and to President Roosevelt at the White House.

Here is the message:

> Since last Thursday evening various groups of marines and soldiers have attacked Mexican zoot suiters throughout the city of Los Angeles. Although the youth did nothing to provoke the attack or for that matter to resist the attack, many were severely wounded, including women and children. Supposedly the attack has been motivated by past conflicts between the two groups and has been amplified by the press claiming that Mexican youths have been disrespectful toward the servicemen, a claim without any foundation.
>
> Despite precautions taken on the part of the military police and local authorities to control the situation, the servicemen continue to walk the streets of Los Angeles armed with clubs and appear to be tacitly supported by many city and local officials in charge of keeping the peace; their attacks have now expanded to include blacks. This situation, which is prompting racial antagonism between the Mexican, Anglo-Saxon and Black communities will undoubtedly have grave international repercussions which will inevitably damage the war effort and thwart the gains made by the Good Neighbor policy. We urge immediate intervention by the Office of War Information so that it moderates the local press which has openly approved of these mutinies and which is treating this situation in a manner that is decidedly inflammatory. . . .

Approximately fifty people, including the members of the Council, attended the meeting in which the decision to send this telegram was reached. . . .

La Opinion, *June 9, 1943* (La Opinion *was a Spanish-language newspaper published in Los Angeles)*

Riot

Washington, June 9, (AP)—Rafael de la Colina, Council Minister of the Mexican Embassy in Washington, was noticeably indignant during an interview dealing with the recent assaults on Mexican American youths by military personnel in Los Angeles. He declared that many innocent Mexican passersby had been beaten.

After receiving news from the Mexican consulate in Los Angeles, the Minister added that it was entirely possible that the Mexican government would present a formal protest to the government of the United States and that the Embassy awaited orders from the Mexican government. . . .

Carey McWilliams, president of the National Lawyers Association in Los Angeles, dispatched a petition to Attorney General Francis H. Biddle calling for an investigation of the events surrounding the recent race conflicts.

"These conflicts are not isolated incidents," said McWilliams. "Evidence indicates that the violence which has occurred during this last weekend is the logical response to the policies and methods used by the local police department against the Mexican community over the last 18 months."

Excelsior, *June 10, 1943* (Excelsior *was published in Mexico City, translated from Spanish.)*

Not a Race Issue, Mayor Says

Los Angeles, June 9—There is no question of racial discrimination involved in the zoot-suit trouble here, Mayor Bowron told State Department officials in a telephonic conversation.

Following his conversation the Mayor issued a statement in which he said:

> I have had a long-distance telephone conversation with the State Department in Washington relative to the local situation. I was advised that the Mexican Embassy had called the matter to the attention of the State Department upon the basis of a report received from the Mexican Consul in Los Angeles.

I informed the State Department that assurances could be given to the Mexican Embassy that the occurrences in this city are not in any manner directed at Mexican citizens or even against persons of Mexican descent. There is no question of racial discrimination involved.

We have here, unfortunately, a bad situation as the result of the formation and activities of youthful gangs, the members of which, probably to the extent of 98 per cent or more, were born right here in Los Angeles. They are Los Angeles youth, and the problem is purely a local one.

We are going to see that members of the armed forces are not attacked. At the same time, we expect cooperation from officers of the Army and Navy to the extent that soldiers and sailors do not pile into Los Angeles for the purpose of excitement and adventure and what they might consider a little fun by beating up young men whose appearance they do not like.

We propose to handle the situation in such a way that there will be no reason for protests on the part of the Mexican Government.

At the same time, I want to assure the people of Los Angeles that there will be no side-stepping and the situation will be vigorously handled. There are too many citizens in this community, some of them good-intentioned and a few whose intentions I question, who raise a hue and cry of racial discrimination or prejudice against a minority group every time the Los Angeles police make arrests of members of gangs or groups working in unison. They all look alike to us, regardless of color and length of their coats.

The police are going to do the job and I propose to back up the police.

New York Times, *June 10, 1943*

Los Angeles Group Insists Riots Halt

BY LAWRENCE E. DAVIES

Los Angeles, June 12—Punishment of the guilty in crimes of violence, "regardless of what clothes they wear, whether they be zoot suits, police, Army or Navy uniforms," was demanded today by a Citizens' Committee appointed by Governor Earl Warren to investigate the Los Angeles outbreaks of the last ten days revolving "zoot-suit" wearers and service men.

Working closely with Robert W. Kenny, State Attorney General, the committee, headed by Bishop Joseph T. McGucken of the Catholic diocese here, declared that the streets of Los Angeles "must be made safe for service men as well as civilians, regardless of national origins."

"The community as well as its visitors," it stated, "must learn that no group has the right to take the law into its own hands."

The committee issued an eight-page report, with demands for immediate and long-range curative action, after hearing testimony for two days behind closed doors from city and police officials, representatives of minority groups, and persons active in social welfare work. Its members plan to meet again on Monday and from time to time issue supplementary reports. . . .

Virtual calm prevailed all over the county during the day after a caravan of fifty-three "zoot suiters" had driven past the City Hall with flags of truce fluttering from the jalopies. Captain Joe Reed of the Police Department, after interviewing them, congratulated them on their frank attitude. . . .

Governor Warren's commitee found it to be "significant" that most of the persons mistreated during the recent incidents in Los Angeles were either persons of Mexican descent or Negroes.

"In undertaking to deal with the cause of these outbreaks," its report said, "the existence of race prejudice cannot be ignored.

"Youth is peculiarly sensitive. To be rejected by the community may throw the youth upon evil companions.

"Any solution of the problems involves among other things an educational program throughout the community designed to combat race prejudice in all its forms." . . .

[The committee] asked for additional facilities for the care and study of delinquent youth and described the problem as "one of American youth, not confined to any racial group."

"The wearers of zoot suits," the report went on, "are not necessarily persons of Mexican descent, criminals or juveniles. Many young people today wear zoot suits.

"It is a mistake in fact and an aggravating practice to link the phrase 'zoot suit' with the report of a crime. Repeated reports of this character tend to inflame public opinion on false premises and excite further outbreaks."

"All juvenile delinquency has increased recently in Los Angeles. This includes crimes committed by youths of Mexican origin. But the fact is that the increase of delinquency in the case of youths of Mexican families has been less than in the case of other national or racial groups and less than the average increase for the community.

"Between 1914 and 1929 all of California, and Los Angeles County in particular, had a rapid increase in Mexican population. The tremendous difficulties experienced by immigrants in making adjustments to their new surroundings are well known. We have learned that the problem is especially acute in the case of the second generation. The foreign-born parent loses authority over his American-born child; families tend to be broken up; and if the children are not completely accepted by their neighbors; they are often without responsible guidance.

"These facts shed light on the youths of Mexican descent in Los Angeles. Many of them are second generation. About 98 percent of them are American born.

"Of the serious crimes committed by persons of Mexican descent, only 25 per cent are committed by minors. Most of the so-called 'zoot-suit' crime amounting to felony has been committed by persons who are fully and legally responsible for their acts."

New York Times, *June 14, 1943*

Memo from Commandant, Eleventh Navy District, to All Units Under His Command, June 10, 1943

. . . The Commandant is seriously concerned over the recent disorders which have occurred in Los Angeles and its vicinity and which have assumed such serious proportion as to be broadcast on the radio and published in newspapers throughout the U.S. The Navy is a disciplined organization composed of loyal and intelligent men and partaking in any activities that are of the nature of mob violence is a direct reflection on the Navy itself and on the individual who wears the uniform. Irrespective of what may have been the original cause of these disorders the enforcement of the law rests in the hands of the civilian police and is not a matter which should be undertaken by any unauthorized groups of Navy personnel. The Commandant believes that the men now engaging in these demonstrations are actuated mainly by a desire for excitement and feels that they have not seriously considered the consequence which may follow from ill considered action. The Commandant suggests that commanding officers bring the substance of the above to the attention of the men of their commands in a personal and unofficial manner having full confidence that an appeal to the individual based on common sense and reasonableness will invoke prompt response. . . .

Letter from San Diego City Councilman Charles C. Dail to Rear Admiral David W. Bagley, U.S. Navy, June 10, 1943

Dear Sir:

The critical situation brought to a head in the Los Angeles area as a result of a lawlessness of certain "zoot suit" wearing gangs is the forerunner of a more serious and widespread condition, and unless exceptional, precautionary methods are undertaken, serious damage to the war effort in civilian-military relations will develop.

The initiative action being taken by soldiers, sailors and marines for the time directed against so-called "zoot suit" wearers is not that alone. It . . . has been aimed at civilians in general. There have been numerous instances in San Diego where members of the military forces have insulted and vilified civilians on public streets; and to cite one instance recently: a Consolidated Aircraft Company official, after objecting to the epithets of a marine, pertaining to his civilian status, was attacked and seriously injured and will be unable to return to his duties for some time, as a result of the injuries sustained. Most civilians just "grin and bear it" rather than precipitate an altercation which would be certain if they resisted.

Every civilian, no matter what type of clothes he is wearing should be safe on the streets, and it is certainly the belief of the writer that the superior officers of service men should vigorously discourage any adverse attitude they may have to civilians, cautioning the personnel that every civilian is not a "draft dodger" and a "slacker," and that a great majority of such civilians in this industrial area are engaged in the building of vital war materials.

The civilian law enforcement officers of this area are capable, ready, willing and able to enforce civilian laws, and any civilian will be dealt with on the basis of the seriousness of his violation. It is the belief of the writer that if steps are taken at this time to correct the derogatory attitude on the part of soldiers, sailors and marines toward civilians, it would go far to relieve the unchecked and developing animosity perpetrated against civilians in general.

Please let me assure you that this letter is prompted solely by a strong patriotic desire to help check a situation which certainly is not conducive to cooperative effort on the part of civilian and military forces.

Memo from Maxwell Murray, Major General, U.S. Army Command, to Headquarters, Southern California Sector, Western Defense Command, Pasadena, California, June 11, 1943

1. The recent incidents connected with the so-called "Zoot Suit" riots involved mob action, and incipient rioting, by many soldiers and other service men.
2. Prompt action to check such action has been taken, and charges are being preferred against those arrested for inciting or actually participating in these riots.
3. It is obvious that many soldiers are not aware of the serious nature of riot charges. Convictions in a recent serious riot have resulted in sentence to death or long confinement.
4. It is desired that the attention of all Military personnel be called immediately to the critical dangers of any form of rioting and that incidents which may start as thoughtless group action in comparatively trivial offenses or boisterous conduct are liable to develop into mob riots of the most serious character. Further, mob rioting usually results in injury to persons in no way connected with the initial causes of the disorder. This is true in the case of the recent disorders, which resulted in affront and injury of some completely innocent civilians.
5. Military personnel of all ranks must understand that no form of mob violence or rioting will be tolerated, and that offenses of this nature will result in immediate and drastic disciplinary action.

QUESTIONS

Defining Terms

Identify in the context of the chapter each of the following:

Nazi ideology	Norman Rockwell
Korematsu v. United States	Pearl Harbor
Four Freedoms	Ted Nakashima
Bracero Program	Internment
Saturday Evening Post	Executive Order #8802

Probing the Sources

1. What were the Four Freedoms? Why did Franklin Roosevelt articulate them? How did Norman Rockwell depict them?
2. How do the sources on the Zoot Suit Riot differ on the causes of the crisis? Which ones do you think are most reliable? Why?
3. What was Japanese Internment? On what grounds did the Supreme Court justify the government's actions?
4. What assumptions underlay the editors' arguments in *The Crisis?*

Interpreting the Sources

1. The Mayor of Los Angeles declared that the Zoot Suit Riots did not spring from racism. Do you agree or disagree? What evidence leads you to your conclusion?
2. From the sources you've read, what was the role of the media in the racial discord of the era?
3. Discuss the conflict between American goals in the war and American racial realities.
4. Why do we often think of World War II as "The Good War," and those who fought it as "the Greatest Generation"? Can you reconcile the idealism of the Four Freedoms with tensions on the homefront?

ADDITIONAL READING

For the war as the fundamental experience of the generation, see Studs Terkel's oral history, *The Good War* (1984), and Tom Brokaw, *The Greatest Generation* (1996). On the leadership of Franklin D. Roosevelt on the eve of and throughout World War II, see James MacGregor Burns, *Roosevelt: The Soldier of Freedom* (1970), and Robert Dallek, *Franklin D. Roosevelt and American Foreign Policy, 1932–1945* (1979). The home front and the battlefront are covered in David M. Kennedy, *Freedom from Fear: The American People in Depression and War, 1929–1945* (1999). Laura Claridge, *Norman Rockwell: A Life* (2001), presents a good case for viewing Rockwell as an important and original American artist. Stuart Murray and James McCabe, *Norman Rockwell's Four Freedoms: Images That Inspire a Nation* (1993), provides important background for the paintings. On Japanese internment, see Peter Irons, *Justice at War: The Story of the Japanese Internment Cases* (1983), Dorothea Lange, Linda Gordon, and Gary Okihiro, *Impounded: Dorothea Lange and the Censored Images of Japanese American Internment* (2006), and Lawson Fusao Inada, *Only What We Could Carry: The Japanese American Internment Experience* (2000). African Americans during the war are examined in Neil Wynn, *The Afro-American and the Second World War* (1976), and Phillip McGuire, *Taps for a Jim Crow Army: Letters from Black Soldiers in World War II* (1993). Mexican Americans during the war, especially in Los Angeles, are studied in Mauricio Mazon, *The Zoot-Suit Riots* (1988), and Eduardo Obregon Pagan, *Murder at the Sleepy Lagoon: Zoot Suits, Race, and Riot in Wartime L.A.* (2006).

11

The Cold War

Historical Context

What is it exactly that we do as historians? As we have suggested throughout this volume, we search through the documentation of the past—looking for patterns and trends, trying to give order to a chaotic jumble of events and thoughts—and then construct stories. We do not write fiction, but neither do we tell the whole truth, for the absolute truth, the capital "T" truth, is unknowable, and perhaps even an illusion itself. In an attempt to understand and organize the past, we construct and use broad generalities to denote the temper or preoccupation of an era. Look at the organization of the earlier chapters of this book. There are separate sections on the eras of Reconstruction, the Progressive period, World War I, the Twenties, the Great Depression, and World War II. The implication is that, for example, during the Progressive era, notions of progress and the improvement of life consumed America. But we know that not all people were involved in progressive crusades—perhaps only the smallest minority were—and that for some people, such as African Americans and many immigrants, the very idea of the Progressive era was a cruel irony. Nevertheless, textbooks and lectures on America in the early twentieth century usually stress Progressivism as the grand organizing principle of the early twentieth century.

The Cold War forms the organizing principle for the period after World War II. On one level, the rivalry between the United States and the Soviet Union—or between West and East, capitalism and communism—was quite real. The foreign policies of both countries emphasized some form of expansion, whether economic or military or both, and the two world powers generally opposed each other on crucial issues. How and why this rivalry developed is still debated by historians. After all, the two countries had been allies between 1941 and 1945 in the war against Nazi Germany. How had allies become opponents within months of the end of World War II? Without an overtly hostile act by either side, why did they become bitter enemies?

Like most events, the answer is complex. The rivalry began with the November 1917 revolution in Russia. Although United States officials had favored the liberal revolution earlier that year in Russia, a revolution that had overthrown Czar Nicholas and installed a moderate republican government, they did not support the October revolutionaries led by Vladimir Ilyich Lenin, a communist who opposed Russia's participation in World War I. Lenin and his Bolshevik supporters ended Russia's experimentation with democracy and republicanism, pulled their country out of the war, and established the Soviet Union. American leaders reacted by briefly joining a multinational force to overthrow the Bolsheviks and by supporting a propaganda campaign that placed the Soviet Union in the worst possible light. Catching the temper of the moment, historian David M. Oshinsky observed, "It was claimed that the Soviets had an electric guillotine that chopped off hundreds of heads an hour; Bolshevik leaders drove around in fancy automobiles while businessmen were starving to death; and Russia had nationalized women by requiring them to register at 'bureaus of free love.' The message was the always the same: the Bolsheviks were hated by the people and represented only themselves."

During the 1920s the United States government tried to ignore the Soviet Union as much as possible. Occasionally a popular novelist would criticize the Soviet Union, or a left-leaning idealist would praise Lenin and the Russians, but there was little intellectual or financial commerce between the countries. That changed slightly in November of 1933, sixteen years after the establishment of the communist state, when the Franklin Roosevelt administration officially recognized and established diplomatic relations with the Soviet Union. Mired in the Great Depression, President Roosevelt hoped that the recognition of the Soviet Union would open new markets for American products. The dream of the great Russian market proved largely chimerical. In 1933, American diplomat and Soviet authority George Kennan had argued against recognition of the Soviet Union. Over 30 years later, in his memoirs, he saw no reason to change his position: "Never—neither then nor at any later date—did I consider the Soviet Union a fit ally or associate, actual or potential, for this country."

Some Americans, however, began to regard the Soviet Union in a new light during the 1930s. Faced by economic hardships at home and the growing threat of Nazi Germany in Europe, many Americans, especially those on the political left, believed that the Soviet Union offered the best solution for both problems. Communism appeared more humane than capitalism during the depression, and collective security seemed more effective than isolationism. Yet other Americans—probably most—continued to view the Soviets as an enemy that would subvert religion, democracy, capitalism, and all that was decent in the world. They pointed to two events as keys to Soviet behavior. The first was a series of purges conducted by Soviet Premier Joseph Stalin. From his first years in office, Stalin had demonstrated a heightened sense of suspicion; he distrusted his own military leaders and government officials; he feared betrayal from those in power, close to power, and far from power. His solution was the ruthless elimination of all suspected enemies. Historians of the purges estimate that about one million people were executed and another twelve million died in labor camps. The purges made Americans question Stalin's methods and the morality of his regime. The questioning turned to outright hatred after the announcement of the German-Soviet Nonaggression Pact in late August 1939. After opposing the Nazis throughout most of the 1930s, Stalin cynically ignored his own expressed beliefs and entered into a pact with Hitler. Making matters worse, in early September the Soviet Union joined Germany in invading and dividing Poland. For most Americans, the purges and the Nonaggression Pact stripped the Soviet Union of its thin veneer of idealism and showed it to be a ruthless, cynical totalitarian state.

But morality is often an inconvenient basis for foreign policy, and in 1941 America's official position with the Soviet Union did an abrupt about-face. First, Hitler violated the 1939 Nonaggression Pact and invaded the Soviet Union. Then—after the Japanese attacked American forces at Pearl Harbor—Germany declared war on the United States. Suddenly the United States and the Soviet Union were allies, partners in an odd marriage of convenience in which neither country really liked or trusted the other. But until Hitler was defeated, it was a marriage in which there could be no divorce.

During World War II, American opinion makers gave Joseph Stalin and the Soviet Union a face lift. Reporters dubbed Stalin "Uncle Joe" and portrayed him as a kindly, if stern, father figure, the sort of patriarch who always had the best interests of the family in mind. In the movie *Mission to Moscow,* Hollywood characterized him as a thoughtful, pipe-smoking, farsighted political leader concerned with collective security, Nazi aggression, and the prosperity and well-being of his country. Other World War II films—*Three Russian Girls, Song of Russia, Boys from Stalingrad, The North Star,* and *Days of Glory*—presented similar views of Stalin and his people. "War has put Hollywood's traditional conception of the Moscovites through the wringer," noted a 1942 *Variety* columnist, "and they have come out shaved, washed, sober, good to their families, Rotarians, brother Elks, and 33rd Degree Masons." In short, popular culture reinforced official political culture.

After the end of the war relations between the United States and the Soviet Union chilled rapidly. Disputes over the fates of Poland and Eastern Europe, the division of Germany, control over atomic weapons, and other issues divided the two countries, leading to a war of rhetoric and a mood of suspicion. In February 1946, Stalin warned Soviet citizens that there could never be a lasting peace with the capitalistic West, suggesting that economic sacrifices, and even war, lay ahead. Supreme Court Justice William O. Douglas called the speech "the declaration of World War III." And so it went—tough talk on one side resulted in equally strident language on the other, difficult issues assumed insurmountable proportions, and the gulf between the two world superpowers widened.

The result was the Cold War, the central fact of American foreign policy between the end of World War II in 1945 and the end of communist rule in the Soviet Union in 1991. During that 45 year period, thought of one another dominated the foreign policies of the United States and the Soviet Union. Through a series of flashpoints ranging from Greece, Turkey, and Berlin to Korea, Vietnam, and Cuba, the two sides jockeyed for advantage in a deadly, global game of chess. Without actually ever going to war against each other, they were never fully at peace. To each, the other was an implacable enemy bent on total world domination.

During that period the Cold War also dominated and defined American life. It became the organizing principle of our popular culture, which boiled down to a series of "us" against "them" confrontations. Hollywood parlayed the theme into successful movies, from such "B" films as *I Was a Communist for the FBI, My Son John,* and *Big Jim McLain* to acclaimed works like *Fail Safe, On the Beach,* and *Dr. Strangelove.* From John Wayne's westerns to James Bond's action adventures the Cold War helped to define the plots. Popular writers and television producers also capitalized on the Cold War. John Le Carre, William F. Buckley, Jr., and Tom Clancy wrote best-sellers that revolved around the Cold War, and television shows such as *The Man from U.N.C.L.E.* and *I Spy* used the Cold War to sell consumer products. Even in international sporting events, the Cold War defined the rules of the game, making winning and losing of monumental importance.

The following documents helped define and portray the Soviet Union for the American people. As you read them consider the authorship and the underlying agenda. How did they contribute to the construction of a Cold War mentality? How did they reinforce or call into question the dominant Cold War paradigm? How did they give shape and meaning to the lives of millions of Americans?

THE DOCUMENTS

Introduction to Document 1

During America's honeymoon period with the Soviet Union in the early 1940s, Hollywood made several films that attempted to place Stalin and Russians in the best possible light. *Mission to Moscow,* released by Warner Brothers in 1943, purports to be the story of American ambassador Joseph Davies' mission to the Soviet Union on the eve of war. In reality, it was an attempt to rewrite Soviet history, justify Stalin's purges, and attack American isolationists. The following section of the script portrays Stalin as a far-sighted statesman and hints that he had no choice but to sign the German-Soviet Nonaggression Pact. Try to imagine how the scene was shot and what impact it would have had on Americans in 1943.

DOCUMENT 1 *Mission to Moscow*

Med. Long Shot Stalin from their angle as he walks toward the camera. (NOTE: In his book, Mr. Davies describes Stalin as follows: "His demeanor is kindly, his manner almost deprecatingly simple, his personality and expression of reserved strength and poise very marked." In the writer's opinion these characteristics for the part are even more important than physical verisimilitude.)
Med. Shot the Group as Stalin walks directly to Davies, dispensing with the formality of an introduction. The two men shake hands.

Stalin: Mr. Davies, I am happy to know you.

Davies: Thank you, Mr. Stalin. This is a great pleasure for me . . . (smiles) also considerable of a surprise.
They all smile at this frankness and the ice is broken.

Kalinin: Gentlemen, won't you please have chairs?

Stalin (as they are seated): Besides your work here in Moscow, I understand you have visited many other sections of the Soviet Union.

Davies: And I've been deeply impressed by what I've seen—your industrial plants, the development of your natural resources, and the work being done to improve living conditions everywhere in your country. I believe history will record you as a great builder for the benefit of common men.

Stalin (with sincere modesty): It is not my achievement, Mr. Davies. Our five-year plans were conceived by Lenin and carried out by the people themselves.

Davies: Well, the results have been a revelation to me. I confess I wasn't prepared for all I've found here. (With a smile.) You see, Mr. Stalin, I'm a capitalist, as you probably know.

Stalin (laughingly): Yes, we know you are a capitalist—there can be no doubt about that.
They all join in the laughter.

Kalinin: We also know this about you, Mr. Davies—the worst things you've had to say, you have said to our faces, the best things you have said to our enemies.

Stalin: We want you to realize that we feel more friendly toward the government of the United States than any other nation. If there are any matters that are not settled between us, please take them up with Molotov.

Davies: Thank you . . . Well, gentlemen, I know how busy you are. I mustn't take up more of your time.

He rises, and the others follow suit, but Stalin interposes before the ambassador can move toward the door.

Stalin: Mr. Davies, do you have another appointment?

Davies: No, I don't.

Stalin: Then please do not hurry away.

The CAMERA PANS with the two men as Stalin leads Davies by the arm toward the door of his own office.

Stalin (as they walk): There are some things on my mind that I would like you to know—and your great president to know.

Full Shot Stalin's Office An austere room with maps on the wall and a large conference table in the middle of the room. We should give the impression here of two men surrounded by the problems of the world. They should be seen at first as very small in contrast with the table at which they are seated. As Stalin talks, the CAMERA PULLS UP to them.

Stalin: The outlook for European peace is bad—very bad. England and France have allowed Hitler to take Austria without a struggle. They will probably allow him to do the same with Czechoslovakia. They have repudiated their pledges to the League and are throwing the defenseless countries on the mercies of bandits.

Davies: It's clear what they're doing. What I don't understand is *why* they're doing it.

Stalin: I will tell you why, Mr. Davies, and I will tell you frankly because this is a time for plain words—the reactionary elements in England, represented by the Chamberlain government, have determined upon the deliberate policy of making Germany strong. And at the same time they shout lies in their press about the weakness of the Russian army and disorder in the Soviet Union.

Davies: You mean, Mr. Stalin, that these elements are actually encouraging German aggression?

Stalin: There is no doubt that their plan is to push Hitler into a war with this country. Then when the combatants exhaust themselves they will step in to make "peace"—yes, the kind of peace that will serve their own interests.

Davies: But I am sure the English people do not approve of such a policy.

Stalin: In my opinion the present governments of England and France do not represent their people. Finally the Fascist dictators will drive too hard a bargain and the people will call their governments to account—but by then it may be too late.

Davies: Mr. Stalin, may I ask you a very direct question?

Stalin: Of course.

Davies: If Hitler *does* attack Czechoslovakia and if France and England go to her aid—is Russia willing and ready to join them in war against Germany?

Stalin: We have a commitment with France to fight in the event they go to the aid of Czechoslovakia. The Soviet Union has never repudiated a treaty obligation. She would not repudiate this one.

Davies: Your past record speaks well for the future.

Stalin: But we are not going to be put in the position of pulling other people's chestnuts out of the fire. Either we must be able to rely on our mutual guarantees with the other democracies or . . . well, we may be forced to protect ourselves in another way.

Davies: Mr. Stalin, on my way home I'm stopping off in England. May I quote what you have just told me?

Stalin: If you could convince them and your own government that peace or war is in the balance, you would do us all a great service.

At this point Davies rises and Stalin walks with him slowly toward the door.

Davies: I feel as keenly as you and Mr. Litvinov that collective security is the last bulwark against war.

Stalin: Litvinov has done all he can to make the world realize it. . . .

Davies (earnestly): Mr. Stalin, a while ago I made the remark that my job was finished. After talking with you, I wonder if it hasn't only begun.

Stalin looks pleased and gratified.

Introduction to Document 2

On March 12, 1947, President Harry Truman addressed a joint session of Congress in an attempt to win approval for a defense aid package for the governments of Greece and Turkey, which were fighting against internal communist movements. One congressman told Truman that he would have to "scare the hell out of the American people" to get congress to appropriate the money. Consider how Truman tried to successfully achieve that end. How did he characterize the Cold War between East and West, communism and capitalism? How does his language serve to enlarge the nature of the struggle?

DOCUMENT 2 *The Truman Doctrine March 12, 1947*

(*Congressional Record*, March 12, 1947)

The gravity of the situation which confronts the world today necessitates my appearance before a joint session of the Congress. The foreign policy and the national security of this country are involved.

One aspect of the present situation, which I wish to present to you at this time for your consideration and decision, concerns Greece and Turkey.

The United States has received from the Greek Government an urgent appeal for financial and economic assistance. . . .

The very existence of the Greek state is today threatened by the terrorist activities of several thousand armed men, led by Communists, who defy the Government's authority at a number of points, particularly along the northern boundaries. . . .

Greece must have assistance if it is to become a self-supporting and self-respecting democracy. The United States must supply this assistance. We have already extended to Greece certain types of relief and economic aid but these are inadequate. There is no other country to which democratic Greece can turn. No other nation is willing and able to provide the necessary support for a democratic Greek Government.

The British Government, which has been helping Greece, can give no further financial or economic aid after March 31. Great Britain finds itself under the necessity of reducing or liquidating its committments in several parts of the world, including Greece. . . .

Greece's neighbor, Turkey, also deserves our attention. The future of Turkey as an independent and economically sound state is clearly no less important to the freedom-loving peoples of the world than the future of Greece. . . .

As in the case of Greece, if Turkey is to have the assistance it needs, the United States must supply it. We are the only country able to provide that help.

I am fully aware of the broad implications involved if the United States extends assistance to Greece and Turkey, and I shall discuss these implications with you at this time.

One of the primary objectives of the foreign policy of the United States is the creation of conditions in which we and other nations will be able to work out a way of life free from coercion. This was a fundamental issue in the war with Germany and Japan. Our victory was won over countries which sought to impose their will, and their way of life, upon other nations.

To ensure the peaceful development of nations, free from coercion, the United States has taken a leading part in establishing the United Nations. The United Nations is designed to make possible lasting freedom and independence for all its members. We shall not realize our objectives, however, unless we are willing to help free peoples to maintain their free institutions and their national integrity against aggressive movements that seek to impose on them totalitarian regimes. This is no more than a frank recognition that totalitarian regimes imposed on free peoples, by direct or indirect aggression, undermine the foundations of international peace and hence the security of the United States.

The peoples of a number of countries of the world have recently had totalitarian regimes forced upon them against their will. The Government of the United States has made frequent protests against coercion and intimidation, in violation of the Yalta Agreement, in Poland, Rumania and Bulgaria. I must also state that in a number of other countries there have been similar developments.

At the present moment in world history nearly every nation must choose between alternative ways of life. The choice is too often not a free one.

One way of life is based upon the will of the majority, and is distinguished by free institutions, representative government, free elections, guarantees of individual liberty, freedom of speech and religion, and freedom from political oppression.

The second way of life is based upon the will of the minority forcibly imposed upon the majority. It relies upon terror and oppression, a controlled press and radio, fixed elections, and the suppression of personal freedoms.

I believe that it must be the policy of the United States to support free peoples who are resisting attempted subjugation by armed minorities or by outside pressures.

I believe that we must assist free peoples to work out their own destinies in their own way. . . .

The seeds of totalitarian regimes are nurtured by misery and want. They spread and grow in the evil soil of poverty and strife. They reach their full growth when the hope of a people for a better life has died. We must keep that hope alive. The free peoples of the world look to us for support in maintaining their freedoms.

If we falter in our leadership, we may endanger the peace of the world—and we shall surely endanger the welfare of this nation.

Great responsibilities have been placed upon us by the swift movement of events. I am confident that the Congress will face these responsibilities squarely.

Introduction to Document 3

On February 12, 1950, Senator Joseph McCarthy of Wisconsin gave a Lincoln's Birthday speech in Wheeling, West Virginia. After briefly extolling the virtues of the 16th American president, McCarthy quickly turned to his real theme, the subversion of the American government by traitors from within. Note whom he accuses. How did social class play into his charges of treason? The speech, which was inserted into the *Congressional Record,* was a bombshell. For the next few years,

McCarthy and his accusations were constantly in the news. (Note that the number of subversives changed depending on where McCarthy gave the speech and where it was reported.)

DOCUMENT 3 *Senator Joseph McCarthy's Speech in Wheeling, West Virginia*

(Congressional Record)

Joseph McCarthy

. . . Five years after a world war has been won, men's hearts should anticipate a long peace, and men's minds should be free from the heavy weight that comes with war. But this is not such a period—for this is not a period of peace. This is a time of the "cold war." This is a time when all the world is split into two vast, increasingly hostile armed camps—a time of a great armaments race.

Today we can almost physically hear the mutterings and rumblings of an invigorated god of war. You can see it, feel it, and hear it all the way from the hills of Indochina, from the shores of Formosa, right over into the very heart of Europe itself.

The one encouraging thing is that the "mad moment" has not yet arrived for the firing of the gun or the exploding of the bomb which will set civilization about the final task of destroying itself. There is still a hope for peace if we finally decide that no longer can we safely blind our eyes and close our ears to those facts which are shaping up more and more clearly. And that is that we are now engaged in a show-down fight—not the usual war between nations for land areas or other material gains, but a war between two diametrically opposed ideologies.

The great difference between our western Christian world and the atheistic Communist world is not political, ladies and gentlemen, it is moral. There are other differences, of course, but those could be reconciled. For instance, the Marxian idea of confiscating the land and factories and running the entire economy as a single enterprise is momentous. Likewise, Lenin's invention of the one-party police state as a way to make Marx's idea work is hardly less momentous.

Stalin's resolute putting across of these two ideas, of course, did much to divide the world. With only those differences, however, the East and the West could most certainly still live in peace.

The real, basic difference, however, lies in the religion of immoralism—invented by Marx, preached feverishly by Lenin, and carried to unimaginable extremes by Stalin. This religion of immoralism, if the Red half of the world wins—and well it may—this religion of immoralism will more deeply wound and damage mankind than any conceivable economic or political system. . . .

Today we are engaged in a final, all-out battle between communistic atheism and Christianity. The modern champions of communism have selected this as the time. And, ladies and gentlemen, the chips are down—they are truly down. . . .

Lest there be any doubt that the time has been chosen, let us go directly to the leader of communism today—Joseph Stalin. Here is what he said—not back in 1928, not before the war, not during the war—but 2 years after the last war was ended: "To think that the Communist revolution can be carried out peacefully, within the framework of a Christian democracy, means one has either gone out of one's mind and lost all normal understanding, or has grossly and openly repudiated the Communist revolution."

And this is what was said by Lenin in 1919, which was also quoted with approval by Stalin in 1947:

"We are living," said Lenin, "not merely in a state, but in a system of states, and the existence of the Soviet Republic side by side with Christian states for a long time is unthinkable. One or the other must triumph in the end. And before that end supervenes, a series of frightful collisions between the Soviet Republic and the Bourgeois states will be inevitable."

Ladies and gentlemen, can there by anyone here tonight who is so blind as to say that the war is not on? Can there be anyone who fails to realize that the Communist world has said, "The time is now"—that this is the time for the show-down between the democratic Christian world and the Communist atheistic world?

Unless we face this fact, we shall pay the price that must be paid by those who wait too long.

Six years ago, at the time of the first conference to map out peace—Dumbarton Oaks—there was within the Soviet orbit 180,000,000 people. Lined up on the antitotalitarian side there were in the world at that time roughly 1,625,000,000 people. Today, only 6 years later, there are 800,000,000 people under the absolute domination of Soviet Russia—an increase of over 400 percent. On our side, the figure has shrunk to around 500,000,000. In other words, in less than 6 years the odds have changed from 9 to 1 in our favor to 8 to 5 against us. This indicates the swiftness of the tempo of Communist victories and American defeats in the cold war. As one of our outstanding historical figures once said, "When a great democracy is destroyed, it will not be because of enemies from without, but rather because of enemies from within."

The truth of this statement is becoming terrifyingly clear as we see this country each day losing on every front.

At war's end we were physically the strongest nation on earth and, at least potentially, the most powerful intellectually and morally. Ours could have been the honor of being a beacon in the desert of destruction, a shining living proof that civilization was not yet ready to destroy itself. Unfortunately, we have failed miserably and tragically to arise to the opportunity.

The reason why we find ourselves in a position of impotency is not because our only powerful potential enemy has sent men to invade our shores, but rather because of the traitorous actions of those who have been treated so well by this Nation. It has not been the less fortunate or members of minority groups who have been selling this Nation out, but rather those who have had all the benefits that the wealthiest nation on earth has had to offer—the finest homes, the finest college education, and the finest jobs in Government we can give.

This is glaringly true in the State Department. There the bright young men who are born with silver spoons in their mouths are the ones who have been worst. . . . In my opinion the State Department, which is one of the most important government departments, is thoroughly infested with Communists.

I have in my hand 57 cases of individuals who would appear to be either card carrying members or certainly loyal to the Communist Party, but who nevertheless are still helping to shape our foreign policy.

One thing to remember in discussing the Communists in our Government is that we are not dealing with spies who get 30 pieces of silver to steal the blueprints of a new weapon. We are dealing with a far more sinister type of activity because it permits the enemy to guide and shape our policy. . . .

As you hear this story of high treason, I know that you are saying to yourself, "Well, why doesn't the Congress do something about it?" Actually, ladies and gentlemen, one of the important reasons for the graft, the corruption, the dishonesty, the disloyalty, the treason in high Government positions—one of the most important reasons why this continues is a lack of moral uprising on the part of the 140,000,000 American people. In the light of history, however, this is not hard to explain.

It is the result of an emotional hang-over and a temporary moral lapse which follows every war. It is the apathy to evil which people who have been subjected to the tremendous evils of war feel. As the people of the world see mass murder, the destruction of defenseless and innocent people, and all of the crime and lack of morals which go with war, they become numb and apathetic. It has always been thus after war.

However, the morals of our people have not been destroyed. They still exist. This cloak of numbness and apathy has only needed a spark to rekindle them. Happily, this spark has finally been supplied.

As you know, very recently the Secretary of State proclaimed his loyalty to a man guilty of what has always been considered as the most abominable of all crimes—of being a traitor to the people who gave him a position of great trust. The Secretary of State in attempting to justify his continued devotion to the man who sold out the Christian world to the atheistic world, referred to Christ's Sermon on the Mount as a justification and reason therefor, and the reaction of the American people to this would have made the heart of Abraham Lincoln happy.

When this pompous diplomat in striped pants, with a phony British accent, proclaimed to the American people that Christ on the Mount endorsed communism, high treason, and betrayal of a sacred trust, the blasphemy was so great that it awakened the dormant indignation of the American people.

He has lighted the spark which is resulting in a moral uprising and will end only when the whole sorry mess of twisted, warped thinkers are swept from the national scene so that we may have a new birth of national honesty and decency in Government.

Introduction to Document 4

Joseph McCarthy made the fear of internal subversion palpable, but many Americans, especially those in the arts, responded with strong words of their own. Allan Ginsberg's most famous poem, *America,* published in 1956, was a rebuke in verse to what he perceived as the nation's hypocrisy and paranoia. "Go fuck yourself with your atom bomb," Ginsberg wrote, reacting against America's disingenuous sense of its own innocence and victimization. Even before McCarthy, the House Committee on UnAmerican Activities (known as HUAC) began in earnest to investigate Americans for their radical political connections in the late 1940s. Filmmakers and actors, singers, writers, and university people, all came before the Committee. Those who cooperated–gave testimony implicating colleagues for radical activities, often with little evidence–believed they were defending America against an insidious communist enemy. Those who refused to testify–and some of them served prison time for contempt of Congress, while others were blacklisted and had difficulty getting work for years–believed they were defending the rights of citizens against a rogue government. Charges that the former were dupes of the commies and the latter, rats spilling their guts for careerist gain, poisoned life among intellectuals for decades. In this document, the poet Thomas McGrath explains to the Committee in 1953 why he would not cooperate with them. McGrath was born in Sheldon, North Dakota, in 1916, the son of poor Irish farmers. He eventually attended the University of North Dakota, won a Rhodes scholarship, served in World War II, did graduate work at Louisiana State University, and finally landed a position at Los Angeles State University in 1950. His refusal to testify three years later cost him his job. When he gave his testimony, McGrath was not well known, but by the end of his life, many critics considered him a great poet

in the tradition of Walt Whitman. Why did McGrath refuse to "name names"? Do you agree or disagree with his decision?

DOCUMENT 4 *Thomas McGrath's Statement to the House Committee on Un-American Activities*

After a dead serious consideration of the effects of this committee's work and of my relation to it, I find that for the following reasons I must refuse to cooperate with this body.

In the first place, as a teacher, my first responsibility is to my students. To cooperate with this committee would be to set for them an example of accommodation to forces which can only have, as their end effect, the destruction of education itself. Such accommodation on my part would ruin my value as a teacher, and I am proud to say that a great majority of my students—and I believe this is true of students generally—do not want me to accommodate myself to this committee. In a certain sense, I have no choice in the matter—the students would not want me back in the classroom if I were to take any course of action other than the one I am pursuing.

Secondly, as a teacher, I have a responsibility to the profession itself. We teachers have no professional oath of the sort that doctors take, but there is a kind of unwritten oath which we follow to teach as honestly, fairly and fully as we can. The effect of the committee is destructive of such an ideal, destructive of academic freedom. As Mr. Justice Douglas has said: "This system of spying and surveillance with its accompanying reports and trials cannot go hand in hand with academic freedom. It produces standardized thought, not the pursuit of truth." A teacher who will tack and turn with every shift of the political wind cannot be a good teacher. . . .

Thirdly, as a poet I must refuse to cooperate with the committee on what I can only call esthetic grounds. The view of life which we receive through the great works of art is a privileged one—it is a view of life according to probability or necessity, not subject to the chance and accident of our real world and therefore in a sense truer than the life we see lived all around us. I believe that one of the things required of us is to try to give life an esthetic ground, to give it some of the pattern and beauty of art. I have tried as best I can to do this with my own life, and while I do not claim any very great success, it would be anti-climactic, destructive of the pattern of my life, if I were to cooperate with the committee.

These, then are reasons for refusing to cooperate, but I am aware that none of them is acceptable to the committee. When I was notified to appear here, my first instinct was simply to refuse to answer committee questions out of personal principle and on the grounds of the rights of man and let it go at that. On further consideration, however, I have come to feel that such a stand would be mere self-indulgence and that it would weaken the fight which other witnesses have made to protect the rights guaranteed under our Constitution. Therefore I further refuse to answer the committee on the grounds of the fourth amendment. I regard this committee as usurpers of illegal powers and my enforced appearance here as in the nature of unreasonable search and seizure.

I further refuse on the grounds of the first amendment, which in guaranteeing free speech also guarantees my right to be silent. Although the first amendment expressly forbids any abridgement of this and other freedoms, the committee is illegally engaged in the establishment of a religion of fear. I cannot cooperate with it in this unconstitutional activity. Lastly, it is my duty to refuse to answer this committee, claiming my rights under the fifth amendment as a whole and in all its parts, and understanding that the fifth amendment was inserted in the Constitution to bulwark the first amendment against the activities of committees such as this one, that no one may be forced to bear witness against himself.

Introduction to Document 5

In 1961, 14 years after Truman addressed Congress about the communist crisis in Greece and Turkey and 11 years after McCarthy emphasized the communist crisis in the State Department, John F. Kennedy was sworn in as president of the United States. The day was bitterly cold in Washington, D.C., but the country enjoyed a springtime of peace. Not only were American troops not engaged in combat, there were no wars looming on the horizon. But like Truman and McCarthy, Kennedy spoke the language of crisis, giving the impression that war might–just might–be close at hand.

DOCUMENT 5 *John F. Kennedy's Inaugural Address, January 20, 1961*

(Department of State Bulletin, February 6, 1961)

We observe today not a victory of party but a celebration of freedom—symbolizing an end as well as a beginning—signifying renewal as well as change. For I have sworn before you and Almighty God the same solemn oath our forebearers prescribed nearly a century and three-quarters ago.

The world is very different now. For man holds in his mortal hands the power to abolish all forms of human poverty and all forms of human life. And yet the same revolutionary beliefs for which our forebearers fought are still at issue around the globe—the belief that the rights of man come not from the generosity of the state but from the hand of God.

We dare not forget today that we are the heirs of that first revolution. Let the word go forth from this time and place, to friend and foe alike, that the torch has been passed to a new generation of Americans—born in this century, tempered by war, disciplined by a hard and bitter peace, proud of our ancient heritage—and unwilling to witness or permit the slow undoing of those human rights to which this nation has always been committed, and to which we are committed today at home and around the world.

Let every nation know, whether it wishes us well or ill, that we shall pay any price, bear any burden, meet any hardship, support any friend, oppose any foe to assure the survival and the success of liberty.

This much we pledge—and more.

To those old allies whose cultural and spiritual origins we share, we pledge the loyalty of faithful friends. United, there is little we cannot do in a host of co-operative ventures. Divided, there is little we can do—for we dare not meet a powerful challenge at odds and split asunder.

To those new states whom we welcome to the ranks of the free, we pledge our word that one form of colonial control shall not have passed away merely to be replaced by a far more iron tyranny. We shall not always expect to find them supporting our view. But we shall always hope to find them strongly supporting their own freedom—and to remember that, in the past, those who foolishly sought power by riding the back of the tiger ended up inside.

To those people in the huts and villages of half the globe struggling to break the bonds of mass misery, we pledge our best efforts to help them help themselves, for whatever period is required—not because the Communists may be doing it, not because we seek their votes, but because it is right. If a free society cannot help the many who are poor, it cannot save the few who are rich.

To our sister republics south of our border, we offer a special pledge—to convert our good words into good deeds—in a new alliance for progress—to assist free men and free governments in casting off the chains of poverty. But this peaceful revolution of hope cannot become the prey of hostile powers. Let all our neighbors know that we shall join with them to oppose aggression or subversion anywhere in the Americas. And let every other power know that this hemisphere intends to remain the master of its own house.

To that world assembly of sovereign states, the United Nations, our last best hope in an age where the instruments of war have far outpaced the instruments of peace, we renew our pledge of support—to prevent it from becoming merely a forum for invective—to strengthen its shield of the new and the weak—and to enlarge the area in which its writ may run.

Finally, to those nations who would make themselves our adversary, we offer not a pledge but a request: that both sides begin anew the quest for peace, before the dark powers of destruction unleashed by science engulf all humanity in planned or accidental self-destruction.

We dare not tempt them with weakness. For only when our arms are sufficient beyond doubt can we be certain beyond doubt that they will never be employed.

But neither can two great and powerful groups of nations take comfort from our present course—both sides overburdened by the cost of modern weapons, both rightly alarmed by the steady spread of the deadly atom, yet both racing to alter that uncertain balance of terror that stays the hand of mankind's final war.

So let us begin anew—remembering on both sides that civility is not a sign of weakness, and sincerity is always subject to proof. Let us never negotiate out of fear. But let us never fear to negotiate.

In your hands, my fellow citizens, more than mine, will rest the final success or failure of our course. Since this country was founded, each generation of Americans has been summoned to give testimony to its national loyalty. The graves of young Americans who answered the call to service surround the globe.

Now the trumpet summons us again—not as a call to bear arms, though arms we need—not as a call to battle, though embattled we are—but a call to bear the burden of a long twilight struggle, year in and year out, "rejoicing in hope, patient in tribulation"—a struggle against the common enemies of man: tyranny, poverty, disease, and war itself.

Can we forge against these enemies a grand and global alliance, North and South, East and West, that can assure a more fruitful life for all mankind? Will you join in that historic effort?

In the long history of the world, only a few generations have been granted the role of defending freedom in its hour of maximum danger. I do not shrink from this responsibility—I welcome it. I do not believe that any of us would exchange places with any other people or any other generation. The energy, the faith, the devotion which we bring to this endeavor will light our country and all who serve it—and the glow from that fire can truly light the world.

And so, my fellow Americans: ask not what your country can do for you—ask what you can do for your country.

My fellow citizens of the world: ask not what America will do for you, but what together we can do for the freedom of man.

Finally, whether you are citizens of America or citizens of the world, ask of us here the same high standards of strength and sacrifice which we ask of you. With a good conscience our only sure reward with history the final judge of our deeds let us go forth to lead the land we love, asking His blessing and His help, but knowing that here on earth God's work must truly be our own.

Introduction to Document 6

In Vietnam, Kennedy extended the Cold War policies of his predecessors, Truman and Eisenhower. Though most Americans had barely heard of the small nation that

had been part of the French empire in Southeast Asia, Kennedy and his advisors worried about a communist takeover. More precisely, Cold War strategists considered the southern part of the country vulnerable to incursions from the communist North. If South Vietnam fell, the logic went, other Southeast Asian countries—Laos, Cambodia, Thailand—would also fall, just like dominoes. Kennedy inherited an American military presence of under one thousand troops in 1961, but by the time he was assassinated in November 1963, he had increased that number to sixteen thousand.

Shortly after Kennedy's death, President Lyndon Johnson began sending troops in ever-increasing numbers; over half a million were on the ground by 1968, and American forces remained there until 1975.

Comic books helped fight the war. The American comic book emerged in the 1930s, and reached a peak of popularity during World War II, when millions of readers, mostly young men, followed the exploits of Superman, Batman, Captain America, and Captain Marvel. Patriotic themes predominated, as these superheroes defended American interests and foiled the Nazis and Japanese. With their unequivocal support of the Allied War effort (even before the Japanese attack on Pearl Harbor), comic books worked to justify American entry into the conflict and propagate the government's wartime policy.

After the war, the industry relied mostly on horror stories and crime themes to sell their wares. DC comics captured the largest market share, but a small upstart company, Marvel, run by Stan Lee, became increasingly successful during the 1960s with the Fantastic Four, Spider-Man, the Incredible Hulk, Daredevil, and Iron Man. Marvel heroes were a bit more human than DC's lineup, with their own insecurities and failings, and the settings of the stories were more identifiable—New York, the Soviet Union, even Vietnam.

The March 1963 Iron Man comic—the very first one to appear—endorsed a national Cold War consensus against a monolithic communist menace embodied by such stereotypical red villains as the Crimson Dynamo, the Red Barbarian, and General Fang. Iron Man reflected the naive assumptions and expectations that many held about Vietnam. The complex political, economic, military, and cultural issues at stake in the conflict were reduced to a simplistic moral struggle of good against evil. Iron Man's victory over the tyrant Wong-Chu is a triumph of Western technology over communist barbarism, and of American valor over Asian treachery.

DOCUMENT 6 *Iron Man Is Born, 1963 Stan Lee*

Iron Man Is Born, 1963 Stan Lee (Marvel Comics)

IRON MAN
IS BORN!
WATCH HIS AWESOME APPROACH! LISTEN TO HIS PONDEROUS FOOTSTEPS AS HE LUMBERS CLOSER... CLOSER... FOR TODAY YOU ARE DESTINED TO ENCOUNTER-- THE INVINCIBLE IRON MAN!!
PLOT: STAN LEE
SCRIPT: LARRY LIEBER
ART: DON HECK
LETTERING: ART SIMEK
X-51
1

IN A SECLUDED AREA SOMEWHERE IN THE U.S. DEFENSE PERIMETER, THERE STANDS A CLOSELY GUARDED BUILDING... THE LABORATORY OF ANTHONY STARK!
BOY! THAT GUY STARK MUST REALLY RATE, TO GET A TWENTY-FOUR HOUR GUARD!
HE RATES, ALL RIGHT! THE COMMIES WOULD GIVE THEIR EYETEETH TO KNOW WHAT HE'S WORKING ON NOW!
AND, INSIDE...
GENERAL, YOU WILL SEE MY TINY TRANSISTOR INCREASE THE POWER OF THIS SMALL MAGNET SO TREMENDOUSLY THAT IT WILL OPEN THAT LOCKED VAULT!
OH, COME NOW, STARK! THAT JUST ISN'T POSSIBLE!
THINK SO? THERE! I'VE SWITCHED ON THE TRANSISTOR! IT'S ENERGIZING THE MAGNET!
CLICK
THE DOOR --IT'S BEGINNING TO BUDGE!
NATURALLY! MY TINY TRANSISTORS ARE SO POWERFUL THAT...
URRHHHHH
--THEY CAN INCREASE THE FORCE OF ANY DEVICE...
URRRRRHHHHHHHHH
URRRHHHHH
--A THOUSANDFOLD!
CRACK
NOW DO YOU BELIEVE THAT THE TRANSISTORS I'VE INVENTED ARE CAPABLE OF SOLVING YOUR PROBLEM IN VIETNAM?
STARK, AFTER WHAT I'VE JUST SEEN, I'M READY TO BELIEVE ANYTHING!
YES, IT WAS AN AMAZING DEMONSTRATION! BUT NOW, LET US LEARN MORE ABOUT THE MAN WHOSE GENIUS MADE IT POSSIBLE! LET US LEARN MORE ABOUT ANTHONY STARK, THE ONE WHO IS FATED TO BECOME... IRON MAN!
2

ANTHONY STARK... RICH, HANDSOME, KNOWN AS A GLAMOROUS PLAYBOY, CONSTANTLY IN THE COMPANY OF BEAUTIFUL, ADORING WOMEN...
LOOK! THERE'S TONY STARK!
UMMMNN... HE'S THE DREAMIEST THING THIS SIDE OF ROCK HUDSON!
THE RIVIERA WAS A REAL DRAG TILL YOU SHOWED UP, DARLING!
YES, ANTHONY STARK IS BOTH A SOPHISTICATE AND A SCIENTIST! A MILLIONAIRE BACHELOR, AS MUCH AT HOME IN A LABORATORY AS IN HIGH SOCIETY!
BUT, THIS MAN WHO SEEMS SO FORTUNATE, WHO'S ENVIED BY MILLIONS -- IS SOON DESTINED TO BECOME THE MOST TRAGIC FIGURE ON EARTH!
OUR TALE REALLY HAS ITS BEGINNING HALFWAY AROUND THE WORLD, IN A SOUTH VIETNAM JUNGLE, MENACED BY WONG-CHU, THE RED GUERRILLA TYRANT!
HAH! I HAVE BROUGHT ANOTHER VILLAGE TO ITS KNEES!
NOW FOR THE WRESTLING MATCH! IF ANY PRISONER CAN DEFEAT WONG-CHU, I FREE WHOLE VILLAGE!
DESPERATE TO SAVE THEIR VILLAGE, THE STRONGEST OF THE NATIVES ACCEPTS THE WAR LORD'S CHALLENGE...
AH, YOU ARE GOOD! BUT WONG-CHU BETTER!
ANOTHER, AND ANOTHER, TRIES IN VAIN...
I AM STRONGEST OF ALL! NEXT TO WONG-CHU OTHER MEN ARE BUT FLEAS!
IT IS OVER! NOW LET US PLUNDER THE TOWN! FOR NONE CAN STOP THE VICTORIOUS WONG-CHU!
3

MEANWHILE, ON THE OUTSKIRTS OF THE JUNGLE...
THE RED GUERRILLAS OUTNUMBER US! OUR HEAVY ARTILLERY COULD BEAT THEM, BUT WE CAN'T TRANSPORT SUCH BIG WEAPONS THROUGH THE DENSE JUNGLE!
SO, THAT'S WHERE MY MIDGET TRANSISTORS COME IN, EH?
RIGHT! THANKS TO YOUR INVENTIONS, OUR MORTARS ARE NO LARGER OR HEAVIER THAN FLASHLIGHTS! OUR MEN CAN CARRY THEM ANYWHERE!
TAKE COVER! THERE'S THE ENEMY! YOU'LL SEE YOUR GUNS IN ACTION NOW!
THAT'S WHY I WAS SENT HERE! TO MAKE SURE THEY WORK AS WELL AS PLANNED! IF NOT, I'LL FIX 'EM ON THE SPOT!
JUST LOOK AT THE REDS RETREAT!
STARK, YOUR WEAPONS ARE EVERY-THING WE HOPED FOR!
BATTLE-FILLED MINUTES LATER...
THE REDS NEVER KNEW WHAT HIT THEM!
BUT, THE JUNGLE HOLDS A THOUSAND PERILS! SOME NATURAL, OTHERS MAN-MADE...
AND, TRIPPING OVER A SMALL, CONCEALED STRING LEADS TO DISASTER...
BAROOM
A BOOBY-TRAP! OHHH...
MINUTES LATER...
YANKEE CIVILIAN STILL ALIVE! HIM MAYBE IMPORTANT OFFICIAL OF GOVERNMENT! I BRING HIM TO WONG-CHU! MAYBE GET REWARD!
OHHHH!
LATER, AT THE GUERRILLA CHIEF'S HEADQUARTERS...
HIS PAPERS REVEAL HE IS FAMOUS YANKEE WEAPONS INVENTOR! HOW IS HE?
BAD! MUCH SHRAPNEL NEAR HIS HEART! IMPOSSIBLE TO OPERATE! CANNOT LIVE LONGER THAN ONE WEEK!
4

IN A FEW DAYS SHRAPNEL WILL REACH HIS HEART-- THEN HE WILL DIE! NOTHING CAN SAVE HIM!
BAH! WE CAN USE HIS GENIUS! WONG-CHU WILL TRICK HIM INTO SPENDING HIS LAST DAYS ON EARTH WORKING FOR US! IS HE STRONG ENOUGH NOW?
YES, HE CAN WORK TILL SHRAPNEL REACHES HEART!
WE KNOW YOU ARE AMERICAN WEAPONS INVENTOR! IF YOU DESIGN POWERFUL NEW WEAPON FOR ME, AFTERWARDS I HAVE SURGEON SAVE YOUR LIFE!
HE'S LYING... IF THEY COULD THEY'D DO IT NOW, TO BE SURE I LIVE LONG ENOUGH TO DESIGN WEAPONS FOR THEM!
I KNOW I'VE ONLY DAYS TO LIVE, BUT MY LAST ACT WILL BE TO DEFEAT THIS GRINNING, SMIRKING, RED TERRORIST!
ALL RIGHT, WONG-CHU, I'LL DO IT!
I KNEW YOU WOULD NOT HESITATE TO BETRAY YOUR COUNTRY TO SAVE YOURSELF!
HERE ROOM WHERE YOU WORK! PLENTY OF SCRAP IRON! PLENTY TOOLS!
THIS I PROMISE YOU... I SHALL BUILD THE MOST FANTASTIC WEAPON OF ALL TIME!
I'LL BUILD IT, ALL RIGHT, BUT IT WILL BE MINE...
--MADE FOR ONLY ONE PURPOSE-- TO KEEP ME ALIVE!
CLICK!
EVERY TICK OF THE CLOCK BRINGS THE DEADLY PIECE OF SHRAPNEL CLOSER TO MY HEART! I'VE GOT TO WORK FASTER THAN I'VE EVER WORKED BEFORE! CAN'T AFFORD A SINGLE MISTAKE!
THEN, ON THE SECOND DAY OF TONY STARK'S RACE AGAINST TIME...
THIS OLD ONE, PROFESSOR YINSEN! ONCE GREAT SCIENTIST! NOW LOWLY MAN-SERVANT OF WONG-CHU.. ...WILL HELP YOU BUILD WEAPON!
NO! I WILL NEVER HELP THE EVIL RED TYRANTS! NEVER!!
5

PROFESSOR YINSEN, IN COLLEGE I READ YOUR BOOKS! YOU WERE THE GREATEST PHYSICIST OF ALL!! THEN, EVERY-ONE THOUGHT YOU HAD DIED!
I'D HAVE BEEN BETTER OFF IF I HAD! I WAS PRESSED INTO SLAVE LABOR BY THE REDS, AND WHEN I RESISTED, WONG-CHU TOOK ME PRISONER!
NO LONGER ABLE TO WORK IN SECRET, ANTHONY STARK MUST REVEAL HIS PLAN TO THE AGED SCHOLAR, THE ONLY HUMAN HE DARES TRUST!
AN IRON MAN! FANTASTIC! A MIGHTY, ELECTRONIC BODY, TO KEEP YOUR HEART BEATING AFTER THE SHRAPNEL REACHES IT! WE JUST MIGHT SUCCEED! THINK WHAT A CREATURE WE COULD CREATE! WHAT WONDERS HE SHALL PERFORM!
AND THE REDS THEMSELVES GAVE US ALL THE MATERIALS WE WILL NEED!
THUS, A DYING MAN'S DESPERATE RACE AGAINST TIME CONTINUES...
I'VE DONE EXTENSIVE WORK WITH TRANSISTORS! I CAN DESIGN THEM IN ANY SIZE TO PERFORM ANY FUNCTION!
WE SHALL USE THEM TO OPERATE THE MACHINE ELECTRONICALLY TO MOVE COUNTLESS GEARS AND CONTROL LEVERS!
ALL ACTIVITY MUST BE COORDINATED PERFECTLY! THE IRON FRAME MUST DUPLICATE EVERY ACTION OF THE HUMAN BODY!
IT SHALL, MY FRIEND! IT SHALL! THIS SHALL BE THE CROWNING ACHIEVEMENT OF MY LIFE!
HOURS PASS INTO DAYS, AS THE SHRAPNEL MOVES CLOSER AND CLOSER TO ANTHONY STARK'S HEART...
I CAN FEEL THE PRESSURE! MY TIME IS RUNNING OUT! WE MUST WORK FASTER!
THERE! THE SELF-LUBRICATION SYSTEM IS COMPLETED! JUST A LITTLE LONGER! YOU MUST HAVE COURAGE!
AND THEN, WHEN THE DOOMED AMERICAN'S CONDITION BECOMES CRITICAL--WHEN HE CAN NO LONGER STAND...
THE LIFE-GIVING HEART OF YOUR IRON BODY IS READY! QUICKLY... CLAMP IT AROUND YOUR CHEST!
6

THERE! IT IS DONE! WHEN I ACTIVATE THE MACHINE, YOUR OWN AMAZING TRANSISTORS WILL FURNISH THE POWER TO KEEP YOUR HEART BEATING! YOU SHOULD LIVE AS LONG AS THE IRON BODY OPERATES!
THIS GENERATOR WILL SOON BUILD UP ENOUGH ENERGY TO FURNISH ALL THE POWER YOU'LL NEED TO MOVE!
BUT SUDDENLY...
THE WARNING LIGHT WE INSTALLED-- IT FLASHES! SOMEONE IS APPROACHING!
IT MUST BE WONG-CHU! IF HE ENTERS NOW, ALL OUR WORK WILL HAVE BEEN IN VAIN!!
WONG-CHU MUST BE KEPT AWAY UNTIL THE MIGHTY ELECTRONIC BODY BEGINS TO POWER THE HEART OF ANTHONY STARK!
MY LIFE IS OF NO CONSEQUENCE! BUT I MUST GAIN TIME FOR IRON MAN TO LIVE!
THEN, BEFORE THE REDS CAN ENTER THE ROOM, THE BRAVE PROFESSOR YINSEN MAKES ONE DESPERATE LAST EFFORT...
DEATH TO WONG-CHU! DEATH TO THE EVIL TYRANT!
HE HAS GONE MAD! AFTER HIM! END HIS MISERABLE LIFE! HE IS OF NO FURTHER USE TO ME!
SLAM!
CLICK!
AND THUS THE GALLANT CHINESE SCIENTIST BUYS PRECIOUS SECONDS FOR ANTHONY STARK... WHILE THE LIFE-SUSTAINING MACHINE BUILDS UP MORE AND MORE POWER BEHIND THE LOCKED DOOR!!!
BANG!
IT IS DONE! DRAG HIM AWAY!
YOU WILL NOT HAVE DIED IN VAIN, MY FRIEND! I SWEAR IT! THE IRON MAN SWEARS IT!
7

THEN, EVEN AS PROFESSOR YINSEN BREATHES HIS LAST, THE ELECTRONIC MARVEL BEGINS TO STIR...
THE TRANSISTORS HAVE SUFFICIENT ENERGY NOW! MY HEART IS BEATING NORMALLY! THE MACHINE IS KEEPING ME ALIVE! ALIVE!!
AND THE TRANSISTOR-POWERED CIRCUITS ARE COORDINATED WITH MY BRAIN WAVES, JUST AS ANY LIVING HUMAN'S BRAIN CONTROLS HIS OWN BODY!
B-BUT I'M LOSING MY BALANCE!
THUD!
I'M LIKE A BABY LEARNING TO WALK! BUT I HAVEN'T TIME! I MUST LEARN QUICKLY! I MUST GET THE KNACK OF MANIPULATING THIS MASSIVE, UNBELIEVABLY POWERFUL IRON SHELL BEFORE THE REDS FIND ME--OR ELSE I'LL BE AT THEIR MERCY!
BUT THE BRAIN WHICH HAS MASTERED THE SECRETS OF SCIENCE IS ALSO CAPABLE OF MASTERING ITS NEW BODY! AND SO...
I HAVE THE FEEL OF IT NOW! I CAN STAND--MOVE--EVEN WALK WITHOUT TOPPLING!
MEANWHILE, OUTSIDE THE LOCKED DOOR...
BREAK IT DOWN! SMASH IT! I MUST LEARN WHAT HAS HAPPENED IN THERE!
WHAM
WH
8

THEY'RE COMING! THIS IS MY GREATEST TEST! CAN THE THING I HAVE CREATED SURVIVE? THE THING WHICH IS LESS THAN HUMAN...YET, FAR MORE THAN MERELY HUMAN! THIS THING WHICH IS NOW-- ANTHONY STARK!!
WHAM
MY BRAIN STILL THINKS! MY HEART STILL BEATS! BUT, IN ORDER TO REMAIN ALIVE, I MUST SPEND THE REST OF MY LIFE IN THIS IRON PRISON!!
BUT, THIS BITTER REALIZATION IS SUDDENLY INTERRUPTED, AS THE IRON MAN SNAPS BACK TO REALITY...
THEY'LL SOON BE THRU THE DOOR... I MUST CONCEAL MYSELF UNTIL I CAN PLAN MY NEXT MOVE!
FORTUNATELY, YINSEN AND I EQUIPPED MY IRON BODY WITH MANY ATTACH-MENTS, SUCH AS THESE!
I'LL FASTEN THESE SUCTION CUPS TO MY PALMS AND TURN ON MY TRANSISTOR-POWERED AIR-PRESSURE JETS!
THEY WORK! THEY GIVE ME THE POWER TO SOAR INTO THE AIR!
THEY DON'T DREAM OF LOOKING UP HERE IN THE SHADOWS!
THE YANKEE IS GONE! AND HE HAS BUILT US NO WEAPONS!
HE CANNOT BE FAR! FIND HIM AND DISPOSE OF HIM AS YOU DID THE OTHER WHO DARED DEFY ME!
THEY KILLED THE PROFESSOR-- A MAN WHO NEVER HARMED ANYONE IN HIS LIFE! THE MURDERING SWINE! THEY'LL PAY FOR IT! I SWEAR IT! IRON MAN SWEARS IT!
WHILE YOU HUNT DOWN YANKEE, I SHALL AMUSE MYSELF AT MY FAVORITE SPORT
THEN, SECONDS AFTER THE REDS DEPART...
YES, WONG-CHU, AMUSE YOURSELF WHILE YOU STILL CAN! FOR OUR MOMENT OF RECKONING IS ALMOST AT HAND!
9

IN THE COURTYARD...
HAH! I WIN AGAIN!
NONE CAN DEFEAT THE MIGHTY WAR LORD!
I SAY HE IS A COWARD! I CHALLENGE WONG-CHU!
WHO DARES SPEAK THUS TO WONG-CHU? SHOW YOURSELF! LET ME SEE THE FACE OF THE ONE I AM ABOUT TO DESTROY!
AS YOU WISH, TYRANT! FIRST, I SHALL REMOVE MY CLOTHES--
WHY DO YOU STARE, WONG-CHU? WHAT IS WRONG?
HAVE YOU NEVER SEEN AN IRON MAN BEFORE?!
YOU--YOU ARE NOT HUMAN! YOU ARE MACHINE!!
AND YOU ARE A HEARTLESS MAN OF EVIL WHO IS ABOUT TO PAY FOR HIS MISDEEDS!
THEN, BEFORE THE STARTLED EYES OF THE RED HORDES, TWO ELECTRONICALLY-POWERED ARMS SEIZE WONG-CHU, LIFTING HIM EASILY AS THEY WOULD A TOY!
YOU ARE NOT FACING A WOUNDED, DYING MAN NOW...
--OR AN AGED, GENTLE PROFESSOR!
THIS IS IRON MAN WHO OPPOSES YOU, AND ALL YOU STAND FOR!
10

YOU MAKE ME LOSE FACE! I DESTROY YOU!! EVEN YOU CAN BE SLAIN!
GUARDS--OPEN FIRE!! DESTROY IRON MAN!
IT WILL TAKE MORE THAN SMALL ARMS FIRE TO PENETRATE MY CAST-IRON BODY!
PHANG
KAPOW!
KAPOW!
PAING
GET GRENADES!! BRING BAZOOKAS!! QUICKLY, YOU FOOLS! QUICKLY!
BUT, BEFORE THE HEAVIER WEAPONS CAN BE BROUGHT INTO PLAY...
I'LL JUST REVERSE THE CHARGE ON THIS MAGNETIC TURBO-INSULATOR...
...AND USE A TOP-HAT TRANSISTOR TO INCREASE ITS REPELLING POWER A THOUSANDFOLD!
THERE! REVERSE MAGNETISM --IT WORKS LIKE A CHARM!
STOP! COME BACK! THE MAGNET AFFECTS ONLY METAL! SHEER MAN-POWER CAN STILL DEFEAT HIM!
PANICKED BY THE INCREDIBLE DEMONSTRATION, THE GUERRILLAS FLEE...
RUSHING INTO THE NEAREST BUILDING, WONG-CHU HEADS FOR THE STAIRS...
UPSTAIRS, THERE IS A LOUDSPEAKER! IN ALL THIS CONFUSION AND NOISE, THEY CAN-NOT HEAR ME! I MUST TALK OVER LOUD-SPEAKER!
LISTEN, MY WARRIORS! TEN THOUSAND YEN TO THE ONE WHO DESTROYS IRON MAN!
AWWKKK WWKKK BBBRRRK!
AN EASY MATTER FOR ME TO CREATE ELECTRICAL INTERFERENCE TO DROWN OUT HIS WORDS WITH STATIC!
11

AND THEN, TO FRUSTRATE THE WAR LORD'S EFFORTS EVEN FURTHER...
NOW I'LL SWITCH MY OWN VOICE ONTO THE LOUDSPEAKER!
DESERT WONG-CHU FLEE INTO THE JUNGLE!
WHA--WHAT IS HAPPENING?? THOSE NOT MY WORDS!
NONE CAN DEFEAT IRON MAN! FLEE, BEFORE HE SLAYS YOU ALL!!
IN PANIC, AND WITHOUT LEADERSHIP, THEY'LL SOON BE CAPTURED BY SOUTH VIETNAM TROOPS!
AND NOW TO SETTLE WITH WONG-CHU!
HE'S LOCKED THE DOOR BUT THAT WON'T KEEP ME OUT!
MY POWERFUL TRANSISTOR MAKES THIS MINIATURE BUZZ SAW INSIDE MY INDEX FINGER-CONTAINER OUT-PERFORM ANYTHING A DOZEN TIMES ITS SIZE!
ZZZZZZZZZ
ALL RIGHT, WAR LORD! YOU'RE FINISHED! COME DOWN HERE!
YOU MIGHT TERRIFY MY TROOPS! BUT NOT WONG-CHU!
TAKE THIS, MONSTER!
SMASH
NOW TO ORDER THE EXECUTION OF ALL MY PRISONERS!
UGH!! HE WEIGHTED EACH DRAWER OF THIS CABINET WITH ROCKS!
12

BUT NO DRAWERS FILLED WITH ROCKS CAN HOLD BACK IRON LIMBS POWERED BY ELECTRONIC TRANSISTORS!
KNOWING HE'S DEFEATED, WONG-CHU IS TRYING TO MURDER ALL HIS PRISONERS BEFORE HE'S STOPPED! I CANNOT ALLOW THAT!
I'M FREE! BUT IT TOOK ALMOST ALL MY ELECTRICAL POWER! I'VE GOT TO RECHARGE! I'M TOO LOW ON ENERGY TO PURSUE WONG-CHU!
YET, I CAN'T LET HIM GET AWAY! WAIT! I HAVE IT!
UNFASTENING HIS LUBRICATING APPARATUS, THE IRON MAN SQUIRTS OUT A THIN STREAM OF OIL...
I ESTIMATED IT JUST RIGHT! THE PRESSURE'S GREAT ENOUGH FOR IT TO REACH THE AMMO DUMP!
GUARDS! GUARDS! SLAY THE PRISONERS! NOW!
BARROOM
13
SECONDS LATER, IRON MAN HAS RECHARGED HIS BATTERIES, AND THEN...
I HAVE SET THE PRISONERS FREE, AND THE REDS HAVE FLED IN BLIND PANIC!
IT'S ALL OVER! NOW, PROFESSOR YINSEN, REST EASY! YOU, WHO SACRIFICED YOUR LIFE TO SAVE MINE, HAVE BEEN AVENGED!
AS FOR THE IRON MAN, THAT METALLIC HULK WHO ONCE WAS ANTHONY STARK... WHO KNOWS WHAT DESTINY AWAITS HIM? TIME ALONE WILL PROVIDE THE ANSWER! TIME ALONE...
THE END
DON'T MISS MORE OF IRON MAN IN THE NEXT GREAT ISSUE OF... TALES of SUSPENSE!

QUESTIONS

Defining Terms

Identify in the context of the chapter each of the following:

Cold War	Kennedy's Inaugural Address
List of 57 names	Greece and Turkey
Wong-Chu	*Mission to Moscow*
Truman Doctrine	Joseph Stalin
Anthony Stark	

Probing the Sources

1. How and why did Harry Truman try to "scare the hell" out of the American people in order to achieve his foreign policy ends?
2. Did Joseph McCarthy believe that internal or external threats posed the gravest danger for the United States? Did he offer a solution?
3. How did John Kennedy try to give an impression of crisis in his inaugural address?
4. Why did Thomas McGrath refuse to testify before HUAC?
5. What was Iron Man fighting for and against?

Interpreting the Sources

1. Were there points on which Harry Truman, Joe McCarthy, and John Kennedy, agreed? Was the Cold War a Democratic or Republican policy?
2. Why was Joseph McCarthy so controversial?
3. How did the threat of communism compare to the 21st century threat of terrorism?
4. What forces shaped the Cold War and accounts for its long life? Was the communist threat real or imaginary?

ADDITIONAL READING

The origin of the Cold War has been one of the most hotly debated topics in American history. An outstanding overview of the Cold War is provided in Walter LaFeber, *America, Russia, and the Cold War* (1985). Daniel Yergin, *Shattered Peace* (1982), recounts the early years of the Cold War. Gar Alperovitz, *Atomic Diplomacy* (1985), suggests that the Cold War began even before the end of World War II, while John L. Goddis, *The United States and the Origins of the Cold War, 1941–1947* (1972), argues that it evolved and deepened over time. Also see Goddis's *Strategies of Containment* (1982). A view from the Soviet Union is provided in Vojtech Mastny, *Russia's Road to the Cold War, 1941–1945* (1979). Many of the leading American actors of the period have written memoirs. Among the best are Dean Acheson, *Present at Creation: My Years in the State Department* (1969), and George F. Kennan, *Memoirs, 1925–1950* (1967). For more general works, see James T. Patterson, *Grand Expectations: The United States, 1945–1974* (1996), and Melvin Leffler, *A Preponderance of Power: National Security, The Truman Administration, and the*

Cold War (1992). The impact of the Cold War on domestic politics and culture has also been considered in depth. David M. Oshinsky, *A Conspiracy So Immense: The World of Joseph McCarthy* (1983) shows how the Cold War worked its way into politics. Stephen J. Whitfield, *The Culture of the Cold War* (1996) traces the impact of the Cold War on American life. Larry Ceplair and Steven Englund, *The Inquisition in Hollywood: Politics of the Film Industry, 1930–1960* (1983) is a detailed study of the relationship between Washington and Hollywood. On comic books, see Bradford Wright, *Comic Book Nation* (2001). For a broad synthesis of the era, see John Lewis Gaddis, *The Cold War* (2005).

12

The Civil Rights Movement

Freedom Summer, 1964

Historical Context

In June 1964, two hundred college students from some of the most prestigious universities in America gathered at the campus of Western College for Women in Oxford, Ohio. They spent several days getting ready for their summer vacations. All were going to Mississippi to participate in one of the most important mass movements in American history. The fact that two hundred *white* students planned to go into the deep South to work in the civil rights movement stirred massive attention in the media. But the fight for equality had already been in high gear for a decade; it was a movement by and for black Americans, with profound consequences for whites.

In 1954, the United States Supreme Court decided unanimously in the landmark case *Brown v. the Board of Education of Topeka, Kansas* that the segregationist doctrine of "separate but equal" public schools for blacks and whites inherently violated constitutional guarantees because segregated black schools were underfunded and inferior. The decision implicitly questioned the entire southern Jim Crow legal system that formally kept blacks and whites apart in schools, hotels, trains, public swimming pools, restrooms, and a variety of other locations. It takes a leap of historical imagination to feel what it must have been like for a black person to confront two drinking fountains—one labeled "White" and the other, probably an inferior facility, labeled "Colored." Most of the time, blacks tried not to notice; but by the mid-1950s, increasing numbers of African Americans stopped looking the other way. It was impossible for them not to be heartened by the *Brown* decision and other court cases in which their rights were upheld; it was equally impossible not to be let down when the federal government hesitated to come through with enforcement of its own laws and judicial decisions. The raising of hopes on the one hand and the failure of fulfillment on the other energized many African Americans to mobilize themselves. Their underlying assumption was that, as Americans, they deserved all of the rights and privileges of other citizens.

Nonviolent direct action became the main technique of the movement for the decade or so beginning with the *Brown* decision and ending with the Mississippi Freedom Summer. Simply put, this technique meant refusing to acquiesce to unjust laws, many of which the courts had overturned. Sit-ins, demonstrations, boycotts, civil disobedience, breaking the law, and filling the jails—all done without committing violence or retaliating against others' aggressions—these were the essence of nonviolent direct action.

The most dramatic early example of such techniques came in Montgomery, Alabama, in December 1955. Mrs. Rosa Parks, a black seamstress, rode the bus home after a long day's work. A white man got on, but she refused to give up her seat to him as law and custom required. When she was arrested, blacks began a mass boycott of Montgomery's bus system. Local residents like E. D. Nixon, who had been active in the labor movement as a railroad porter, and 27-year-old Martin Luther King, Jr., of Atlanta, freshly graduated from divinity school at Boston University, helped organize and inspire the year-long boycott. The protesters won their point when the Supreme Court ruled that laws forcing blacks to sit at the back of the bus or to give up their seats to whites were illegal. Once again, however, enforcement was slow.

In 1960, the movement took a new turn as four black students from North Carolina Agricultural and Technical College simply sat down at a segregated lunch counter and waited to be served. Whites berated, abused, then arrested them. For the next few years, sit-ins occurred at public accommodations throughout the South. Protesters requested their rights as citizens and maintained their Gandhian mode of nonviolence; whites responded with increasing levels of bloodshed. Demonstrators were killed and wounded as they registered at previously segregated universities, rode previously segregated buses, and checked into all-white hotels. Boycotts brought local economies to a standstill; massive sit-ins tied up criminal justice systems by filling the jails with protesters; and, above all, evening news images of people protesting peacefully for their rights and being met by police dogs, water cannons, and bludgeons brought considerable sympathy. Even President Kennedy was cautiously supporting new civil rights legislation by the time of his assassination.

Yet, as the summer of 1964 approached, the civil rights movement was coming to a crossroads. The right to be served a cup of coffee, to swim in public pools, or even to go to good schools (and ten years after the *Brown* decision, southern schools remained segregated) were important, but increasingly, the movement was forced to confront issues of politics and power. African Americans in the southern states constituted an enormous potential electorate, yet old legal barriers kept them from voting. This ultimate right of citizenship was next on the movement's agenda, and the Freedom Summer was part of the proposed solution.

Organizational leadership of the movement had been evolving all along. The National Association for the Advancement of Colored People (NAACP) had led the way in bringing civil rights cases to courts, especially in the 1950s, but as the movement turned toward nonviolent direct action, other groups with new leaders such as the Southern Christian Leadership Conference (SCLC) led by Martin Luthur King Jr., and James Farmer's Congress on Racial Equality (CORE) took center stage. Early in the 1960s, however, another organization emerged, the Student Nonviolent Coordinating Committee (SNCC). SNCC was the most militant of these organizations. Its membership drew heavily on young black southerners, many of whom had grown up poor, had seen the rising tide of white resistance, and were skeptical that integration was the answer. SNCC was active in various ways, but concern with

Sit-in in Jackson, Mississippi, in June 1963. (AP/Wide World)

issues of power led its members to undertake a massive voter registration drive. The Freedom Summer project was part of this new emphasis.

Under the leadership of Robert Moses, SNCC, CORE, and the NAACP banded together in an umbrella organization known as the Congress of Federated Organizations (COFO). However, the money and manpower for COFO came mainly from SNCC, and the Freedom Summer was effectively a SNCC project. Simply put, the goal was to put hundreds of field-workers in Mississippi to educate poor rural African Americans in their elementary rights and to help them register to vote. Massive participation by idealistic white college students would bring increased press coverage and highlight the oppressive social conditions of the Deep South.

As SNCC planned the Freedom Summer, some leaders objected to involvement by whites. They argued that nonblacks came south, then departed when things got rough; that they stole all of the publicity; and that they monopolized leadership roles. Moses, however, insisted that integration was the ultimate goal and that he would not be a party to any form of segregation. As for whites getting too much media attention, the movement depended on stirring public opinion against segregation, and since the press was more interested in white protesters than black, the whites were useful allies out of proportion to their relatively small numbers.

The following news stories, editorials, photographs, memoranda, and other documents give a sense of the forces at work in Mississippi in the summer of 1964 and of the contending factions and ideologies. The events of that summer shattered the faith of many in nonviolent direct action, and in the coming years, civil rights protests grew increasingly bloody. After 1964, the movement's goals became much more concerned with economic and political power, and its methods more militant.

The results of those early years were mixed. Local governments seemed intransigent, acts of white violence went unpunished, and those sworn to uphold the law, such as the Federal Bureau of Investigation, often took the side of whites who attacked blacks. On the other hand, Congress passed the Civil Rights Act of 1964, which banned discrimination in public accommodations. The pain and indignity of legal apartheid had ended. One year later, President Lyndon Johnson signed the Voting Rights Act of 1965, a law that was gradually enforced, fulfilling (with exceptions) the demonstrators' goal of bringing the vote to southern blacks. Since its passage, thousands of African Americans have been elected to political office. So those who sacrificed so much for equality brought important changes to the South and even to the North, where segregation, by custom if not always by law, was the norm.

Events like the Freedom Summer of 1964—with televised scenes of black martyrdom in the face of white violence—challenged the old power structure and shocked some people into supporting the goals of the movement. Much of the discriminatory legacy of the Jim Crow era remained then and still remains. Especially in the field of economic opportunity, African Americans continue to face obstacles born of racial prejudice. Nonetheless, an ongoing tradition of activism that began in the 1950s continues to this day. Furthermore, that legacy did not remain confined to the field of African Americans' rights, but extended to other racial minorities, to the women's movement, and to the protest against the Vietnam War. The civil rights struggle, then, opened a whole new era of activist politics.

THE DOCUMENTS

The documents in this chapter tell the story of the Freedom Summer as it unfolded. Remember that this was only one episode in a drama that developed over several years. Note the range of opinion expressed by journalists and commentators (for example, the old 1950s technique of red-baiting—making unfounded allegations that individual leaders were communists—was still going strong). Note, too, how the civil rights debate covered a broad area of contested ground: states' rights versus the need for federal intervention; southern folkways versus racial equality; individual security versus group advancement; court cases versus direct action; and nonviolence versus greater militancy.

Introduction to Document 1

Document 1 provides some background for the events of 1964. Anne Moody grew up in Centreville, Mississippi, during the 1940s and 1950s. Her autobiography, *Coming of Age in Mississippi,* published in 1968, described her confusion, agony, and anger as she slowly became conscious of the racism and violence that surrounded her. Moody fought segregation with everything she had, risking her life and pushing herself to the edge of a nervous breakdown. The following passages capture how it felt to work in the civil rights movement in the summer of 1963. Moody

was a student at Tougaloo College, but she devoted most of her time to community organizing. Document 1 is excerpted from a chapter in Moody's autobiography; here she describes the situation in Canton, Mississippi.

DOCUMENT 1 *From Coming of Age in Mississippi*

Anne Moody

In July, CORE opened up an office in Canton, Mississippi, to start a voter registration campaign in Madison County. By this time, I was so fed up with the fighting and bickering among the organizations in Jackson, I was ready to go almost anywhere, even Madison County, where Negroes frequently turned up dead. Shortly before Christmas a man's headless corpse had been found on the road between Canton and Tougaloo with the genitals cut off and with K's cut into the flesh all over his body. Around the time the body was found, Tougaloo College had received a lot of threats, so an inventory was made of all the males on campus to see if any were missing.

When Reverend [Ed] King discovered that I had agreed to work with CORE in the area, he was very much concerned. He discussed Canton with me, telling me he thought the place was too rough for girls. Some of my girlfriends also begged me not to go. But I just had to. I don't know why I felt that way, but I did.

Because I had come from Wilkinson County, I just didn't think Madison could be any worse. Things might even be a little better, I thought, since in Madison there were three Negroes to every white. I remembered that in Jackson there had been one point when I could see the white folks actually tremble with fear. At times when we were having mass demonstrations we had them so confused they didn't know that to do. Whenever I could detect the least amount of fear in any white Mississippian, I felt good. I also felt there was a chance of winning the battle regardless of how costly it turned out to be.

Disregarding all acts of violence, Madison County was considered a place with a possible future for Negroes. In addition to the fact that our records showed that there was a population of twenty-nine thousand Negroes as against nine thousand whites, Negroes owned over 40 percent of the land in the county. However, there were only about one hundred and fifty to two hundred registered to vote, and these had registered as a result of a campaign conducted by a few local citizens a couple of years earlier. Of this number, less than half were actually voting.

I arrived in Canton with Dave Dennis one Friday evening, and was taken straight to the CORE office, a small room adjoining a Negro café. The café was owned by C. O. Chinn and his wife, a well-established Negro family. It was located on Franklin Street in the center of one of Canton's Negro sections. Dave and I were just in time to have supper there with George Raymond, the project director, and Bettye Poole, my old Tougaloo buddy.

Dave introduced me to Mrs. Chinn. She was a stout lady with a warm and friendly smile. I liked her right away. I spent the entire evening sitting around the office talking to her and George Raymond about Madison County.

The office had been open only a few weeks, and in that time, Mrs. Chinn had already had her liquor license taken away. The place had been broken into twice, and many Negroes had been physically threatened. George reported that so far mostly teen-agers were involved in the Movement. He said that about fifty dedicated teen-age canvassers showed up each day. They were sent out daily, but had little success. Most of the Negroes just didn't want to be bothered, Mrs. Chinn told me. "That's the way it is all over," I thought. "Most Negroes have been thoroughly brainwashed. If they aren't brainwashed, they are too insecure—either they work for Miss Ann or they live on Mr. Charlie's place."

I just didn't see how the Negroes in Madison County could be so badly off. They should have had everything going for them—out-numbering the whites three to one and owning just about as much land as they did. When I discussed this point with Mrs. Chinn, I discovered that, although they did own the land, they were allowed to farm only so much of it. Cotton is the main crop in Mississippi, and, as Mrs. Chinn explained that night, the federal government controls cotton by giving each state a certain allotment. Each state decides how much each county gets and each county distributes the allotments to the farmers. "It always ends up with the white people getting most of the allotments," Mrs. Chinn said. "The Negroes aren't able to get more, regardless of how much land they have." Most of the farmers in Madison County were barely living off what they made from their land. Besides, they were never clear from debt. The independent farmers were practically like sharecroppers, because they always had their crop pledged in advance. The more I thought about it, the more it seemed that the federal government was directly or indirectly responsible for most of the segregation, discrimination, and poverty in the South. . . .

By the beginning of August . . . Dave Dennis decided to bring in three . . . workers—two girls, who were students from Jackson, and a boy called Flukie, a CORE task force worker. There were now six of us, but there was still more work than we could handle. George and Flukie went out in the country each day to talk with farmers and to scout for churches to conduct workshops in. The rest of us were left to canvass and look after the office.

So far we had only been able to send a handful of Negroes to the courthouse to attempt to register, and those few that went began to get fired from their jobs. This discouraged others who might have registered. Meanwhile, we were constantly being threatened by the whites. Almost every night someone came running by to tell us the whites planned to bump us off.

One evening just before dark, someone took a shot at a pregnant Negro woman who was walking home with her two small sons. This happened in a section where a few poor white families lived. The woman stood in the street with her children, screaming and yelling for help. A Negro truck driver picked them up and drove them to the Boyd Street housing project, which was right across the street from the Freedom House. She was still yelling and screaming when she got out of the truck, and people ran out of all the project houses. The woman stood there telling everyone what had happened. She was so big it looked as though she was ready to have the baby any minute. As I looked at the other women standing around her, I didn't like what I saw in their faces. I could tell what they were thinking—"Why don't you all get out of here before you get us all killed?"

After this incident, Negro participation dropped off to almost nothing, and things got so rough we were afraid to walk the streets. In addition, our money was cut off. We were being paid twenty dollars a week by the Voter Education Project, a Southern agency which supported voter registration for Negroes. They said that since we were not producing registered voters, they could not continue to put money into the area. It seemed things were getting rough from every angle. We sometimes went for days without a meal. I was getting sick and losing lots of weight. . . .

Sunday, September 15, 1963, was my twenty-third birthday. I got up about nine that morning feeling like one hundred and three. Everyone else was sleeping so I just decided to let them sleep. After a shower, I started to fix breakfast even though Mattie had promised to cook that morning. As soon as I finished, I got them up because we were supposed to have a staff meeting later. . . .

We were all eating and listening to the radio when the music stopped abruptly in the middle of a record. "A special news bulletin just in from Birmingham," the DJ was saying. "A church was just bombed in Birmingham, Alabama. It is believed that several Sunday-school students were killed." We all sat glued to our seats, avoiding each other's eyes. No one was eating now. Everyone was waiting for the next report on the bombing. The second report confirmed that four girls had been killed. I looked at George; he sat with his face buried in the palms of his hands. Dave sat motionless with tears in his eyes. Mattie looked at Dave as if she had been grounded by an electric shock. I put my hand up to my face. Tears were pouring out of my eyes, and I hadn't even known I was crying.

"Why! Why! Why! Oh, God, why? Why us? Why us?" I found myself asking. "I gotta find myself some woods, trees, or water—anything. I gotta talk to you, God, and you gotta answer. Please don't play Rip Van Winkle with me today."

I rushed out of the house and started walking aimlessly. I ran up a hill where there were trees. I found myself in a graveyard I didn't even know was there. I sat there looking up through the trees, trying to communicate with God. "Now talk to me, God. Come on down and talk to me.

"You know, I used to go to Sunday school when I was a little girl. I went to Sunday school, church, and B.T.U. every Sunday. We were taught how merciful and forgiving you are. Mama used to tell us that you would forgive us seventy-seven times a day, and I believed in you. I bet you those girls in Sunday school were being taught the same as I was when I was their age. Is that teaching wrong? Are you going to forgive their killers? You not gonna answer me, God, hmm? Well, if you don't want to talk, then listen to me.

"As long as I live, I'll never be beaten by a white man again. Not like in Woolworth's. Not any more. That's out. You know something else, God? Nonviolence is out. I have a good idea Martin Luther King is talking to you, too. If he is, tell him that nonviolence has served its purpose. Tell him that for me, God, and for a lot of other Negroes who must be thinking it today." . . .

A few days later, a Negro high school girl, picking cotton after school out in the country, was raped by a white farmer. The news was whispered throughout Canton. All the Negroes thought it was horrible, but none of them stopped sending their children to pick cotton. They had no choice—the little money the teen-agers made from picking cotton kept them in school. In Madison County, the use of teen-aged labor during the cotton-picking season was an institution. The Negro schools actually closed at noon the first two months of the school year, so that the students would be available to work for the white farmers. Their own parents, who had almost as much land as the whites but received much smaller allotments from the government, practically starved. Most of them couldn't even afford to give their children lunch money and buy them school supplies. . . .

Because the girl came to the CORE office and filled out an affidavit, her father had to resort to packing a gun to protect his family. After that, several open assaults were made on young Negro girls by the white men in the area. The assaults provoked a lot of talk concerning other affairs. . . . It came out in the open that some of the top officials of Madison County had Negro mistresses that they lived with almost full-time. . . .

It was now three weeks since the Birmingham church bombing, and during this time the Klan had been extremely busy. What I feared most was that the threats would stop, and action would begin—that I would see a bunch of Klansmen riding through Canton. If this ever happened, I was sure the streets of Canton would flow with blood for days.

Introduction to Documents 2 through 4

The following internal documents from leaders of the civil rights groups that organized the Freedom Summer set forth the strategy and rationale for the project.

Document 2 is from a pamphlet distributed by SNCC in Spring 1964. It details the conditions of voting rights for blacks in Mississippi. Document 3 is an undated (probably early 1964) summary of SNCC's plans for the Freedom Summer and the reasons for the project. The document is too long to reprint in its entirety; what is left out here goes into great detail about the need to establish "freedom schools," designed to educate black youth in basic literacy skills, and also to identify potential

young leaders to strengthen the future of the civil rights movement. Document 4 is a memorandum from Robert Moses to the "Friends of Freedom in Mississippi"—mostly leaders in the movement—asking them to write to President Lyndon Johnson and urge protection for civil rights workers. Documents 3 and 4 were circulated among organizers of the movement; they were not for public consumption.

DOCUMENT 2 *SNCC Pamphlet on Voting Rights*

For the first time in United States history colored citizens are organizing across an entire state to overthrow white supremacy. In Mississippi national and local civil rights, civic and church organizations, through the Council of Federated Organizations, are pulling together for the right to demand changes in the Mississippi Way of Life.

At the same time there are whites throughout the state organizing to crush the movement for change. The dominant white supremacy group is known as the White Citizens' Councils, organized by Mississippi's "leading" citizens in 1954 to combat colored voting rights and resist the Supreme Court school decision that same year.

The Citizens' Councils now maintain a firm stranglehold on the governorship, the state legislature and the federal and state courts. They control local and state education throughout most of the state, and dominate the economic base and activity in the state. . . .

In 1890 there were many more colored citizens than white citizens who were eligible to become qualified electors in Mississippi. Therefore, in that year a Mississippi Constitutional Convention was held to adopt a new State Constitution.

Section 244 of the new Constitution required a new registration of voters starting January 1, 1892. This section also established a new requirement for qualification as a registered voter: a person had to be able to read any section of the Mississippi Constitution, or understand any section when read to him, or give a reasonable interpretation of any section. . . .

Under the new registration the balance of voting power shifted. By 1899 approximately 122,000 (82 percent) of the white males of voting age were registered. But only 18,000 (9 percent) of the colored males qualified. Since 1899 a substantial majority of whites of voting age have become registered voters. But the percentage of colored registered voters declined. . . .

On April 22, 1954, the State Legislature again passed a resolution to amend Section 244. This time however, several new qualifications were included in the proposal.

FIRST, that a person must be able to read and write any section of the Mississippi Constitution; and give a reasonable interpretation of the Constitution to the county registrar.

SECOND, a person must be able to demonstrate to the county registrar a reasonable understanding of the duties and obligations of citizenship under a constitutional form of government.

THIRD, that a person make a sworn written application for registration on a form which would be prescribed by the State Board of Election Commissioners.

FOURTH, that all persons who were registered before January 1, 1954, were expressly exempted from the new requirements. . . .

The burden of the new requirements had to fall on colored citizens because a substantial majority of whites were already registered and therefore exempted from the amendment. Most would still have to apply for registration and therefore have to fulfill the new requirements. In 1954 at least 450,000 (63 percent) of the voting-age whites were registered.

Approximately 22,000 (five percent) of the voting-age colored citizens were registered. With 95 percent of the 472,000 eligible voters white, the proposed amendment to Section 244 was adopted on November 2, 1954. . . .

Without the right to register and vote we cannot take part in any phases of Mississippi's form of republican government.

What recourse do the white supremacists leave Mississippi colored citizens, if they cannot voice their opinions at the polls?

DOCUMENT 3 *Prospectus for the Mississippi Freedom Summer*

It has become evident to the civil rights groups involved in the struggle for freedom in Mississippi that political and social justice cannot be won without the massive aid of the country as a whole, backed by the power and authority of the federal government. Little hope exists that the political leaders of Mississippi will steer even a moderate course in the near future (Governor Johnson's inaugural speech notwithstanding); in fact, the contrary seems true: as the winds of change grow stronger, the threatened political elite of Mississippi becomes more intransigent and fanatical in its support of the status quo. The closed society of Mississippi is, as Professor Silver asserts, without the moral resources to reform itself. And Negro efforts to win the right to vote cannot succeed against the extensive legal weapons and police powers of local and state officials without a nationwide mobilization of support.

A program is planned for this summer which will involve the massive participation of Americans dedicated to the elimination of racial oppression. Scores of college students, law students, medical students, teachers, professors, ministers, technicians, folk artists and lawyers from all over the country have already volunteered to work in Mississippi this summer—and hundreds more are being recruited. . . .

Since 1964 is an election year, the clear-cut issue of voting rights should be brought out in the open. Many SNCC and CORE workers in Mississippi hold the view that Negroes will never vote in large numbers until Federal marshals intervene. At any rate, many Americans must be made to realize that the voting rights they so often take for granted involve considerable risk for Negroes in the South. In the larger context of the national civil rights movement, enough progress has been made during the last year that there can be no turning back. Major victories in Mississippi, recognized as the stronghold of racial intolerance in the South, would speed immeasurably the breaking down of legal and social discrimination in both North and South. . . .

This summer's work in Mississippi is sponsored by COFO, the Council of Federated Organizations, which includes the Student Nonviolent Coordinating Committee (SNCC), the Southern Christian Leadership Conference (SCLC), the Congress of Racial Equality (CORE), and the NAACP, as well as Mississippi community groups. Within the state COFO has made extensive preparations since mid-January to develop structured programs which will put to creative use the talents and energies of the hundreds of expected summer volunteers. . . .

Voter registration workers will be involved in an intensive summer drive to encourage as many Negroes as possible to register. They will participate in COFO's Freedom Registration, launched in early February, to register over 400,000 Negroes on Freedom Registration books. These books will be set up in local Negro establishments and will have simplified standards of registration (the literacy test and the requirement demanding an interpretation of a section of the Mississippi Constitution will be eliminated). Freedom Registration books will serve as the basis of a challenge of the official books of the state and the validity of "official" elections this fall. Finally, registration workers will assist in the campaigns of Freedom candidates who are expected to run for seats in all five of the State's congressional districts and for the seat of Senator John Stennis, who is up for re-election. . . .

DOCUMENT 4 **Robert Moses Memorandum**

Memo to "Friends of Freedom in Mississippi"
Roy Wilkins, James Farmer, Martin Luther King,
James Forman, A. Philip Randolph, Bayard Rustin,
John Lewis, Harry Belafonte, James Baldwin,
Dick Gregory, Ossie Davis, Marlon Brando,
Aaron Henry, Ed King, Robert Spike, Jesse Gray,
Larry Landry, Clyde Ferguson, Noel Day, Ella Baker.

From: Bob Moses

Re: Mississippi Freedom Summer

Dear Sirs:

I am writing on request of the Executive Committee of the Student Nonviolent Coordinating Committee and in my function as Program Director of the Council of Federated Organizations (COFO).

You are all aware of the summer program COFO is sponsoring in Mississippi this summer. We expect to field over two thousand workers in Freedom schools, community centers, voter registration drives in every county, and projects in selected white communities. We anticipate up to one thousand volunteers from across the country to join us in this program, including ministers, teachers, lawyers and students.

We have learned through bitter experience in the past three years that the judicial, legislative and executive bodies of Mississippi form a wall of absolute resistance to granting civil rights to Negroes. It is our conviction that only a massive effort by the country backed by the full power of the President can offer some hope for even minimal change in Mississippi.

We have already been accused of launching this project to incite violence and chaos in Mississippi this summer. We have two answers to this charge. For one, violence is prevalent throughout the state; at least six Negroes have been killed by whites in the past three months. And, more important, the responsibility for maintaining law and guaranteeing, at the same time, the right to peaceful protest, must rest, in the final analysis, in the case of Mississippi, with the President of the United States.

The President must be made to understand that this responsibility rests with him, and him alone, and that neither he nor the American people can afford to jeopardize the lives of the people who will be working in Mississippi this summer by failing to take the necessary precautions before the summer begins.

We are writing this letter now to you, to join together as the "Friends of Freedom in Mississippi" to seek a meeting with President Johnson to ask him to do the following things to insure peaceful change in Mississippi this summer.

President Johnson should:

1. Meet in early May with Governor Johnson of Mississippi and extract from Governor Johnson the pledge that he will call together all state and local law enforcement leaders and lay down certain ground rules for the summer. Under these rules the following activities will not only be permitted, but will be protected: peaceful orderly picketing; voter registration; orderly distribution of leaflets; peaceful assembly; free-

dom of inter-racial groups to live in the Negro communities and to move around the state without molestation.

2. President Johnson will inform the governor that these are clearly established constitutional rights which the federal government has the responsibility to protect, and that if the governor will not do this, the federal government, will before the summer, establish at key points throughout the state constellations of federal marshalls who will be ready on call to protect these rights by preventive action, including on-the-spot arrests; and that the full power of the federal government stands behind these marshalls. If the governor agrees, but then there is an obvious breaking of the agreement, these marshalls will be immediately moved into Mississippi.
3. President Johnson should pledge to the committee in advance that he will take these actions if the governor refuses. . . .

Introduction to Document 5

Document 5 is a group of news reports on the incidents of Freedom Summer 1964. These reports not only tell us information about events but also give us a sense of how newspapers and magazines both influenced and reflected popular opinion. There are editorials, features, and news stories here, from sources north and south, liberal and conservative, local and national. Note how widely opinions about events ranged, and how even the "facts" were controversial. Try to see how far you can go in reconstructing the known details of the case. Where did ideological positions, value judgments, and clashing perspectives come into play? How did they shape the writers' perceptions of events?

DOCUMENT 5 *Reporting Freedom Summer*

Mississippi: Allen's Army
NEWSWEEK, FEBRUARY 24, 1964

The second summer of the Negro revolt was still months off. But ever since the first, Allen Thompson, the graying, satin-smooth mayor of unreconstructed Jackson, Miss., has been acting as though Armageddon were just around the corner.

Girding for a new wave of civil-rights demonstrations this summer, Thompson is massing an impressive—and expensive—deterrent force of men and military hardware. To defend the capital city of 144,422, he is building up his young, tough, riot-trained police force from 390 to 450, plus two horses and six dogs. The force is "twice as big as any city our size," Thompson boasted last week—and it will be backed by a reserve pool of deputies, state troopers, civilian city employees, and even neighborhood citizen patrols.

With a hefty $2.2 million budget to spend, the department recently bought 200 new shotguns, stockpiled tear gas, and issued gas masks to every man. Its motor fleet includes three canvas-canopied troop lorries, two half-ton searchlight trucks, and three giant trailer trucks to haul demonstration POW's [prisoners of war] off to two big detention compounds. "I think we can take care of 25,000," the mayor said.

But the pride of Allen's Army is Thompson's Tank—the already popular nickname for a 13,000-pound armored battlewagon built to the mayor's specifications at roughly $1 a pound. The twelve-man tank, abristle with shotguns, tear-gas guns, and a submachine gun, flopped on its first mission—putting down a demonstration at all-Negro Jackson State College two weeks ago. As it rolled up, a tear-gas shell went off inside, and all twelve men stumbled out crying. Nevertheless, Thompson says reverently: "It's a wonderful thing."

Would a collision come? Thompson thought so—and so did the young warhawks of the Student Nonviolent Coordinating Committee, already mapping a massive summer campaign in Mississippi. SNCC was dispatching questionnaires last week to prospective recruits for its own nonviolent army of 500 to 1,000—mostly college students—to staff "freedom schools," community centers, and voter-registration drives. "The summer of 1964," SNCC chairman John Lewis said, "could really be *the* year for Mississippi. Before the Negro people get the right to vote, there will have to be a massive confrontation, and it probably will come this summer. . . ."

The mayor insists his army is only a second-strike force designed to preserve law and order. "We have to wait," he told *Newsweek's* Karl Fleming, "until they start trouble." But Thompson is certain trouble will come. "This is it," he said. "They are not bluffing and we are not bluffing. We're going to be ready for them. . . . They won't have a chance."

Western College to Host Civil Rights School

Oxford Press, Oxford, Ohio, June 4, 1964

The National Council of Churches' Commission on Religion and Race will conduct a two-week instructional program at Western College for Women, June 12–27, President Herrick B. Young announced today.

College students from Yale, Harvard, Oberlin, the University of Illinois, and the University of North Carolina, among other institutions, will be prepared for a civil rights program to be conducted this summer throughout the South.

In making this announcement, President Young stated, "We have made our facilities available for this training program upon the request of the Council. As an institution with a Christian emphasis and an integrated student body, the Western campus is an appropriate setting for such a program."

The students participating in the program will be trained in two groups of three hundred each. The duration of each session will be one week. A staff of approximately fifty lawyers, social workers and educators will conduct the program.

The program will emphasize skills-training, in such matters as voter education, voter registration, remedial reading, how to teach, citizenship education, and the development of community centers. . . .

One-third of those recruited and trained will work in community centers and another third will teach such subjects as reading in summer schools. The rest will work in voter education and registration.

The students also will be trained in nonviolent discipline, because in many cases they may be called on to work under adverse circumstances, a spokesman of the National Council of Churches said.

The week-long course will also screen out those who should not be sent into situations that could become tense, the spokesman said.

Along with the students, the Council plans to send lawyers and ministers. The lawyer will advise on voter rights and other problems and the ministers will act as counselors.

Students Told Dixie Has Perils, Warned Jailing, Death Possible in Rights Invasion

Chicago Daily News, June 16, 1964

Raymond R. Coffey

OXFORD, Ohio—The barefoot and Bermuda shorts legion of white college students training here for a civil rights invasion of Mississippi will never be able to say they weren't warned.

Still miles and days away from the borders of the Magnolia State, they're ingesting a heavy diet of blood and thunder lectures about what they are likely to encounter before the summer is gone.

They are also being told bluntly that they are being counted on to provide a kind of shield of political protection for the local Negroes they'll be working with.

The students, around 200 of them, from all over the country, are being sent into Mississippi at the end of the week to work in a program of voter registration, "freedom schools" and community centers sponsored jointly by several major civil rights groups.

Their first training sessions—on techniques, security precautions, the politics and economics of Mississippi and so on—were held on the campus of Western College for Women here Monday.

At the first general meeting, James Forman, executive secretary of the Student Nonviolent Co-ordinating Committee (SNCC), and a key figure in the program, put it on the line.

At the beginning, he said, the students should be made aware of three things:

They should expect to get beaten up, they should expect to go to jail and they should be aware of the possibility that some one is going to get killed.

"This should be discussed now," he said. "So if anyone wants to turn back, they can turn back now."

Robert Moses, Negro director of the whole project, told the students, many of them from well-to-do families and the nation's top colleges:

"The fact is, you have political influence through your mothers and fathers and congressmen and other people back home. Mississippi Negroes don't."

This influence, he and other speakers indicated, is being counted on to get the federal government to flood Mississippi with agents who will be able to provide some measure of safety for the civil rights workers, white and Negro.

At a section meeting for a small group of students, Stokely Carmichael, 22, a Negro college graduate and veteran of four years in the Mississippi civil rights movement, was more explicit.

The only safe way to "work a plantation," when trying to get Negro field hands to register as voters, he said, "is to have two guys, one of whom stays in the car and keeps the motor running."

Also essential, he said, is a car that can hit at least 85 miles an hour when the time comes to escape.

Matter-of-factly he noted that most plantation roads are privately owned, which gives the white manager the feeling that he can shoot trespassers freely.

"All plantation trucks now carry rifles and some of them have two-way radios," Carmichael explained, because "until about 1962 the boss man's job was just to get the cotton picked, but now he also has to make sure there's no civil rights activity among the field hands."

U.S. Puts Rights Army on Its Own in Dixie
Chicago Daily News, June 20, 1964

Nicholas Von Hoffman

OXFORD, Ohio—They got the word straight from Uncle Sam. It hit with a shock wave of fear and anger.

Some 200 college students, civil rights volunteers bound for Mississippi, have been told to their faces that the Justice Department can't guarantee their physical safety.

The word came from John Doar, a Justice official—and the students responded with catcalls, sarcastic laughter and loud, angry questions. . . .

Doar told the students, the first contingent of 1,000 expected to work on various civil rights and education programs with Mississippi Negroes, that "I admire what you intend to do. The real heroes in this country today are the students."

He said that Mississippi is "a state that has gotten off the track."

"It appears to me," Doar said, "that there are a great many people (in Mississippi) who recognize that Mississippi is part of the United States and want to change, but for the most part they have been silent.

Doar stated that the power of the Ku Klux Klan, the White Citizens' councils and of other extremist groups is being used to "fight at any cost to the country to resist any encroachment on white supremacy."

He said that the extremists are trying to mark the students as people bent on "creating mass disorder in the streets of Mississippi."

He warned the students that, since under the federal system it is the State of Mississippi's job to keep law and order, that it is "impossible for Negroes to be protected" by the federal government.

"I suggest that for now you accept that as a fact," he quietly told the students who listened with tense expressions on their faces until they erupted during the question-answer period. . . .

"The FBI will do its best to keep track of where everybody is in Mississippi," said Doar, "but we cannot protect you in the sense of preventing a crime from occuring against you."

Over 100 Students—Civil Rights Workers Arrive in Mississippi

Shreveport [Louisiana] *Journal*, June 22, 1964

JACKSON, Miss. (AP)—The first wave of Northern and Eastern college students was in Mississippi today to begin work among Negroes.

The Council of Federated Organizations (COFO) said more than 100 students came by bus and car over the weekend, and more were expected.

More than 200 volunteer student workers finished a week of indoctrination for the Mississippi Summer Project conducted by the National Conference of Churches at Oxford, Ohio. They were told how to hold voter registration drives and set up remedial schools.

COFO, which includes major civil rights groups working in the state, has estimated some 1,000 students will come to staff workshops for Negroes this summer.

3 Rights Workers Are Freed After Paying $20 Fines

Baton Rouge [Louisiana] *State Times*, June 22, 1964

JACKSON, Miss. (AP)—The Neshoba County sheriff's office said today three civil rights workers were arrested Sunday and released after paying a $20 fine.

The Council of Federated Organizations said the trio has been unaccounted for since Sunday afternoon.

Bill Light, a COFO public information officer, said two white workers and a Meridian Negro left Meridian Sunday for Philadelphia in Neshoba County to check on a report of a Negro church being burned last week.

Light identified the three as Mickey Schwener, 24, New York City, a Congress of Racial Equality field secretary; James Cheney, 22, a Meridian Negro CORE worker; and Allen Goodman, 20, a New York City summer volunteer.

Light said they learned through calling police departments between Jackson and Philadelphia that the three were arrested Sunday for speeding and held briefly. He said they posted a $20 bond and were released.

COFO said they have not been heard from since.

"Freedom" to the Delta

CHARLESTON [SOUTH CAROLINA] *POST*, JUNE 24, 1964

This week the vanguard of a youthful army left the rolling hill country of southwestern Ohio, where volunteers had spent several weeks being indoctrinated and incensed, for the flat Delta land of Mississippi. The Summer Project, a joint effort of the Student Non-Violent Coordinating Committee (SNICK) and the National Council of Churches, was on the march. . . .

"The real aim of SNICK and the other more extreme Negro organizations is to secure the military occupation of Mississippi by federal troops." This is not the expressed judgment of Mississippi Governor Paul Johnson or even of Senator James Eastland. The words are those of Joseph Alsop, the liberal columnist. Mr. Alsop, however much he may desire civil rights for Negroes, knows that no good can come from this Summer Project, controlled as it is by the most militant of the many civil rights groups and the one whose ranks include, according to Mr. Alsop, more than a few dedicated Communists. . . .

The crusade leaders say publicly that the main thrust of the summer invasion will be directed at voter discrimination in Mississippi, where only 6.6 percent of Negroes of voting age are registered to vote. Such an effort, conducted with forbearance and directed at helping the Negro improve himself, might produce some good. Judging by the record, however, SNICK is short on forbearance and uncommonly long on making trouble. Nor is the National Council of Churches likely to provide much in the way of restraint.

The Council has invested $260,000 in this project, and it wants more out of that investment than a handful of votes. At a Baltimore meeting last February, during which the Summer Project was under discussion, Council members talked of "social redevelopment" in Mississippi, of applying "corrective treatment" to the Delta region.

"The main problem at this point," the Council's own report of the Baltimore meeting said, "is the concentration of wealth among the few, e.g., on an average, 5 percent of the farms control 50 percent of all the farmland."

Voting? This has nothing to do with voting. The Council is speaking of agrarian reform of the sort that socialists promote.

From this, the goals of the Summer Project appear to be two-fold: first, indoctrination in socialist economics; second, military occupation of Mississippi if that can be arranged. This is no longer a struggle of black and white. If the reports of even the most liberal observers are to be believed, the Reds predominate and the nation can anticipate a long, hot summer indeed.

Charred Hulk of Car Spurs Intense Search

NEW HAVEN [CONNECTICUT] *REGISTER*, JUNE 24, 1964

WASHINGTON (AP)—President Johnson conferred today with Allen Dulles, who is flying to Mississippi this afternoon as the President's personal representative to evaluate law observance in the face of an organized civil rights campaign there.

Sitting in on the meeting of Johnson and Dulles, former head of the Central Intelligence Agency, was Atty. Gen. Robert F. Kennedy.

Johnson asked Dulles to undertake the assignment after three civil rights workers disappeared in Mississippi and the car in which they were riding was found burned. . . .

PHILADELPHIA, Miss. (AP)—Three-man teams combed the bayous and red clay hill countryside of east-central Mississippi today for three young civil rights workers who vanished Sunday night.

Federal agents teamed with state and local police in checking every house, shack and barn around the Bogue Chitto swamp, where the youth's fire-gutted station wagon was found by the FBI Tuesday.

Missing are Andy Goodman, 20, and Michael Schwerner, 24, both white from New York City, and James Cheney, a 22-year-old Negro from nearby Meridian.

They vanished mysteriously Sunday night after Cheney paid a $20 fine for speeding. The trio headed southeast toward Meridian but the burned station wagon was found 13.5 miles northeast here.

Mississippi's Lawless Invaders

SHREVEPORT [LOUISIANA] *JOURNAL*, JUNE 26, 1964

Before summer is over, the country is likely to experience student lawlessness in various places as a result of mixing holiday leisure with too much alcohol. Police in New York, Wisconsin and other states have had to deal firmly with such juvenile riots in the last few years.

This kind of unorganized lawlessness, which violates the rights of peaceful communities, is bad enough. It is symptomatic of rising disrespect for law.

Much worse, however, is the planned lawlessness for which students are training on the campus of the Western College for Women in Oxford, Ohio. We refer to the so-called "student army" that is begining to enter Mississippi to break state laws and foment strife. This "army" of young integrationists was described recently in The Chicago Daily News. Many of the students never have seen Mississippi, the Chicago newspaper reports, but they want to break its laws, nevertheless.

It is shocking that college students should want to devote a summer to lawlessness. It is even more shocking that a college would offer its campus for a course in civil disobedience. Most shocking of all is that a church group, namely the National Council of Churches—as revealed last March 27 in The Journal's editorial, "Mississippi Marked for New Invasion"—should be behind the force of law-breaking demonstrators.

The type of person with whom the National Council of Churches is involved must astonish some of its more innocent supporters. We refer to Myles Horton, head of the Highlander Center in Knoxville, Tenn.

"Horton," says *The Chicago Daily News*, "is helping the orientation program set up by the National Council of Churches on the campus of Western College for Women for the hundreds of students going into Mississippi to work on civil rights this summer."

As noted by the Charleston, S.C., News and Courier, it would require a book to recount Myles Horton's record of involvement in leftwing causes over the years.

Important documentation of his career was made available last November when Louisiana's Joint Legislative Committee on UnAmerican Activities released a special report. The committee report, based on sworn testimony, included affidavits signed by persons who stated that they had seen Young Communist League cards in the possession of Myles Horton and other Highlander Folk School leaders. Other affidavits told of the Soviet government being praised at Highlander, and of the Russian flag being saluted at that training school.

The appointment of Myles Horton is the strongest indictment we can imagine of the National Council of Churches as a radical action force in politics, masquerading as religious.

As a result of initial forays into the so-called "civil rights" field in Mississippi, three young integrationists—two whites and a Negro—today are the objects of an intensive search. They disappeared mysteriously after paying a traffic fine in Philadelphia, Miss., Sunday. A station wagon in which they were traveling was later found burned, but no trace of the missing trio was detected.

If violence has befallen the invading integrationists, the State of Mississippi can be counted upon to work with federal investigators in bringing the criminals to justice.

But until there is definite proof that harm has befallen the three outsiders, judgment in the case should be withheld. As has been pointed out by Mississippi authorities, it is possible that the missing men are alive and well—and maybe even in another section of the country. President Johnson's unwarranted grandstand action in sending federal forces into Mississippi to "aid" in the search for the missing men is another affront to the South. . . .

Traded: A Birthright for a Mess

CHARLOTTE [NORTH CAROLINA] *OBSERVER*, JULY 11, 1964

Nine years ago, William Faulkner wrote these words about the South:

> The question is no longer of white against black. It is no longer whether or not white blood shall remain pure, it is whether or not white people remain free.

Faulkner's point has been largely overlooked while the attention of a nation is focused on a more visible struggle of Negro Americans to get their first deep draughts of freedom. Yet today, so soon after Faulkner wrote the question, it no longer can be reasonably asked about his native Mississippi.

For the answer has already been made in Mississippi—the white people have not remained free. Clearly, nowhere in all America has the white citizen been so thoroughly shorn of his native rights as he has in Mississippi.

Of freedom to worship, for example:

"I can't even say God is love without seeing people in the pews getting red and showing signs of anger," said one Jackson minister. "That meant love your brother. And if you love your brother, they think, your daughter will marry a Negro." . . .

White Americans in many locales are in danger of social ostracism or worse if they express praise for the President of the United States, the past President or the preceding President. And if Mississippi goes the route of Alabama, no white American will even be able to vote for the current President.

A petition expressing support for "the governor and city officials in maintaining law and order" was passed around to prominent Jackson businessmen after an outbreak of Ku Klux Klan activities. None dared sign it.

While conversing with a friend, one-time Baptist and native Mississippian Frank Trippett of Newsweek magazine referred to "card-carrying Baptists" in light humor. His friend quickly said, "Shhhh. Man, you're back in the South now."

Thus has a pall of fear stifled any but the most orthodox expression, to a degree that has little parallel in American history.

Of freedom of the press:

Most newspapers dare not cross the invisible line of dissent. Editorials endorsing "law and order" often read like apologies, laced with attacks on everything else it is safe to attack, for insurance against angry reader reaction.

A cross recently was burned at the home of the managing editor of the McComb Daily Enterprise-Journal—not because the paper advocated desegregation, but because it printed stories of Klan terrorism on the front page. . . .

In one respect, the white American in Mississippi has made himself the virtual slave of the Negro. He has so relentlessly pursued the policy of white supremacy that the Negro question has come to dominate almost every aspect of his life—the thinking, the speech, the business, the politics, the education. Everywhere a Mississippian turns, he bumps against the issue he has created.

The cost of keeping the state a "white man's land" was always high, but it has finally taken from the native white American there much of his basic heritage. Until he realizes what he has traded away, his is the central tragedy of American life.

White Moderate Lives in Fear, Very Real Danger in Mississippi

MINNEAPOLIS TRIBUNE, JULY 12, 1964

Dick Cunningham

Jack Hill is not his real name. But he is a real person and he lives in Jackson, Miss., with a very real fear.

He's a white man who has stepped out of line twice.

He stopped paying dues to the White Citizens' Council when the council solicited funds for the defense of Byron De La Beckwith, accused slayer of Negro leader Medgar Evers.

More recently he and his wife went to a play at Negro Tougaloo College near Jackson. They stayed for an integrated dinner and found some of the Negro faculty members "a lot smarter than some of the white people we spend time with.

"But if you print that," Hill said quickly, "I'll call you a liar."

What does Hill fear?

All the things anyone fears who defies convention anywhere plus a specific Mississippi fear.

"There's a man in my area—a funeral director—who keeps his eye on things like this. If he knew what I said, he could ruin my business in a month."

One of the goals of the Council of Federated Organizations (COFO), the alliance of groups that is sponsoring the Negro civil rights drive in Mississippi this summer, is to reach such white moderates as Jack Hill.

A team of white students, mostly Southerners, is seeking to talk to them in churches, business groups, labor unions and college groups.

Talking may be as far as they get this summer, but the ultimate aim, according to COFO director Rober Moses, "is to give the white moderate some relief from his impotence."

Heart of Darkness

NEW YORK TIMES, AUGUST 6, 1964

Only two weeks ago we were blandly assured by Sen. James O. Eastland of Mississippi that the disappearance of three civil rights workers in his state might well turn out to be a hoax. Now three bodies have been found, and the FBI has identified two of them as Mickey Schwerner and Andy Goodman. The third corpse is probably all that is mortal of James Chaney, the Negro companion of the two white youths. Some hoax.

It is true that the North has no right to affect superior airs in lecturing Mississippi on civil rights; bigotry is no respecter of the Mason-Dixon line. But the attitude to murder sets Mississippi apart. A year ago, Medgar Evers [a civil rights leader] was shot in the back. Since then, at least 11 Negroes have been killed in mysterious circumstances in Mississippi, including two whose bodies were believed to have been found in the Mississippi River during the search for three civil rights workers.

Though this bloody business horrifies the rest of the country, the tendency in Mississippi is to shrug it off. In Philadelphia, Miss., a resident who declined to give his name to the Associated Press was quoted as laconically remarking of the three boys, "if they had stayed home where they belonged nothing would have happened to them." Implicit in this attitude is the feeling that Mississippi is not "home" to an American but an alien place to be visited at one's own peril. . . .

These Are the Times . . . That Challenge the South

THE NEW REBEL, NEWSLETTER OF THE SOUTHERN STUDENT ORGANIZING COMMITTEE, OCTOBER 1964

Jim Williams

. . . What are the values we cherish? Most of us grew up in the fifties. In a sense we grew up in a very special and a very fine way. For most of us, the fifties provided an abundance which our parents never shared during their childhood, but which we did receive and take almost for granted. From our middle class and Christian heritage we received these traditions of the South.

We cherish the values of freedom, of liberty and democracy. We strive toward the virtues of charity, compassion and humanity. We thirst after decency, the taste of the Great Society which is a democracy of the whole people with abundance and freedom for all. Many "yankees" poke fun of what seems to them to be an exaggerated sense of manners on the part of southerners. Yet, underlying our obvious mannerism, is a deep sense of values.

Another set of values challenges us today. This new doctrine emphasizes personal aggrandisement versus public comfort, selfishness and callowness in place of altruism. This new doctrine, in the name of "freedom" seeks to destroy freedom by flaunting the constitution and the courts and the laws of the land. Men like George Wallace and Ross Barnett espouse freedom and states' rights on one hand—and deny these by force to their Negro brothers. Along with their friends in the Citizens' Councils, they espouse the freedom to starve, the freedom to be shot by segregationist police, and the freedom to rot in jail for exercising the right to vote.

This view has come to be accepted as that representing the South. And, what else could people think as lynching after lynching continued, after firehoses and police dogs, beatings and burnings and bombings? This, too, has come to be "southern tradition."

We must ask ourselves what part of the southern tradition do we wish to emulate? That of compassion, of the heroism of thousands of southerners in working for a better world through the labor movement and now the civil rights movement—or, the dark tradition of the KKK, the Citizens' Councils and assassination?

Introduction to Document 6

Document 6 contains excerpts from interviews (published in the December 18, 1964, issue of *The Nation*) with civil rights workers who participated in voter registration. Note that the article is not about how Freedom Summer changed the lives of black Mississippians. Rather, the focus is on the feelings of those who went south.

DOCUMENT 6 *Journey to Understanding*

Howard Zinn

Four Witnesses to a Mississippi Summer

THE LAWYER . . . WILLIAM M. KUNSTLER

. . . Recently, I was exchanging views with one of the many young lawyers who had volunteered to serve in Mississippi. "I didn't get a chance to practice much law," he said, "but I never felt more like a lawyer in my life.". . .

In private practice, the lawyer is a detached being who views the conflicts that swirl about him as laboratory problems to be solved by the arts of his ancient profession. He is the ringmaster who, by the toot of his whistle or the snap of his whip, brings order out of chaos. For this performance, he expects and receives recognition in the form of money and prestige.

But the movement lawyer, once he has acclimated himself to the demands and dimensions of his new practice, sees a horizon utterly different from the one that defined his activities back in New York City or Chicago. He is activated, not by the promise of fame and fortune, but by the sharing of a common cause with those he represents.

The transformation does not come overnight. I can still recall with shame my earnest recommendation to a brother attorney during the Freedom Rider trials that he not address our clients at a mass meeting. "A lawyer must remain aloof," I told him. "If we become emotionally involved in our clients' problems we will not be able to be dispassionate courtroom advocates."

Three years later I realized that I was playing a fool's game and that my advice was worse than worthless. No remember of a great social movement can remain untouched by the forces that drive it. When Clarence Darrow left his lucrative job as general counsel to the Chicago & Northwestern Railroad to defend Debs and his American Railway Union, his resignation was testimony that attorneys who would serve humanity rather than individual clients must do so with their hearts as well as their heads. . . .

Mississippi in the summer of 1964 was the catalyst of a growing awareness that the law does not exist in a vacuum but is grounded in life. The young men and women who offered their bodies as a witness to the attainability of a just society shamed the American bar into standing beside them. For generations lawyers had looked aside while Negroes in the Deep South had been systematically dehumanized. All in the name of the law, black men had been driven away from the polls, segregated out of community life, forced back into a slavery every bit as intense as that which had theoretically been lifted from them 100 years earlier. Yet the legal profession uttered not one word of collective protest.

That lawyers should have ignored the plight of the Negro is the bitterest of paradoxes, for lawyers have a special obligation to create and preserve the equality on which our entire system of jurisprudence is expressly founded. On courthouse friezes across the land is engraved some form of the motto: "Equal Justice Under Law."

The law did not change in Mississippi last summer, but the lawyers who journeyed there did. All of us, suddenly and starkly conscious that we had failed in one way or another to live up to the solemn responsibilities of our profession, were grateful for the chance to justify our existences. What had started out as an adventure for many of us had abruptly changed into the lesson of our lives.

THE MINISTER . . . BEVERLY ALLEN ASBURY

. . . Something has happened to my theological thinking as a result of the trip to Mississippi. Nearly twenty years ago at the University of Georgia I started considering the Christian ministry from a real concern for human beings. Later I found a theology to express that concern and to give it definition. Later still, perhaps, theological considerations somewhat replaced the human concern, but Mississippi brought me back to people again and helped me put the theological understanding in a new perspective. The "established" churches I saw in Mississippi, and many of the "established" churches I see in the North, can be described only as religious ghettos. They have to be endured with a great deal of fatigue and boredom, and if I were faced with the attitude which exists in so many of them, I doubt that I could "go to church." I see in them too much of a desire to evangelize the world only when it will yield a direct return to the church in increased membership and financial contributions. The established church I saw in Mississippi holds itself aloof from the world, and the established church I see in Ohio and elsewhere too often refuses to risk itself for the sake of the world.

What I saw caused me to turn, as I turned years before, to an understanding of Jesus. My present theological mood looks increasingly to this Man, the "Man-for-Others." I look to Him as the paradigm of my faith, as the one who gives Himself to suffer at the hands of a godless world precisely out of love for that world. The church must use the persuasion and power of love to bring about reconciliation at every level of human and national life. It must pay whatever the price may be to create a faithful and effective structure for the alleviation of every human need. When it becomes the Church of Jesus Christ, it can do no other than follow its Lord into the suffering of those who cannot cry out for themselves. . . .

THE EDUCATOR . . . RICHARD J. BERNSTEIN

In the early fifties, when I started teaching at Yale, there was a general uneasiness among the politically liberal members of the faculty. The lament at that time centered upon the state of mind of the students. They seemed intimidated by, or indifferent to, the poisoned atmosphere created by [Senator Joseph R.] McCarthy, they were "out for themselves," lacked a developed social conscience, were without a cause. Many of the liberal teachers—the attitude was characteristic of campuses throughout the country—were nostalgic for the thirties. That had been a time of heated political discussion, with students in the thick of radical movements. Why wasn't this generation of students more like what we had been (or like what we conceived ourselves to have been)?

There was an element of bad faith in this pose. Besides romanticizing and exaggerating the effectiveness of the radical past, it betrayed an unwillingness and inability to come to grips with new political realities. It was a time when liberals, of whatever generation, were seized by political impotence. They talked about the ills of modern society and were vociferous in decrying the forms of alienation and estrangement, but when it came down to what to do, they offered few concrete proposals.

In the decade since then, the outlook of American youth has changed dramatically. Out of a generation that never knew the depression, out of a generation nurtured on the myth of American affluence, has emerged a group sensitive to social injustice, committed to do something about it, and with a good practical sense of what must be done. I believe that the influence of this group is far greater than its numbers, and that their activity is re-educating America, reawakening our social conscience, and most important, pointing the way toward effective social action It is from this perspective that we can begin to appreciate the value of the Mississippi Summer Project.

The situation in Mississippi last summer was fully reported, but the press did a good deal to distort what actually took place. The incidents judged noteworthy were those of violence and intimidation. In part, the Council of Federated Organizations was also responsible for playing up this aspect of the situation. Violence is nothing new in Mississippi, but for the first time the national spotlight was focused on it. However, the real heart of the project hardly ever hit the news; that was the day-to-day interaction between COFO workers and the Negro community working together for a common cause. Furthermore, the significance of the experience for the doctors, ministers, lawyers and others who went to participate, or just to see the project in operation, cannot be underestimated. My few days in Mississippi last summer were among the most intense, vital and meaningful in my life. And my experience was certainly not unique. Almost everyone I have met who spent some time in Mississippi, no matter how brief, came away with a similar feeling. This project did as much for the participants as for civil rights. It re-educated us about what civil rights really are. And through those who participated and observed, the spirit of the project is spreading across the country.

THE DOCTOR . . . AARON O. WELLS

. . . Four physicians were selected as an advanced committee to confer in Mississippi with leaders of the Council of Federated Organizations, the National Council of Churches and other leaders in the state. Their task was to determine how our medical presence in Mississippi could be made most effective. They returned with an enthusiastic report, and we assigned medical teams to initiate the program. Before the first team entered Mississippi, this nucleus of dedicated persons found a name—the Medical Committee on Human Rights.

Looking back, I realize that I was slow to decide how I could best serve these obviously dedicated people. A woman colleague whose opinion I have always held invaluable was one of the original members, and her enthusiasm and interest influenced me. Then, too, I had asked my wife, who is a registered nurse, to represent me at an early meeting. Her immediate reaction was to enlist in the project, and soon thereafter she was in Mississippi as the nurse with a medical team.

The response of these two women forced me to consider very seriously my own level of participation. I asked myself whether financial contributions to the various civil rights organizations was sufficient. Would attendance at conferences and occasional health lectures in the context of civil rights fulfill my moral obligation to my people? I decided that these responses were not enough, that I must go to Mississippi.

POSTSCRIPT

After Chaney, Goodman, and Schwerner disappeared, the Johnson administration sent additional federal personnel to aid in the search, protect other civil rights workers, and enforce the law. Not only were these efforts minuscule given the enormity of the problem, but those in positions of power, like FBI chief J. Edgar Hoover, remained openly hostile to the civil rights movement. Nonetheless, several months after the bodies of the three men were found, twenty white men, including the sheriff and a deputy of Nashoba County, were indicted for conspiracy to deprive Chaney, Goodman, and Schwerner of their civil rights. (The state of Mississippi would not charge them with murder, so the federal courts indicted them for the lesser crime.) Evidence procured by a large payoff to an anonymous informant revealed that Deputy Sheriff Cecil Price deliberately released the three, whom he had charged with speeding, into the hands of waiting Klansmen. In 1967, seven of those indicted were convicted and began prison sentences.

Within the movement itself, the Freedom Summer had mixed results. The knowledge that all of the publicity about the three missing men—not to mention the massive federal effort to find them—occurred because two were white, further polarized the movement. Many African Americans resented those who returned at the end of summer to suburban homes or prestigious colleges; most whites could barely begin to comprehend the depths of black fear and rage. Some in the movement turned away from nonviolence to a more militant stance.

But as part of a long-term process, Freedom Summer had lasting results. Roughly fifty freedom schools and fifty community centers opened throughout Mississippi, and those institutions became bases of political power and a training ground for new leaders. Certainly the examples of Chaney, Goodman, and Schwerner, as well as of the hundreds of volunteers who joined the Freedom Summer, inspired many others to labor in the movement. Moreover, the tragedy of that summer focused national attention on the Deep South and helped forge a consensus that the most blatant denial of rights must end.

Perhaps most important, the Freedom Summer began a long chain of events that led to African Americans' gaining not just voting rights, but a share of *political* power, north and south. The most visible sign of this rising tide was the political emergence of a middle-aged black woman, Fanny Lou Hamer, and the Mississippi Freedom Democratic party in late summer 1964.

Ms. Hamer had worked all of her life on plantations. In the early 1960s, despite threats, then beatings, and even attempted murder by the Klan, she put down her hoe to lead local voter registration drives for SNCC. When the Mississippi Democratic party remained unresponsive to African-American citizens, COFO established a rival group, the Freedom Democratic party. The Freedom Democrats enrolled 60,000 members, elected a slate of delegates to the Democratic National Convention, and sent them to Atlantic City in late August 1964 to challenge the right of the regular Democratic delegation to represent the state. The old-line Democrats won at the insistence of party nominee President Lyndon Johnson, but not before the Freedom Democrats made their case before the credentials committee and, more important, before a national television audience. Hamer's account, in her plain-spoken English, of the "woesome time" in Winona, Mississippi, when she and other voter registration workers were taken into the county jail and beaten nearly to death moved Americans as few events of the era. The political process—voting, holding office, participating in the major parties—would never again be so closed to African Americans.

QUESTIONS

Defining Terms

Identify in the context of the chapter each of the following:

Brown v. Board of Education	Rosa Parks
CORE	SNCC
Anne Moody	"freedom schools"
National Council of Churches	voter registration
COFO	Robert Moses

Probing the Sources

1. Describe the social and economic conditions of African Americans in the South of the 1950s.
2. What were the goals of the Freedom Summer of 1964?
3. Discuss the role of violence in the civil rights movement, particularly during the Freedom Summer. What was nonviolent direct action, and how effective was it?
4. How did the Freedom Summer of 1964 fit into the earlier and later history of the civil rights movement?
5. What role did white students have in the Freedom Summer? Why did they participate?
6. How and why were African Americans kept from voting in the South?

Interpreting the Sources

1. Some critics called the leaders of the civil rights movement un-American, yet others responded that the movement was in the mainstream of American democratic traditions. Discuss these points.
2. How successful was the Freedom Summer in particular and the civil rights movement in general?
3. What comparisons do you see between Freedom Summer and the era of Reconstruction? Think about voting rights, federal intervention, and the uses of terrorism.
4. Does reading about the Freedom Summer make you optimistic or pessimistic about the ability of people to reform their world?
5. Were white participants "victimized" by the movement? Why did they join, and what did they receive?

ADDITIONAL READING

One of the best general introductions to the civil rights movement is Harvard Sitkoff, *The Struggle for Black Equality, 1954–1980* (1981). Claybome Carson's *In Struggle: SNCC and the Black Awakening of the 1960s* (1981) provides outstanding background for the Freedom Summer; Doug McAdam's *Freedom Summer* (1988) documents the incidents of 1964 as does Charles Marsh, *God's Long Summer* (1997); and Charles Payne, *I've Got the Light of Freedom* (1995). For good case studies of the movement, see William H. Chafe, *Civilities and Civil Rights: Greensboro, North Carolina, and the Black Struggle for Freedom* (1980); and Robert J. Norrell, *Reaping the Whirlwind: The Civil Rights Movement in Tuskegee* (1985). On the role of federal agents in the movement, try David Garrow, *The FBI and Martin Luther King, Jr.* (1981). For King and his times, see Taylor Branch, *Parting the Waters* (1988) and Branch, *Pillar of Fire* (1998), and Branch *At Canann's Edge* (2006). For international context, see Mary Dudziak, *Cold War Civil Rights* (2000). For a moving oral history by those who participated, see Howell Raines, *My Soul Is Rested* (1977). On the movement after 1964, try William L. Van De Berg, *New Day in Babylon* (1993). For a dramatic account of a key moment, see Raymond Arsenault, *Freedom Riders* (2006).

13

My Lai

The Nadir of the Vietnam War

Historical Context

On March 16, 1968, units of the United States Army's Americal Division assaulted the Vietcong in an area designated "Pinkville," a strip of Quang Ngai province along the South China Sea. Press releases and combat action reports filed in the days after the assault described the confrontation between the United States forces and Vietcong—South Vietnamese supporters of communist Ho Chi Minh—as a resounding American victory. Sergeant Jay Roberts, a reporter who covered the assault for the Army's Public Information Department, noted that U.S. forces killed 128 enemy troops and captured enemy weapons and documents. "The combat assault went like clockwork," Lieutenant Colonel Frank Barker, the commander of the task force that conducted the maneuver, told Roberts.

Barker said as much to his superiors in his combat action report, noting that the "operation was well planned, well executed and successful." To be sure, a few civilians in the hamlet of My Lai were caught in the cross fire of the opposing forces, but "the infantry unit on the ground and helicopters were able to assist civilians in leaving the area and in caring for and/or evacuating the wounded."

Army and American newspapers picked up on Roberts's and Barker's comments and printed them in small stories about the fighting in Vietnam, and General William Westmoreland, commander of U.S. forces in Vietnam, issued an official congratulatory message to Barker. In truth, what had happened in "Pinkville" that March day created hardly any interest. It seemed just the slightest ripple in a very large sea, a minor assault on a minor hamlet far from the center of the action—really nothing important enough to occupy anyone's thoughts.

But the men who took part in the assault stored memories very different from the official one. Some had recorded their thoughts in journal entries and letters. Thomas R. Partsch scribbled in his journal during a water break:

> Mar. 16 Sat. got up at 5:30 left at 7:15 we had 9 choppers. 2 lifts first landed had mortar team with us. We started to move slowly through the village shooting everything in sight children men and women and animals. Some was sickening. The[ir] legs were shot off

> and they were still moving it was just hanging there. I think the[ir] bodies were made of rubber. I didn't fire a round yet and I didn't kill anybody not even a chicken I couldn't.

That evening, Captain Brian Livingston, a helicopter commander, wrote his wife and expressed his disgust with the operation:

> Well its been a long day, saw some nasty sights. I saw the insertion of infantrymen and were they animals. . . . I've never seen so many people dead in one spot. Ninety-five percent were women and kids. We told the grunts on the ground of some injured kids. They helped them alright. A captain walked up to this little girl, he turned away took five steps, and fired a volley of shots into her. . . . I'll tell you something it sure makes you wonder why we are here.

Others told friends what they had seen. A month after the attack, Private Charles "Butch" Gruver gave his version of that day to an army buddy named Ronald Ridenhour. Seated in a bar, relaxing with a few bottles of beer, Gruver asked Ridenhour, "Did you hear about Pinkville?" When Ridenhour answered that he had not, Gruver commented, "We went in there and killed everybody." As they drank, more details emerged. Gruver's Charlie Company had gone into My Lai expecting a real fight, but they encountered no hostile Vietcong, only a village full of frightened women, old men, and children, many of whom they herded into small groups for security reasons. But then orders were given to kill the civilians, and some soldiers went on a rampage. There were mass murders, rapes, torture. It was horrible. Ridenhour could not believe what he was hearing, but Gruver swore it was all true. In the next few months, Ridenhour met and quizzed other soldiers who had been at My Lai. Each confirmed Gruver's tale, adding more details about the terrible day.

The same event, two very different versions; one official, the other unofficial. In an odd way, that had always been the American story in Vietnam. From the start there had been a confusion between the official and the unofficial, between what the American people back home heard about the conflict and what the American soldiers knew was the nasty reality of war. The United States had become involved in Vietnam during the late 1940s, purportedly as part of an effort to contain communism throughout the world; in reality President Harry Truman had agreed to help the French recapture their former colony in return for their pledge to join the North Atlantic Treaty Organization (NATO). During the 1950s, America's commitment to fighting Ho Chi Minh's communist forces in Vietnam increased. Rather than see Vietnam "fall" to the communists, the administration of President Dwight Eisenhower scuttled free elections and supported the unpopular, anticommunist regime of Ngo Dinh Diem.

When he took office in 1961, President John Kennedy continued the Cold War policies and strategies of Truman and Eisenhower. He even increased American military involvement in Vietnam, slowly raising troops levels there from 1,000 in January 1961 to 16,000 in November 1963. Vietnam, his policy makers insisted, was the key to all of Southeast Asia. If it "fell," Laos, Cambodia, and Thailand would follow, threatening Japan and Australia. It would be like a line of dominoes: topple the first and the rest would also go down.

President Lyndon Johnson continued the logic inherited from Kennedy: He would not be the first American to lose a war, nor would he preside over a communist victory. Despite the South Vietnamese government's corruption and incompetence;

despite his own pledges during the 1964 election not to involve America in a land war in Asia; and despite the lack of international support for the war, he increased American troop levels: 25,000 at the end of 1964; nearly 200,000 one year later, which doubled after another year; 500,000 by the beginning of 1968; and 550,000 before the end of the year. Moreover, these soldiers were no longer "advisers" to South Vietnam, as they had been termed in the Eisenhower-Kennedy years. Now they were initiating combat, dropping unprecedented numbers of bombs. They also used new substances such as chemical defoliants to clear away the jungle, and napalm, a flammable jelly that was dropped burning from airplanes and clung to everything it hit. Still, the war was a stalemate. Hundreds of thousands of Vietnamese and tens of thousands of Americans were dying, landscapes were being turned into moonscapes, and many American citizens, sensing a gap between official pronouncements and unofficial reality, could not understand why. Protests—on college campuses, in churches, on the streets—grew in size and strength during the late 1960s.

No event more clearly showed the difference between official and unofficial versions of the war than the January 31, 1968, Tet Offensive—a massive, coordinated North Vietnamese and Vietcong assault against major cities and towns in South Vietnam. The Tet Offensive began shortly after General William Westmoreland's much-publicized visit to Washington, D.C. An end to the war, Westmoreland had told Johnson and the American people, was in sight; the Vietcong had been overwhelmed and North Vietnam was suffering terribly. But the Tet Offensive seemed to belie Westmoreland's rosy optimism. And although American forces turned back the communist offensive, many American civilians no longer fully believed the pronouncements of their leaders. President Johnson realized as much. After the Tet Offensive he no longer spoke about winning the war; rather he simply wanted it ended.

The My Lai massacre occurred less than two months after the start of the Tet Offensive. It took place during a period of low morale and high frustration, a time when many soldiers had lost faith in their mission and questioned why they were fighting and dying. But the sad event underscores some of the grim realities of the war in Vietnam, including the nature of the warfare, American attitudes toward the Vietnamese, the gap between the official pronouncements about the war and the realities of the war, and the psychological impact of battle. In the following documents, consider these issues and ask yourself exactly what happened in My Lai, and why?

THE DOCUMENTS

Introduction to Documents 1, 2, and 3

The first three documents present the official and unofficial versions of the My Lai assault. Sergeant Jay A. Roberts's press release is a sanitized version of what happened at My Lai. Next Colonel Oran K. Henderson reports to his superiors on the investigation he conducted concerning an alleged massacre at My Lai. The final document is Ronald Ridenhour's letter detailing what he had learned about the assault on My Lai. Together they illustrate the gap between what was officially reported about the event and what the soldiers themselves said about the event. Ridenhour's letter, incidentally, was sent a year after the My Lai incident to prominent politicians and military leaders, and became the first instance of public exposure.

DOCUMENT 1 **Press Release, March 17, 1968**

Jay A. Roberts

CHU LAI, VIETNAM (Americal IO)—For the third time in recent weeks, the Americal Division's 11th Brigade infantrymen from Task Force Barker raided a Viet Cong stronghold known as "Pinkville" six miles northeast of Quang Ngai, killing 128 enemy in a running battle.

The action occurred in the coastal town of My Lai where, three weeks earlier, another company of the brigade's Task Force Barker fought its way out of a VC ambush, leaving 80 enemy dead.

The action began as units of the task force conducted a combat assault into a known Viet Cong stronghold. "Shark" gunships of the 174th Aviation Company escorted the troops into the area and killed four enemy during the assault. Other choppers from the 123d Aviation Battalion killed two enemy.

"The combat assault went like clockwork," commented LTC Frank Barker, New Haven, Conn., the tack force commander. "We had two entire companies on the ground in less than an hour."

A company led by [Captain] Ernest Medina, Schofield Barracks, Hawaii, killed 14 [Viet Cong] minutes after landing. They recovered two M1 rifles, a carbine, a shortwave radio and enemy documents.

DOCUMENT 2 **Report of Investigation, April 24, 1968**

Oran K. Henderson

1. An investigation has been conducted of the allegations cited in Inclosure 1. The following are the results of this investigations.

2. . . . This area has long been an enemy strong hold, and Task Force Barker had met heavy enemy opposition in this area on 12 and 23 February 1968. All persons living in this area are considered to be VC or VC sympathizers by the District Chief. Artillery and gunship preparatory fires were placed on the landing zones used by the two companies. Upon landing and during their advance on the enemy positions, the attacking forces were supported by gunships. By 1500 hours all enemy resistance had ceased and the remaining enemy forces had withdrawn. The results of this operation were 128 VC soldiers KIA. During preparatory fires and the ground action by the attacking companies 20 noncombatants caught in the battle area were killed. Interviews revealed that at no time were any civilians gathered together and killed by US soldiers. The civilian habitants of the area began withdrawing to the southwest as soon as the operation began and within the first hour and a half all visible civilians had cleared the area of operations.

3. The Son Tinh District Chief does not give the allegations any importance and he pointed out that the two hamlets where the incidents is alleged to have happened are in an area controlled by the VC since 1964. [He] reported that the making of such allegations against US Forces is a common technique of the VC propaganda machine.

4. It is concluded that 20 non-combatants were inadvertently killed when caught in the area of preparatory fires and in the cross fires of the US and VC forces on 16 March 1968. It is further concluded that no civilians were gathered together and shot by US soldiers. The allegation that US Forces shot and killed 450–500 civilians is obviously a Viet

Cong propaganda move to discredit the United States in the eyes of the Vietnamese people in general and the ARVN soldier in particular.

5. It is recommended that a counter-propaganda campaign be waged against the VC in eastern Son Tinh District.

DOCUMENT 3 *Letter to Military and Political Leaders, March 29, 1969*

Ronald Ridenhour

Gentlemen:

It was late in April, 1968 that I first heard of "Pinkville" and what allegedly happened there. I received that first report with some skepticism, but in the following months I was to hear similar stories from such a wide variety of people that it became impossible for me to disbelieve that something rather dark and bloody did indeed occur sometime in March, 1968 in a village called "Pinkville" in the Republic of Viet Nam.

In late April, 1968 I was awaiting orders for a transfer . . . when I happened to run into Pfc "Butch" Gruver, whom I had known in Hawaii. . . . During the course of our conversation he told me the first of many reports I was to hear of "Pinkville."

"Charlie" Company 1/20 had been assigned to Task Force Barker in late February, 1968 to help conduct "search and destroy" operations on the Batangan Peninsula, Barker's area of operation. The task force was operating out of L. F. Dottie, located five or six miles north of Quant Nhai [*sic*] city on Viet Namese National Highway 1. Gruver said that Charlie Company had sustained casualties; primarily from mines and booby traps, almost everyday from the first day they arrived on the peninsula. One village area was particularly troublesome and seemed to be infested with booby traps and enemy soldiers. It was located about six miles northeast of Quant Nhai city at approximate coordinates B.S. 728795. It was a notorious area and the men of Task Force Barker had a special name for it: they called it "Pinkville." One morning in the latter part of March, Task Force Barker moved out from its firebase headed for "Pinkville." Its mission: destroy the trouble spot and all of its inhabitants.

When "Butch" told me this I didn't quite believe that what he was telling me was true, but he assured me that it was and went on to describe what had happened. The other two companies that made up the task force cordoned off the village so that "Charlie" Company could move through to destroy the structures and kill the inhabitants. Any villagers who ran from Charlie Company were stopped by the encircling companies. I asked "Butch" several times if all the people were killed. He said that he thought they were, men, women and children. He recalled seeing a small boy, about three or four years old, standing by the trail with a gunshot wound in one arm. The boy was clutching his wounded arm with his other hand, while blood trickled between his fingers. He was staring around himself in shock and disbelief at what he saw. "He just stood there with big eyes staring around like he didn't understand; he didn't believe what was happening. Then the captain's RTO (radio operator) put a burst of 16 (M-16 rifle) fire into him." It was so bad, Gruver said, that one of the men in his squad shot himself in the foot in order to be medi-vac-ed out of the area so that he would not have to participate in the slaughter. Although he had not seen it, Gruver had been told by people he considered trustworthy that one of the company's officers, 2nd Lieutenant Kally (this spelling may be incorrect) had rounded up several groups of villagers (each group consisting of a minimum of 20 persons of both sexes and all ages). According to the story, Kally then machine-gunned each group. Gruver estimated that the population of the village had been 300 to 400 people and that very few, if any, escaped.

After hearing this account I couldn't quite accept it. Somehow I just couldn't believe that not only had so many young American men participated in such an act of barbarism, but that their officers had ordered it. There were other men in the unit I was soon to be assigned to, "E" Company, 51st Infantry (LRP), who had been in Charlie Company at the time that Gruver alleged the incident at "Pinkville" had occurred. I became determined to ask them about "Pinkville" so that I might compare their accounts with Pfc Gruver's.

When I arrived at "Echo" Company, 51st Infantry (LRP) the first men I looked for were Pfc's Michael Terry, and William Doherty. Both were veterans of "Charlie" Company, 1/20 and "Pinkville." Instead of contradicting "Butch" Gruver's story they corroborated it, adding some tasty tidbits of information of their own. Terry and Doherty had been in the same squad and their platoon was the third platoon of "C" Company to pass through the village. Most of the people they came to were already dead. Those that weren't were sought out and shot. The platoon left nothing alive, neither livestock nor people. Around noon the two soldiers' squad stopped to eat. "Billy and I started to get out our chow," Terry said, "but close to us was a bunch of Vietnamese in a heap, and some of them were moaning. Kally (2nd Lt. Kally) had been through before us and all of them had been shot, but many weren't dead. It was obvious that they weren't going to get any medical attention so Billy and I got up and went over to where they were. I guess we sort of finished them off." Terry went on to say that he and Doherty then returned to where their packs were and ate lunch. He estimated the size of the village to be 200 to 300 people. Doherty thought that the population of "Pinkville" had been 400 people.

If Terry, Doherty and Gruver could be believed, then not only had "Charlie" Company received orders to slaughter all the inhabitants of the village, but those orders had come from the commanding officer of Task Force Barker, or possibly even higher in the chain of command. Pfc Terry stated that when Captain Medina (Charlie Company's commanding officer Captain Ernest Medina) issued the order for the destruction of "Pinkville" he had been hesitant, as if it were something he didn't want to do but had to. Others I spoke to concurred with Terry on this.

It was June before I spoke to anyone who had something of significance to add to what I had already been told of the "Pinkville" incident. It was the end of June, 1968 when I ran into Sargent [*sic*] Larry La Croix at the USO in Chu Lai. La Croix had been in 2nd Lt. Kally's platoon on the day Task Force Barker swept through "Pinkville." What he told me verified the stories of the others, but he also had something new to add. He had been a witness to Kally's gunning down of at least three separate groups of villagers. "It was terrible. They were slaughtering the villagers like so many sheep." Kally's men were dragging people out of bunkers and hootches and putting them together in a group. The people in the group were men, women and children of all ages. As soon as he felt that the group was big enough, Kally ordered an M-60 (machine-gun) set up and the people killed. La Croix said that he bore witness to this procedure at least three times. The three groups were of different sizes, one of about twenty people, one of about thirty people, and one of about forty people. When the first group was put together Kally ordered Pfc Torres to man the machine-gun and open fire on the villagers that had been grouped together. This Torres did, but before everyone in the group was down he ceased fire and refused to fire again. After ordering Torres to recommence firing several times, Lieutenant Kally took over the M-60 and finished shooting the remaining villagers in that first group himself. Sargent La Croix told me that Kally didn't bother to order anyone to take the machinegun when the other two groups of villagers were formed. He simply manned it himself and shot down all villagers in both groups.

This account of Sargent La Croix's confirmed the rumors that Gruver, Terry and Doherty had previously told me about Lieutenant Kally. It also convinced me that there was a very substantial amount of truth to the stories that all of these men had told. If I needed more convincing, I was to receive it.

It was in the middle of November, 1968 just a few weeks before I was to return to the United States for separation from the army that I talked to Pfc Michael Bernhardt. Bernhardt had served his entire year in Viet Nam in "Charlie" Company 1/20 and he too was about to go home. "Bernie" substantiated the tales told by the other men I had talked to in vivid, bloody detail and added this. "Bernie" had absolutely refused to take part in the massacre of the villagers of "Pinkville" that morning and he thought that it was rather strange that the officers of the company had not made an issue of it. But that evening "Medina (Captain Ernest Medina) came up to me ("Bernie") and told me not to do anything stupid like write my congressman" about what had happened that day. Bernhardt assured Captain Medina that he had no such thing in mind. He had nine months left in Viet Nam and felt that it was dangerous enough just fighting the acknowledged enemy.

Exactly what did, in fact, occur in the village of "Pinkville" in March, 1968 I do not know for certain, but I am convinced that it was something very black indeed. I remain irrevocably persuaded that if you and I do truly believe in the principles, of justice and the equality of every man, however humble, before the law, that form the very backbone that this country is founded on, then we must press forward a widespread and public investigation of this matter with all our combined efforts. I think that it was Winston Churchill who once said "A country without a conscience is a country without a soul, and a country without a soul is a country that cannot survive." I feel that I must take some positive action on this matter. I hope that you will launch an investigation immediately and keep me informed of your progress. If you cannot, then I don't know what other course of action to take.

I have considered sending this to newspapers, magazines, and broadcasting companies, but I somehow feel that investigation and action by the Congress of the United States is the appropriate procedure, and as a conscientious citizen I have no desire to further besmirch the image of the American serviceman in the eyes of the world. I feel that this action, while probably it would promote attention, would not bring about the constructive actions that the direct actions of the Congress of the United States would.

Sincerely,
/s/ Ron Ridenhour

Introduction to Documents 4, 5, and 6

Documents 4, 5, and 6 also explore the gap between the official and the unofficial, between what was supposed to have happened and what did happen. Documents 4 and 5 detail how soldiers were instructed to treat Vietnamese civilians and prisoners. In theory all combat troops were informed of the rules of military engagement regarding the treatment of civilians and prisoners of war. But as Herbert L. Carter attests in Documents 6, many American soldiers in Vietnam had not received such instruction.

DOCUMENT 4 ***Nine Rules for Personnel of US Military Assistance Command, Vietnam***

The Vietnamese have paid a heavy price in suffering for their long fight against the communists. We military men are in Vietnam now because their government has asked us to help its soldiers and people in winning their struggle. The Viet Cong will attempt to turn the Vietnamese people against you. You can defeat them at every turn by the strength, understanding, and generosity you display with the people. Here are nine simple rules:

NINE RULES

1. Remember we are guests here: We make no demands and seek no special treatment.
2. Join with the people! Understand their life, use phrases from their language and honor their customs and laws.
3. Treat women with politeness and respect.
4. Make personal friends among the soldiers and common people.
5. Always give the Vietnamese the right of way.
6. Be alert to security and ready to react with your military skill.
7. Don't attract attention by loud, rude or unusual behavior.
8. Avoid separating yourself from the people by a display of wealth or privilege.
9. Above all else you are members of the US Military Forces on a difficult mission, responsible for all your official and personal actions. Reflect honor upon yourself and the United States of America.

DISTRIBUTION—1 to each member of the United States Armed Forces in Vietnam

DOCUMENT 5 ***The Enemy in Your Hands***

1. *Handle him firmly, promptly, but humanely.* The captive in your hands must be disarmed, searched, secured and watched. But he must also be treated at all times as a human being. He must not be tortured, killed, mutilated, or degraded, even if he refuses to talk. If the captive is a woman, treat her with all respect due her sex.

2. *Take the captive quickly to security.* As soon as possible evacuate the captive to a place of safety and interrogation designated by your commander. Military documents taken from the captive are also sent to the interrogators, but the captive will keep his personal equipment except weapons.

3. *Mistreatment of any captive is a criminal offense. Every soldier is personally responsible for the enemy in his hands.* It is both dishonorable and foolish to mistreat a captive. It is also a punishable offense. Not even a beaten enemy will surrender if he knows his captors will torture or kill him. He will resist and make his capture more costly. Fair treatment of captives encourages the enemy to surrender.

4. *Treat the sick and wounded captive as best you can.* The captive saved may be an intelligence source. In any case he is a human being and must be treated like one. The soldier who ignores the sick and wounded degrades his uniform.

5. *All persons in your hands, whether suspects, civilians, or combat captives, must be protected against violence, insults, curiosity, and reprisals of any kind.* Leave punishment to the courts and judges. The soldier shows his strength by his fairness, firmness, and humanity to the persons in his hands.

DOCUMENT 6 ***". . . You Do What You Want to Do . . ."***

HERBERT L. CARTER TESTIMONY TO THE PEER COMMISSION

Q: Do you recall getting any instructions on how to handle prisoners of war during this time?
A: We had a little instruction on that.
Q: Do you recall what they told you?
A: They told us that if we get a prisoner to hold them until someone, intelligence, was actually supposed to interrogate them. The instructor sort of laughed about this.
Q: Why did they, or he, laugh about this? Do you know?
A: It was just the way they said it, like you do what you want to do with them actually.

Introduction to Documents 7 through 12

The final set of documents detail the days leading up to the My Lai massacre and what happened on March 16, 1968. In Document 7 soldier Michael Bernhardt discusses the way many American G.I.s regarded the Vietnamese, and how racism and the frustrations of fighting an elusive enemy created an atmosphere that made a massacre possible. In Documents 8 and 9 Captain Eugene Kotouc, an intelligence officer, and Gregory Olson, a member of the platoon that assaulted My Lai, discuss the orders Charlie Company, under the command of Lieutenant William Calley, were given the day before the My Lai assault. Documents 10 and 11 detail the day of the massacre, throwing light on what individual soldiers did and thought. Document 12 is the testimony of a My Lai villager who survived the assault. All of these documents are from the *Peer's Report*—an investigation that collected soldiers' testimony—except for the Calley interview which is taken from his court-martial trial.

DOCUMENT 7 ***Michael Bernhardt***

Q: Why were you sent away on detail when the investigating officer was coming?
A: The investigating officer wasn't there to talk to everyone. We were spread out along the area of the perimeter. But I still think I might have been sent away because I might have said something that would have damaged the company.
Q: You mean . . . that you didn't approve of what was going on, or what had been going on [the My Lai attack]?
A: That's what I mean, yes, sir.
Q: And this was known to other people in the company?
A: Yes, sir.
Q: Did you explain why?
A: I believe I did, sir, but it wasn't getting through to too many people.
Q: You believe you did what?

A: Tried to explain why I didn't think it was right. It didn't have strategic value to it at all. I believe that there is an effort on the part of some people in the higher quarters of the military, both allied and American, who want to see the war dragged on. One of the ways that they do this is by cultivating this attitude that someone very aptly called the "dink complex," and that these things that happened as a result of the "dink complex" damage us. The idea I believe in that war is not to kill off the enemy. It would just be too hard to do that. You have got to make them want to stop fighting or else eliminate his means of fighting. When you go out and do something like this, I believe what you are doing is breeding more Viet Cong.
Q: You mean by killing the civilians at My Lai?
A: Yes, sir.
Q: Go ahead.
A: I believe that this breeds Viet Cong and this isn't helping us at all. It is more hurting us. That's also why—and I want to make it clear here—that's why I made these public statements and so on. I wasn't trying to drag anybody down. I think that already now an attitude has changed by men who either are serving or will serve in Vietnam—that they won't get away with this all the time. It was an attitude that was prevalent in my company, and I wanted to see it reduced altogether.
Q: When you speak of a "dink complex" were you referring to how American soldiers look upon the Vietnamese people?
A: Yes, sir.
Q: Could you explain that a little more. I think I know what you mean, but I'm not sure.
A: All right, sir. From the way I look at it, I believe that it is mostly the linguistics bit. Now a person loses a certain aspect for being valued as a human being if you cannot understand him—rather if he doesn't have the means of communication with somebody else. A lot of the men—to their way of thinking, since the Vietnamese were speaking something that we could not understand, felt that they weren't communicating with anyone. It is just a sort of psychological way to look at it. What they thought were these people were a whole lot less than human. They knew, or they at least heard, of their value of human life. I think we're stuck with our values. Also they could get away with just about anything that they wanted to get away with. There is a lot of frustration that is among the men over there, and these frustrations cannot be directed at those responsible for creating them, and so, they're directed at what they can be directed at. In other words, making sort of a whipping boy out of the South Vietnamese population.
Q: In other words, helpless people—they just take it out on them?
A: Yes, sir, it sounds—it's illogical, of course, but we're not going to look for logic in a large member of men that would do this.
Q: Is this attitude related to the practice of referring to the Vietnamese as "dinks," "slopes," and "gooks," and this sort of thing?
A: Yes, sir, right, something like that. These are small manifestations of it. The larger manifestations is this and also the fact that there are a lot of—I said to the press that I thought it was an isolated incident. I didn't think it was an isolated incident, but I didn't think it would be wise to tell the press that I thought it happened all over Vietnam, because, first of all, I didn't know and, second of all, it wouldn't help any to say that it did.
Q: You feel that this is not isolated, but you don't actually have evidence of other—
A: (*Interposing*) Right. All I have is what information I've gathered by talking to other men about this particular incident and also not relating to this incident, but just talking about Vietnam in general. . . .
Q: . . . Did you understand, or did you comprehend the difference between civilians and noncombatants, detainees?

A: I understood myself, sir. I just don't—I don't know about the other men, but I understood myself. I didn't see any reason to ask questions, because it seemed to me that I knew about as much as anybody I could ask. Maybe it sounds presumptuous, but I didn't think that Lieutenant Calley or Captain Medina could have provided me with a better answer than I had myself. . . .

Q: . . . What do you mean by this, you tried something similar to this before or what?

A: No, sir. But, once when we started operating and when we first came into contact with Vietnamese civilians, or whatever they were, apparently civilians, there were several old women with "chogie sticks"—that is, the long stick that they balance on their shoulder with two baskets, one on either end—in front of me. I ordered them to stop, that is "dung lai," which means stop, I think. I never got the right reaction out of "dung lai," and they kept on going only a little bit faster. I fired some shots over their heads. After that time Lieutenant Calley said to me that "the old man" says—which could mean any "old man," the company commander, the battalion commander—said that if they don't stop when you say "dung lai," you shoot them. So I didn't think of this as really being the best way to handle it. There could be any reason why they don't stop when I say "dung lai." Not knowing for sure what "dung lai" means myself, I might be telling them to get lost. It's a tonal language. You have to know the music, not only the words, so I might be saying it wrong. I just couldn't see doing that. I was told that they might have hand grenades in the baskets and I thought they might also have fish, since they were fish baskets, and I didn't really trust the judgment of the people that I had in command of me.

DOCUMENT 8 *Eugene Kotouc*

Q: Were any instructions given concerning the destruction of the village?

A: Yes, sir, there were. Colonel Barker said he wanted the area cleaned out, he wanted it neutralized, and he wanted the buildings knocked down. He wanted the hootches burned, and he wanted the tunnels filled in, and then he wanted the livestock and chickens run off, killed, or destroyed. Colonel Barker did not say anything about killing any civilians, sir, nor did I. He wanted to neutralize the area.

Q: When did he give these instructions?

A: He told me this was what we wanted to do here. When it was, it was prior to the operation. As I recall, it was the night before, or early afternoon before, on 15 March. . . .

Q: Were you familiar with the brigade orders and the division orders concerning the burning and/or destruction of a village or hamlet?

A: I am familiar with Colonel Henderson saying that when we get through down there, there would not be any 48th left, or any place for them to live.

Q: Specifically what did Colonel Henderson say?

A: To the best of my recall, he said that when we get through with that 48th Battalion, they won't be giving us any more trouble. We're going to do them in once and for all. I thought, personally, that was a real fine thing to say.

Q: Did he give any instructions to burn the village?

A: Not to my knowledge, sir.

Q: To destroy the area?

A: Not to my knowledge. . . .

Q: I would like you to again state, to the best of your ability, what Colonel Barker said that you would do with respect to that village, My Lai?

A: Colonel Barker said he wanted the defensive positions destroyed, the bunkers, and the trench work, and the tunnels, if we could find them. He wanted the hootches knocked down, and in a case where they could burn them to burn them up. He wanted the livestock and chickens to be run off, or else destroy them. Run them off and get them out of the area.

Q: Did he say anything about the wells, the water?

A: No, sir, he definitely did not. Colonel Barker never did say anything about polluting wells, or to do anything with the wells, not to my knowledge. I never heard him say anything about that.

Q: Did he say anything about destruction of other villages in later parts of the operation?

A: He spoke in general terms, and frankly, the village My Lai was not given a whole lot—we did not talk constantly about My Lai. The operation was not for My Lai per se. It was for the area there. The reason we went to My Lai was because that is where we thought the headquarters and the two battalions were. They were to sweep through and move, and as my memory serves me, they moved through the north-northeast. There would be a blocking company up there. The idea was that anything that could be used in the defensive position or blocking position to give aid and cover was to be destroyed. . . .

Q: Were the company commanders given to understand that they had a chance to encounter the 48th VC Battalion in and around My Lai? Were they given to understand that they had a chance to trap the 48th VC Battalion in My Lai and around there?

A: That was the hope of the whole thing, that we could get them into there, pinch them in, and do battle with them right there, and that Michles' company would be in a position where they could not get away if they ran. They would just take off, they would scatter to the winds. It was the whole picture that we could suck them in, pinch them in, and destroy them.

Q: In the discussion of the plans, you planned to destroy the base of operations in and around My Lai. Could that have been given in such terms that the company commanders got the idea that this should include that part of the civilian population which supported the VC?

A: To do away with them, sir?

Q: Yes.

A: No, I do not believe so, sir. It certainly wasn't—

Q: (*Interposing*) I understand you testified this certainly was not said specifically.

A: Sir, I do not think it was inferred, sir.

Q: Included in the field order, were there instructions, specific instructions, to watch out for them the best you could, and to see that no harm came to non-combatant civilians. Was that discussed on the 15th?

A: Sir, I do not think it was referred to, sir. . . .

Q: We will come back to the civilians. But going back to the planning stages, the directive stages of the operation. Were there not any considerations given to the care and handling of the civilians? If the order of Colonel Barker had just been issued to destroy the place, it would have been obvious that you were going to have—that there was going to be a refugee problem of considerable magnitude. Was any consideration given to that?

A: Yes, sir, there was. It was an SOP (standard operating procedure) for the unit when civilians were present in the area, if a fight was going on, the civilians would be taken and moved down the road, in this case to Quang Ngai City. We told them to please get out of the area, and go down to Quang Ngai City. We had been telling those people for a long time to get out of there and live in Quang Ngai City where they had refugees places. It was a policy, and I personally saw it happen when they take the people and just move them through the lines and go down the road. Normally, with all the shooting, they were scared, and they would go on down the road. We did not appoint, and say: "You take civilians down the road." We did not do that.

Q: Were there any instructions issued by Colonel Barker or Colonel Calhoun, or anybody, to take . . . adequate provisions for marching these civilians out of the area, moving them down in an orderly fashion to Quang Ngai City, and assuring that they were adequately cared for?

A: There was not, because I brought it up myself. I wanted to know what kind of release point they wanted for the civilian population. And they said to do it like normally, and move them down the road.

DOCUMENT 9 *Greogry T. Olsen*

Q: Prior to the assault on My Lai did the Company receive a briefing?

A: Yes the company did. The briefing was given by CPT Medina and I attended the briefing. At the time everybody was down in the dumps, because just previous due to various operations in the past few weeks we had lost about 25 men. 7 of them had been killed and the rest wounded. The briefing was given at LZ Dottie, where CPT Medina, drew a map on the ground and explained the entire procedures. We had instructions to shoot on sight any military age male, running from us, or shooting at us. We were then told, that we are to clear all the people out of the village. He (CPT Medina) did not say anything about the disposition of the people that we had or would clear out of the village. We were told, to destroy all the food supplies and the animals in the area. I do not remember if in the initial briefing we were told to burn all the huts. CPT Medina made the statement that we owed the enemy something. The troops had a feeling that they should revenge their fallen comrades.

Q: Did CPT Medina ever order during the aforementioned briefing to kill all the inhabitants of the village? With all the inhabitants I mean also women and children.

A: Negative. He did not. CPT Medina, was in my opinion an outstanding Commander. He was always concerned with the welfare of his men. Sometimes we did things the hard way, but in the end it was always the best for us. CPT Medina would never have given an order to kill women and children.

Q: Was LT Calley present during the briefing?

A: I assume he was.

Q: Did you attend a briefing on the operation My Lai by LT Calley?

A: I only remember that he told us on which helicopters we were supposed to go on. I do not remember LT Calley giving us a specific briefing on My Lai after CPT Medina had briefed us. I do not remember who my squadleader was during the Pinkville Operation. It is quite a long time ago.

DOCUMENT 10 ***Herbert L. Carter***

We were picked up by helicopters at LZ Dottie early in the morning and we were flown to My Lai. We landed outside the village in a dry rice paddy. There was no resistance from the village. There was no armed enemy in the village. We formed a line outside the village.

The first killing was an old man in a field outside the village who said some kind of greeting in Vietnamese and waved his arms at us. Someone—either Medina or Calley—said to kill him and a big heavy-set white fellow killed the man. I do not know the name of the man who shot this Vietnamese. This was the first murder.

Just after the man killed the Vietnamese, a woman came out of the village and someone knocked her down and Medina shot her with his M16 rifle. I was 50 or 60 feet from him and saw this. There was no reason to shoot this girl. Mitchell, Conti, Meadlo, Stanley, and the rest of the squad and the command group must have seen this. It was a pure out and out murder.

Then our squad started into the village. We were making sure no one escaped from the village. Seventy-five or a hundred yards inside the village we came to where the soldiers had collected 15 or more Vietnamese men, women, and children in a group. Medina said, "Kill everybody, leave no one standing. Wood was there with an M-60 machine gun and, at Medina's orders, he fired into the people. Sgt Mitchell was there at this time and fired into the people with his M16 rifle, also. Widmer was there and fired into the group, and after they were down on the ground, Widmer passed among them and finished them off with his M16 rifle. Medina, himself, did not fire into this group.

Just after this shooting, Medina stopped a 17 or 18 year old man with a water buffalo. Medina said for the boy to make a run for it—he tried to get him to run—but the boy wouldn't run, so Medina shot him with his M16 rifle and killed him. The command group was there. I was 75 or 80 feet away at the time and saw it plainly. There were some demolition men there, too, and they would be able to testify about this. I don't know any other witnesses to this murder. Medina killed the buffalo, too.

Q: I want to warn you that these are very serious charges you are making. I want you to be very sure that you tell only the truth and that everything you say is the truth?

A: What I have said is the truth and I will face Medina in court and swear to it. This is the truth: this is what happened.

Q: What happened then?

A: We went on through the village. Meadlo shot a Vietnamese and asked me to help him throw the man in the well. I refused and Meadlo had Carney help him throw the man in the well. I saw this murder with my own eyes and know that there was no reason to shoot the man. I also know from the wounds that the man was dead.

Also in the village the soldiers had rounded up a group of people. Meadlo was guarding them. There were some other soldiers with Meadlo. Calley came up and said that he wanted them all killed. I was right there within a few feet when he said this. There were about 25 people in this group. Calley said when I walk away, I want them all killed. Meadlo and Widmer fired into this group with his M16 on automatic fire. Cowan was there and fired into the people too, but I don't think he wanted to do it. There were others firing into this group, but I don't remember who. Calley had two Vietnamese with him at this time and he killed them, too, by shooting them with his M16 rifle on automatic fire. I didn't want to get involved and I walked away. There was no reason for this killing. These were mainly women and children and a few old men. They weren't trying to escape or attack or anything. It was murder.

A woman came out of a hut with a baby in her arms and she was crying. She was crying because her little boy had been in front of her hut and between the well and the hut and someone had killed the child by shooting it. She came out of the hut with her baby and Widmer shot her with an M16 and she fell. When she fell, she dropped the baby and then Widmer opened up on the baby with his M16 and killed the baby, too.

I also saw another woman come out of a hut and Calley grabbed her by the hair and shot her with a caliber 45 pistol. He held her by the hair for a minute and then let go and she fell to the ground. Some enlisted man standing there said, "Well, she'll be in the big rice paddy in the sky."

Q: Do you know any witnesses to these incidents?

A: Stanley might have [seen] the one Calley killed. There were a lot of people around when Widmer shot the woman with the baby. I can't definitely state any one person was there, but there were a lot of people around.

I also saw a Vietnamese boy about 8 years old who had been wounded, I think in the leg. One of the photographers attached to the company patted the kid on the head and then Mitchell shot the kid right in front of the photographer and me. I am sure the boy died from the fire of Mitchell.

About that time I sat down by a stack of dying people and Widmer asked me if he could borrow my caliber .45 pistol and finish off the people. I gave him my pistol and he walked in among the people and would stand there and when one would move, he would shoot that person in the head with the pistol. He used three magazines of caliber 45 ammunition on these people. These were men, children, women, and babies. They had been shot by machinegunners and riflemen from Company C, 1/20th Infantry. This was at a T-junction of two trails on the outskirts of the village. I got my pistol back from Widmer and holstered it again.

Q: How many people do you figure Widmer finished off when he used your pistol?

A: I know he shot some twice, so I figure he shot fifteen or so with my pistol. I know he shot one guy in the head and I imagine that was where he was shooting them all.

Q: What happened then?

A: We went on through the village and there was killing and more killing. I was with Stanley, mainly. I sat down with Stanley and Widmer came up again and asked to borrow my pistol again. I gave it to him. I saw a little boy there—wounded, I believe in the arm—and Widmer walked up close to the kid and shot him with my pistol. Widmer said something like, "Did you see me shoot that son of a bitch," and Stanley said something about how it was wrong. My gun had jammed when Widmer shot the kid. As far as I could tell, the kid died as a result of this gunshot. Then Widmer gave me my pistol back and walked off. I was trying to clean it when it accident[al]ly went off and I was shot in the left foot. Stanley gave me medical aid and then the medics came. Medina and some of the command group came up and then I was flown out in a helicopter. The next day the medics brought Meadlo into the hospital. He had stepped on a booby-trap and had lost his foot. He said he thought God might be punishing him for what he had done in My Lai. . . .

Q: Did you murder anyone in Vietnam?

A: The only people I killed in Vietnam I killed in combat. I didn't kill any women or kids or unarmed persons at all, ever.

Q: How many people do you think were killed in My Lai?

A: There were more than 100, but I couldn't tell you accurately how many people were killed. I don't believe there were any people left alive.

DOCUMENT 11 ***William L. Calley***

A: . . . Meadlo was still standing there with a group of Vietnamese, and I yelled at Meadlo and asked him—I told him if he couldn't move all those people to "get rid of them."
Q: Did he give you any reply to that, any audible reply that you heard?
A: He gave me a reply—I don't know what it was, sir.
Q: And then what did you do?
A: I continued over to Mitchell's location, sir.
Q: Did you hear any firing at that time?
A: There was firing, yes, sir.
Q: From where?
A: At Mitchell's location, back behind me, the gunships were still placing—they were still—I could hear heavy volumes of fire starting back up in the village. Apparently the third element was starting to come into the village.
Q: All right. Then what did you do?
A: I continued over to Sergeant Mitchell's location, sir.
Q: Did you fire into that group of people?
A: No, sir, I did not.
Q: All right, go on with relating what happened and what you did.
A: I went up and I told—talked to Sergeant Mitchell, told him to get his men together, get on the other side of the ditch and showed him where I wanted his machine gun emplaced and told him to link up his men with Sergeant Bacon, sir.
Q: Now during or approximately at that same time, was there an incident that occurred which you did some firing?
A: Yes, sir, there is.
Q: Now I am specifically referring to an individual. Was there an individual man involved somewhere around there or killed about that time?
A: No, sir, there wasn't.
Q: After you had this conversation up there with Mitchell, what happened and what did you do?
A: I heard a considerable amount of firing to my north, and I moved up along the edge of the ditch and around a hootch, and I broke out in the clearing and my men were—had a number of Vietnamese in the ditch and were firing upon them, sir.
Q: Now when you say your men, can you identify any of the men?
A: I spoke to Dursi and I spoke to Meadlo, sir.
Q: Was there anybody else there that you can identify by name?
A: No, sir. There was a few other troops but it was insignificant to me at that time.
Q: What's your best impression of how many there were at the ditch?
A: Four to five, sir.
Q: Two of whom you can specifically identify, Meadlo and Dursi?
A: Yes, sir. I spoke to those two.
Q: Now what did you do after you saw them shooting in the ditch?
A: Well, I fired into the ditch, also, sir. . . .
Q: All right. Then when it was up in there—after you moved up along side the ditch, that's when you started firing into the ditch, is that correct?
A: Yes, sir.
Q: After that incident, what did you do?
A: Well, I told my men to get on across the ditch and to get in position after I had fired into the ditch.

Q: Prior to that time, had you received any other message from Captain Medina?
A: Still to hurry up and get my men out in position where they were supposed to be.
Q: Was that the full extent of that conversation?
A: That's all I can remember him saying the whole time—from the time the second platoon broke and I got out in my position, sir.
Q: All right. After, did you leave the vicinity of the ditch—shortly thereafter, after you fired in the ditch, when did you leave it? Was it shortly—did you stay there a long time, or did you stay there a long while—a short time or what did you do?
A: I don't take it—it was a very rapid period of time to me. I can't say basically what time it was. It seemed like it was only a matter of half a minute, maybe a full minute at the most. I fired in the ditch and the men started moving across. Sergeant Bacon's men were coming out of the village, moving forward at that time. I started moving over to his location.
Q: Did you have a chance to look and observe what was in the ditch?
A: Yes, sir.
Q: What did you see?
A: Dead people, sir.
Q: All right. Did you see any appearance of anybody being alive in there?
A: No, sir.
Q: Let me ask you—at any time that you were along near that ditch, did you push or have anybody push people into the ditch?
A: Yes and no, sir.
Q: Give us the yes part first.
A: When I came out of the hedgerow, I came right out. The last man to go into the ditch—and I didn't physically touch him—if he would have stopped, I guess I would have.
Q: Was somebody there with him that was ordering him in or pushing him?
A: They had been ordered to go to the ditch, sir.
Q: Do you know who gave them that information?
A: Indirectly, I did, sir.
Q: Indirectly, what do you mean by that? Was it through somebody?
A: I had told Meadlo to get them people on the other side of the ditch, sir.
Q: After the incident where you went and you saw this one man and you fired into the ditch, what did you then do?
A: I continued moving northwardly along the edge of the ditch, sir.
Q: And for how far and where did you go?
A: Well, I went up to about the end of the ditch and about that time Warrant Officer Thompson, I believe he is Lieutenant Thompson now, landed his helicopter, sir. . . .
Q: All right. Now aside from what you said about the shooting into the ditch, was there any other shooting you did in that general vicinity?
A: The next time I fired, the helicopter had lifted off and I started walking over to the machine gun position and I fired on a head moving through the rice somewhere over in this area here (indicating). . . .
Q: There has been some information disclosed that you heard before the court that you stood there at the ditch for a considerable period of time, that you waited and had your troops organize groups of Vietnamese, throw them in the ditch or knock them in the ditch or pushed them in the ditch, and that you fired there for approximately an hour and a half as those groups were marched up. Did you participate in any such a shooting or any such an event?
A: No, sir, I did not.

Q: Did you at any time direct anybody to push people in the ditch?
A: Like I said, sir, I gave the order to take those people through the ditch and had also told Meadlo if he couldn't move them to "waste them" and I directly—other than that—it was only that one incident. I never stood up there for any period of time. My main mission was to get my men on the other side of that ditch and get in that defensive position and that's what I did, sir.
Q: Now why did you give Meadlo a message or the order that if he couldn't get rid of them to "wasted them"?
A: Because that was my order. That was the order of the day, sir.
Q: Who gave you that order?
A: My commanding officer, sir, Captain Medina, sir.
Q: And stated in that posture, in substantially those words, how many times did you receive such an order from Captain Medina?
A: The night before in the company briefing, the platoon leaders' briefing, the following morning before we lifted off, and twice there in the village, sir. . . .

DOCUMENT 12 *Nguyen Hieu*

Q: What is your name?
A: Nguyen Hieu.
Q: How old are you?
A: Twenty-five years old.
Q: Are you native of Tu Cung?
A: Yes. . . .
Q: . . . Were you in your house on the morning of 16 March 1968 when the Americans came?
A: Yes, I lived there in 1968.
Q: Were you there on the morning of 16 March 1968 when the Americans came?
A: Yes, I was there that morning.
Q: How many other members of your family were there with you in the house that morning?
A: Five.
Q: What did you do when you heard the artillery fire?
A: For the first time early in the morning I heard artillery come in here (indicating) and American helicopters come into here (indicating) on the west side of the village. They came here and they look us from the bunker.
Q: Was the bunker near your house?
A: Yes, right here (*indicating*).
Q: Did all the members of your family go in the bunker?
A: My mother stayed in the house. I and the children went to the bunker.
Q: How long did you stay in the bunker?
A: About 2 hours.
Q: Did the Americans come near the bunker?
A: Yes, they came into the bunker.
Q: They came into the bunker?
A: Yes.
Q: And did they make you come out of the bunker?
A: When the Americans came to the house my mother came out of house, and the Americans then raped my mother and they shot her.

Q: They shot and raped your mother?
A: Yes, shot and raped my mother. My sister ran out of the bunker and they shot my sister and two children. . . .
Q: How many Americans were there?
A: Two Americans.
Q: Were they Caucasians or Negroes?
A: I saw only one black and one yellow.
Q: One black and one yellow. No white?
A: I saw one black, one yellow, and another I don't know exactly.
Q: Which one raped your mother?
A: The black soldier. . . .
Q: What did the white soldier do while the Negro solider was raping your mother?
A: After they shot my mother, the white soldier checked the house to see that everybody was dead and then he went out. . . .
And later, a second group of Americans came in to burn the house.
Q: Were you the only one that stayed in the bunker?
A: Yes, I stayed alone.
Q: And your sister went out of the bunker and was shot?
A: My sister went out to help my mother and was shot.
Q: Were they all shot right around your house or did they take them some place else and shoot them?
A: They were all shot in the house.
Q: After the soldiers that shot the people left, how long were you in the bunker before the other soldiers came that burned the house?
A: About 40 minutes.
Q: About 40 minutes?
A: Yes.
Q: Did you see the soldiers that burned the house?
A: No, I did not see the Americans that burned the house.
Q: Did they shoot any livestock? Any animals, chickens, pigs?
A: They killed two buffalo.
Q: What did you do after the soldiers left?
A: After the Americans left I burned my mother and sister.
Q: I am sorry that your family was killed like this. Thank you for coming here today to help us.

Postscript

Three years after the My Lai Massacre, a young war hero gave testimony before the Senate Committee on Foreign Relations. Massachusetts native John Kerry served on a gunboat in the Mekong Delta, and he received the Silver Star, the Bronze Star, and three Purple Hearts for valor. But by 1971, after he left the Navy, he was a leader of Vietnam Veterans Against the War. He told the Committee that American soldiers knew the horrors of the war, even if many American people wanted to avoid the truth: "We saw America lose her sense of morality as she accepted very coolly a My Lai and refused to give up the image of American soldiers who hand out chocolate bars and chewing gum."

My Lai eventually became shorthand for the hell of war, but it almost escaped the notice of the American people. Chief Warrant Officer Hugh Thompson—who literally put himself between American troops and the Vietnamese, then flew wounded civilians out of the combat zone—kept the case alive by filing a complaint. The military brass, however, preferred to treat the case as an unfortunate but inadvertent killing of a dozen or two dozen civilians. Another soldier, Ronald Ridenhour from Phoenix, would not let the story die. He did his own investigation and pursued eye witness accounts. Then in March 1969, he wrote to President Nixon, the Joint Chiefs, the State Department, and several Congressmen—among whom Representative Morris Udall pushed for a full investigation.

The case was finally turned over to the Army's Inspector General, and as witnesses were interviewed, the enormity of the crime became apparent. By the end of the year, My Lai made the cover of both *Time* and *Newsweek,* and graphic photographs of the massacre filled the pages of *Life Magazine.* The Pentagon appointed a commission headed by three-star General William Peers for a closed-door investigation. The Commission interviewed nearly 400 witnesses and produced 20,000 pages of testimony (some of which you read in this chapter). The Peers Commission recommended action against dozens of soldiers for rape and murder, but also singled out several officers for covering up crimes.

Twenty-five men initially were to be prosecuted, but due to a combination of circumstances, only a few were charged, and one tried. The case against Lieutenant William Calley was overwhelming—too many eye-witnesses identified him mowing down dozens of unarmed civilians. Upwards of 500 people died at My Lai. Calley's defense attorney argued that the lieutenant was being made a scapegoat for higher-ups like Captain Ernest Medina. Medina, who, it was alleged, gave the orders to leave no one alive. But the military tribunal, after deliberating thirteen days, found Calley—and Calley alone—guilty of premeditated murder, and sentenced him to be confined to prison and hard-labor for life.

Opinion polls indicated that the American public strongly disapproved of the verdict. President Nixon soon intervened to take Calley out of confinement and move him to house arrest. Calley's prosecutor, Aubrey Daniel, crusaded against what he considered the political expediency that prevented those who murdered innocent civilians from receiving justice. Nonetheless, William Calley, the only man who served any time at all for the massacre, was paroled at the end of 1974.

QUESTIONS

Defining Terms

Identify in the context of the chapter each of the following:

Pinkville	William Westmoreland
domino theory	Tet Offensive
"Charlie" Company	Vietcong
Nine Rules	Butch Gruver
Ronald Ridenhour	William Calley
court-martial	Captain Medina

Probing the Sources

1. How did the official version of the My Lai assault differ from the soldiers' testimonies? Why were they so different from each other?

2. How were soldiers supposed to treat civilians and prisoners of war? Why didn't they follow the book?
3. What were William Calley's and Charlie Company's orders for March 16, 1968? Did they follow orders or take the law into their own hands? Or both?

Interpreting the Sources

1. What does the My Lai massacre tell us about the nature of warfare in Vietnam? Do you think My Lai was an isolated case or part of a larger problem?
2. Given various codes of warfare, who were guilty of war crimes? Why was only William Calley convicted of a war crime?
3. Why was the Vietnam War so controversial?
4. Why should Americans today be interested in what happened at My Lai?

ADDITIONAL READING

The documents in this section come from *My Lai: A Brief History with Documents* (1998), edited by James S. Olson and Randy Roberts. Two fine books on the massacre are Seymour Hersh, *My Lai 4: A Report on the Massacre and Its Aftermath* (1970) and Michael Bilton and Kevin Sim, *Four Hours in My Lai* (1992). For the experience of a combat veteran, try Tim O'Brien, *If I Die in the Combat Zone* (1988), and *The Things They Carried* (1990). The literature on the war in Vietnam is extensive, but anyone interested in the nature of the combat and the experiences of the soldiers should read Neil Sheehan, *A Bright Shining Lie* (1988); Christian Appy, *Working-Class War* (1993); Michael Herr, *Dispatches* (1977); Mark Baker, *'Nam* (1982); Stewart O'Nan, *The Vietnam Reader* (1998); and Davis Maraniss, *They Marched Into Sunlight* (2003). Stanley Karrow's *Vietnam: A History* (1999) remains a useful introduction

14

The Rise of Liberalism in the 1960s and 1970s

Historical Context

When young Southerners began their sit-ins to integrate lunch counters and buses, they started something that reached beyond the civil rights movement. By the late 1960s, as the Vietnam War raged on, hundreds of thousands of Americans took to the streets in protest. Draft-age college students, clergymen, even Vietnam veterans, turned out by the hundreds of thousands. But even beyond the antiwar movement, the 1960s launched an experiment in mass, participatory politics. Protests, community organizing, and street demonstrations focused on a range of issues. Activists saw themselves as attempting to fulfill America's democratic promise. New groups organized as never before, and "rights consciousness," as some have called it, proceeded from the assumption that democracy involves much more than mere voting. Social change happened when the excluded—often defined by ethnicity, gender, and sexual orientation—became aware of their plight and asserted themselves.

The new activism was different from the old organizing efforts of the labor movement, which had its roots deep in the nineteenth century, and found its greatest triumphs during the Great Depression and its aftermath. During the 1930s, intense work by unionists in America's basic industries led to the formation of the Congress of Industrial Organizations. Massive new unions like the United Auto Workers were legitimated by the New Deal, which, under the Wagner Act, for the first time gave federal sanction and protection to workers' right to collective bargaining. During the postwar era, roughly a third of America's workers belonged to labor unions, and they led the way in setting a remarkably high standard of living for working people.

But economic justice was not the only motive for activism. An unusual cultural tone pervaded the 1960s; America's affluence and the upbeat rhetoric of the Kennedy and Johnson administrations gave a sense of limitless possibilities. More, a distinct spirituality pervaded many of the era's reforms. The civil rights movement, with its base in the black churches, was the most obvious example. New organizing among Native Americans also gained energy from spiritual sources, as did efforts among Mexican farm workers, and from American women. Beyond the specific groups, the era was characterized by remarkable utopian hopes, as if humankind stood at the verge of a social, spiritual, and personal millenium that for centuries tantalized yet eluded the faithful.

What became known as the counterculture was the era's most obvious manifestation of utopian dreams. The shock troops of the counterculture, the so-called hippies, sought not so much political or economic solutions to American problems but cultural ones. During the 1960s countless youths responded to the call to "turn-on, tune-in, drop-out," an ambiguous phrase that implied leaving behind the world of school, work, and career for a freer life centered on the open expression of impulses and desires, all made easier with recreational drugs such as marijuana and LSD. A very popular book of the era, Charles Reich's *Greening of America,* argued that the counterculture foretold a change of consciousness in America—youths were leading the way toward abandoning the work ethic, the obsession with success, and the destructiveness of American business culture. The phrase "sex, drugs, and rock and roll" implied a hedonism that was real enough, but the counterculture also embodied important ideological commitments. The new order would be founded on communal consciousness, freedom, play, and the sacredness of the world; it opposed the 1950s image of "the organization man," or "the man in the gray flannel suit."

The counterculture had its attractions for many youthful Americans, and certainly "hippie" styles quickly entered consumer awareness. Long hair, bell-bottom pants, and psychedelic displays grew common by the seventies, long after the numbers of hippies in meccas like the Haight-Ashbury district of San Francisco declined. But equally important, and perhaps more profound than the counterculture was America's tilt toward the political Left. Within the federal government, the Kennedy and Johnson administrations sponsored a range of new programs that extended the old social welfare interventions of the New Deal—civil rights and voting rights laws, Medicare and Medicaid, expanded versions of Aid to Families with Dependent Children and unemployment compensation, equal opportunity programs, the Environmental Protection Agency, the Occupational Safety and Health Administration, and so forth. Such policies did not end with the sixties, but continued long into the seventies, as the Republican administration of Richard M. Nixon added Affirmative Action, strong new environmental laws, and the Endangered Species Act.

But it was outside of mainstream politics that some of the most interesting developments took place. For example, the long history of women attempting to gain full recognition and equality reignited in the 1960s. A founding document of the renewed feminist movement was the unlikely bestseller, Betty Friedan's The *Feminine Mystique* (1963). Friedan, a journalist with experience in the labor movement, asked why it was that after participating broadly in American society and economy during the forties, American women found themselves shunted back into the home as wives and mothers, caretakers of new postwar suburban households. By "feminine mystique" she meant that women were now valued only for their "sex functions," which in American culture meant traditionally female attributes—beauty, nurturance, housekeeping—rather than careers or creativity. For many women, it was the sense of achievement that came from working in the civil rights or antiwar movements, followed by the frustration of not having their contributions acknowledged by the men who dominated those movements, that led toward feminism.

Two dozen women founded the National Organization for Women in 1966 to lobby the federal government for enforcement of antidiscrimination laws. From there the movement grew. In 1971, the very first issue of *Ms.* magazine sold over a quarter million copies. Women founded new groups, some of them overtly political, some of them dedicated to "consciousness raising." Like most of the movements of this era, there was no single voice, point-of-view, or organization representing everyone. Many women considered lack of opportunity in the workplace to be the most compelling problem; others focused on inequalities in relationships between men and women. Health issues, daycare, and the cult of beauty all came under scrutiny. Equal opportunity and equal pay remained fundamental concerns of the women's movement, but "cultural issues" grew increasingly prominent, and often very divisive. Many women believed that laws making abortion a crime must be overturned, and the United States Supreme Court agreed in 1973 with the *Roe v. Wade* decision. Despite this ruling, not only has the issue not gone away, positions have become ever more entrenched, dividing Americans along lines of religion, gender, and region.

A new movement also began among Latino Americans. In California's central valley, the United Farm Workers gained unexpected success organizing poor itinerant farm laborers, mostly Mexicans and the children of Mexicans. Inspired in part by the civil rights movement under Martin Luther King Jr. and led by the equally charismatic Cesar Chavez, this AFL-CIO affiliate began with grape pickers in the town of Delano in 1965, and quickly gained converts in California's enormous "factories in the fields." This was no simple union movement, however. The farm workers' rallies took place in both English and Spanish, they borrowed anthems from the civil rights movement like "We Shall Overcome," and they featured banners with the symbolism of an Aztec eagle and of the Virgin of Guadalupe. Chavez received considerable support from other unions like the United Auto Workers, from student groups, and from the Catholic Church. Above all, the farm workers melded their commitment to economic justice with ethnic nationalism, with the recognition that they were mostly of Mexican descent; they made "la causa" and "la huelga" their own. Soon Latino organizing spread beyond the farm workers to urban battles for quality schools in Western cities, and to other groups, especially Puerto Ricans in New York and Chicago.

The breaking down of the old Cold War concensus—which included increasingly militant protest for African American equality and growing street demonstrations against the Vietnam War—continued to manifest itself as a rising tide of dissent among other groups. After decades of relative calm, Native Americans began a cycle of protest in the 1960s and 1970s. New challenges regarding tribal rights and land claims began to enter the courts. More dramatically, a group of nearly one hundred Indians from various tribes took over and occupied Alcatraz Island—formerly a federal prison—in the middle of San Francisco Bay, and held it for eighteen months. By 1973, three hundred Oglala Sioux, members of a new organization called the American Indian Movement (AIM), occupied Wounded Knee, South Dakota, scene of the massacre where the Plains Wars had ended eighty years before. The American Indian Movement fought FBI and other federal agents to a standoff, and only after more than two months was a truce arranged and shooting stopped.

Also in the late sixties came the beginnings of "Gay Power." Homosexual relationships had been long stigmatized and criminalized. In furtive gay hangouts in large cities, gay bashing by straights and shakedowns by police had been routine for decades. Rather suddenly, it seemed, gays refused to accept this second-class citizenship. The symbolic beginning came in June 1969, at the Stonewall Inn in New York City, where a riot underscored this unwillingness to put up with harassment any more. Equally important, the seventies became a time for "coming out of the closet," not just for individuals, but for homosexuals generally; now was the time to assert themselves, to fight for legislation ending discrimination, and to resist being stigmatized as sick or depraved.

Finally, the ecology movement, or what is more commonly referred to today as environmentalism, received an enormous push during these years. The Clean Air Act, Clean Water Act, Environmental Protection Agency, and Endangered Species Act eventually received broad-based support, but much of the impetus for this legislation came from mass organizing. Hundreds of thousands of Americans celebrated the first annual Earth Day on April 22, 1970, while rallies, teach-ins, and sit-ins, especially on college campuses, alerted people to ecological dangers. More, environmentalism caused Americans to question the assumptions of constant economic growth and technological progress. The movement pushed the ideas of the early twentieth-century conservation movement—which gave us the national forests and parks—further than ever. Now the focus shifted to dealing with the environmental damage caused by mass production and consumption.

The burst of activism on so many fronts did not simply end with the 1970s. Environmental issues, for example, continue to be a strong presence on the political landscape. The gay rights movement still garners headlines in the twenty-first century, as courts rule on the subject of same-sex marriage, and the political parties stake out positions on the desirability of civil unions. Certainly by the 1980s, however, with the election of Ronald Reagan and the rightward drift of Congress, the courts, and state governments, Americans in general shifted toward more conservative positions. Progressive, Left, or liberal causes found themselves increasingly on the defensive as the century waned. Still, the existence today of a substantial black middle class, the presence of women not just in the workforce but in positions of authority, and the cleaner air and water in our environment, are all important legacies of earlier activism.

THE DOCUMENTS

Introduction to Documents 1 through 3

Although the rhetoric of the family farm still reasonates in American culture, rural life in the post–New Deal era has been dominated by large, consolidated "agribusinesses." California led the way in the creation of "factories in the fields," with massive public works programs bringing water into the enormous Imperial, Sacramento, and San Joaquin Valleys. Farms that grew into hundreds, thousands, even tens of thousands of acres employed a succession of immigrant laborers—Chinese, Japanese, South Asian, Filipino, and especially Mexican. In the postwar era, the federal "Bracero" program opened Western farms to Mexican nationals explicitly working as migratory, temporary labor. Entire families worked brutal hours for poverty wages. They covered thousands of miles each year, planting and harvesting not only in the West but often also in Midwestern states, riding buses from job to job and living in primitive labor camps. Sometimes they wintered in Mexico, sometimes in California towns like Salinas. But a permanent home, regular schooling for their children, health care, all were impossible dreams.

Cesar Chavez grew up in Arizona on a tiny family farm. The Great Depression made it impossible for his family to pay back taxes, and they were forced into migratory labor when their farm was taken and their home bulldozed. Years later, after struggling with issues of how best to aid farm workers and their families, Chavez joined the union movement, eventually helping to found the United Farm Workers of America (UFW). Towns in California's Central Valley such as Fresno,

Merced, Visalia, and Bakersfield, were consistently ranked among those with the lowest income in America. Farm workers, mostly Mexican or Mexican American, earned roughly $1.50 per hour during the 1960s. Migrants had life expectancies twenty years shorter than the American average, and infant mortality rates that doubled national norms. Their work-related injuries came not just from stoop-labor, but also from exposure to highly toxic pesticides and herbicides. In California alone, 100,000 of hired farm laborers were children.

After several years of organizing, a 1965 strike of Filipino grape pickers began near Delano. This turned out to be the beginning of the UFW's great organizing drive, which, after a decade of effort, resulted in the signing of collective bargaining agreements between union and major growers. Document 1, the "Plan of Delano," printed as a single sheet broadside, set forth the assumptions of those who joined the movement. Note here how the boundaries between religion, politics, and history blurred. Document 2, a Western Union telegram sent March 5, 1968 from Martin Luther King, Jr. to Cesar Chavez, reveals how the farm workers struggle drew strength from the tactics of the Civil Rights Movement. Document 3 is a speech, "Cesar Chavez on Money and Organizing," delivered in a church in Keene, California, on October 4, 1971. Here Chavez reveals his belief that sacrifice was the glue holding the movement together. As you read these documents, ask yourself about the connections between politics, culture, and religion.

DOCUMENT 1 *The Plan of Delano*

We, the undersigned, gathered in Pilgrimage to the capital of the State in Sacramento in penance for all the failings of Farm Workers as free and sovereign men, do solemnly declare before the civilized world which judges our actions, and before the nation to which we belong, the propositions we have formulated to end the injustice that oppresses us.

We are conscious of the historical significance of our Pilgrimage. It is clearly evident that our path travels through a valley well known to all Mexican farm workers. We know all of these towns of Delano, Madera, Fresno, Modesto, Stockton and Sacramento, because along this very same road, in this very same valley, the Mexican race has sacrificed itself for the last hundred years. Our sweat and our blood have fallen on this land to make other men rich. This Pilgrimage is a witness to the suffering we have seen for generations.

The Penance we accept symbolizes the suffering we shall have in order to bring justice to these same towns, to this same valley. The Pilgrimage we make symbolizes the long historical road we have travelled in this valley alone, and the long road we have yet to travel, with much penance, in order to bring about the Revolution we need, and for which we present the propositions in the following PLAN:

1. This is the beginning of a social movement in fact and not in pronouncements. We seek our basic, God-given rights as human beings. Because we have suffered—and are not afraid to suffer—in order to survive, we are ready to give up everything, even our lives, in our fight for social justice. We shall do it without violence because that is our destiny....
2. We seek the support of all political groups and protection of the government, which is also our government, in our struggle. For too many years we have been treated like the lowest of the low.... We are tired of words, of betrayals, of indifference. To the politicians we say that the years are gone when the farm worker said nothing and did

nothing to help himself. From this movement shall spring leaders who shall understand us, lead us, be faithful to us, and we shall elect them to represent us. WE SHALL BE HEARD.

3. We seek, and have, the support of the Church in what we do. At the head of the Pilgrimage we carry LA VIRGEN DE LA GUADALUPE because she is ours, all ours, Patroness of the Mexican people. We also carry the Sacred Cross and the Star of David because we are not sectarians, and because we ask the help and prayers of all religions. All men are brothers, sons of the same God; that is why we say to all men of good will, in the words of Pope Leo XIII, "Everyone's first duty is to protect the workers from the greed of speculators who use human beings as instruments to provide themselves with money. It is neither just nor human to oppress men with excessive work to the point where their minds become enfeebled and their bodies worn out." GOD SHALL NOT ABANDON US.
4. We are suffering. We have suffered, and we are not afraid to suffer in order to win our cause. We have suffered unnumbered ills and crimes in the name of the Law of the Land. Our men, women, and children have suffered not only the basic brutality of stoop labor, and the most obvious injustices of the system; they have also suffered the desperation of knowing that that system caters to the greed of callous men and not to our needs. Now we will suffer for the purpose of ending the poverty, the misery, and the injustice, with the hope that our children will not be exploited as we have been....
5. We shall unite. We have learned the meaning of UNITY. We know why these United States are just that—united. The strength of the poor is also in union. We know that the poverty of the Mexican or Filipino worker in California is the same as that of all farm workers across the country, the Negroes and poor whites, the Puerto Ricans, Japanese, and Arabians; in short, all of the races that comprise the oppressed minorities of the United States. The majority of the people on our Pilgrimage are of Mexican descent, but the triumph of our race depends on a national association of all farm workers....
6. We shall Strike. We shall pursue the REVOLUTION we have proposed. We are sons of the Mexican Revolution, a revolution of the poor seeking bread and justice. Our revolution will not be armed, but we want the existing social order to dissolve; we want a new social order. We are poor, we are humble, and our only choice is to Strike in those ranches where we are not treated with the respect we deserve as working men, where our rights as free and sovereign men are not recognized....

Across the San Joaquin Valley, across California, across the entire Southwest of the United States, wherever there are Mexican people, wherever there are farm workers, our movement is spreading like flames across a dry plain. Our PILGRIMAGE is the MATCH that will light our cause for all farm workers to see what is happening here, so that they may do as we have done. The time has come for the liberation of the poor farm worker.

History is on our side.

MAY THE STRIKE GO ON! VIVA LA CAUSA!

DOCUMENT 2 ***Martin Luther King, Jr. to Cesar Chavez***

Cesar Chaves, United Farm Workers PO Box 130 Delano Calif

I am deeply moved by your courage in fasting as your personal sacrifice for justice through nonviolence. Your past and present commitment is eloquent testimony to the constructive power of nonviolent action and the destructive impotence of violent reprisal. You stand today as a living example of the Ghandian tradition with its great force for social progress and its healing spiritual powers. My colleagues and I commend you for your bravery, salute you for your indefatigable work against poverty and injustice, and pray for your health and your continuing service as one of the outstanding men of America. The plight of your people and ours is so grave that we all desperately need the inspiring example and effective leadership you have given.

Martin Luther King Jr President
Southern Christian Leadership Conference

DOCUMENT 3 *Cesar Chavez on Money and Organizing*[1]

What I'm going to say may not make much sense to you. On the other hand, it may make an awful lot of sense. This depends on where you are in terms of organizing and what your ideas are about that elusive and difficult task of getting people together—to act together and to produce something....

We started with two principles: First, since there wasn't any money and the job had to be done there would have to be a lot of sacrificing. Second, no matter how poor the people, they had a responsibility to help the union. If they had $2.00 for food, they had to give $1.00 to the union. Otherwise, they would never get out of the trap of poverty. They would never have a union because they couldn't afford to sacrifice a little bit more on top of their misery. The statement: "They're so poor they can't afford to contribute to the group," is a great cop-out. You don't organize people by being afraid of them. You never have. You never will. You can be afraid of them in a variety of ways. But one of the main ways is to patronize them. You know the attitude; Blacks or browns or farm workers are so poor that they can't afford to have their own group. They hardly have enough money to eat. This makes it very easy for the organizer. He can always rationalize, "I haven't failed. They can't come up with the money so we were not able to organize them."

We decided that workers wanted to be organized and could be organized. So the responsibility had to be upon ourselves, the organizers. Organizing is one place where you can easily get away with a failure. If you send a man to dig a ditch 3 feet by 10 feet, you'll know if he did it or not. Or if you get someone to write a letter, you'll know if he wrote it. In most areas of endeavor, you can see the results. In organizing, it's different. You can see results years later, but you can't see them right away. That's why we have so many failures. So many organizers that should never be organizers go in and muddy the waters. Then good organizers have to come in and it's twice as hard for them to organize.

We knew we didn't have the money. We knew farm workers could be organized and we were going to do it. We weren't going to accept failure. But we were going to make sure that workers contributed to the doing of this organizing job. That has never been done in the history of this country.

We started out by telling workers, "We are trying to organize a union. We don't have money but if you work together it can be done." 95% of the workers we talked to were very kind. They smiled at us. 5% asked us questions and maybe 1% had the spirit and really wanted to do something.

We didn't have any money for gas and food. Many days we left the house with no money at all. Sometimes we had enough gas to get there but not enough to come back. We were determined to go to the workers. In fact at the very beginning of the organizing drive, we looked for the worst homes in the barrios where there were a lot of dogs and kids outside. And we went in and asked for a handout. Inevitably, they gave us food. Then they made a collection and gave us money for gas. They opened their homes and gave us their

[1]Transcribed from a talk given by Cesar Chavez to a group of church people on October 4, 1971, at La Paz, the farm workers retreat center in Keene, California.

hearts. And today, they are the nucleus of the union's leadership. We forced ourselves to do this. We kept telling ourselves, "If these workers don't get organized, if we fail, it's our fault not theirs."

Then the question came up, how would we survive? My wife was working in the fields. We used to take the whole family out on Sundays and earn a few dollars to be able to survive the following week. We knew we couldn't continue that way. And we knew that the money had to come not from the outside but from the workers. And the only way to get the money was to have people pay dues.

So we began the drive to get workers to pay dues so we could live, so we could just survive. We were very frank, very open. At a farm worker's convention, we told them we had nothing to give them except the dream that it might happen. But we couldn't continue unless they were willing to make a sacrifice. At that meeting everyone wanted to pay \$5.00 or \$8.00 a month. We balked and said "No, no. Just \$3.50. That's all we need." There were about 280 people there, and 212 signed up and paid the \$3.50 in the first month.

90 days from that day, there were 12 people paying \$3.50. By that time we had a small community. There were 6 of us—four of us working full time. There were a lot of questions being asked. Some said, "They're very poor and can't afford it. That's why they're not paying." And a few of us said, "We're poor too. We're poorer than they are. And we can afford to sacrifice our families and our time. They have to pay."

I remember many incidents when I went to collect dues. Let me tell you just one. I'd been working 12 years with the mentality that people were very poor and shouldn't be forced to pay dues. Keep that in mind. Because that comes in handy in understanding what you go through when you're not really convinced that this is the way it should be.

I went to a worker's home in McFarland, 7 miles south of Delano. It was in the evening. It was raining and it was winter. And there was no work. I knew it. And everyone knew it. As I knocked on the door, the guy in the little two room house was going to the store with a \$5.00 bill to get groceries. And there I was. He owed \$7.00 because he was one full month behind plus the current one. So I'd come for \$7.00. But all he had was \$5.00. I had to make a decision. Should I take \$3.50 or shouldn't I? It was very difficult. Up to this time I had been saying, "They should be paying. And if they don't pay they'll never have a union." \$3.50 worth of food wasn't really going to change his life one way or the other that much. So I told him, "You have to pay at least \$3.50 right now or I'll have to put you out of the union." He gave me the \$5.00. We went to the store and changed the \$5.00 bill. I got the \$3.50 and gave him the \$1.50. I stayed with him. He bought \$1.50 worth of groceries and went home.

That experience hurt me but it also strengthened my determination. If this man was willing to give me \$3.50 on a dream, when we were really taking the money out of his own food, then why shouldn't we be able to have a union—however difficult. There had never been a successful union for farm workers. Every unionizing attempt had been defeated. People were killed. They ran into every obstacle you can think of. The whole agricultural industry along with government and business joined forces to break the unions and keep them from organizing. But with the kind of faith this farm worker had why couldn't we have a union? …

When you sacrifice, you force others to sacrifice. It's an extremely powerful weapon. When somebody stops eating for a week or ten days, people come and want to be part of that experience. Someone goes to jail and people want to help him. You don't buy that with money. That doesn't have any price in terms of dollars.

Those who are willing to sacrifice and be of service have very little difficulty with people. They know what they are all about. People can't help but want to be near them—to help them and work with them. That's what love is all about. It starts with you and radiates out. You can't phoney it. It just doesn't go. When you work and sacrifice more than anyone else around you, you put others on the spot and they have to do at least a bit more than they've been doing. And that's what puts it together.

These observations tie in directly with the whole question of organizing. Why do we have leaders? We put some people out in the fields and all of a sudden they hit, they click. Everyone's happy with them and they begin to move mountains. With other people there are problems and heartaches. They just don't go. When we look and see what's happening, almost invariably the differences are along the lines of willingness to sacrifice and work long hours.

We didn't start out knowing these things. We have discovered them. During those six years of strike and boycott it never seemed like that much of a struggle. We accepted it as a fact. Now that we're over that big hurdle, we look back and say, "My God. People really sacrificed. And the things that I asked them to do! Did I really ask them to do that much?" I asked them to do it to the maximum and they did it....

Introduction to Documents 4 through 7

When Betty Friedan published *The Feminine Mystique* women's wages were less than three-fifths of those earned by men, and fewer than ten percent of American professionals—doctors, lawyers, architects, college professors—were women. Increasingly in the late 1960s and into the 1970s, women organized and demonstrated for greater equity on the job. One result was the revival of the Equal Rights Amendment (ERA), which was first proposed in 1923.

In Document 4, Shirley Chisolm, one of the only women in Congress during the 1960s, argues before her colleagues for the ERA, and Document 5 is the amendment itself. The amendment's aim was to grant constitutional guarantees of equal rights and full citizenship to women. Social conservatives who felt women were incapable of equality opposed the measure, as did some progressives who wanted to maintain protective workplace legislation. Finally, though, in 1972, with both Democrat and Republican backing, the proposed Twenty-Seventh Amendment to the Constitution passed both houses of Congress. But getting ratification from three-quarters of the states was another matter. Thirty-five states—seventy percent of the total, just three shy of approval—were on board by 1975. But then the country slowly drifted toward greater conservatism, and the opposition became better organized. Claims that the amendment jeopardized wives' rights to be supported by husbands, that it opened the door to greater leniency on abortion, that women might be sent into combat, all took their toll. Time ran out on the ratification process before another state mustered the votes in favor of the amendment.

The women's movement focused on a range of issues, but Document 6, Kathi Roche's "The Secretary: Capitalism's House Nigger," makes clear by its incendiary title the author's anger that the role of secretary was as high as most women could aspire in the white-collar world. In Document 7, " 'Women's Liberation' Aims to Free Men Too," Gloria Steinem—one of the most visible and important leaders of the movement—argues that the largest aims of the movement were to create not just equality for women, but a more humane society. Her article appeared in the Sunday *Washington Post,* June 7, 1970. What do you find most surprising in the arguments put forward in these documents?

DOCUMENT 4 *Equal Rights for Women*

Hon. Shirley Chisholm of New York, in the House of Representatives, May 21, 1969

Mrs. CHISHOLM. Mr. Speaker, when a young woman graduates from college and starts looking for a job, she is likely to have a frustrating and even demeaning experience ahead of her. If she walks into an office for an interview, the first question she will be asked is, "Do you type?"

There is a calculated system of prejudice that lies unspoken behind that question. Why is it acceptable for women to be secretaries, librarians, and teachers, but totally unacceptable for them to be managers, administrators, doctors, lawyers, and Members of Congress.

The unspoken assumption is that women are different. They do not have executive ability, orderly minds, stability, leadership skills, and they are too emotional.

It has been observed before, that society for a long time, discriminated against another minority, the blacks, on the same basis—that they were different and inferior. The happy little homemaker and the contented "old darkey" on the plantation were both produced by prejudice.

As a black person, I am no stranger to race prejudice. But the truth is that in the political world I have been far oftener discriminated against because I am a woman than because I am black.

Prejudice against blacks is becoming unacceptable although it will take years to eliminate it. But it is doomed because, slowly, white America is beginning to admit that it exists. Prejudice against women is still acceptable. There is very little understanding yet of the immorality involved in double pay scales and the classification of most of the better jobs as "for men only."

More than half of the population of the United States is female. But women occupy only 2 percent of the managerial positions. They have not even reached the level of tokenism yet. No women sit on the AFL-CIO council or Supreme Court. There have been only two women who have held Cabinet rank, and at present there are none. Only two women now hold ambassadorial rank in the diplomatic corps. In Congress, we are down to one Senator and 10 Representatives.

Considering that there are about 3 1/2 million more women in the United States than men, this situation is outrageous.

It is true that part of the problem has been that women have not been aggressive in demanding their rights. This was also true of the black population for many years. They submitted to oppression and even cooperated with it. Women have done the same thing. But now there is an awareness of this situation particularly among the younger segment of the population.

As in the field of equal rights for blacks, Spanish-Americans, the Indians, and other groups, laws will not change such deep-seated problems overnight. But they can be used to provide protection for those who are most abused, and to begin the process of evolutionary change by compelling the insensitive majority to reexamine its unconscious attitudes.

It is for this reason that I wish to introduce today a proposal that has been before every Congress for the last 40 years and that sooner or later must become part of the basic law of the land—the equal rights amendment.

Let me note and try to refute two of the commonest arguments that are offered against this amendment. One is that women are already protected under the law and do not need legislation. Existing laws are not adequate to secure equal rights for women.

Sufficient proof of this is the concentration of women in lower paying, menial, unrewarding jobs and their incredible scarcity in the upper level jobs. If women are already equal, why is it such an event whenever one happens to be elected to Congress?

It is obvious that discrimination exists. Women do not have the opportunities that men do. And women that do not conform to the system, who try to break with the accepted patterns, are stigmatized as "odd" and "unfeminine." The fact is that a woman who aspires to be chairman of the board, or a Member of the House, does so for exactly the same reasons as any man. Basically, these are that she thinks she can do the job and she wants to try.

A second argument often heard against the equal rights amendment is that it would eliminate legislation that many States and the Federal Government have enacted giving special protection to women and that it would throw the marriage and divorce laws into chaos.

As for the marriage laws, they are due for a sweeping reform, and an excellent beginning would be to wipe the existing ones off the books. Regarding special protection for working women, I cannot understand why it should be needed. Women need no protection that men do not need. What we need are laws to protect working people, to guarantee them fair pay, safe working conditions, protection against sickness and layoffs, and provision for dignified, comfortable retirement. Men and women need these things equally. That one sex needs protection more than the other is a male supremacist myth as ridiculous and unworthy of respect as the white supremacist myths that society is trying to cure itself of at this time.

DOCUMENT 5 *The Equal Rights Amendment*

Section 1. Equality of rights under the law shall not be denied or abridged by the United States or by any state on account of sex.
Section 2. The Congress shall have the power to enforce, by appropriate legislation, the provisions of this article.
Section 3. This amendment shall take effect two years after the date of ratification.

DOCUMENT 6 *The Secretary: Capitalism's House Nigger*

Kathi Roche

How many secretaries do you know who rose "through the ranks" to a job which, after years of experience, they were qualified to hold? Damn few. The very concept of the secretarial role imposes limitations that prohibit rising above "one's class" and these limitations work effectively, with few exceptions. That is because a secretary is, first and foremost, a servant, in the most servile sense of the word, and any spark of creativity one may glean from the job is pure cream. We are the cleaner-uppers, the keepers of the office, the human processing machines for work that is not ours or, if it is, we receive no credit for it. Every piece of creative work involves mundane tasks for its administration and application, and that's the end assigned to us. Years of experience contribute only to the prospect of a better, higher-paying *secretarial* job, perhaps something administrative, but creative . . . ? Heaven forbid! Let's leave that to the thinkers and the doers.

How does one come to be considered a thinker or a doer? Certainly not by being a secretary. Yet women are still told that the best-way-to-break-into-business-is-to-learn-typing-and-shorthand, and we continue to buy that line. Indeed, a whole educational curriculum has established itself on this myth, and many of us who wanted to really "get somewhere" actually shelled out near-college-rate tuition to attend private business schools that would make us the envy of every poor file clerk. Those of us whose potential might have produced a real thinker sold out, dumbly accepting our preassigned place behind the typewriter, and, once there, worked ever harder at self-fulfillment by steadily perfecting our self-images as Gals Friday. Overlooking the "deadend" signs on this road to self-defeat, we increased our "efficiency," perfected our smiles and our bottled beauty, the-better-to-serve-you-coffee-with-my-dear.

And when things got bad, and we couldn't understand why we felt stifled by the humdrum of it all, we reassured ourselves of our worth. We reminded ourselves of that "special place" behind The Man, never questioning the psychology of the role and what it was doing to us. The majority of our bosses were, no doubt, well-intentioned men, whose praise for our work, unfortunately, was bestowed on sponges. For, however momentarily uplifting it may have been, that praise came to mean little in the face of a larger source of morale that went beyond The Man himself: we had learned to vicariously experience The Man's own status and prestige, and perceived those attributes as our (counterfeit) own. The more important and powerful he became, the more smugly we basked in the afterglow. Our "maternal instincts," carefully conditioned in years past, were put to work as we eagerly, and with a sense of duty and reverent responsibility, became supporters for the egos of the Creators. (The poor man, what would he do without me.) And the more we supported, the more we became subconsciously aware of our own diminishing importance before that Bestower of All Good, until we had come full circle, from stove to typewriter, still desperately identifying with that which we could never become. And so, in the interests of selfish survival, we settled for second best, and continued to cater to our Image.

And of course, the system has succeeded in once again dividing us and turning us against one another. We all know the infighting, bickering and sniping that goes on among "those impossible girls at the office." As a matter of fact, our submergence in the competitive, backbiting ambience of the business world has succeeded in honing to perfection our ability to head for each other's jugular, lest we lose our few hard-won goodies and get edged out of our job as the vp's secretary by some young, sexy female from the steno pool. Our carefully nurtured image as the woman behind the throne must not be jeopardized at any cost, and so we continue to hate and fear one another, further isolating ourselves from reminders of what we are, or could have been, or might be, if that girl from the steno pool gets a toehold.

For you see, we have not changed one iota in status since the day we entered the office. Whether we're in the steno[graphy] pool or behind the Chairman of the Board, we're all in the same time-honored bag (for women) of servitude, and the forecast for the future doesn't herald a change. I can see the day (as a matter of fact, I think it's here) when women are informed that the world of computers "needs" women who are "experienced and qualified" to help run the brave new world. We'll march ahead, armed with our degrees and flourishing an air of professionalism, only to find that, instead of typing letters, we'll have been relegated to—you guessed it—programming the computers.

A word of warning here. The well documented ability of technology to free humans for creative existence has served as a panacea for many of us at one time or another. Unfortunately, the mere growth of technology does not assure us that, willy-nilly, we will all be freed sooner or later. Like any other system, technology can be twisted by the abuse of power to create a new prison for certain classes. Only until we abolish the corporate class system that is maintained by the creators of technology can we be assured of a free and unfettered future. If we don't abolish it, we'll have come an even longer way, baby, but don't you ever forget that the token surprises The Man holds in store for us will only be alternative routes to service at the dinner table.

DOCUMENT 7 *Women's Liberation Aims to Free Men, Too*

The Washington Post Sunday, June 7, 1970

By Gloria Steinem

This is the year of Women's Liberation. Or at least, it's the year the press has discovered a movement that has been strong for several years now, and reported it as a small, privileged, rather lunatic event instead of the major revolution in consciousness—in everyone's consciousness, male or female—that I believe it truly is.

It is a movement that some call "feminist" but should more accurately be called humanist; a movement that is an integral part of rescuing this country from its old, expensive patterns of elitism, racism and violence.

The first problem for all of us, men and women, is not to learn, but to unlearn. We are filled with the popular wisdom of several centuries just past, and we are terrified to give it up. Patriotism means obedience, age means wisdom, woman means submission, black means inferior: these are preconceptions imbedded so deeply in our thinking that we honestly may not know that they are there.

Unfortunately, authorities who write textbooks are sometimes subject to the same popular wisdom as the rest of us. They gather their proof around it, and end by becoming the theoreticians of the status quo. Using the most respectable of scholarly methods, for instance, English scientists proved definitively that the English were descended from the angels while the Irish were descended from the apes....

It wasn't easy for the English to give up their mythic superiority. Indeed, there are quite a few Irish who doubt that they have done it yet. Clearing our minds and government policies of outdated myths is proving to be at least as difficult, but it is also inevitable. Whether it's woman's secondary role in society or the paternalistic role of the United States in the world, the old assumptions just don't work any more.

Part of living this revolution is having the scales fall from our eyes. Every day we see small obvious truths that we had missed before. Our histories, for instance have generally been written for and about white men. Inhabited countries were "discovered" when the first white male set foot there, and most of us learned more about any one European country than we did about Africa and Asia combined.

I confess that, before some consciousness-changing of my own, I would have thought that the women's history courses springing up around the country belonged in the same cultural ghetto as home economics. The truth is that we need Women's studies almost as much as we need Black Studies, and for exactly the same reason: too many of us have completed a "good" education believing that everything from political power to scientific discovery was the province of white males....

Before we go on to other reasons why Women's Liberation Is Men's Liberation, too—and why this incarnation of the women's movement is inseparable from the larger revolution—perhaps we should clear the air of a few more myths—the myth that women are biologically inferior, for instance. In fact, an equally good case could be made for the reverse.

Women live longer than men. That's when the groups being studied are always being cited as proof that we work them to death, but the truth is that women live longer than men even when the groups being studied are monks and nuns. We survived Nazi concentration camps better, are protected against heart attacks by our female hormones, are less subject to many diseases, withstand surgery better and are so much more durable at every stage of life that nature conceives 20 to 50 percent more males just to keep the balance going....

A second myth is that women are already being treated equally in this society. We ourselves have been guilty of perpetuating this myth, especially at upper economic levels where women have grown fond of being lavishly maintained as ornaments and children. The chains may be made of mink and wall-to-wall carpeting, but they are still chains.

The truth is that a woman with a college degree working full time makes less than a black man with a high school degree working full time. And black women make least of all. In many parts of the country—New York City, for instance—a woman has no legally guaranteed right to rent an apartment, buy a house, get accommodations in a hotel or be served in a public restaurant. She can be refused simply because of her sex.

In some states, women get longer Jail sentences for the same crime. Women on welfare must routinely answer humiliating personal questions; male welfare recipients do not. A woman is the last to be hired, the first to be fired. Equal pay for equal work is the exception. Equal chance for advancement, especially at upper levels or at any level with authority over men, is rare enough to be displayed in a museum.

As for our much-touted economic power, we make up only 5 percent of the Americans receiving $10,000 a year or more, and that includes all the famous rich widows. We are 51 percent of all stockholders, a dubious honor these days, but we hold only 18 percent of the stock—and that is generally controlled by men....

I don't want to give the impression, though, that we want to join society exactly as it is. I don't think most women want to pick up briefcases and march off to meaningless, depersonalized jobs. Nor do we want to be drafted—and women certainly should be drafted; even the readers of Seventeen magazine were recently polled as being overwhelmingly in favor of women in national service—to serve in a war like the one in Indochina.

We want to liberate men from those inhuman roles as well. We want to share the work and responsibility, and to have men share equal responsibility for the children. Probably the ultimate myth is that children must have fulltime mothers, and that liberated women make bad ones. The truth is that most American children seem to be suffering from too much mother and too little father.

Women now spend more time with their homes and families than in any other past or present society we know about. To get back to the sanity of the agrarian or joint family system, we need free universal day care. With that aid, as in Scandinavian countries, and with laws that permit women equal work and equal pay, man will be relieved of his role as sole breadwinner and stranger to his own children.

No more alimony. Fewer boring wives. Fewer childlike wives. No more so-called "Jewish mothers," who are simply normally ambitious human beings with all their ambitiousness confined to the house. No more wives who fall apart with the first wrinkle because they've been taught that their total identity depends on their outsides. No more responsibility for another adult human being who has never been told she is responsible for her own life, and who sooner or later says some version of, "If I hadn't married you, I could have been a star." Women's Liberation really is Men's Liberation, too....

Much of the trouble this country is in has to do with the masculine mystique: The idea that manhood somehow depends on the subjugation of other people. It's a bipartisan problem.

The challenge to all of us is to live a revolution, not to die for one. There has been too much killing, and the weapons are now far too terrible. This revolution has to change consciousness, to upset the injustice of our current hierarchy by refusing to honor it. And it must be a life that enforces a new social justice.

Because the truth is that none of us can be liberated if other groups are not. Women's Liberation is a bridge between black and white women, but also between the construction workers and the suburbanites, between Mr. Nixon's Silent Majority and the young people it fears....

Introduction to Document 8

What today is called the environmental movement has a long history. Theodore Roosevelt was associated in image and in fact with the American West, and his administration was the first actively to "conserve" the land, most spectacularly in Expanding National Park System. Many of the early efforts aimed to manage resources, to use them efficiently. Over the years, a range of naturalist thinkers, from Henry David Thoreau to John Muir, and from Aldo Leopold to Edward Abbey, sought a less calculating vision of the environment; wilderness was not a resource to be mined but humankind's foundation in the natural world. One book in particular, Rachel Carson's *Silent Spring,* published in 1962, brought environmental issues to the front of Americans' awareness. For years Carson had been writing popular books about the new science of ecology—about the relationships and interdependencies of species with each other. *Silent Spring,* however, did not so much describe the "web of life," as raise in alarming detail the possibility that humankind was slowly poisoning itself. Carson focused especially on the chemical DDT, an unusually effective insecticide used during the postwar era, that helped farmers control pests. She revealed that a growing body of research demonstrated the long-term, cumulative effects of such sprays. *Silent Spring* was the beginning of environmental consciousness for many Americans because it demonstrated so powerfully that the benefits of progress came at an enormous cost—in the case of DDT, poisoning the earth and water. Within a few years, grassroots pressure caused the federal government to establish the Environmental Protection Agency, and to pass the Clean Air and Clean Water Acts. States and local communities created their own environmental agencies, while militant activist groups like Green Peace and Earth First pressed hard for change.

Citizen participation took many forms, most spectacularly the first Earth Day on April 22, 1970. The idea of a day devoted to celebrating nature and pondering ecological issues had been around for a while, but an environmental activist, Democratic Senator Gaylord Nelson of Wisconsin, took a leading role in bringing the federal government into the act. Earth Day was a series of mass meetings in hundreds of cities and college campuses across the country. These were modeled on the demonstrations against the Vietnam War, with speeches and music; above all, the idea was to bring people out, and in fact, roughly twenty million Americans attended, providing striking footage on the evening news. Most of the organizers were college students, and the National Coordinator of Activities was Dennis Hayes, a graduate of Stanford University, who was then a student at Harvard. He gave Earth Day's opening speech in Washington, D.C. Pay attention to how his remarks were not simply about environmental issues. How and why does he link ecological degradation to the Vietnam War, the profit motive, and corporate public relations?

DOCUMENT 8 ***Dennis Hayes, Earth Day Speech, Washington D.C., April 22, 1970***

I suspect that the politicians and businessmen who are jumping on the environmental bandwagon don't have the slightest idea what they are getting into. They are talking about filters on smokestacks while we are challenging corporate irresponsibility. They are bursting with pride about plans for totally inadequate municipal sewage treatment plants; we are challenging the ethics of a society that, with only 6 percent of the world's population, accounts for more than half of the world's annual consumption of raw-materials.

Our country is stealing from poorer nations and from generations yet unborn. We seem to have a reverse King Midas touch. Everything we touch turns to garbage—142 tons of smoke, 7 million junked cars, 30 million tons of paper, 28 billion bottles, 48 billion cans each year....

We're spending insanely large sums on military hardware instead of eliminating hunger and poverty. We squander our resources on moon dust while people live in wretched housing. We still waste lives and money on a war that we should never have entered and should get out of immediately.

We have made Vietnam an ecological catastrophe. Vietnam was once capable of producing a marketable surplus of grain. Now America must feed her. American bombs have pockmarked Vietnam with more than 2.6 million craters a year, some of them thirty feet deep. We spent $7.3 million on defoliation in Vietnam last year alone, much of it on 2,4,5–T, a herbicide we've now found causes birth defects. We dumped defoliants on Vietnam at the rate of 10,000 pounds a month, and in the last fiscal year alone we blackened 6,600 square miles. We cannot pretend to be concerned with the environment of this or any other country as long as we continue the war in Vietnam or wage war in Cambodia, Laos, or anywhere else.

But even if that war were over tomorrow, we would still be killing this planet. We are systematically destroying our land, our streams, and our seas. We foul our air, deaden our senses, and pollute our bodies. And it's getting worse.

America's political and business institutions don't seem yet to have realized that some of us want to live in this country thirty years from now. They had better come to recognize it soon. We don't have very much time. We cannot afford to give them very much time.

When it comes to salvaging the environment, the individual is almost powerless. You can pick up litter, and if you're diligent, you may be able to find some returnable bottles. But you are forced to breathe the lung-corroding poison which companies spew into the air. You cannot buy electricity from a power company which does not pollute. You cannot find products in biodegradable packages. You cannot even look to the manufacturer for reliable information on the ecological effects of a product.

You simply can't live an ecologically sound life in America. That is not one of the options open to you. Go shopping and you find dozens of laundry products; it seems like a tremendous array unless you know that most are made by three companies, and the differences in cleaning power are almost negligible. If you really want to be ecologically sound, you won't buy any detergents—just some old-fashioned laundry soap and a bit of soda. But there's nothing on those packages to tell you the phosphate content, and there's nothing in the supermarket to tell you, only meaningless advertising that keeps dunning you.

We are learning. In response, industry has turned the environmental problem over to its public relations men. We've been deluged with full-page ads about pollution problems and what's being done about them. It would appear from most of them that things are fine and will soon be perfect. But the people of America are still coughing. And our eyes are running, and our lungs are blackening, and our property is corroding, and we're getting angry. We're getting angry at half-truths, angry at semitruths, and angry at outright lies.

We are tired of being told that we are to blame for corporate depredations. Political and business leaders once hoped that they could turn the environmental movement into a massive antilitter campaign. They have failed. We have learned not to place our faith in regulatory agencies that are supposed to act in the public interest. We have learned not to believe the advertising that sells us presidents the way it sells us useless products.

We will not appeal any more to the conscience of institutions because institutions have no conscience. If we want them to do what is right, we must make them do what is right. We will use proxy fights, lawsuits, demonstrations, research, boycotts, ballots—whatever it takes. This may be our last chance. If environment is a fad, it's going to be our last fad.

Things as we know them are falling apart. There is an unease across this country today. People know that something is wrong. The war is part of it, but most critics of the war have, from the beginning, known that the war is only a symptom of something much deeper. Poor people have long known what is wrong. Now the alley garbage, the crowding and the unhappiness and the crime have spread beyond the ghetto and a whole society is coming to realize that it must drastically change course.

We are building a movement, a movement with a broad base, a movement which transcends traditional political boundaries. It is a movement that values people more than technology, people more than political boundaries and political ideologies, people more than profit. It will be a difficult fight. Earth Day is the beginning.

QUESTIONS

Defining Terms

Identify in the context of the chapter each of the following:

hippies	counterculture
Betty Friedan	American Indian Movement
Cesar Chavez	United Farm Workers Union
Earth Day	Gloria Steinem
Equal Rights Amendment	Rachel Carson

Probing the Sources

1. On what basis did farm workers claim the right to unionize and strike?
2. Why did Cesar Chavez consider it important for activists to make sacrifices?
3. What did Gloria Steinem mean by saying that women's liberation would free men too?
4. Why, according to Dennis Hayes, was there a need for Earth Day?

Interpreting the Sources

1. Why did individuals like Cesar Chavez think unionizing farm workers was necessary?
2. What was at stake in the Equal Rights Amendment?
3. Why do you think Roche singles out secretaries as especially vulnerable?
4. Do you believe that much has changed since Earth Day? Has the environment gotten better or worse?
5. Why do you suppose the 1960s and 1970s were so filled with activism?

ADDITIONAL RREADING

The literature on the 1960s and 1970s is enormous, but some good titles to begin with include Todd Gitlin, *The Sixties: Years of Hope, Days of Rage* (1987), and Maurice Isserman, *If I Had a Hammer: The Death of the Old Left and the Birth of the New* (1987). Other works include James Miller, *"Democracy Is in the Streets": From Port Huron to the Siege of Chicago* (1987), and David Farber, Chicago '68 (1987). On the women's movement, a now classic work is Sara Evans, *Personal Politics: The Roots of Women's Liberation in the Civil Rights Movement and the New Left* (1979). Also see Alice Echols, *Daring to Be Bad: Radical Feminism in America, 1967–1975* (1989). Other important works include Alexander Bloom, ed., Longtime Gone: Sixties America Then and Now (2001); James J. Farrell, *The Spirit of the Sixties* (1997); Martin Duberman, *Stonewall* (1993); Frederick John Dalton, *The Moral Vision of Cesar Chavez* (2003); William Cronon, *Uncommon Ground* (1995), and Beth Bailey and David Farber, *America in the Seventies* (2004).

15

The Conservative Revolution

HISTORICAL CONTEXT

Two of the most frequently used, but also intellectually slippery, adjectives we employ are *liberal* and *conservative.* Each word implies both a political position and a way of life. Spend a night watching political talk shows on television and you will come away convinced that liberals are Democrats who support activist government; racial, gender, and gay rights issues; freedom of choice in the abortion debate; and the belief that wealthy businessmen probably have something to hide. Conservatives, on the other hand, are portrayed as Republicans who advocate small government; believe that racial, gender, and gay rights issues mask other agendas; oppose abortion; and argue that wealthy businessmen are agents of economic good, creating wealth, which benefits all Americans. The problem for any student of American history is that the terms *liberal* and *conservative* have not always meant the same thing, that in the last two hundred and fifty years their meanings have changed radically.

Ambrose Bierce, a turn-of-the-century writer noted for his sardonic humor, defined *conservative* in his *Devil's Dictionary* as "A statesman who is enamored of existing evils, as distinguished from a Liberal, who wishes to replace them with others." Bierce was right—the idea of inherent, recognizable evil is part of traditional conservatism. In its modern form the term *conservative* is as much a product of the French Revolution as the idea of liberty, equality, and fraternity. For many thinkers and writers in England and the United States, the French Revolution came to symbolize the excesses of freedom, the idea that if people were cut loose from traditions, chaos and anarchy would result. In England, Edmund Burke, the father of modern conservatism, wrote *Reflections on the Revolution in France* (1789), a work that predicted where revolutionary freedom would lead. Burke believed that social and political stability rested on a foundation of traditions and time-proven institutions. Any change, he maintained, had to be slow and gradual. He detested grand, utopian ideas, asserting that imperfect people could never create a perfect society, and that radical change will always end in disaster. At best, humans can find a modicum of order, justice, and freedom, but they can never create a society free from evil, suffering, and inequality. This, conservatives argue, has been the mistake of all social and political revolutions, from the French and Russian to the Chinese and Cuban.

The ideas of Burke found their way into the United States Constitution, the Bill of Rights, the Federalist Papers, and many state constitutions. But in the United States liberalism also had powerful advocates. Where conservatives placed faith in

God, distrusted human nature, and feared too much freedom, liberals tended to deemphasize religion, trusted in the goodness of people, and reveled in certain kinds of freedom. At least in the nineteenth century, it was a strong central government that liberals feared. Thomas Jefferson's notion that "the government that governed least governed best" captured this fear. And many liberals maintained that their distrust of a strong government has a basis in economic fact. They adhered to the economic ideas of Adam Smith, articulated in his influential book *Wealth of Nations* (1776). Smith was a proponent of economic freedom, arguing that a marketplace freed from any government control or interference functioned the best. Free people making free choices promoted economic well-being, Smith observed, and archaic institutions and governmental meddling created more problems than they solved.

In the nineteenth century, the primary battleground for liberals and conservatives was the marketplace. Jefferson's and Andrew Jackson's Democratic Party generally supported the "laissez-faire" principle that the government should stay out of the economy. Alexander Hamilton's Federalist Party, followed by Henry Clay's Whig Party and Abraham Lincoln's Republican Party, countered with proposals for a more activist federal government. Hamilton, Clay, and Lincoln consistently supported a national bank, protective tariffs, and federally funded internal improvements. By 1912 the Republican Party was clearly the party of a strong central government; it had created a national bank, legislated protective tariffs and internal improvements, and established the principle that the federal government had the right to regulate business activity. The Democratic Party, which only managed to elect two presidents between 1860 and 1932, generally supported a weaker federal government with more limited powers. In short, the conservative position tended to be more government and the liberal position less government.

In the late-nineteenth century and the first half of the twentieth century, however, other issues complicated the liberal–conservative debate. The arrival of millions of immigrants, the emergence of labor unrest, the growth of cities, the increasing awareness of racial inequalities, and a host of other social problems disturbed many Americans. Severe depressions in the 1890s and 1930s and violent revolutions in Russia and Mexico raised the specter of social and political convulsions. During the Great Depression, President Franklin Roosevelt and his Democratic coalition made an ideological about-face. Roosevelt abandoned the laissez-faire ideas of nineteenth-century Democrats and embraced the notion of an activist government. In an effort to preserve capitalism and democracy—to prevent radical social and political upheaval—he expanded programs designed to promote social justice. Out of his presidency came the idea of an American welfare state. His party, the Democratic Party, became the agent of activism, regulating economic activity and promoting social justice.

From the 1930s through the 1960s, conservatism floundered through an identity crisis, as Roosevelt's New Deal set the course of American politics. FDR's America had, in the words of one historian, "a rendezvous with destiny." The New Deal was followed by Harry Truman's Fair Deal, John F. Kennedy's New Frontier, and Lyndon Johnson's Great Society. The Democratic Party became the home of social justice, racial advancement, and gender equality. It promoted itself as the advocate for the poor and disenfranchised, the safeguard against the powerful and the greedy. Even Dwight Eisenhower, the single Republican president between 1932 and 1968, spoke the language of liberalism. Rather than reject the legacy of FDR, he accepted it. Ike said he was a conservative, "but an extremely liberal conservative," and defined his political philosophy as "dynamic conservatism." He combined fiscal prudence with a concern for social justice, a position squarely in line with Democrats FDR, Truman, JFK, and LBJ. By the end of the 1950s, traditional conservatives seemed out of step with the march of the times.

In the early 1960s, however, the conservatives found a new voice and a fresh agenda. Barry Goldwater, Republican Senator from Arizona, had no interest in Eisenhower's dynamic conservatism. America's problem, he felt, was too much government, not too little. In *The Conscience of a Conservative* (1960), Goldwater articulated a new conservative agenda. He was committed to "achieving the maximum amount of freedom for individuals that [was] consistent with the maintenance of social order." His enemy was the burgeoning federal bureaucracy, "a Leviathan, a vast national authority out of touch with the people, and out of control." He absolutely rejected the legacy of the New Deal, the politics of subsidies, price supports, closed shops, and special interest legislation, all administered from Washington, D.C. "I have little interest in streamlining government or making it more efficient, for I mean to reduce its size," he wrote. "I do not undertake to promote welfare, for I propose to extend freedom. My aim is not to pass laws, but to repeal them." Ironically, Goldwater conceived of a modern alternative to New Deal liberalism that expanded on Jefferson's distrust of a distant and unchecked federal government. Between 1960 and 1964, Goldwater's thin manifesto sold 3.5 million copies, and although voters rejected him by a landslide in the 1964 presidential race, his message did not suffer a similar fate. Goldwater's book became, as conservative writer Patrick Buchanan observed, "our new testament; it contained the core beliefs of our political faith. . . . We read it, memorized it, quoted it. . . . For those of us wandering around in the arid desert of Eisenhower Republicanism, it hit like a rifle shot."

The Conscience of a Conservative was the starting point for modern conservativism. But the conservative movement, like the liberal movement, was a broad-based coalition of groups with different agendas. Such Republican politicians as Ronald Reagan and Newt Gingrich championed Goldwater's demands for fiscal restraint, lower taxes, deregulation, welfare cuts, and reduced bureaucracy. Others joined the movement for different reasons. Southern conservatives resented such federal actions as desegregation and "forced" busing. Religious conservatives questioned the Supreme Court's ruling on abortion, prayer in schools, and other social issues. Western conservatives demanded state control of federally held western lands and relief from federal restrictions on logging and extraction industries. And Libertarians simply wanted more freedom from government interference. Uniting these ideological strands was a grassroots movement, particularly strong in the sun belt, intent on pushing the Republican Party to the right.

Although Lyndon Johnson soundly defeated Barry Goldwater in 1964, and ideological conservatives like Reagan and Gingrich did not emerge until the 1980s, the Republican party gained ground steadily in the late 1960s and in the 1970s. Richard Nixon, although a centrist Republican himself, capitalized on America's racial backlash and demographic shifts. Goldwater demonstrated that the South and West were most receptive to his message; and once president, Nixon courted those sections of the country. During the 1970s, an increasing number of white Southerners and working-class Catholics—traditionally Democratic loyalists—voted Republican.

In addition, the shift in the population to the "Sun Belt" added to the political strength of the Republican Party. The elections of Reagan and the two George Bushes underscored these changes.

In the last thirty years, the conservative movement has fashioned an alternative to the welfare state. Certainly what Roosevelt began has not disappeared, but it no longer stands as an unquestioned "rendezvous with destiny." The elections of Ronald Reagan, George Bush, and George W. Bush demonstrate the vitality of the conservative movement, as does the acceptance of much of its economic agenda by Bill Clinton. The following documents give a sampling of conservative ideas about political philosophy, the economy, foreign policy, religion and the state, and cultural values.

THE DOCUMENTS

Introduction to Documents 1 and 2

Central to understanding modern American conservatism is Barry Goldwater's brief book *The Conscience of a Conservative.* Franklin Roosevelt's New Deal and Dwight Eisenhower's Modern Republicanism had cast a long shadow. Most mainstream Democrats and mainstream Republicans in the 1950s accepted the legacy of the New Deal. They generally agreed on the role government should play in the economy and society. They did not view the growth or power of the central government with alarm, believing it was an agent of good for the majority of Americans.

Goldwater challenged these notions. He called for greater economic freedom and individual liberty. For him, the government in Washington, D.C., was not the solution but the problem. He proposed not to reaffirm and extend the New Deal traditions, but to eradicate them. Running for the presidency on the Republican ticket in 1964, he promised, "I will not change my beliefs to win a vote. I will offer a choice, not an echo." Lyndon Johnson soundly defeated Goldwater in the 1964 presidential election, but the ideas Goldwater espoused energized the conservative movement.

Document one comes from Chapter Two, "The Perils of Power." Taking issue with liberal Democrats and Republicans, Goldwater calls for significant changes in the very nature of government. In the second document, Chapter Ten, "The Soviet Menace," Goldwater addresses foreign policy, an area where he believes the federal government should be active. He presents a conservative critique of the Soviet Union and a new plan for conducting the Cold War.

DOCUMENT 1 *The Perils of Power*

The New Deal, Dean Acheson wrote approvingly in a book called *A Democrat Looks At His Party*, "conceived of the federal government as the whole people organized to do what had to be done." A year later Mr. Larson wrote *A Republican Looks At His Party*, and made much the same claim in his book for Modern Republicans. The "underlying philosophy" of the New Republicanism, said Mr. Larson, is that "if a job has to be done to meet the needs of the people, and no one else can do it, then it is the proper function of the federal government."

Here we have, by prominent spokesmen of both political parties, an unqualified repudiation of the principle of limited government. There is no reference by either of them to the Constitution, or any attempt to define the legitimate functions of government. The government can do whatever *needs* to be done; note, too, the implicit but necessary assumption that it is the government itself that determines *what* needs to be done. We must not, I think underrate the importance of these statements. They reflect the view of a majority of the leaders of one of our parties, and of a strong minority among the leaders of the other, and they propound the first principle of totalitarianism: that the State is competent to do all things and is limited in what it actually does only by the will of those who control the State.

It is clear that this view is in direct conflict with the Constitution which is an instrument, above all, for *limiting* the functions of government, and which is as binding today as when it was written. But we are advised to go a step further and ask why the Constitution's framers restricted the scope of government. Conservatives are often charged, and in a sense rightly so, with having an overly mechanistic view of the Constitution: "It is America's enabling document; we are American citizens; therefore," the Conservatives' theme runs, "we are morally and legally obliged to comply with the document." All true. But the Constitution has a broader claim on our loyalty than that. The founding fathers had a *reason* for endorsing the principle of limited government; and this reason recommends defense of the constitutional scheme even to those who take their citizenship obligations lightly. The reason is simple, and it lies at the heart of the Conservative philosophy.

Throughout history, government has proved to be the chief instrument for thwarting man's liberty. Government represents power in the hands of some men to control and regulate the lives of other men. And power, as Lord Acton said, *corrupts* men. "Absolute power," he added, "corrupts absolutely."

State power, considered in the abstract, need not restrict freedom: but absolute state power always does. The *legitimate* functions of government are actually conducive to freedom. Maintaining internal order, keeping foreign foes at bay, administering justice, removing obstacles to the free interchange of goods—the exercise of these powers makes it possible for men to follow their chosen pursuits with maximum freedom. But note that the very instrument by which these desirable ends are achieved *can* be the instrument for achieving undesirable ends—that government can, instead of extending freedom, restrict freedom. And note, secondly, that the "can" quickly becomes "will" the moment the holders of government power are left to their own devices. This is because of the corrupting influence of power, the natural tendency of men who possess *some* power to take unto themselves *more* power. The tendency leads eventually to the acquisition of *all* power—whether in the hands of one or many makes little difference to the freedom of those left on the outside.

Such, then, is history's lesson, which Messrs. Acheson and Larson evidently did not read: release the holders of state power from any restraints other than those they wish to impose upon themselves, and you are swinging down the well-travelled road to absolutism.

The framers of the Constitution had learned the lesson. They were not only students of history, but victims of it: they knew from vivid, personal experience that freedom depends on effective restraints against the accumulation of power in a single authority. And that is what the Constitution is: *a system of restraints against the natural tendency of government to expand in the direction of absolutism*. We all know the main components of the system. The first is the limitation of the federal government's authority to specific, delegated powers. The second, a corollary of the first, is the reservation to the States and the people of all power not delegated to the federal government. The third is a careful division of the federal government's power among three separate branches. The fourth is a prohibition against impetuous alteration of the system—namely, Article V's tortuous, but wise, amendment procedures.

Was it then a *Democracy* the framers created? Hardly. The system of restraints, on the face of it, was directed not only against individual tyrants, but also against a tyranny of the masses. The framers were well aware of the danger posed by self-seeking demagogues—

that they might persuade a majority of the people to confer on government vast powers in return for deceptive promises of economic gain. And so they forbade such a transfer of power—first by declaring, in effect, that certain activities are outside the natural and legitimate scope of the public authority, and secondly by dispersing public authority among several levels and branches of government in the hope that each seat of authority, jealous of its own prerogatives, would have a natural incentive to resist aggression by the others.

But the framers were not visionaries. They knew that rules of government, however brilliantly calculated to cope with the imperfect nature of man, however carefully designed to avoid the pitfalls of power, would be no match for men who were determined to disregard them. In the last analysis their system of government would prosper only if the governed were sufficiently determined that it should. "What have you given us?" a woman asked Ben Franklin toward the close of the Constitutional Convention. "A Republic," he said, *"if you can keep it!"*

We have not kept it. The Achesons and Larsons have had their way. The system of restraints has fallen into disrepair. The federal government has moved into every field in which it believes its services are needed. The state governments are either excluded from their rightful functions by federal preemption, or they are allowed to act at the sufferance of the federal government. Inside the federal government both the executive and judicial branches have roamed far outside their constitutional boundary lines. And all of these things have come to pass without regard to the amendment procedures prescribed by Article V. The result is a Leviathan, a vast national authority out of touch with the people, and out of their control. This monolith of power is bounded only by the will of those who sit in high places. . . .

How did it happen? How did our national government grow from a servant with sharply limited powers into a master with virtually unlimited power?

In part, we were swindled. There are occasions when we have elevated men and political parties to power that promised to restore limited government and then proceeded, after their election, to expand the activities of government. But let us be honest with ourselves. Broken promises are not the major causes of our trouble. *Kept* promises are. All too often we have put men in office who have suggested spending a little more on this, a little more on that, who have proposed a new welfare program, who have thought of another variety of "security." We have taken the bait, preferring to put off to another day the recapture of freedom and the restoration of our constitutional system. We have gone the way of many a democratic society that has lost its freedom by persuading itself that if "the people" rule, all is well. . . .

I am convinced that most Americans now want to reverse the trend. I think that concern for our vanishing freedoms is genuine. I think that the people's uneasiness in the stifling omnipresence of government has turned into something approaching alarm. But bemoaning the evil will not drive it back, and accusing fingers will not shrink government.

The turn will come when we entrust the conduct of our affairs to men who understand that their first duty as public officials is to divest themselves of the power they have been given. It will come when Americans, in hundreds of communities throughout the nation, decide to put the man in office who is pledged to enforce the Constitution and restore the Republic. Who will proclaim in a campaign speech: "I have little interest in streamlining government or in making it more efficient, for I mean to reduce its size. I do not undertake to promote welfare, for I propose to extend freedom. My aim is not to pass laws, but to repeal them. It is not to inaugurate new programs, but to cancel old ones that do violence to the Constitution, or that have failed in their purpose, or that impose on the people an unwarranted financial burden. I will not attempt to discover whether legislation is 'needed' before I have first determined whether it is constitutionally permissible. And if I should later be attacked for neglecting my constituents' 'interests,' I shall reply that I was informed their main interest is liberty and that in that cause I am doing the very best I can."

DOCUMENT 2 *The Soviet Menace*

And still the awful truth remains: We can establish the domestic conditions for maximizing freedom, along the lines I have indicated, and yet become slaves. We can do this by losing the Cold War to the Soviet Union.

American freedom has always depended, to an extent, on what is happening beyond our shores. Even in Ben Franklin's day, Americans had to reckon with foreign threats. Our forebearers knew that "keeping a Republic" meant, above all, keeping it safe from foreign transgressors; they knew that a people cannot live and work freely, and develop national institutions conducive to freedom, except in peace and with independence. In those early days the threat to peace and independence was very real. We were a fledgling-nation and the slightest misstep—or faint hearts—would have laid us open to the ravages of predatory European powers. It was only because wise and courageous men understood that defense of freedom required risks and sacrifice, as well as their belief in it, that we survived the crisis of national infancy. As we grew stronger, and as the oceans continued to interpose a physical barrier between ourselves and European militarism, the foreign danger gradually receded. Though we always had to keep a weather eye on would-be conquerors, our independence was acknowledged and peace, unless we chose otherwise, was established. Indeed, after the Second World War, we were not only master of our own destiny; we were master of the world. With a monopoly of atomic weapons, and with a conventional military establishment superior to any in the world, America was—in relative and absolute terms—the most powerful nation the world had ever known. American freedom was as secure as at any time in our history.

Now, a decade and half later, we have come full circle and our national existence is once again threatened as it was in the early days of the Republic. Though we are still strong physically, we are in clear and imminent danger of being overwhelmed by alien forces. We are confronted by a revolutionary world movement that possesses not only the will to dominate absolutely every square mile of the globe, but increasingly the capacity to do so: a military power that rivals our own, political warfare and propaganda skills that are superior to ours, an international fifth column that operates conspiratorially in the heart of our defenses, an ideology that imbues its adherents with a sense of historical mission; and all of these resources controlled by a ruthless despotism that brooks no deviation from the revolutionary course. This threat, moreover, is growing day by day. And it has now reached the point where American leaders, both political and intellectual, are searching desperately for means of "appeasing" or "accommodating" the Soviet Union as the price of national survival. The American people are being told that, however valuable their freedom may be, it is even more important to live. A craven fear of death is entering the American consciousness. . . .

The temptation is strong to blame the deterioration of America's fortunes on the Soviet Union's acquisition of nuclear weapons. But this is self-delusion. The rot had set in, the crumbling of our position was already observable, long before the Communists detonated their first Atom Bomb. Even in the early 1950s, when America still held unquestioned nuclear superiority, it was clear that we were losing the Cold War. Time and again in my campaign speeches of 1952 I warned my fellow Arizonans that "American Foreign Policy has brought us from a position of undisputed power, in seven short years, to the brink of possible disaster." And in the succeeding seven years, that trend, because its cause remains, has continued.

The real cause of the deterioration can be simply stated. Our enemies have understood the nature of the conflict, and we have not. They are determined to win the conflict, and we are not.

I hesitate to restate the obvious—to say again what has been said so many times before by so many others: that the Communists' aim is to conquer the world. I repeat it because it is the beginning and the end of our knowledge about the conflict between East and West. I repeat it because I fear that however often we have given lip-service to this central political fact of our time, very few of us have *believed* it. If we had, our entire approach to foreign policy over the past fourteen years would have been radically different, and the course of world events radically changed.

If an enemy power is bent on conquering you, and proposes to turn all of his resources to that end, he is at war with you; and you—unless you contemplate surrender—are at war with him. Moreover—unless you contemplate treason—your objective, like his, will be victory. Not "peace," but victory. Now, while traitors (and perhaps cowards) have at times occupied key positions in our government, it is clear that our national leadership over the past fourteen years has favored neither surrender nor treason. It is equally clear, however, that our leaders have not made *victory* the goal of American policy. And the reason that they have not done so, I am saying, is that they have never believed deeply that the Communists are in earnest. . . .

I suggest that we look at America's present foreign policy, and ask whether it is conducive to victory. There are several aspects of this policy. Let us measure each of them by the test: Does it help defeat the enemy? . . .

1. The key guidepost is the Objective, and we must never lose sight of it. It is not to wage a struggle against Communism, but to win it.

2. Our strategy must be primarily offensive in nature. Given the dynamic, revolutionary character of the enemy's challenge, we cannot win merely by trying to hold our own. In addition to paring his blows, we must strike our own. In addition to guarding our frontiers, we must try to puncture his. In addition to keeping the free world free, we must try to make the Communist world free. To these ends, we must always try to engage the enemy at times and places, and with weapons, of our own choosing.

3. We must strive to achieve and maintain military superiority. Mere parity will not do. Since we can never match the Communists in manpower, our equipment and weapons must more than offset his advantage in numbers. We must also develop a limited war capacity. For this latter purpose, we should make every effort to achieve decisive superiority in small, clean nuclear weapons.

4. We must make America economically strong. We have already seen why economic energy must be released from government strangulation if individual freedom is to survive. Economic emancipation is equally imperative if the nation is to survive. America's maximum economic power will be forged, not under bureaucratic direction, but in freedom.

5. In all of our dealings with foreign nations, we must behave like a great power. Our national posture must reflect strength and confidence and purpose, as well as good will. We need not be bellicose, but neither should we encourage others to believe that American rights can be violated with impunity. We must protect American nationals and American property and American honor—everywhere. We may not make foreign peoples love us—no nation has ever succeeded in that—but we can make *them respect us*. And *respect* is the stuff of which enduring friendships and firm alliances are made.

6. We should adopt a discriminating foreign aid policy. American aid should be furnished only to friendly, anti-Communist nations that are willing to join with us in the struggle for freedom. Moreover, our aid should take the form of loans or technical assistance, not gifts. And we should insist, moreover, that such nations contribute their fair share to the common cause.

7. We should declare the world Communist movement an outlaw in the community of civilized nations. Accordingly, we should withdraw diplomatic recognition from all Communist governments including that of the Soviet Union, thereby serving notice on the world that we regard such governments as neither legitimate nor permanent.

8. We should encourage the captive peoples to revolt against their Communist rulers. This policy must be pursued with caution and prudence, as well as courage. For while our enslaved friends must be told we are anxious to help them, we should discourage premature uprisings that have no chance of success. The freedom fighters must understand that the time and place and method of such uprisings will be dictated by the needs of an overall world strategy. To this end we should establish close liaison with underground leaders behind the Iron Curtain, furnishing them with printing presses, radios, weapons, instructors: the paraphernalia of a full-fledged Resistance.

9. We should encourage friendly peoples that have the means and desire to do so to undertake offensive operations for the recovery of their homelands. For example, should a revolt occur inside Red China, we should encourage and support guerrilla operations on the mainland by the Free Chinese. Should the situation develop favorably, we should encourage the South Koreans and the South Vietnamese to join Free Chinese forces in a combined effort to liberate the enslaved peoples of Asia.

10. We must—ourselves—be prepared to undertake military operations against vulnerable Communist regimes. Assume we have developed nuclear weapons that can be used in land warfare, and that we have equipped our European divisions accordingly. Assume also a major uprising in Eastern Europe, such as occurred in Budapest in 1956. In such a situation, we ought to present the Kremlin with an ultimatum forbidding Soviet intervention, and be prepared, if the ultimatum is rejected, to move a highly mobile task force equipped with appropriate nuclear weapons to the scene of the revolt. Our objective would be to confront the Soviet Union with superior force in the immediate vicinity of the uprising and to compel a Soviet withdrawal. An actual clash between American and Soviet armies would be unlikely; the mere threat of American action, coupled with the Kremlin's knowledge that the fighting would occur amid a hostile population and could easily spread to other areas, would probably result in Soviet acceptance of the ultimatum. The Kremlin would also be put on notice, of course, that resort to long-range bombers and missiles would prompt automatic retaliation in kind. On this level, we would invite the Communist leaders to choose between total destruction of the Soviet Union, and accepting a local defeat. . . . Had we the will and the means for it in 1956, such a policy would have saved the Hungarian Revolution.

This is hard counsel. But it is hard, I think, not for what it says, but for saying it openly. Such a policy involves the risk of war? Of course; but any policy, short of surrender, does that. Any policy that successfully frustrates the Communists' aim of world domination runs the risk that the Kremlin will choose to lose in a kamikaze-finish. It is hard counsel because it frankly acknowledges that war may be the price of freedom, and thus intrudes on our national complacency. But is it really so hard when it goes on to search for the most likely means of safeguarding both our lives *and* our freedom? Is it so hard when we think of the risks that were taken to create our country?—risks on which our ancestors openly and proudly staked their "lives, fortunes, and sacred honor." Will we do less to *save* our country?

The risks I speak of are risks on our terms, instead of on Communist terms. *We*, not they, would select the time and place for a test of wills. *We*, not they, would have the opportunity to bring maximum strength to bear on that test. *They*, not we, would have to decide between fighting for limited objectives under unfavorable circumstances, or backing down. And these are immense advantages.

The future, as I see it, will unfold along one of two paths. Either the Communists will retain the offensive; will lay down one challenge after another; will invite us in local crisis after local crisis to choose between all-out war and limited retreat; and will force us, ultimately, to surrender or accept war under the most disadvantageous circumstances. Or *we* will summon the will and the means for taking the initiative, and wage a war of attrition against them—and hope, thereby, to bring about the internal disintegration of the Communist empire. One course runs the risk of war, and leads, in any case, to probable defeat. The other runs the risk of war, and holds forth the promise of victory. For Americans who cherish their lives, but their freedom more, the choice cannot be difficult.

Introduction to Document 3

One of the central beliefs of conservatives, and particularly religious conservatives, is the existence of evil. Conservatives since the time of Edmund Burke have tended to frame questions in terms of good and evil, and to their minds, among the most evil of forces are revolutionary movements that overthrow traditions, radically change governments, and challenge religious authority. Ronald Reagan viewed the Soviet Union as just such a revolutionary movement. For him the Cold War was not just a geopolitical battle between two superpowers. It was a contest between good and evil. In a speech before the National Associations of Evangelicals, a conservative Christian organization, Reagan introduced the notion of the "evil empire." He called on his listeners to use a moral yardstick in foreign policy, and never to accept the idea that one sort of government is as good as the next.

DOCUMENT 3 *President Ronald Reagan on Russia as an "Evil Empire," 1983*

During my first press conference as President, in answer to a direct question, I pointed out that, as good Marxist-Leninists, the Soviet leaders have openly and publicly declared that the only morality they recognize is that which will further their cause, which is world revolution. I think I should point out I was only quoting Lenin, their guiding spirit, who said in 1920 that they repudiate all morality that proceeds from supernatural ideas—that's their name for religion—or ideas that are outside class conceptions. Morality is entirely subordinate to the interests of class war. And everything is moral that is necessary for the annihilation of the old, exploiting social order and for uniting the proletariat.

Well, I think the refusal of many influential people to accept this elementary fact of Soviet doctrine illustrates an historical reluctance to see totalitarian powers for what they are. We saw this phenomenon in the 1930's. We see it too often today.

This doesn't mean we should isolate ourselves and refuse to seek an understanding with them. I intend to do everything I can to persuade them of our peaceful intent, to remind them that it was the West that refused to use its nuclear monopoly in the forties and fifties for territorial gain and which now proposes 50-percent cut in strategic ballistic missiles and the elimination of an entire class of land-based, intermediate-range nuclear missiles.

At the same time, however, they must be made to understand we will never compromise our principles and standards. We will never give away our freedom. We will never abandon our belief in God. And we will never stop searching for a genuine peace. . . .

A number of years ago, I heard a young father, a very prominent young man in the entertainment world, addressing a tremendous gathering in California. It was during the time of the cold war, and communism and our own way of life were very much on people's minds. And he was speaking to that subject. And suddenly, though, I heard him saying, "I love my little girls more than anything—" And I said to myself, "Oh, no, don't. You can't—don't say that." But I had underestimated him. He went on: "I would rather see my little girls die now, still believing in God, than have them grow up under communism and one day die no longer believing in God."

There were thousands of young people in that audience. They came to their feet with shouts of joy. They had instantly recognized the profound truth in what he had said, with regard to the physical and the soul and what was truly important.

Yes, let us pray for the salvation of all of those who live in that totalitarian darkness—pray they will discover the joy of knowing God. But until they do, let us be aware that while they preach the supremacy of the state, declare its omnipotence over individual man, and predict its eventual domination of all peoples on the Earth, they are the focus of evil in the modern world.

It was C. S. Lewis who, in his unforgettable "Screwtape Letters," wrote: "The greatest evil is not done now in those sordid 'dens of crime' that Dickens loved to paint. It is not even done in concentration camps and labor camps. In those we see its final result. But it is conceived and ordered (moved, seconded, carried and minuted) in clear, carpeted, warmed, and well-lighted offices, by quiet men with white collars and cut fingernails and smooth-shaven cheeks who do not need to raise their voice."

Well, because these "quiet men" do not "raise their voices," because they sometimes speak in soothing tones of brotherhood and peace, because, like other dictators before them, they're always making "their final territorial demand," some would have us accept them at their word and accommodate ourselves to their aggressive impulses. But if history teaches anything, it teaches that simple-minded appeasement or wishful thinking about our adversaries is folly. It means the betrayal of our past, the squandering of our freedom.

So, I urge you to speak out against those who would place the United States in a position of military and moral inferiority. . . . I urge you to beware the temptation of pride—the temptation of blithely declaring yourselves above it all and label both sides equally at fault, to ignore the facts of history and the aggressive impulses of an evil empire, to simply call the arms race a giant misunderstanding and thereby remove yourself from the struggle between right and wrong and good and evil.

I ask you to resist the attempts of those who would have you withhold your support for our efforts, this administration's efforts, to keep America strong and free, while we negotiate real and verifiable reductions in the world's nuclear arsenals and one day, with God's help, their total elimination.

While America's military strength is important, let me add here that I've always maintained that the struggle now going on for the world will never be decided by bombs or rockets, by armies or military might. The real crisis we face today is a spiritual one; at root, it is a test of moral will and faith.

Whittaker Chambers, the man whose own religious conversion made him a witness to one of the terrible traumas of our time, the Hiss-Chambers case, wrote that the crisis of the Western World exists to the degree in which the West is indifferent to God, the degree to which it collaborates in communism's attempt to make man stand alone without God. And then he said, for Marxism-Leninism is actually the second oldest faith, first proclaimed in the Garden of Eden with the words of temptation, "Ye shall be as gods."

The Western World can answer this challenge, he wrote, "but only provided that its faith in God and the freedom He enjoins is as great as communism's faith in Man."

I believe we shall rise to the challenge. I believe that communism is another sad, bizarre chapter in human history whose last pages even now are being written. I believe this because the source of our strength in the quest for human freedom is not material, but spiritual. And because it knows no limitation, it must terrify and ultimately triumph over those who would enslave their fellow man. For in the words of Isaiah: "He giveth power to the faint; and to them that have no might He increased strength. . . . But they that wait upon the Lord shall renew their strength; they shall mount up with wings as eagles; they shall run, and not be weary. . . . "

Yes, change your world. One of our Founding Fathers, Thomas Paine, said, "We have it within our power to begin the world over again." We can do it, doing together what no one church could do by itself.

God bless you, and thank you very much.

Introduction to Document 4

It's been called the religious right, the moral majority, and the fundamentalist revolt. But by whatever name, conservative Christians have provided votes for conservative, mostly Republican, candidates. They have also advocated and fought for a series of social, political, and moral positions, from antiabortion legislation and the right to school prayer to balanced budgets and defense spending. Such conservative Christians as Jerry Falwell and Pat Robertson have used mass media, particularly television, to preach their message, and they have demonstrated an ability to form and run grassroots organizations.

Conservative Christians have decided the outcomes of many elections, especially when "cultural" issues–abortion, gay rights, the theory of evolution, school prayer, for examples–became salient. Marion Gordon "Pat" Robertson, founder and chairman of the Christian Broadcasting Network (CBN), was one of the most powerful conservative Christian voices in the second half of the twentieth century. A son of a congressman and senator, a Marine during the Korean War, and an author of numerous books, Robertson is known to his viewers for his warm smile and his iron opinions. In 1988, he made a bid for the presidency. In the following speech, he summarized what he and other conservative Christians believed was wrong–and right–about America. When his candidacy faltered, he endorsed the Republican candidate George Bush.

DOCUMENT 4 *Pat Robertson Launches His Presidential Bid, September 17, 1986*

Constitution Hall, Sept. 17, 1986

On September 17, 1787, just 199 years ago today, 391 men meeting in solemn assembly at Independence Hall in Philadelphia voted their approval of a document drafted on behalf of the people of the United States to "form a more perfect union, establish justice, insure domestic tranquility, provide for the common defense, promote the general welfare, and secure the blessings of liberty to ourselves and our posterity."

In 1788 the first elections were held under this newly drafted Constitution and in 1789 our first president, George Washington, placed his hand upon the Holy Bible and swore a solemn oath that to the best of his ability he would "preserve, protect, and defend the Constitution of the United States. . . ."

A Vision Was Born

The Constitution adopted on this date moved a nation from the brink of anarchy to the threshold of stability and prosperity. A vision was born on this date of a nation united—a nation whose official motto was E Pluribus Unum—out of many one. The vision born on September 17 was of one nation—under God—with liberty and justice for all.

- These men knew all too well that there was only one source of our liberty. Tonight we do well to listen to their words:

Our First President who had presided over the Constitutional Convention in his farewell address declared, "Reason and experience forbid us to expect public morality in the absence of religious principal."

- Our Second President, John Adams, whose wisdom was key to the drafting of our Constitution said, "We have not government armed with power capable of contending with human passions unbridled by morality and religion. Our Constitution was made only for a moral and religious people. It is wholly inadequate to the government of any other."
- And our Third President, Thomas Jefferson, the author of our Declaration of Independence, gave us solemn warning, "And can the liberties of a nation be thought secure, when we have removed their only firm basis—a conviction in the minds of the people that these liberties are the gift of God? And they are not to be violated but with His wrath."

Warnings Disregarded

Yet despite these warnings, we have permitted during the past 25 years an assault on our faith and values that would have been unthinkable to past generations of Americans. We have taken virtually all mention of God from our classrooms and textbooks. Using public funds we have begun courses in so called "values clarification" which tend to undermine our historic Judeo-Christian faith. We have taken the Holy Bible from our young and replaced it with the thoughts of Charles Darwin, Karl Marx, Sigmund Freud, and John Dewey. A small elite of lawyers, judges, and educators have given us such a tortured view of the establishment of religion clause of the First Amendment to our Constitution that it has been called by one United States Senator "an intellectual scandal."

Instead of absolutes, our youth have been given situational ethics and the life centered curriculum. Instead of a clear knowledge of right and wrong, they have been told "if it feels good do it." Instead of self-restraint they are often taught self-gratification and hedonism.

What We Have Paid

Our motion pictures, our television, our radio, our youth concerts, with a few outstanding exceptions, seem to have a single message—God is out, casual sex, infidelity and easy divorce, the recreational use of drugs, and radical lifestyles are in. . . .

- There are 1,000,000 illegitimate pregnancies to unwed teenagers every year in our country. Of these, 400,000 babies are aborted—yet 600,000 babies are born each year to youngsters hardly old enough to be away from their parents. In the black community, according to a CBS report, 60% of all births are to women without a man in residence.
- On the darker side of society an estimated 1/4 of all our children are sexually assaulted while they are growing up, and each year between 1.2 and 1.5 million teenagers are either runaways or throwaways. And to match our new sexual freedom this year there will be an estimated 8.6 million new cases of venereal disease in our country, and the dread incurable killer AIDS may have already infected 1,000,000 Americans.
- Our schools, with what is called "progressive education," have become progressively worse. We have in our society 27 million functional illiterates. Each year we add 2.3 million to their number. Instead of being the most literate nation on earth, we rank number 14 among the developed nations in literacy and we are falling fast.

What the Liberal Elite Say

Now in 1986 the same liberal elite's that gave us the problem deny the cause and tell us that this is a problem for government. Ladies and gentlemen, what we are facing is not a governmental problem, it is a moral problem.

Human cruelty, human selfishness, alcoholism, drug addiction, and sexual promiscuity will always bring poverty and the disintegration of society. The answer for us does not lie in institutionalizing aberrant behavior—whether that behavior is substance abuse or sexual perversion. And certainly the answer does not lie in once again penalizing the productive sector of our society with high taxes and wasteful spending.

A New Vision Is Born

Ladies and gentlemen, the answer lies in—a new rise of faith and freedom that will give to every American a vision of hope—a vision of opportunity—a vision that will take us past these troubled days and show us the promise that lies ahead for each of us.

Even as the framers of our Constitution gave our forefathers a vision of a new land blessed with liberty, I would like for all of us on this special day to hold out A NEW VISION FOR AMERICA—A NEW VISION of hope for ourselves and our posterity.

Our children and our grandchildren are our greatest treasure. First of all we owe them a secure and loving family environment. We owe them strong homes and a mother and father who care for them, spend time with them, and truly love them. We owe to them the excitement and future potential offered by education and job training that is second to none in the world.

To accomplish this goal we must guarantee

1. New tougher discipline in drug and alcohol free schools. For our children and grandchildren we will eliminate once and for all from our land the mob supported drugs and pornography which is destroying and debasing their dream of the future.
2. We will insure to them a return to a basic broad based phonics approach to reading. Our children must learn basic language and basic math. They must know the facts of history—the facts of geography—the facts of science. The "progressive education" advocated by John Dewey and his followers is a colossal failure and must be abandoned.
3. For our children's and grandchildren's sake we must insure that control of education is returned to their parents and caring teachers in local communities, and taken away from a powerful union with leftist tendencies.
4. There can be no education without morality, and there can be no lasting morality without religion. For the sake of our children, we must bring God back to the classrooms of America!

What Critics Say

Of course some would say, wouldn't that upset the atheists in our midst. Studies done for us by George Gallup show that 94 percent of all Americans believe in God. Only 6 percent are atheists. Ladies and gentlemen, I passionately believe that the atheists among us should have every right of citizenship—the right to print, to broadcast, to speak, to persuade, to own businesses, to organize politically, to run for office—but I do not believe that the 94 percent of us who believe in God have any duty whatsoever to dismantle our entire public affirmation of faith in God just to please a tiny minority who don't believe in anything.

And ladies and gentlemen, as we struggle to see a new birth of faith and freedom in our nation, we pledge ourselves without reservation to maintain religious liberty for all people. Speaking for myself, and I am sure for all of you, we affirm that we will preserve, protect, and defend with all our strength the First Amendment to the Constitution of the United States as it was given us by the founders of our nation.

Several weeks ago my lovely daughter-in-law gave birth to a redheaded, blue-eyed baby boy. My first grandson. As I looked down at that little fellow, I knew we had placed on his tiny shoulders a share of a \$2.3 trillion national debt. As I thought more about it, I realized that before he began kindergarten he would owe a share of \$3 trillion.

Why So Much Debt?

Why have we done this to him? Was our nation at war? Not recently. Were we in the throes of a great depression? Hardly. Was there some natural calamity to justify such extraordinary spending? None that I am aware of. In times of extraordinary prosperity we have become the first generation ever to plunder the patrimony of its children and grandchildren. We have robbed them to pay for our wasteful excesses.

Why then did we do it? We did it because Federal spending is out of control. We did it because we have a Congress controlled by politicians who lack the will to say no to the clamor of special interest groups. We did it because we have as a people forgotten the words of John Kennedy who said, "Ask not what your country can do for you, but rather ask what you can do for your country."

We must have a new vision of lean, efficient government freed from the bloated excesses of the past—providing for the people those things they cannot do for themselves. Gone will be wasteful procurement; gone will be unnecessary departments and agencies; gone will be the frenzy to spend budget allocations before the next appropriation comes due; gone will be tax paid subsidies to the rich; and gone will be the hordes of favor seekers who have come for their piece of what Donald Lambro calls "Fat City."

Pursuit of Happiness the Goal

Government will guarantee to every citizen the right to pursue happiness. No longer will it try to guarantee happiness for every citizen.

Government will be our servant not our master. The Federal Budget will be balanced and we will lay the foundation for a new era of prosperity.

Ladies and gentlemen, in 1978 I was shocked when America's trade deficit hit what was then an alarming $33 billion.

Now, eight years later, that trade deficit is projected this year to reach a staggering $168 billion. We cannot sit idly by and watch the industrial might of America overcome by foreign competition.

Fine honest men and women who have labored all their lives to produce our steel—our automobiles—our television sets—our petroleum—are now out of work.

Goods Still Key to Well-Being

We are told not to worry because we are moving from an industrial to a service and information economy. But I do worry, because I know and you know, that in order to survive, an economy must produce tangible goods. No economy can survive which buys its goods from other countries and sells services and information on computer screens to itself.

Our new vision of America must include a partnership between the government, American business, and the American working men and women. We can no longer count each other as adversaries, but allies in a worldwide struggle. We are all Americans and working together with our great reservoir of ingenuity, hard work, and the entrepreneurial spirit we will make "made in America" synonymous with "the best in the world."

We believe in free trade and open markets. We are against protective walls to shield outmoded or monopolistic industries.

Fair Trade Is Vital

But we also believe in fair trade—and we serve due notice on the Japanese and our other trading partners. . . .

Either give us free and fair access to your markets—or we will shut down America's markets to you.

One year ago this Spring I visited a refugee camp in Honduras near the Nicaraguan border. I took my camera crew inside a dark tent with a dirt floor. Sitting on a rough cot was a Nicaraguan woman less than five feet tall.

She told a tale of horror at the hands of the Sandinistas. Her husband had been a bus driver. The Sandinistas accused him of being sympathetic to the Contras. Without a trial they seized him, and before her eyes they dismembered his body. Then they raped her and lowered her into a well half-dead with shock and fear. She regained consciousness, struggled out of her confinement, and made her way across the border to freedom.

As I think about this little woman, I realize that she is just one victim of the communist tyranny that since 1917 has claimed through war, starvation, murder, and torture an estimated 250 million lives.

We Cannot Ignore Oppression

President Abraham Lincoln wrote these unforgettable words, "Familiarize yourself with the chains of bondage and you prepare your own limbs to wear them."

Can we craft a new vision for our own society while ignoring the chains of bondage of one billion of our fellow human beings?

Can we allow armed aggression from outside or armed aggression from within a country to extinguish freedom for its people? Can we turn a deaf ear to the cries for material help from those brave freedom fighters in Angola, in Afghanistan, in Mozambique, in Nicaragua, who would take to the field of battle at the risk of their own lives to bring freedom and democracy to their people?

COMMUNISM MUST FALL

We must be strong enough to resist any further spread of communist tyranny. We must hold forth the dream that one day this terrible blight on the world will fall through its own corruption and violation of human nature. And while we wait we must make it our goal that no longer will communist tyranny be financed by loans and credits from bankers and industrialists in the free world.

Yes, together we share a dream. . . . A new vision for America. A vision of a great nation. A shining city on a hill. The undisputed leader of the free world. And together as we join our hands, our hearts, and our voices as one—we will once again see this great land truly one nation under God!

Now a Personal Word

For the past three years, people have come to me and said, "your vision for America is our vision, will you be our champion and stand tall for the values millions of us share. Will you run for the presidency of the United States?"

What began as a trickle has become a torrent. Tens of thousands of wonderful people on their feet saying "Go for it."

But those across America who know me know that this is not enough. The question for me on this or for that matter on any major decision is simple . . . "What is God's will for me in this?"

Let me assure you that deep in my heart I know God's will for me in this crucial decision and I have His further assurance that He will care for, continue, and enlarge the ministry of CBN which is so dear to my heart.

So now to all of you assembled on this 17th of September, I give you my decision.

If by September 17, 1987, one year from today, three million registered voters have signed petitions telling me that they will pray—that they will work—that they will give toward my election, then I will run as a candidate for the nomination of the Republican Party for the office of President of the United States of America.

Introduction to Document 5

P. J. O'Rourke is known for his biting wit and satire. As a writer for the *National Lampoon,* he revels in taking on the most sensitive subjects. Some writers looked at America's problems and asked how they could exist in a wealthy country like the United States. O'Rourke looked at the same problems and said that things could be a lot worse if the government was more involved. The following document is a speech he made celebrating the opening of the Cato Institute building in Washington, D.C. The Cato Institute promotes the "defense of the traditional American principles of individual liberty, limited government, free markets, and peace." O'Rourke used his speech to discuss the recently elected Clinton Administration.

DOCUMENT 5 *Speech Given to Libertarians*

May 6, 1993

The Cato Institute has an unusual political cause—which is no political cause whatsoever. We are here tonight to dedicate ourselves to that cause, to dedicate ourselves, in other words, to . . . nothing.

We have no ideology, no agenda, no catechism, no dialectic, no plan for humanity. We have no "vision thing," as our ex-president would say, or, as our current president would say, we have no Hillary.

All we have is the belief that people should do what people want to do, unless it causes harm to other people. And that had better be clear and provable harm. No nonsense about secondhand smoke or hurtful, insensitive language, please.

I don't know what's good for you. You don't know what's good for me. We don't know what's good for mankind. And it sometimes seems as though we're the only people who don't. It may well be that, gathered right here in this room tonight, are all the people in the world who don't want to tell all the people in the world what to do.

This is because we believe in freedom. Freedom—what this country was established upon, what the Constitution was written to defend, what the Civil War was fought to perfect.

Freedom is not empowerment. Empowerment is what the Serbs have in Bosnia. Anybody can grab a gun and be empowered. It's not entitlement. An entitlement is what people on welfare get, and how free are they? It's not an endlessly expanding list of rights—the "right" to education, the "right" to health care, the "right" to food and housing. That's not freedom, that's dependency. Those aren't rights, those are the rations of slavery—hay and a barn for human cattle.

There is only one basic human right, the right to do as you damn well please. And with it comes the only basic human duty, the duty to take the consequences.

So we are here tonight in a kind of antimatter protest—an unpolitical undemonstration by deeply uncommitted inactivists. We are part of a huge invisible picket line that circles the White House twenty-four hours a day. We are participants in an enormous nonmarch on Washington—millions and millions of Americans *not* descending upon the nation's capital in order to demand *nothing* from the United States government. To demand nothing, that is, except the one thing which no government in history has been able to do—leave us alone.

There are just two rules of governance in a free society:

- Mind your own business.
- Keep your hands to yourself.

Bill—keep your hands to yourself. Hillary—mind your own business.

We have a group of incredibly silly people in the White House right now, people who think government works. Or that government *would* work, if you got some real bright young kids from Yale to run it.

We're being governed by dorm room bull session. The Clinton administration is over there right now pulling an all-nighter in the West Wing. They think that, if they can just stay up late enough, they can create a healthy economy and bring peace to former Yugoslavia.

The Clinton administration is going to decrease government spending by increasing the amount of money we give to the government to spend.

Health care is too expensive, so the Clinton administration is putting a high-powered corporate lawyer—Hillary—in charge of making it cheaper. (This is what I always do when I want to spend less money—hire a lawyer from Yale.) If you think health care is expensive now, wait until you see what it costs when it's free.

The Clinton administration is putting together a program so that college graduates can work to pay off their school tuition. As if this were some genius idea. It's called *getting a job*. . . .

You know, if government were a product, selling it would be illegal.

Government is a health hazard. Governments have killed many more people than cigarettes or unbuckled seat belts ever have.

Government contains impure ingredients—as anybody who's looked at Congress can tell you.

On the basis of Bill Clinton's 1992 campaign promises, I think we can say government practices deceptive advertising.

And the merest glance at the federal budget is enough to convict the government of perjury, extortion, and fraud.

There, ladies and gentlemen, you have the Cato Institute's program in a nutshell: government should be against the law.

Term limits aren't enough. We need jail.

Introduction to Document 6

The mid-1990s represented the high-water mark of the conservative movement. Under Reagan and Bush, conservatives held the White House, but the election of Bill Clinton ushered a new group into power—men and women who disagreed with conservatives about the role of government in the economy and society. Though a centrist Democrat, Clinton certainly believed in traditional Democratic policies that clashed with the ideas of conservative Republicans in the House of Representatives and the Senate. During the 1994 elections, Congressman Newt Gingrich proposed a plan to "restore the bonds of trust between the people and their elected representatives." It was a plan to make government less expensive and more responsible; it combined many of conservatives' favorite economic, political, social, and cultural themes. As such, it was an extension of the ideas of Barry Goldwater. The Contract With America helped the Republicans regain control of the House and Senate in 1994. The entire plan, however, was never enacted, and Clinton was reelected in 1996.

DOCUMENT 6 *Contract With America, 1994*

As Republican Members of the House of Representatives and as citizens seeking to join that body we propose not just to change its policies, but even more important, to restore the bonds of trust between the people and their elected representatives.

That is why, in this era of official evasion and posturing, we offer instead a detailed agenda for national renewal, a written commitment with no fine print.

This year's election offers the chance, after four decades of one-party control, to bring to the House a new majority that will transform the way Congress works. That historic change would be the end of government that is too big, too intrusive, and too easy with the public's money. It can be the beginning of a Congress that respects the values and shares the faith of the American family.

Like Lincoln, our first Republican president, we intend to act "with firmness in the right, as God gives us to see the right." To restore accountability to Congress. To end its cycle of scandal and disgrace. To make us all proud again of the way free people govern themselves.

On the first day of the 104th Congress, the new Republican majority will immediately pass the following major reforms, aimed at restoring the faith and trust of the American people in their government:

FIRST, require all laws that apply to the rest of the country also apply equally to the Congress;

SECOND, select a major, independent auditing firm to conduct a comprehensive audit of Congress for waste, fraud or abuse;

THIRD, cut the number of House committees, and cut committee staff by one-third;

FOURTH, limit the terms of all committee chairs;

FIFTH, ban the casting of proxy votes in committee;

SIXTH, require committee meetings to be open to the public;

SEVENTH, require a three-fifths majority vote to pass a tax increase;

EIGHTH, guarantee an honest accounting of our Federal Budget by implementing zero base-line budgeting.

Thereafter, within the first 100 days of the 104th Congress, we shall bring to the House Floor the following bills, each to be given full and open debate, each to be given a clear and fair vote and each to be immediately available this day for public inspection and scrutiny.

1. THE FISCAL RESPONSIBILITY ACT
   A balanced budget/tax limitation amendment and a legislative line-item veto to restore fiscal responsibility to an out-of-control Congress, requiring them to live under the same budget constraints as families and businesses.
2. THE TAKING BACK OUR STREETS ACT
   An anti-crime package including stronger truth-in-sentencing, "good faith" exclusionary rule exemptions, effective death penalty provisions, and cuts in social spending from this summer's "crime" bill to fund prison construction and additional law enforcement to keep people secure in their neighborhoods and kids safe in their schools.
3. THE PERSONAL RESPONSIBILITY ACT
   Discourage illegitimacy and teen pregnancy by prohibiting welfare to minor mothers and denying increased AFDC for additional children while on welfare, cut spending for welfare programs, and enact a tough two-years-and-out provision with work requirements to promote individual responsibility.
4. THE FAMILY REINFORCEMENT ACT
   Child support enforcement, tax incentives for adoption, strengthening rights of parents in their children's education, stronger child pornography laws, and an elderly dependent care tax credit to reinforce the central role of families in American society.
5. THE AMERICAN DREAM RESTORATION ACT
   A $500 per child tax credit, begin repeal of the marriage tax penalty, and creation of American Dream Savings Accounts to provide middle class tax relief.

6. THE NATIONAL SECURITY RESTORATION ACT
   No U.S. troops under U.N. command and restoration of the essential parts of our national security funding to strengthen our national defense and maintain our credibility around the world.
7. THE SENIOR CITIZENS FAIRNESS ACT
   Raise the Social Security earnings limit which currently forces seniors out of the work force, repeal the 1993 tax hikes on Social Security benefits and provide tax incentives for private long-term care insurance to let Older Americans keep more of what they have earned over the years.
8. THE JOB CREATION AND WAGE ENHANCEMENT ACT
   Small business incentives, capital gains cut and indexation, neutral cost recovery, risk assessment/cost-benefit analysis, strengthening the Regulatory Flexibility Act and unfunded mandate reform to create jobs and raise worker wages.
9. THE COMMON SENSE LEGAL REFORM ACT
   "Loser pays" laws, reasonable limits on punitive damages and reform of product liability laws to stem the endless tide of litigation.
10. THE CITIZEN LEGISLATURE ACT

A first-ever vote on term limits to replace career politicians with citizen legislators.

Further, we will instruct the House Budget Committee to report to the floor and we will work to enact additional budget savings, beyond the budget cuts specifically included in the legislation described above, to ensure that the Federal budget deficit will be less than it would have been without the enactment of these bills.

Respecting the judgment of our fellow citizens as we seek their mandate for reform, we hereby pledge our names to this Contract with America.

QUESTIONS

Defining Terms

Identify in the context of the chapter each of the following:

Edmund Burke	Moral Majority
Adam Smith	evil empire
Barry Goldwater	liberal elite
laissez-faire	Cato Institute
dynamic conservatism	Contract With America

Probing the Sources

1. Why does Barry Goldwater want to reduce the size and the power of the federal government? How does he use the United States Constitution in his argument?
2. What is Barry Goldwater's view of the Soviet Union? How does he think the United States should conduct its relations with the Soviet Union?
3. How does Ronald Reagan view the Soviet Union? What does he mean by the phrase "evil empire"?
4. Pat Robertson offers a critique of contemporary America. What does he consider the problems of the country? And what are the solutions?
5. What basic political and personal beliefs lead to P. J. O'Rourke's critique of President Bill Clinton?

6. How is Newt Gingrich's Contract With America a fundamentally conservative document?

Interpreting the Sources

1. In what ways do Barry Goldwater and Ronald Reagan agree on foreign policy? What is the role of morality and fundamental religious belief in foreign policy?
2. Why would the Religious Right support the Republican Party more than the Democratic Party or some third party movement? What role does religious ideology play in modern conservatism?
3. What ideas in the Contract With America seem straight out of the political philosophy of Barry Goldwater?
4. Goldwater, Reagan, Robertson, and Gingrich speak the same political language, expressing similar ideas in much the same way. P. J. O'Rourke's mode of expression is obviously different. But are his ideas different? Is he a "traditional" conservative or some sort of new breed?

ADDITIONAL READING

A very good introduction to the history of modern conservative thought is Russell Kirk, editor, *The Portable Conservative Reader* (1982); it includes selections from such conservative thinkers as Edmund Burke, Alexander Hamilton, John C. Calhoun, Henry Adams, and Irving Kristol. Rowland Berthoff, *An Unsettled People: Social Order and Disorder in American History* (1971) presents a conservative interpretation of American history. Recent works on conservativism include, Michael Kazin, *The Populist Persuasion* (1995); Lisa McGirr, *Suburban Warriors* (2001); Dan T. Carter, *The Politics of Rage* (1995); John Andrew, *The Other Side of the Sixties* (1997); Mary C. Brennan, *Turning Right in the Sixties* (1995); and Harvey Kaye, *The Powers of the Past* (1992). Also see Lee Edwards, *The Conservative Revolution: The Movement That Remade America* (1999); Robert Alan Goldwater, *Barry Goldwater* (1995); and George Will, *The Woven Figure: Conservatism and the American Fabric* (1997). New works include Robert Brent Toplin *Radical Conservatism* (2006), and Gregory Schneider, *Conservatism in America since 1930* (2003).

CREDITS

Page 29: Excerpted from Samuel Gompers, *Seventy Years of Life and Labor* (New York: E.P. Dutton & Co., 1925); pp. 134-135, 137-141, 155-157. Copyright 1925 by E.P. Dutton, renewed 1953 by Gertrude Gleaves Compers. Reprinted by permission of the publisher, Dutton, an imprint of New American Library, a division of Penguin Books USA Inc.

Page 32: Excerpted from Mary Harris Jones, *The Autobiography of Mother Jones,* ed., Mary Field Parton (Chicago: Charles H. Kerr Co., 1925); pp. 14-16. © 1925, 1953, 1990 by Charles H. Kerr Publishing Company. Reprinted by permission.

Page 168: From H. L. Mencken, *A Mencken Chrestomathy*. Copyright © 1926 by Alfred A. Knopf, Inc. and renewed 1954 by H. L. Mencken. Used by permission of Alfred A. Knopf, a division of Random House, Inc.

Page 177: From Robert S. McElvane, *Down and Out in the Great Depression: Letters from the Forgotten Man*. Copyright © 1983 by the University of North Carolina Press. Used by permission of the publisher.

Page 180: Reprinted with permission from Tom Kromer, from *Waiting for Nothing and Other Writings*, edited by Arthur D. Casciato and James L.W. West. Copyright by The University of Georgia Press.

Page 189: Reprinted from *Jews Without Money*, by Michael Gold.

Page 203: "The Army Must Act," reprinted with permission from *The Crisis,* September 1941, p. 279.

Page 204: "An Open Letter to President Roosevelt – An Editorial," reprinted with permission from *The Crisis,* January 1943, p. 8.

Page 209: Ted Nakashima, "Concentration Camp: U.S. Style," first printed in *The New Republic,* June 15, 1942.

Page 211: Reprinted with permission of the *Los Angeles Times.*

Page 212: Reprinted with permission of the *New York Times.*

Page 214: Published in Mexico City and translated from Spanish – Fair Use.

Page 222: From David Cuthbert, *Mission to Moscow.* Copyright © 1980. Reprinted with permission of the University of Wisconsin Press.

Page 253: From Anne Moody, *Coming of Age in Mississippi*. Copyright © 1968 by Anne Moody. Used by permission of Doubleday, a division of Random House, Inc.

Page 256: Excerpted from the *Baltimore Afro-American,* October 3, 1964. Reprinted courtesy of Afro-American Company of Baltimore City T/A Afro-American Newspapers.

Page 267: From Howard Zinn, "Journey to Understanding," from *The Nation,* December 18, 1964.

Page 305: Kathi Roche, "The Secretary: Capitalism's House Nigger." Documents from the Women's Liberation Movement. Duke University Rare Book, Manuscript, and Special Collections Library.

Page 307: Gloria Steinem, "'Women's Liberation' Aims to Free Men, Too." First appeared in *The Washington Post,* June 7, 1970. Reprinted by permission of Gloria Steinem.

INDEX

Note: page numbers in *italics* refer to illustrations